Taken To Heaven
— in AD 70!

Taken To Heaven — in AD 70!

*A Preterist Study of the Eschatological Blessings
Expected by the First Christians
at the Parousia of Christ circa AD 70*

Ian D. Harding

About the Front Cover: (by the publisher) –
Our desire was to depict the Parousia in the style of a Biblical Theophany as it would have been understood in the Hebrew cosmology of the first century. Included are the key visible aspects of the resurrection of the dead and the "snatching away" of the living mentioned in various Parousia texts (esp. 1 Thess. 4:13-17; Matt. 24:31). We wanted to help modern Christians have a more Biblical concept of what it must have been like for the first century Christians to see the Parousia and experience this final Theophany in the redemptive drama.

© Copyright 2005 by Ian D. Harding
First Edition, May 2005
Printed in the United States of America

First printing – May 2005 – 2,000 copies

ISBN 1-932844-01-5

All rights reserved by the author, Ian D. Harding. No part of this publication may be reproduced, stored in a retrieval system, or transmitted in any form by any means, electronic, mechanical, photocopy, recording, or otherwise, without the prior express written permission of the author, except for brief quotations in critical reviews in various media. Such quotations must be used with proper reference to their context and give appropriate credit to their authorship.

All Bible quotes are taken from the *New King James Version*, Thomas Nelson Publishers, unless otherwise indicated. Used by permission. The copyright and all other rights are retained by Thomas Nelson Publishers.

Abbreviations for Bible translations and versions used herein:
 NKJV – *New King James Version*
 ASV – *American Standard Version*
 AV – Authorized Version (King James Version)
 GLT – J. P. Green's Literal Translation (Online Bible)
 KJV – *King James Version*
 YLT – *Young's Literal Translation of the Holy Bible*, Robert Young
 Weymouth – *New Testament in Modern Speech*, Richard Weymouth

Published By
International Preterist Association, Inc.
122 Seaward Avenue
Bradford, Pennsylvania 16701-1515 USA

TABLE OF CONTENTS

Autobiographical Sketch and Photo vi
Foreword by Arthur Melanson vii
Foreword by Walt Hibbard ix
Preface xi

PART 1
The New Testament Theme of *Deposit and Fullness* in regard to the Measure Of New Covenant Blessedness Already Experienced by The First Christians Before the Parousia

1. The New Covenant in the Days of the Apostles 3
2. New Covenant Blessings - Deposit and Fullness 27
3. The Good Things To Come 65

PART 2
The *Nature of the Fullness* Of New Covenant Blessedness Expected by the First Christians to be received at the Parousia of Christ Jesus circa AD 70

4. The God of *Glory* and the Hope of *Glory* 87
5. Going to the Father and into His *Glory* 109
6. Crowned and Presented Before the *Presence* of God at the Parousia 125

PART 3
New Testament Scriptures which reveal the *Expectation of Consummation* held by the First Christians, that was about to be fulfilled at the Parousia of Jesus Christ, circa AD 70

7. Relevant Scriptures Regarding the First Christians' Hope of Consummation at the Parousia of Jesus Christ, circa AD 70 (Part 1) 145
8. Relevant Scriptures Regarding the First Christians' Hope of Consummation at the Parousia of Jesus Christ, circa AD 70 (Part 2) 179

PART 4
The Significance of the *New Jerusalem* in the Book of Revelation, and the *Victory of the Lord Jesus Christ* as the Heir of the Nations

9. The New Jerusalem and the Consummation for the Saints (Part 1) 219
10. The New Jerusalem and the Consummation for the Saints (Part 2) 247
11. Firstfruits and Harvest – Pre-Parousia and Post-Parousia Christians 291

Appendix 307
    "The Perfect" in 1 Cor. 13:10 and its non-relation to the Canon

Autobiographical Sketch

I first put my trust in Jesus as Lord and Saviour about 30 years ago in my second year at University (studying Engineering). After finishing and working for over a year, I was led to the Baptist Theological College of Queensland, where I completed a two year Diploma of Biblical Studies. I have been a keen student of the Bible ever since. It was at the Baptist College that I first met a very special lady, Kay, my wife-to-be.

Since that time I have been mainly employed in administrative and customer service positions. Our church involvement has mainly been in Baptist churches both in Brisbane and overseas (London and Scotland). I have served in diaconate and eldership roles, and have had opportunities to do some lay preaching – particularly in Britain where we spent nearly 9 years in total out of the last 16. I enjoy fellowship with Christians from a variety of denominations. Kay and I have been married for nearly 23 years, and have a special son and daughter-in-law who have given us a lovely granddaughter.

Up until I found it on the internet about 4 years ago (2000), I had never heard of preterism – not in Bible College, not from a pulpit, nor seen any books on the subject. I was helped by the many articles on the www.preteristarchive.com website, and especially by James Stuart Russell's book *The Parousia*. It changed my whole understanding of eschatology, aiding me to see that according to the apostles' inspired expectation, the parousia of Christ must have occurred before that generation expired.

After a year's further study, I began to find that some of the teaching by some preterist writers about the fulfilments expected at the parousia did not seem to match up with what I understood the New Testament epistles to be saying. I became convinced that the expectation expressed in the epistles was that at the parousia both the then-living saints and the deceased saints (composed of deceased Christians and deceased OT believers) of pre-AD 70 history all together would experience the same consummate glorification together with Christ in heaven. I was helped in reading Ernest Hampden-Cook's and Russell's books, both of which confirmed this understanding.

I did not set out to write a book at all. I simply began (2002-2003) to prepare some articles for my own benefit, to crystallize my own beliefs on what the New Testament predicted would really happen to the pre-parousia saints at the parousia of Christ. Those articles were then collected (2003) and published in this present volume (2004).

Foreword by Arthur Melanson

God, in His times and purposes, calls forth certain individuals for a special work. Ian Harding is such a man. It is a joy to read this Christian writer who so faithfully follows the admonition of staying true to the simplicity that is in Christ Jesus. Harding carefully builds his case on the solid support of the word of God. If any fault be sought, it might be said the author "overbuilds" his case (writing is akin to building). It is easily forgivable when we think of the winds and waves of dissension that will beat on this literary structure.

This work by Ian Harding is more than a book on eschatology; it is an illumination of God's divine purpose in Christ. This book defines the ultimate purpose of God—the perfection and glorification of fallen man. How God accomplishes that goal is the adventure story of this text.

The author is a Christ centered man. This book is Christ centered. Christ centered teaching produces Christ centered people. Harding keeps Jesus Christ in exactly the same place God the Father keeps Him—in the exact center of everything He does, yesterday, today and forever. The reader will find that 'Christ in you, the hope of glory' is as important today as it was in the days of the Apostle Paul. Much of modern preterism misses this truth.

Under Harding's tutelage the reader will come to appreciate 'audience relevance' in a new light. If we are ever to know what our Bibles are truly saying then we must know what it meant to the divinely inspired author and to those who read his words. That does not mean, however, that our Bibles are not for our spiritual instruction as well. As you follow the author's teaching in the enclosed pages, you will glean a deeper love and appreciation for the word of God than perhaps you have ever known.

Ian Harding's insights from the original languages of Scripture are *outstanding*. He often supplies the reader with his own translation in difficult to understand passages. He also uses the renderings from other translators. In doing this Harding does not lose his readers. One has the sense of seeing a valuable truth because the author cares about them knowing.

The title of this tome will cause consternation to some. A good honest consideration of the material herein, however, will show that Harding is on solid ground. It will become obvious that we fail to understand the *Taken To Heaven! –In AD 70* view because we also fail to understand the nature of the resurrection promises. Which of us can say we have nothing left to learn on these matters?

Ian Harding's teaching shatters some of the traditional structures of men. The reader will discern that Harding's purpose is not to attack these man-made constructs, but rather to deliver the strait word of the Lord. The ideologies of man fail in comparison.

A great strength of this book is the inclusion of comments from futuristic but insightful authors of centuries past. They did not appreciate the significance of the timing of first century events, but they did display a remarkable understanding of the afterlife and the consummation phase of our Christianity—glorification in the living presence of God. Harding recognizes the value of their contributions and includes selections from their writings. We are richer for it.

All readers will learn something new. More importantly, though, the reader will get a fresh look at God's great plan of salvation and see how the glorification of man in the heavenly city, the new Jerusalem, vindicates the reputation of our Savior, Jesus Christ. The final stage of God's amazing grace is *glorification!* I learned that from this book.

Many will fiercely oppose this publication. Many more will find comfort for the heart and nourishment for the soul. This is a major work. Amid controversy, it will be a classic in our time and a treasure-trove for generations to come.

Arthur Melanson
Joy of the Lord Radio Ministry
Audubon, New Jersey
January, 2004

Foreword by Walt Hibbard

A body of dynamic and groundbreaking literature surrounds every new theological movement. The Protestant Reformation in the sixteenth century spread rapidly under God's grace as He used the scholarly efforts of Martin Luther and John Calvin, followed by the great theological works of the seventeenth century Puritan writers, to propel the greatest revival in the history of the church of Jesus Christ. Yet, undergirding this awakening, more than any other single element, was the prior invention of Gutenberg's printing press, placing the Holy Bible for the first time into the hands of the people. No longer would Scripture be limited to the clergy. The man in the pew could study the Bible for himself, unshackled from the fetters of church controlled popes and bishops. He could become a Berean (Acts 17:10-11), and many since that day have done exactly that.

In the last quarter of the 20th century, an eschatological movement largely hidden from the church since the first century, began to emerge. Entitled "Preterism," this view taught that all Bible prophecy was fulfilled by the destruction of Jerusalem by the Romans in AD 70. With eschatological studies at that time firmly settled into a morass of interpretative shambles and scholars unable to agree on many important aspects of "the last things," the timing was right for a book to appear in 1971 by a "Church of Christ" minister in Warren, Ohio, Max King. It was entitled *The Spirit of Prophecy*. Unknown to Mr. King at the time, nearly a century earlier (1878), a Congregational minister in England, James Stuart Russell, had written a book entitled, *The Parousia*, which was to become the most influential and earth-shaking book on Bible prophecy from a preterist viewpoint to date. Baker Book House published the first American reprint of it in 1983. Dr. Russell's book has helped many thousands of searching Bible students, pastors and scholars to find a more scriptural and exegetically accurate understanding of the often-difficult eschatological passages.

Other significant preterist books followed, by authors such as Don K. Preston, Edward E. Stevens, R. C. and J. E. Leonard, Gene Fadeley, John Noe, Daniel E. Harden, Randall Otto, Kenneth M. Davies, Kelly N. Birks, Jessie E. Mills, and Tom and Steve Kloske. Several of these authors have earned doctorate degrees, including Otto, Noe, Birks and Mills.

Then suddenly, out of nowhere it seemed, in 2002, a lengthy manuscript arrived from a preterist scholar then in Australia (now in England), Mr. Ian Harding. Several of us were asked to evaluate it. Each reviewer agreed this was a major exegetical study that needed to be published! What made this manuscript so special? Why did it excite all of us so much?

It helps answer these questions to mention another groundbreaking book just previously written by Edward E. Stevens, entitled *Expectations Demand a First Century Rapture*. Since the Stevens book taught a view of the Second Coming different from that of many contemporary preterists (but similar to Dr. Russell's view) it sparked some controversy and challenged us to restudy. What an encouragement it was to Ian Harding to learn of Mr. Stevens' new book over the Internet and to read his insightful exegesis. Unwittingly (in God's providence), Mr. Harding's independent studies had brought him to a position very similar to that of Mr. Stevens! Isn't it amazing how our Lord brings men from different continents together, both studying His Word, and leading them to similar conclusions?

There are a number of things that impressed me about Mr. Harding and this book:

1. Mr. Harding's faithful reliance on inerrant, inspired, and infallible Scripture.
2. The integrity and thoroughness of his exegesis; he has done his homework.
3. His humility in acknowledging the often-overlooked good work done by futurists, although he differs on various points and final conclusions.
4. His word studies such as "hope," "inheritance," "glory," and "New Jerusalem" provide deep insight often missed even in preterist circles.
5. Applies the interpretative principle of "audience relevancy" to a higher level of consistency than exhibited in most other preterist books.
6. Mr. Harding's adherence to the doctrines of the Reformed faith.

It was a thrilling experience for me in being privileged to review Mr. Harding's articles. As I read and re-read the material, I found my own understanding of the preterist view greatly enlightened. In respect to the deceased pre-Parousia saints, the living pre-Parousia Christians, and the post-Parousia Christians (like you and me living today), Mr. Harding's book fits it all together in a way that I had never before witnessed. Because of all of these reasons, I treasure this book and anxiously await its publication. The *International Preterist Association* is to be commended for publishing this book.

For the open-minded inquirer into the preterist view, Dr. Russell's book remains unchallenged as a giant salvo of powerfully convincing arguments for abandoning futurism in favor of preterism. For the confirmed preterist who has already read Russell and seeks a fuller and richer exposition of Scripture relating to what actually happened at the Second Coming in AD 70, both on earth and in heaven, Mr. Harding's new book provides, to my heart and mind, a definitive and satisfying answer.

May I be permitted to make a prediction? I really expect that *Taken to Heaven! – In AD 70* by Ian Harding will take its place, alongside James Stuart Russell's *The Parousia*, as one of the two most influential and significant preterist books to be published in the last two centuries.

Walt Hibbard
Wilmington, Delaware
April 27, 2004

Preface

Let me firstly share with you a story.

The sun and the moon quarreled once.

The sun said, "The leaves on the trees are green," whereas the moon said, "They are silver."
The moon said, "Men usually sleep," whereas the sun said, "They are usually in motion."
"Why then is there such a silence on the earth?" the moon asked.
"Who told you this?" the sun wondered. "There is much noise on earth."

So they debated.

And then the wind appeared.

He heard the talk and laughed. "What is this whole quarrel about? I blow when both the sun and the moon are in the firmament. During the day, when the sun shines, it is as the sun says. There is noise on earth, all men move, and the leaves are green. But during the night, when the moon shines, everything changes. Men sleep, silence reigns, and the leaves get a silver color. When clouds cover the moon, the leaves even become black. Neither you, sun, nor you, moon, know the whole truth.

(From: Richard Wurmbrand, *Little Notes Which Like Each Other*, Hodder and Stoughton, London, 1974, p. 53)

Modern preterism and futurism do not get along. Advocates of both types of eschatological belief claim to be adhering to the truth of Scripture.

Without wishing to cause offence to either side, may I suggest that they are like the sun and the moon in the story — both right, and yet both wrong. Let me explain it in point form, as I perceive things:

Point 1 = a scriptural truth, that is right.
Point 2 = a subsequent deduction, that is not right.
Point 3 = an unwarranted accommodation of the Scriptural language, in order to weld together Points 1 and 2.

The modern preterist* says:
    1. The Parousia of Jesus occurred circa AD 70, in keeping with all the time imminency statements in the New Testament as spoken by

Jesus and the apostles — (which I believe IS a true statement) — and then on the basis of this truth the modern preterist makes what he thinks is a logical deduction:
2. Therefore it follows that the hope of glory and resurrection and final salvation, etc, that was promised to occur at the Parousia of Christ must be now fulfilled in us post-Parousia (post-AD 70) Christians while we are still in this life on earth, while we are still carrying the legacy of the fall of Adam within ourselves — (which I believe is NOT a correct deduction) —
3. And to reconcile the truth of an AD 70 Parousia of Christ with their deduction of perfection now in the post-Parousia church on earth, the NT language of a real glorification and real deliverance from corruption expected at the Parousia, is accommodated down to give it a covenantal, non-experiential meaning.

*(I am referring to the modern preterists who espouse the most popularly held preterist belief that the Christians alive at the time of the Parousia actually remained on earth following the Parousia in a condition like us modern Christians, and that the eschatological consummation promised in the New Testament is fulfilled "covenantally" in this life on earth in the post-Parousia church).

The modern futurist says:
1. The eschatological hope of glory and resurrection and final salvation, etc, that was promised in the NT to occur at the Parousia of Christ, by the very language and meaning of words, describes a real, experientially perfecting matter to do with a real glorification in heaven with Christ, which is certainly not manifested in the church while Christians are in this life on earth, for the fulfillment expected in the New Testament is not compatible with the thought of Christians still bearing the legacy of the fall, still subject to sin, the flesh, the world, the devil — (which I believe IS a true statement) — and then on the basis of this truth the futurist makes what he thinks is a logical deduction:
2. Therefore since such a real experiential glorification is not manifested in Christians on earth, then the Parousia of Christ cannot yet have occurred — (which I believe is NOT a correct deduction)
3. And to reconcile the truth that we do not see the promised eschatological fulfillments of glory, etc., in our churches with their deduction that the Parousia has not occurred, the language of imminency in the NT regarding the expectancy that the coming of the Lord would be fulfilled before that generation passed away, is accommodated down to give it non-imminency meanings and double meanings, etc.

Without wishing in any way to pretend omniscience, I wish to peacefully present this study, *hoping that it will act like the wind in the above story to somewhat reconcile matters.* I believe God has enlightened both preterists and futurists with eschatological truths to be shared. This book shows from Scripture, I believe, that in regard to the Points 1, 2 and 3 of both preterists and futurists, the following conclusions can be made:

- BOTH, the preterist AND the futurist, are *right* in making scripturally TRUE statements in their respective Points 1.
- BOTH, the preterist AND the futurist, are *wrong* in making INCORRECT deductions in their respective Points 2, based on their true statements in Point 1.
- BOTH, the preterist AND the futurist, have unwittingly resorted to accommodating down the plain meaning of language in the NT in order to support their deductions in Points 2; although, strangely enough, each has adopted the plain meaning of language in arriving at their respective true statements in their Points 1.

I am writing as one who holds to the truth of both Points 1, above; who seeks to avoid what I consider the incorrect deductions of both Points 2, and who seeks not to reduce or accommodate down the clear meaning of language of Scripture as is done in both Points 3. "Impossible!" says the preterist and the futurist together. This book will, I believe, show there is no impossibility, but rather, consistency, in my taking these positions.

It is not my intention to prove an AD 70 Parousia of Christ. I myself am convinced from the NT scriptures, that the *Parousia* (second coming) of Christ took place in the first century, circa AD 70. The words of Jesus that he would come again before that generation passed away, and other statements by Jesus, plus the Holy Spirit's witness through the other NT writers that the Parousia was near, at hand, at the very door, and that some of their number would be alive when it arrived ... — all of these have been examined in full detail by other writers, and I will not go into these matters in this book. James Stuart Russell's *The Parousia* is a classic treatment of the first century Parousia of Christ, which I recommend.

The Purpose of this book.

Operating upon (what I believe to be) the scriptural basis that the Parousia of Christ occurred circa AD 70 the purpose of this book is to show that a consistent study of the NT confirms that the first Christians (deceased and living) were expecting on the occasion of the Parousia to receive from their great Savior a real experiential resurrection/change and glorification in heaven with Christ. They were *not* expecting to remain on earth in mortal bodies after the Parousia, because the consummation to be brought by Christ at his Parousia is in no way compatible with believers still remaining with mortality, sin, the flesh, dullness, etc., within them.

I will also show how we imperfect post-Parousia Christians relate to the glorious inheritance that the pre-Parousia saints entered into at the Parousia, thereby encouraging us and enabling us to see *our* exciting hope.

For this preterist view presented herein, I have coined the name: *the preterist "taken-to-heaven" view*, (also called the *preterist rapture view*). Perfection and glory came to the living pre-Parousia saints when they were literally taken to heaven at the Parousia. Perfection and glory will likewise come to each of us post-Parousia Christians when we are also literally taken to heaven at our individually allotted times.

Two groups of Christians that I especially hope to help in this study:

1. I trust this book will take away a stumbling block to Christian futurists taking a proper look at preterism. For futurists can rightly feel that modern preterism, with its emphasis on an eschatological fulfillment in this life on a fallen earth, denies what they (the futurists) see as the scriptural NT hope of a real experiential glory and resurrection for Christians; and so I can't blame them for not looking any further into preterism, with such a stumbling block put before them. *I will show that the futurists' eschatological hope of glory in heaven is not diminished, but enhanced, by the view of the AD 70 Parousia of Christ.*
2. I also pray it helps my fellow preterists who, thinking that the great consummation promised in the NT must be fulfilled in them now in this life on earth, honestly still groan within like the apostle Paul, knowing experientially they are no more really spiritual than their futurist brethren, and that for all Christians in this life on earth the presence of sin, the flesh, weakness, sorrow, death, etc., make it very obvious that they are far from being experientially perfected. Such preterists have no other scriptures to cling to that offer them any higher experience than what they have now. They believe all the expectation-of-glory promises are already being enjoyed by the post-AD 70 church, so they have reinterpreted all those glorious heavenly blessings to suggest that we Christians today after AD 70 have no more than a covenantal, "positional" (in Christ), or non-experiential inheritance of those blessings. Where are they to look for a *real* experiential reward after this life on earth is over? This book shows that we modern post-Parousia preterists (indeed, all Christians) have a very real hope of glory when we die, and that the expectation scriptures *really* mean being *taken to heaven* to have a real, experiential glorification together with Christ in the presence of the Father, "far better" than anything we experience on earth after the AD 70 Parousia.

I wish to acknowledge the help and encouragement and patience of special American Christian friends: Garrett Brown, Arthur Melanson, Walt Hibbard, and Ed Stevens in the production of this book. I also wish to acknowledge the patience and loving support of my wife, Kay, during my countless hours at my computer.

Ian D Harding
Brisbane, Australia
November 2003

PART 1

In Which is Examined the
New Testament Theme of
Deposit and Fullness in regard to
the Measure Of New Covenant Blessedness
Already Experienced by The First Christians
Before the Parousia

Chapters 1 to 3

Chapter 1

The New Covenant in the Days of the Apostles

Prior to examining the expectations of the first Christians regarding the coming blessings at the Parousia of Christ, it is necessary firstly to ground ourselves in the fact that the first Christians, (i.e. those existing prior to the Parousia of the Lord in about AD 70), regarded themselves as living under God's new covenant established in the Lord Jesus Christ.

To the great joy of the followers of Jesus, the new covenant had come! It had commenced its operation on earth on the Day of Pentecost, when the exaltation, victory and rule of Jesus the Messiah was testified by the coming of the Holy Spirit to his disciples. This was the gospel that was preached by the apostles. They knew they were no longer under the old covenant laws, sacrifices and priesthood, but under the new covenant.

The first Christians were under a unique situation for, while they were experiencing the new covenant with the new life of peace and fellowship with God the Father through Christ, all around them an old covenant Judaism was still continuing with its old ceremonies oblivious to the significance of the coming of Jesus and his atoning work. The new fabric had come, and couldn't blend with the old fabric. Their Judaic opponents accused the new Christians of dishonoring the traditional Mosaic system. Most Jews couldn't comprehend that Jesus was the fulfillment of that system. The New Testament epistles are full of exhortation to the Christians to hold to their faith in Christ and his new covenant with its new creation life, and not fall back into the Judaic way of bondage under law-works.

Listed below are some of the new covenant blessings experienced by the first Christians. Dear reader, a careful perusal of these Scriptures will refresh your soul. Oh, the wonder of God's grace in providing a life-giving new covenant through and in the Lord Jesus for us. We see in these Scriptures that the apostles and first Christians were well aware of the major change that had occurred in God's dealings with mankind following the life, death, resurrection and ascension of the Lord Jesus Christ.

1. The New Testament proclaims a fulfillment of Old Testament prophecies regarding a New Covenant

Throughout the Old Testament, we have the repeated themes of a promised Shepherd-King of David's line who would minister a salvation based on a new and everlasting covenant. The gospel proclaimed by the apostles after Pentecost is where Jesus is shown to be this promised Messiah. They understood that the Old Testament prophecies of a new covenant salvation through the Seed of David were being fulfilled in their day, through the exalted Jesus Christ.

The theme of a Shepherd-King of David's line bringing a new and everlasting covenant and salvation may be exemplified in the following OT scriptures: (Emphasis in following is mine - IH).

Isa. 9:6-7 for *unto us a Child is born, unto us a Son is given*; and the government will be upon His shoulder. ... Of the increase of *His* government and peace *there will be* no end, *upon the throne of David* and over His kingdom, to order it and establish it....

Isa. 42:1, 6-7, 9 "Behold! *My Servant* whom I uphold, *My Elect One* in whom my soul delights! I have put my Spirit upon him...*I give You as a covenant to the people, As a light to the Gentiles*, 7 To open blind eyes... 9 Behold...new *things* I declare."

Jer. 23:5-6 "Behold, days are coming," says the LORD, "That *I will raise to David a Branch of righteousness; A King shall reign and prosper*, and execute judgment and righteousness in the earth. 6 In His days Judah will be saved, And Israel will dwell safely; *Now this is His name ... the LORD our righteousness.*

Jer. 31:31,33-34; 33:14-17 "Behold, *the days are coming, says the LORD, when I will make a new covenant with the house of Israel and with the house of Judah...* 33 "*...this is the covenant that I will make* with the house of Israel after those days, says the LORD:... 33:14 'Behold, the days are coming,' says the LORD, 'that *I will perform that good thing* which I have promised to the house of Israel and to the house of Judah: 15 '*In those days and at that time I will cause to grow up to David A Branch of righteousness*; He shall execute judgment and righteousness in the earth. 16 In those days Judah will be *saved*, And Jerusalem will dwell safely. *And this is the name by which she will be called: the LORD our righteousness.' 17 "For thus says the LORD: 'David shall never lack a man to sit on the throne of the house of Israel*;

Ezek. 34:23-25 "*I will establish one shepherd* over them, and he shall feed them—*My servant David. He shall feed them and be their shepherd.* 24 "And I, the LORD, will be their God, and My servant David a prince among them; I, the LORD, have spoken. 25 "I will make a covenant of peace with them....

Ezek 36:25-28 [speaks of the new covenant in the power of the Holy Spirit]. "I will give you *a new heart and put a new spirit within you...I will put My Spirit within you and cause you to walk in My statutes*, and you will keep My judgments and do *them*.... you shall be My people, and I will be your God.

Ezek 37:23-26 "...Then they shall be My people, and I will be their God. *24 David My servant shall be king over them, and they shall all have one shepherd*; they shall also walk in My judgments and observe My statutes, and do them. 25 ...and *My servant David shall be their prince forever. 26 Moreover I will make a covenant of peace with them, and it shall be an everlasting covenant...*"

Steeped in this OT background, the New Testament writers show that Jesus of Nazareth is that Great Shepherd of the sheep, the Servant of the line of David, who has been enthroned as King, ruler of the New Covenant. This is the Gospel that Paul and the other apostles felt privileged to preach. This is why Paul especially emphasized in his preaching and epistles the fact that Jesus of Nazareth was of the line of David, and was the Messiah, and that gospel days that were now upon them were those witnessed to by the law and the prophets of the OT. Paul regarded himself as a minister of the Gospel, and as a minister of the New Covenant. Below is a sample of scriptures wherein the NT writers convey the significance of Jesus' fulfilling OT prophecies such as those above.

- Lk. 1:31-33, 67-73 "And behold, you will conceive in your womb and bring forth a Son, and shall call His name *JESUS. 32 "He will be great, and will be called the Son of the Highest; and the Lord God will give Him the throne of His father David....* "Blessed *is* the Lord God of Israel, For He has visited and redeemed His people, 69 *And has raised up a horn of salvation for us In the house of His servant David, 70 As He spoke by the mouth of His holy prophets, Who have been since the world began,* 71 That we should be saved from our enemies And from the hand of all who hate us, 72 To *perform the mercy promised to our fathers* and to remember His holy covenant....
- Matt. 21:9 ...the multitudes who went before and those who followed cried out, saying: *"Hosanna to the Son of David! 'Blessed is He who comes in the name of the LORD!'* Hosanna in the highest!"
- Acts 2:29-36 (Words of Peter) "Men *and* brethren, let *me* speak freely to you of the patriarch *David*, that he is both dead and buried, and his tomb is with us to this day. 30 "Therefore, being a prophet, and knowing that God had sworn with an oath to him that of the fruit of his body, according to the flesh, *He would raise up the Christ to sit on his throne,* 31 "he, foreseeing this, spoke concerning the resurrection of the Christ, that His soul was not left in Hades, nor did His flesh see corruption. 32 "This Jesus God has raised up, of which we are all witnesses. 33 *"Therefore being exalted to the right hand of God, and having received from the Father the promise of the Holy Spirit, He poured out this which you now see and hear.* 34 "For David did not ascend into the heavens, but he says himself: *'The LORD said to my Lord, "Sit at My right hand, 35 till I make Your enemies Your footstool."'* 36 *"Therefore let all the house of Israel know assuredly that God has made this Jesus, whom you crucified, both Lord and Christ."*
- Acts 13:23, 32-34, 38-41 (Words of Paul) *"From this man's seed [i.e. King David's seed], according to [the] promise, God raised up for Israel a Savior — Jesus —...* 32 "And we declare to you *glad tidings——that promise which was made to the fathers.* 33 *"God has fulfilled this for us their children,* in that He has raised up Jesus.... 38 "Therefore let it be known to you, brethren, *that through this Man is preached to you the forgiveness of sins; 39 "and by Him everyone who believes is justified from all things from which you could not be justified by the law of Moses.* 40 "Beware there-

fore, lest what has been spoken in the prophets come upon you: 41 "Behold, you despisers, Marvel and perish! For I work a work in your days, A work which you will by no means believe, Though one were to declare it to you.'"

[*Note v. 40 – Paul regarded the "work" of God, the work of salvation through the Messiah Jesus, the new covenant work, as present "in your days," i.e. in the days of his hearers*].

Rom 1:1-6, 16-17 Paul, a bondservant of Jesus Christ, called *to be* an apostle, *separated to the gospel of God 2 which He promised before through His prophets in the Holy Scriptures, 3 concerning His Son Jesus Christ our Lord, who was born of the seed of David according to the flesh,* 4 *and* declared *to be* the Son of God with power according to the Spirit of holiness, by the resurrection from the dead.... 16 *For I am not ashamed of the gospel of Christ, for it is the power of God to salvation for everyone who believes, for the Jew first and also for the Greek.* 17 For in it the righteousness of God is revealed from faith to faith; as it is written, "The just shall live by faith."

Rom 3:21-22 But now the righteousness of God apart from the law is revealed, *being witnessed by the Law and the Prophets,* 22 even the righteousness of God, through faith in Jesus Christ, to all and on all who believe.

2 Tim 2:8 Remember that *Jesus Christ, of the seed of David, was raised from the dead according to my gospel,*

Jesus is the good shepherd of Ezekiel's prophecies.

Jn. 10:10b-11, 14, 16 "...I have come that they may have life, and that they may have *it* more abundantly. I am the good shepherd. The good shepherd gives His life for the sheep.... 14 *"I am the good shepherd...* 16 "And other sheep I have which are not of this fold; them also I must bring, and they will hear My voice; and there will be *one flock and one shepherd.*

Heb 13:20-21 Now may *the God of peace* who brought up our *Lord Jesus* from the dead, *that great Shepherd of the sheep,* through the blood of *the everlasting covenant,* 21 make you complete in every good work to do His will, working in you what is well pleasing in His sight, through Jesus Christ, to whom *be* glory forever and ever.

Here in Heb. 13, we have the themes of God's Shepherd and everlasting covenant and covenant of peace as prophesied by Ezekiel.

Rev. 5:5 But one of the elders said to me, "Do not weep. *Behold, the Lion of the tribe of Judah, the Root of David, has prevailed* to open the scroll and to loose its seven seals."

Rev. 22:16, 17 "*I, Jesus,* have sent My angel to testify to you these things in the churches. *I am the Root and the Offspring of David,* the Bright and Morning Star." 17 ...And let him who thirsts come. And whoever desires let him take the water of life freely."

2. Jesus' High Priesthood, Mediatorship, and Blood — New Covenant Realities

The first Christians were experiencing the salvation provided by Jesus their High Priest and Mediator of the New Covenant. The apostle Paul was appointed a preacher of this great truth which God had revealed (1 Tim 2:7). No longer were the Aaronic priesthood and Mosaic sacrificial system the object of their trust. They now knew Jesus as their High Priest who had gained them access to the Father.

Through Jesus' ministry as high priest and mediator of the new covenant, his people were experiencing cleansed consciences. As their caring high priest he was able to give true aid to those being tested; he was sympathizing with their weaknesses and was the means of their receiving grace and mercy to help in their time of need. How great for these first Christian Jews, coming out of an ineffectual Mosaic covenant, to look to Jesus as the greater-than-Aaron high priest, and say "We have such a high priest who is seated at the right hand of God in the heavenly tabernacle blessing us with his new covenant ministry!"

The early church clearly regarded the sacrificial death of Christ as initiating and dedicating the new covenant; and that, following the entry of Jesus their High Priest into the heavenly Holy of Holies with his own blood, believers in Christ Jesus were experiencing the new covenant blessings purchased by Christ's blood. The old covenant was dedicated by the blood of an animal sacrifice, and animal blood was sprinkled upon the people, symbolizing their reception into that old covenant (e.g. Heb 9:18-20). The new covenant was dedicated by the sacrificial blood of Christ, and the believers' inclusion in that new covenant is figuratively referred to as their being sprinkled by the blood of Christ (Heb 12:24; 1 Pet 1:2).

In the following sample of scriptures, note the wonderful themes of Jesus' high priesthood, mediatorship, and blood — all to do with the ministry of the new covenant operating in those first Christians' lives.

> Matt 26:27-28 Then He took the cup, and gave thanks, and gave *it* to them, saying, "Drink from it, all of you. 28 "For *this is My blood of the new covenant,* which is shed for many for the remission of sins. See also Lk. 22:20.
>
> 1 Cor. 10:16; 11:23-26 The cup of blessing which we bless, is it not *the communion of the blood of Christ*? The bread which we break, is it not the communion of the body of Christ? 11:23 For I received from the Lord what I also delivered to you...

The early Christians were experiencing a new relationship with God through the blood of the new covenant, the blood of Christ. They celebrated the fact of the New Covenant having been inaugurated by Christ's blood, in their communion feasts.

> 1 Tim 2:5-7 *For there is one God and one Mediator between God and men, the Man Christ Jesus*, 6 who gave Himself a ransom for all,

to be testified in due time, 7 *for which I was appointed a preacher and an apostle* – I am speaking the truth in Christ *and* not lying – *a teacher of the Gentiles in faith and truth.*

Heb 2:17 - 3:1 Therefore, in all things He had to be made like *His* brethren, that He might be *a merciful and faithful High Priest in things pertaining to God, to make propitiation for the sins of the people.* 18 For in that He Himself has suffered, being tempted, *He is able to aid those who are tempted.* 1 Therefore, holy brethren, partakers of the heavenly calling, *consider the Apostle and High Priest of our confession, Christ Jesus,*

Heb 4:14-16 "Seeing then *that we have a great High Priest who has passed through the heavens, Jesus the Son of God*, let us hold fast our confession.... 16 Let us *therefore come boldly to the throne of grace, that we may obtain mercy and find grace* to help in time of need." (See also Heb 7:20-28)

Heb. 8:2 Now *this is* the main point of the things we are saying: *We have such a High Priest, who is seated at the right hand of the throne of the Majesty in the heavens,* 2 *a Minister of the sanctuary and of the true tabernacle which the Lord erected, and not man.*

Heb 8:6 But *now* He has obtained a more excellent ministry, inasmuch as *He is also Mediator of a better covenant*, which was established on better promises.

Heb 9:11-15 But *Christ came as High Priest of the good things to come,...* 12 *...with His own blood He entered the Most Holy Place once for all, having obtained eternal redemption....* 15 *And for this reason He is the Mediator of the new covenant, by means of death, for the redemption of the transgressions under the first covenant*, that those who are called may receive the promise of the eternal inheritance.

Heb. 10:29 *...the Son of God... blood of the covenant... Spirit of grace?*

Heb. 12:24 [you have come]... to *Jesus the Mediator of the new covenant, and to the blood of sprinkling* that speaks better things than *that of* Abel.

Heb. 13:20 "Now may the God of peace who brought up our Lord Jesus from the dead, that great Shepherd of the sheep, *through the blood of the everlasting covenant...*" *The blessing of sanctification in Heb 13:20-21 is based on the blood of the new covenant.*

1 Pet. 1:1-2 Peter, an apostle of Jesus Christ, To the... elect according to the foreknowledge of God the Father, in sanctification of the Spirit, for obedience and *sprinkling of the blood of Jesus Christ*. Grace to you and peace be multiplied.

3. The New Covenant and Righteousness and Justification

The early Christians of Paul's day were experiencing the great gift of righteousness by faith, which was a great blessing of the new covenant. In Romans, Paul says the gospel of righteousness by faith he was teaching as then present in his day was in fulfillment of Old Testament prophecies.

Those Old Testament prophecies contained the promise of a new covenant. The old covenant standard of righteousness by works of the law that the Jews were aiming at, is clearly shown by Paul to be futile, and that God's gospel focuses on the new covenant righteousness by faith in Christ. (Actually God's way of righteousness by faith in Christ was present since creation: Romans chapter 4 demonstrates that Abraham was justified by faith. But the justification by faith of old testament saints was in prospect of the full revelation of the atonement to be accomplished by Jesus Christ).

> Jer. 33:14-16 'Behold, the days are coming,' says the LORD, 'that I will perform *that good thing* [emphasis mine, IH] which I have promised to the house of Israel and to the house of Judah: 15 'In those days and at that time I will cause to grow up to David a Branch of righteousness [*a King, Jer 23:5*]; ...And *this is the name by which she will be called: the LORD our righteousness.*'.

"That good thing" or "that good word/matter" (from the Hebrew, הַדָּבָר הַטּוֹב "ha-dabar ha-tov") that the Lord was referring to in Jer 33:14 (quoted just above), which He had promised, was the establishing of a new covenant, an everlasting covenant, as stated clearly in Jer 31:31-34, 40, wherein the Lord's people would have the righteousness of the Seed of David, and remission of sin, and a new spiritual life in fellowship with God. The focus in the above verses is that the promised new covenant would see the Lord's people experiencing the Lord as their righteousness.

Consider also Isaiah's prophecy of the granting of justification through the sacrifice of the Messiah:

> Isa. 53:10-11 Yet it pleased the LORD to bruise Him; He has put *Him* to grief. When You make His soul an offering for sin, He shall see *His* seed, He shall prolong *His* days, And the pleasure of the LORD shall prosper in His hand. 11 He shall see the labor of His soul, *and* be satisfied. *By His knowledge My righteous Servant shall justify many, For He shall bear their iniquities.*
> Isa. 45:24-25 He shall say, '*Surely in the LORD I have righteousness and strength....* 25 In the LORD all the descendants of Israel [*the believers - IH*] *shall be justified, and shall glory.*'

Paul's "gospel," or "good message" which he said was already present in his day, is the same as Jeremiah's "good word" (33:14) – the revelation of the new covenant – the gift of righteousness from God, through faith in the Lord Jesus Christ – salvation and righteousness before God, because of the grace of God. In these blessings Paul gloried, and loved to preach them (all of which wonderful blessings were impossible under the old covenant, e.g., Rom 3:19-20).

> Acts 13:38-39 "Therefore let it be known to you, brethren, that through this Man is preached to you the forgiveness of sins; 39 *"and by*

Him everyone who believes is justified from all things from which you could not be justified by the law of Moses.

Rom. 1:16 ...I am not ashamed of *the gospel... it is the power of God to salvation for everyone who believes, for the Jew first and also for the Greek. 17 For in it the righteousness of God is revealed from faith to faith*; as it is written, "The just shall live by faith."

Rom 3:20 Therefore by the deeds of the law no flesh will be justified in His sight, for by the law *is* the knowledge of sin. 21 *But now the righteousness of God apart from the law is revealed, being witnessed by the Law and the Prophets,* 22 *even the righteousness of God, through faith in Jesus Christ,* to all and on all who believe. For there is no difference; 23 for all have sinned and fall short of the glory of God, 24 *being justified freely by His grace through the redemption that is in Christ Jesus,* 25 whom God set forth *as* a propitiation by His blood, through faith, to demonstrate His righteousness, because in His forbearance God had passed over the sins that were previously committed, 26 to demonstrate at the present time His righteousness, that He might be just and *the justifier of the one who has faith in Jesus.*

Note the "but now" in Rom 3:21. Under the old covenant, justification by faith through the Messiah was only viewed prospectively through the types and figures of the ceremonial system, (for those with spiritual understanding to see the truth). But now, the days of the Messiah and new covenant atonement had been fully revealed and were known and experienced by all who believed in Christ Jesus.

Rom 5:8-9 But God demonstrates His own love toward us, in that while we were still sinners, Christ died for us. 9 Much more then, *having now been justified by His blood*, we shall be saved from wrath through Him. [Which blood? Christ's blood of the everlasting, new covenant - IH].

Rom 5:18-21 Therefore, as through one man's offense *judgment* came to all men, resulting in condemnation, even so *through one Man's righteous act the free gift came to all men, resulting in justification of life.* 19 For as by one man's disobedience many were made sinners, so also *by one Man's obedience many will be made righteous.* 20 Moreover the law entered that the offence might abound. But where sin abounded, grace abounded much more, 21 so that as sin reigned in death, even so *grace might reign through righteousness to eternal life through Jesus Christ our Lord.*

Clearly Paul regards the Christians' present relationship with God through the Lord Jesus as one that is superior to that under old covenant law which "entered in alongside" to reveal the real nature of the sin that came into the world through Adam; this law could never justify anyone (Acts 13:39; 15:10). In Christ Jesus the Christians were experiencing the new covenant righteousness from God through Christ.

Rom 10:3-4, 10-12 For they [the Jews] being ignorant of God's righteousness, and seeking to establish their own righteousness, have not submitted to the righteousness of God. 4 For *Christ is the end of the law* [the law of the old covenant] *for righteousness to everyone who believes.* 10 For with the heart *one believes unto righteousness*, and with the mouth confession is made unto salvation.

1 Cor. 1:30 But of Him *you are in Christ Jesus, who became for us wisdom from God – and righteousness and sanctification and redemption –* 31 that, as it is written, "He who glories, let him glory in the LORD."

Paul says here in Rom 10:4 and 1 Cor. 1:30 that Christ Jesus became the righteousness of believers. This was promised in Jer 23:6 "Now this is His name by which He shall be called, The Lord our Righteousness." And, says Paul, in view of this righteousness believers glory in the Lord, which was prophesied in Isa. 45:25, "In the Lord all the descendants of Israel [who come to Him, believing, IH] shall be justified and shall glory."

See also 2 Cor. 5:21; 6:1-2 - *righteousness and the day of salvation.*

4. The New Covenant and Redemption, Reconciliation and the Remission of Sins

The first Christians were experiencing a redemption involving the remission of sins, which was a major aspect of the promised new covenant, as is pointed out in Jeremiah's prophetic words from Jer 31:33-34. The writer of the letter to the Hebrews takes up Jeremiah's words:

Heb 10:15-18 But the Holy Spirit also witnesses to us *[about true remission of sins through Christ, as per previous context]*; for after He had said before, 16 *"This is the covenant that I will make with them after those days, says the LORD: I will put My laws into their hearts, and in their minds I will write them,"* 17 *then He adds, "Their sins and their lawless deeds I will remember no more." 18 Now where there is remission of these, there is no longer an offering for sin. [Jer. 31:34 adds "I will forgive their iniquity."]*

Under the old covenant animal sacrifices, true remission of sins was not possible; they had merely been "passed over" (Rom 3:25). Under the new covenant, by the blood of Jesus and the High Priesthood of Jesus, there is true remission of sins, true propitiation and true reconciliation with God. The first Christians were experiencing these blessings.

Matt 26:28 "For this is *My blood of the new covenant, which is shed for many for the remission of sins.*

Lk. 24:44-48 *[after His resurrection]* Then He said to them, "These *are* the words which I spoke to you while I was still with you, that *all things must be fulfilled which were written in the Law of Moses and the Prophets and the Psalms concerning Me."* 45 And He opened their understanding, that they might comprehend the Scriptures. 46 Then He said to them, "Thus it is written, and thus it was necessary for the Christ to suffer and to rise from the dead the third day, 47 "and *that repentance and remission of sins should be preached in His name to all nations, beginning at Jerusalem.* 48 "And you are witnesses of these things."

Verse 47 is tantamount to saying that the new covenant promised in the prophet Jeremiah's prophecy should be now preached to all nations.

Acts 2:36-38 [Peter's sermon] "Therefore let all the house of Israel know assuredly that God has made this Jesus, whom you crucified, both Lord and Christ."... 38 Then Peter said to them, *"Repent, and let every one of you be baptized in the name of Jesus Christ for the remission of sins; and you shall receive the gift of the Holy Spirit.* 39 "For *the promise* is to you and to your children, ...all who are afar off, as many as the Lord ... will call."

"The promise" includes Jeremiah's promise of remission of sins, plus Joel and Ezekiel's promises of the Holy Spirit. Lk. 24:47 is being fulfilled - repentance and remission of sins are being preached, beginning at Jerusalem.

Acts 10:43 *[Peter's sermon to the Centurion]* "To Him *[i.e. Jesus] all the prophets witness* that, *through His name, whoever believes in Him will receive remission of sins."*

Eph 1:7 (also Col. 1:14) *In Him we have redemption through His blood, the forgiveness [or, remission] of sins...*

Rom 3:21, 24-25 But now the righteousness of God apart from the law is revealed, being witnessed by the Law and the Prophets... being justified freely by His grace *through the redemption that is in Christ Jesus*, 25 *whom God set forth as a propitiation by His blood, through faith,* to demonstrate His righteousness, because in His forbearance God had passed over the sins that were previously committed *[under the old covenant - see Heb 9:15]*

Rom 5:10-11 For if *when we were enemies we were reconciled to God through the death of His Son,* much more, having been reconciled, we shall be saved by His life. 11 And not only that, but we also rejoice in God through *our Lord Jesus Christ, through whom we have now received the reconciliation.*

Col. 1:19-22 "For it pleased *the Father that* in Him all the fullness should dwell, 20 and by Him to reconcile all things to Himself, by Him, whether things on earth or things in heaven, *having made peace through the blood of His cross.* 21 *And you,* who once were alienated and enemies in your mind by wicked works, *yet now He has reconciled* 22 *in the body of His flesh through death..."* See Col. 2:13f; Heb 1:1ff – forgiveness of sin.

> Heb 9:11-12, 15 ...*with His own blood He entered the Most Holy Place once for all, having obtained eternal redemption....* 15 ...*He is the Mediator of the new covenant, by means of death, for the redemption of the transgressions under the first covenant*, that those who are called may receive the promise of the eternal inheritance.

"With his own blood," - the blood of the eternal covenant (Heb 13:20). The writer clearly regards the first covenant as finished for all those who come to God through Jesus. The transgressions under the first covenant which were previously "passed over" by God (Rom 3:25), and for which no animal sacrifice could really cleanse away the guilt, now have been cleansed by Christ Jesus, the Mediator of the New Covenant (Heb 9:15). Many Jews previously living under the old covenant, such as the 3000 listening to Peter's sermon of Acts chapter 2, now after Pentecost were experiencing the redemption, the remission of sins, as part of the ministry of Jesus, Mediator of the new covenant.

> Heb 10:10-19 ...*we have been sanctified through the offering of the body of Jesus Christ once for all.* 11 And every priest stands ministering daily and offering repeatedly the same sacrifices, *which can never take away sins.* 12 *But this Man, after He had offered one sacrifice for sins forever*, sat down at the right hand of God,... 14 For *by one offering He has perfected forever those who are being sanctified.* 15 But the Holy Spirit also witnesses to us; for after He had said before, 16 *"This is the covenant that I will make with them after those days, says the LORD... "Their sins and their lawless deeds I will remember no more."* 18 Now where *there is remission of these, there is* no longer an offering for sin.

Note the emphasis: the old covenant with its mortal Aaronic priests and animal sacrifices could not give the perfection of remission of sins; but now the new-order, ever-living High Priest, Jesus, has bought this perfection and the set-apartness to God, by the offering of himself as the sacrificial victim for all who believe in him. They are no longer under the old covenant imperfection but under the new covenant perfection in Christ.

> 1 Pet. 1:18 knowing that you were not redeemed with corruptible things, like silver or gold, from your aimless conduct received by tradition from your fathers, but [you were redeemed] *with the precious blood of Christ*, as of a lamb without blemish and without spot. [the blood of the everlasting covenant, Heb 13:20]

5. The New Covenant of New Creation Life — Deliverance from Old Covenant Law

The early Christians regarded themselves as freed from the old covenant law which was a schoolmaster or guardian only until Christ came with his new covenant in which they were now made sons and had received the spirit of sonship. Instead of the letter of the law, they had the Spirit of the life of Christ in them — new covenant life, new creation life — in which the ways of God were written and formed in their hearts and minds. They were now not under law but under grace. They no longer thought in terms of the separation of Jews and gentiles - an old covenant distinction - but in terms of "all one in Christ Jesus."

Old Testament prophecies spoke of the gift of the Spirit and new spiritual life under the Messiah — central features of the new covenant:

> Jer 31:31-34 "...I will make *a new covenant... this is the covenant* that I will make," says the LORD:.... "*I will put My law in their minds, and write it on their hearts;* and I will be their God, and they shall be My people."
>
> Jer 32:38-40 'They shall be My people, and I will be their God; 39 '*then I will give them one heart and one way, that they may fear Me forever,...* 40 'And *I will make an everlasting covenant with them,* that I will not turn away from doing them good; but *I will put My fear in their hearts so that they will not depart from Me.* [*Heb 13:20 declares that the everlasting covenant was through the blood of Christ*].
>
> Ezek 36:26-28 "*I will give you a new heart and put a new spirit within you; I will take the heart of stone out of your flesh and give you a heart of flesh.* 27 "*I will put My Spirit within you and cause you to walk in My statutes, and you will keep My judgments and do them.* 28 ...you shall be My people, and I will be your God.*

Old Testament prophecies such as these, promising a new covenant with the Holy Spirit and new creation life in the heart, were fulfilled in the lives of the first Christians, as shown in the New Testament epistles. Some examples follow:

(i) The New Covenant Ministry and New Creation Life in the Spirit

> 2 Cor. 3:2-6,14 - 4:1 You are our epistle written in our hearts, known and read by all men; 3 clearly *you are an epistle of Christ, ministered by us, written not with ink but by the Spirit of the living God, not on tablets of stone but on tablets of flesh, that is, of the heart....* 5 ...*our sufficiency is from God,* 6 who also made us sufficient as ministers of the new covenant, not of the letter but of the Spirit; for the letter kills, but the Spirit gives life....* 14 But their minds [i.e. of the unbelieving Jews] were blinded. For until this day the same veil remains unlifted in the reading of the Old Testament, because the *veil* is taken away in Christ.... 17 Now *the Lord is the Spirit; and where the Spirit of the Lord is, there is liberty.* 18 But we all, with unveiled face, beholding as in a mirror the glory of the Lord, *are*

being transformed into the same image from glory to glory, just as *by the Spirit of the Lord.* 1 Therefore, since *we have this ministry [of the new covenant, 3:6 - IH]*, as we have received mercy, we do not lose heart.

In Christ, the Old Covenant is fulfilled. Most Jews were veiled to this truth, and never knew the spiritual liberty of the New Covenant. Paul was a preacher of the New Covenant wherein the Spirit of God, as promised in the OT, was writing the very nature of God in their hearts, and transforming their lives.

> 2 Cor. 5:14-18 17 Therefore, *if anyone is in Christ, he is a new creation; old things have passed away; behold, all things have become new.* 18 Now all things *are* of God, *who has reconciled us to Himself through Jesus Christ*, and has given us *the ministry of reconciliation.*
>
> Rom 7:4-6 Therefore, my brethren, you also have become dead to the law through the body of Christ*, that you may be married to another——to Him who was raised from the dead, that we should bear fruit to God.* 5 For when we were in the flesh, the sinful passions which were aroused by the law were at work in our members to bear fruit to death. 6 But now we have been delivered from the law, having died to what we were held by*, so that we should serve in the newness of the Spirit and not in the oldness of the letter.*

As promised by Ezekiel in ch. 36, the new covenant involves the Holy Spirit filling the believers with the newness of a holy life, in contrast with the old covenant which could only bring bondage and death.

> Rom 8:1-4 *There is therefore now no condemnation to those who are in Christ Jesus*, who do not walk according to the flesh, but according to the Spirit. 2 *For the law of the Spirit of life in Christ Jesus has made me free from the law of sin and death.* 3 *For what the law could not do in that it was weak through the flesh, God did* by sending His own Son in the likeness of sinful flesh, on account of sin: ...4 that *the righteous requirement of the law might be fulfilled in us who do not walk according to the flesh but according to the Spirit.*
>
> Rom 8:15-16 For you did not receive the spirit of bondage again to *fear [i.e. that bondage under the law of the old covenant]*, but *you received the Spirit of adoption by whom we cry out, "Abba, Father."* 16 *The Spirit Himself bears witness with our spirit that we are children of God,*
>
> See also Gal 3:13-14; Eph 2:8-10; Eph 3:20-24; Col. 3:9-10 — the gift of the Spirit, God's new creation in Christ Jesus, a being renewed in righteousness and holiness.

> Phil 2:13; 3:1-3 for *it is God who works in you both to will and to do for His good pleasure...* 2 Beware of dogs, beware of evil workers, beware of the mutilation! 3 For *we are the circumcision, who worship God in the Spirit, rejoice in Christ Jesus, and have no confidence in the flesh,*

Paul means by Phil 3:2-3, as the whole context shows, that the Christians are not under the old covenant of fleshly rituals, with a fleshly worship; but that they now have a regenerated heart due to a spiritual circumcision, and worship God in a new spiritual way, just as Jesus promised in Jn. 4:21-24, and as in Ezekiel's prophecy 36:26-27).

> Tit. 3:4-7 But after that the kindness and love of God our Savior toward man appeared, 5 Not by works of righteousness which we have done, but *according to his mercy he saved us, by the washing of regeneration, and renewing of the Holy Ghost*; 6 *Which he shed on us abundantly through Jesus Christ our Savior*; 7 That being justified by his grace, we should be made heirs according to the hope of eternal life.

Here is God's giving them a new spirit (regeneration), and putting His Spirit in them, according to Ezekiel. See also Heb 9:14; 13:20-21 — on the basis of the blood of the new covenant, there is cleansing of conscience to truly serve God, and have God's inward sanctifying work.

(ii) No longer under law, but grace – the grace of the new covenant

> Gal 2:18-21 *[Note Peter's fear of the Judaizers who wanted to bring Christians under the law. Paul said the following as part of his response]* 18 For if I build again the things which I destroyed, I confirm myself *as* a transgressor. 19 *For through the Law I died to the law, that I might live to God. 20 I have been crucified with Christ, and I live; yet no longer I, but Christ lives in me. And that life I now live in the flesh, I live by faith toward the Son of God, who loved me and gave Himself on my behalf.* 21 I do not set aside the grace of God, for if righteousness *is* through law, then Christ died without cause.

The believers in Christ, have the righteousness of the new covenant, given by the grace of God, and are no longer under the law.

> Gal. 3:23 - 4:7 But before the faith came, we were kept under guard by the law, kept for the faith which would afterward be revealed. 24 *Therefore the law was our tutor to bring us to Christ, that we might be justified by faith.* 25 *But after [the] faith has come, we are no longer under a tutor. 26 For you are all sons of God through faith in Christ Jesus....* 4:4 But

when the fullness of the time had come, God sent forth His Son, born of a woman, born under the law, 5 to redeem those who were under the law, that we might receive the adoption as sons. 6 And because you are sons, God has sent forth the Spirit of His Son into your hearts, crying out, "Abba, Father!" *7 Therefore you are no longer a slave but a son, and if a son, then an heir of God through Christ.*

For the believers in Christ Jesus, they were no longer under the tutelage of the old covenant which could never make them sons of God; their subjection to the old covenant was only until "the faith" came, i.e. the gospel of faith in Christ Jesus. Through redemption in Christ they are now sons of God, with the Spirit in their hearts. The presence of the Messiah and the gift of the Spirit were promised in Old Testament prophecies as aspects of the new covenant. The first Christians were members of the new covenant, children of the promise of righteousness by faith in Christ.

See Gal 4:21- 5:2. Paul states clearly: There are two covenants: a Sinai-Hagar-bondwoman covenant of law-works which brings bondage, and a Jerusalem-above-Sarai-freewoman covenant of justification by faith in Christ which gives liberty: an old covenant and a new covenant.

The believers in Christ and his gospel-promise of justification by faith are born of the Spirit and are children of the new gospel covenant, children of promise, in contrast to the non-believing Jews who remain under the yoke of the old covenant as children of bondage. Paul, in Gal 5:1, quoted above, agrees with Peter in Acts 15:10, by both referring to the old covenant system as a "yoke" which none can bear, a yoke of bondage, which gives rise to a spirit of bondage (Rom 8:15). Believers in Christ are free from it and have a new liberty in Christ!

> Rom 6:14 For sin shall not have dominion over you, for *you are not under law but under grace.*
> Rom 7:1-6 Or do you not know, brethren (for I speak to those who know the law), *that the law has dominion over a man as long as he lives?*... 4 Therefore, *my brethren, you also have become dead to the law through the body of Christ, that you may be married to another*—to Him who was raised from the dead, that we should bear fruit to God. 5 For when we were in the flesh, *the sinful passions which were aroused by the law* were at work in our members to bear fruit to death. 6 *But now we have been delivered from the law, having died to what we were held by, so that we should serve in the newness of the Spirit and not in the oldness of the letter.*
> See also Col. 2:8-17 — *Believers in Christ had a completeness of new inner circumcision done by God, new life, forgiveness from all the laws against them – having the "substance" in Christ instead of the previous "shadow" of the law.*

All those "in Christ" have finished with the law covenant; they are now under "grace," that is, the new covenant in Christ which is based on the sheer grace of God. Their life now centers on walking by faith in obedience to Christ as their life. Both in the Philippians passage 3:1-3, and the Colossians passage 2:8-17 Paul is claiming that the Christians are not bound to the old covenant laws any more. They have come to the completeness of forgiveness and new life that is in Christ. They are no longer under the incompleteness of the temporary, figurative, shadowy and condemning nature of the old covenant with its laws and ceremonies, but are under grace in the permanent, spiritual reality and "substance" of the new covenant in Christ.

(iii) The New Covenant church composed of all nationalities of men and women has been formed. The Old Covenant barriers and distinctions are removed in the church of Jesus Christ.

Paul was appointed by God as a minister of the New Covenant, a minister of the gospel of reconciliation between God and sinners, a minister of the mystery, now revealed, of Christ who unites all believers of all nationalities in himself. Paul is declaring that the age of the New Covenant is upon them. The blessings of this mystery of Christ had been hidden in past ages; although there are hints of the union of believing Jews and Gentiles in the OT prophets, "but now" at this time of history, the New Covenant of unity in Christ is revealed and is being preached.

> Eph 2:11-22 Therefore remember that you, once Gentiles in the flesh – who are called Uncircumcision by what is called the Circumcision made in the flesh by hands – 12 that at that time you were without Christ, being aliens from the commonwealth of Israel and strangers from the covenants of promise, having no hope and without God in the world. 13 *But now in Christ Jesus you who once were far off have been brought near by the blood of Christ [= the blood of the New Covenant - IH].* 14 For *He Himself is our peace, who has made both one, and has broken down the middle wall of separation, 15 having abolished in His flesh the enmity, that is, the law of commandments contained in ordinances, so as to create in Himself one new man from the two, thus making peace,* 16 and that He might reconcile them both to God in one body through the cross, thereby putting to death the enmity. 17 And He came and preached peace to you who were afar off and to those who were near. 18 *For through Him we both have access by one Spirit to the Father.* 19 *Now, therefore, you are no longer strangers and foreigners, but fellow citizens with the saints and members of the household of God,* 20 *having been built on the foundation of the apostles and prophets, Jesus Christ Himself being the chief cornerstone,* 21 in whom the whole building, being joined together, grows into a holy temple in

the Lord, 22 in whom you also are being built together for a dwelling place of God in the Spirit.

Note here that the new covenant assembly made up of believers of all types of nationalities has been built, verse 20, on the foundation of the gospel teaching of the apostles and prophets, that is, built onto the Lord Jesus Christ as the chief corner stone. This new covenant assembly which now exists is not a part of the old covenant system, but a fulfillment of the promises given in the Old Testament. Individually, new gentile believers are being built together with Jewish believers for God to have his dwelling place in them by the Spirit. The church is growing as a holy temple in Christ. (See also 1 Cor. 3:16; 6:19).

See a similar text in Eph 3:1-12. For the gentiles to be "partakers [along with believing Jews] of His promise in Christ" (v. 6), it means they are partakers of what was promised in the OT, viz., the new covenant involving the gift of righteousness and eternal life in the Messiah. This mystery is manifested "now," showing forth the manifold wisdom of God.

> Gal 3:27-29 For as many of you as were baptized into Christ *have put on Christ. 28 There is neither Jew nor Greek, there is neither slave nor free, there is neither male nor female; for you are all one in Christ Jesus.* 29 ...if you *are* Christ's, then you are Abraham's seed, and heirs according to the promise.

(iv) "You in Christ" - "Christ in you."

The phrases "in Christ" and "through Christ," which occur many times in the New Testament writings, are New Covenant terms. The believers are not now seen by God as related to the Old Covenant, but are seen as related to Christ Jesus, their Savior, Lord, and Mediator of the New Covenant, in whom they have true reconciliation with God. A wonderful corollary of the fact of this New Covenant relationship with and in Christ is that Christ indwelt his people and Christ was their life.

> Gal 2:19-20 "For I through the law died to the law that I might live to God. 20 "I have been crucified with Christ; it is no longer I who live, but *Christ lives in me*; and the *life* which I now live in the flesh I live by faith in the Son of God, who loved me and gave Himself for me.

The Old Covenant left one desolate (see, e.g. Rom 7), but under the New Covenant Paul had the new life of Christ in him.

> 2 Cor. 13:3-6 since you seek a proof of Christ speaking in me, *[Christ] who is not weak toward you, but [who is] mighty in you.* 4 For though He was crucified in weakness, yet He lives by the power of God. For we also are weak in Him, but we shall live with Him by the power of God toward you. 5 Exam-

ine yourselves *as to* whether you are in the faith. Test yourselves. Do you not know yourselves, that *Jesus Christ is in you?* ——unless indeed you are disqualified. 6 But I trust that you will know that we are not disqualified. *[bracketed parts mine - IH]*

Paul was aware that being a Christian meant having "Jesus Christ in you," and not a weak Christ either, but a "Christ who is mighty in you."

Rom 8:9-10 But you are not in the flesh but in the Spirit, if indeed the Spirit of God dwells in you. Now if anyone does not have the Spirit of Christ, he is not His. 10 And if *Christ is in you*, the body *is* dead because of sin, but the Spirit *is* life because of righteousness.

Gal 4:19-22f My little children, for whom I labor in birth again *until Christ is formed in you*, 20 I would like to be present with you now and to change my tone; for I have doubts about you. 21 Tell me, you who desire to be under the law, do you not hear the law? 22 For it is written that Abraham had two sons: the one by a bondwoman, the other by a freewoman....

For those Galatian believers who were abandoning the true New Covenant gospel of faith and grace in Christ, by returning to the Old Covenant law for justification, Paul said, " My little children, for whom I labor in birth again until Christ is formed in you." (Gal 4:19) He had once travailed over them when he had previously preached the gospel to them, and as a result of his preaching they had embraced Christ as their all sufficient Savior and Righteousness, and Christ was formed in them as their new life. But by their having fallen from the way of grace and returning to the law-works, the presence and life of Christ in them was obviously failing to come forth. Sadly, liberty in Christ was being squashed by bondage under law (cf. Gal 5:1). Paul was having to travail over them AGAIN (like he did the first time) until Christ was formed in them again by their re-embracing him and the true gospel. See the context following, in which Paul demonstrates that they are children of the promise, born of the Spirit, children of the Jerusalem above, symbolizing the new covenant. Christ being formed in them is related to the overall context of the believers tending to resort to Old Covenant rituals instead of progressing in their New Covenant life in Christ, characterized by Christ's indwelling presence, as Paul testified of himself in Gal 2:19-20.

Col. 1:27 To them (to his saints, v. 26) God willed to make known what are the riches of the glory of this mystery among the Gentiles: which is *Christ in you*, the hope of glory.

Contrary to how many preterists interpret Gal 4:19, and Col. 1:27, I don't believe the contexts refer to "Christ in you" as a hope to be fulfilled at the future Parousia of Christ. Rather the verses referred to above show that "Christ in you" was taught as a present reality for Christians of Paul's day. And Col. 1:27 means that the fact of Christ's presence in the believers then, was a sure guarantee of future glory with Christ at his future Parousia. I believe Col. 3:4 contains the same idea: Christ is our life, says Paul; Christ is in us and with us now by his Spirit; and this makes us confident that when he is manifested we will appear with him in glory. The "mystery" of Jew and Gentile being united now in Christ was a special revelation, not so revealed before (see Ephesian passages above). This union in Christ meant that all partook of the one Spirit. And the indwelling of Christ was not just the portion of the Jewish Christians, but, as Paul was excited to preach, also the portion of the Gentiles who believed.

> Eph 3:14-19 For this reason I bow my knees to the Father of our Lord Jesus Christ, 15 from whom the whole family in heaven and earth is named, 16 that He would grant you, according to the riches of His glory, to be strengthened with might through His Spirit in the inner man, 17 *that Christ may dwell in your hearts through faith*; that you, being rooted and grounded in love, 18 may be able to comprehend with all the saints what *is* the width and length and depth and height— 19 to know the love of Christ which passes knowledge; that you may be filled with all the fullness of God.

Paul says he bows in prayer "For this reason..." Which reason? The one he had just mentioned in 2:11 - 3:13, namely, that now God has revealed his mystery in Christ, of uniting Jews and Gentiles, as one body in Christ, wherein all are formed as one temple for the dwelling place of God by the Spirit. This New Covenant reality is according to God's eternal purpose which he accomplished in Christ Jesus. For this reason, Paul prays that the Ephesian believers may be strengthened by the Spirit in their inner man, and that Christ may dwell in their hearts by faith. It seems clear to me that this indwelling of Christ and the knowing the love of Christ were blessings the pre-Parousia Christians were to experience.

6. The New Covenant – Knowledge of and Fellowship with God

A central blessing of the promised New Covenant was a new experience of God revealing himself as his people's God and of his people experiencing a new spiritual knowledge of God himself and a new access to Him and fellowship with Him. The first Christians were experiencing all of this through the mediatorship of the Lord Jesus Christ.

> Heb 8:10-12 [quoting from Jer 31:31-34] *"For this is the covenant that I will make* with the house of Israel after those days, says the LORD: I will put My laws in their mind and write them on their hearts; *and I will be their God, and they shall be My people. 11 "None of them shall teach his neighbor, and*

none his brother, saying, 'Know the LORD,' for all shall know Me, from the least of them to the greatest of them. 12 "For I will be merciful to their unrighteousness, and their sins and their lawless deeds I will remember no more."

This promise of a new covenant union with, and experiential knowledge of God is said to be the experience of the first Christians.

> Rom. 5:5 1-2, 5 Therefore, having been justified by faith, *we have peace with God through our Lord Jesus Christ*, 2 through whom also *we have access by faith into this grace in which we stand*, and rejoice in hope of the glory of God.... 5 Now hope does not disappoint, because *the love of God has been poured out in our hearts by the Holy Spirit who was given to us*.
>
> Eph 1:15-18 Therefore I also, after I heard of your faith in the Lord Jesus and your love for all the saints, 16 do not cease to give thanks for you, making mention of you in my prayers: 17 that *the God of our Lord Jesus Christ, the Father of glory, may give to you the spirit of wisdom and revelation in the knowledge of Him*, 18... your understanding being enlightened...

Note that it is through the Lord Jesus Christ, their Mediator, that the Father of glory now grants a New Covenant knowledge of God.

> Eph 2:11-13, 18 ...remember that you, once Gentiles in the flesh – who are called Uncircumcision by what is called the Circumcision made in the flesh by hands – 12 that *at that time you were without Christ, being aliens from the commonwealth of Israel and strangers from the covenants of promise*, having no hope and *without God* in the world. 13 But *now in Christ Jesus you who once were far off have been brought near by the blood of Christ...* 18 For *through Him we both have access by one Spirit to the Father*.

No longer are they strangers from the covenants of promise. By the blood of Christ, the blood of the new, everlasting covenant, they are in the promised New Covenant, they have been brought near, and have spiritual, experiential access to God as their own loving Father.

> Eph 3:14-19 — *knowing the love of Christ, filled with the fullness of God, by the power of the Spirit.*
>
> Col. 1:9-10 For this reason we... do not cease to pray for you, and to ask that you may be *filled with the knowledge of His will in all wisdom and spiritual understanding*; 10 that you may walk worthy of the Lord, fully pleasing *Him*, being fruitful in every good work and *increasing in the knowledge of God*;

Heb 4:14, 16 *Seeing then that we have a great High Priest* who has passed through the heavens, Jesus the Son of God, let us hold fast *our* confession. 16 *Let us therefore come boldly to the throne of grace*, that we may obtain mercy and find grace to help in time of need.

2 Pet. 1:1-2 Simon Peter, a bondservant and apostle of Jesus Christ, To those who have obtained like precious faith with us by the righteousness of our God and Savior Jesus Christ: 2 *Grace and peace be multiplied to you in the knowledge of God and of Jesus our Lord*

1 Jn. 1:3-4 that which we have seen and heard we declare to you, that you also may have fellowship with us; and *truly our fellowship is with the Father and with His Son Jesus Christ.* 4 And these things we write to you that your joy may be full.

1 Jn. 2:13 I write to you, fathers, Because *you have known Him who is from the beginning.* I write to you, young men, Because you have overcome the wicked one. I write to you, little children, Because *you have known the Father.*

1 Jn. 5:20 And *we know that the Son of God has come and has given us an understanding, that we may know Him who is true*; and we are in Him who is true, in His Son Jesus Christ. This is the true God and eternal life.

Eternal Life in Christ

The ultimate new covenant blessing is eternal life. But what is the essence of that life? The experiential knowledge of God himself (Jn. 17:3). The first believers had this eternal life in Christ whereby they experientially knew God, and were growing in their personal knowledge of God.

Jn. 20:30-31 ...Jesus did many other signs in the presence of His disciples, which are not written in this book; 31 but *these are written that you may believe that Jesus is the Christ, the Son of God, and that believing you may have life in His name.*

1 Jn. 5:11-13, 20 And this is the testimony: that *God has given us eternal life*, and this life is in His Son. 12 *He who has the Son has life*; he who does not have the Son of God does not have life. 13 *These things I have written to you who believe in the name of the Son of God, that you may know that you have eternal life*, and that you may *continue to* believe in the name of the Son of God.... 20 And we know that the Son of God has come *and has given us an understanding, that we may know Him who is true*; and *we are in Him who is true*, in His Son Jesus Christ. *This is the true God and eternal life.*

7. For the first Christians the New Covenant is "now"

May the reader pardon me for perhaps repeating some of the passages already quoted above in this section, but I felt it important to emphasize the wonder in which the first Christians, especially those of Jewish background, regarded the amazing newness of the time of the gospel of Jesus Christ in which they lived.

As pointed out in the first section of this article, the gospel involved the Messiah's coming, and his making atonement for the sins of his people, and their coming under the promised New Covenant of the Messiah, Jesus, who was that greater David promised in the prophecies of Jeremiah and Ezekiel. We cannot imagine the almost incredible wonder of men like the apostle Paul, who were so steeped in the Old Testament scriptures, to suddenly discover that the time of the promised New Covenant, introduced by the long-awaited Messiah had actually come, and that they had the privilege of being a part of this gospel of God.

I have listed just a few verses to illustrate how the apostles regarded the significance of the gospel times they were now living in. The recurrent use of the word "now" (Gr. νῦν and νυνι, *nun* and *nuni, now, present in time*) emphasizes the significance of these times. For them, their connection with Old Covenant systems and their unsaved days were finished; *now* they were a part of something far greater - the gospel of God, the New Covenant age which had *now* been revealed by God. (emphasis mine, IH).

> Rom 3:20-22, 25-26 Therefore by the deeds of the law no flesh will be justified in His sight, for by the law *is* the knowledge of sin. 21 *But NOW the righteousness of God apart from the law is revealed*, being witnessed by the Law and the Prophets, 22 even the righteousness of God, through faith in Jesus Christ, to all and on all who believe.... 25 [Jesus Christ] whom God set forth *as* a propitiation by His blood, through faith, to demonstrate His righteousness, because in His forbearance God had passed over the sins that were previously committed, 26 *to demonstrate at the present time* [lit. in the NOW season, Gr. ἐν τῷ νῦν καιρῷ] *His righteousness, that He might be just and the justifier of the one who has faith in Jesus*.
> Rom 16:25-27 Now to Him who is able to establish you according to *my gospel* and the preaching of Jesus Christ, according to *the revelation of the mystery kept secret since the world began 26 but NOW has been made manifest, and by the prophetic Scriptures has been made known to all nations*, according to the commandment of the everlasting God, for obedience to the faith – 27 to God, alone wise, *be* glory through Jesus Christ forever. Amen.
> 2 Cor. 6:1-2 We then, *as* workers together *with Him* also plead with *you* not to receive *the grace of God* in vain. 2 For He says: "In an acceptable time I have heard you, And in the day of salvation I have helped you." *Behold, NOW is the accepted time; behold, NOW is the day of salvation*.
> Eph 2:11-13 Therefore remember that you, once Gentiles in the

flesh – who are called Uncircumcision by what is called the Circumcision made in the flesh by hands — 12 that *at that time* you were without Christ, being aliens from the commonwealth of Israel and *strangers from the covenants of promise*, having no hope and without God in the world. 13 *But NOW in Christ Jesus you who once were far off have been brought near by the blood of Christ.*

See also Eph 3:2-6, 8-12 — the mystery of Christ NOW revealed by the Spirit; gentiles are partakers; NOW the manifold wisdom of God in Christ is revealed, and Paul is preaching it to help men see it and experience it.

Col. 1:19-21 . . 21 And *you, who once were alienated and enemies in your mind* by wicked works, *yet NOW He has reconciled 22 in the body of His flesh through death*

2 Tim 1:8-11 Therefore do not be ashamed of the testimony of our Lord, nor of me His prisoner, but share with me in the sufferings for *the gospel* according to the power of God, *9 who has saved us and called us with a holy calling, not according to our works, but according to His own purpose and grace which was given to us in Christ Jesus before time began,* 10 *but has NOW been revealed by the appearing of our Savior Jesus Christ, who* has abolished death and brought life and immortality to light through the gospel, 11 to which I was appointed a preacher, an apostle, and a teacher of the Gentiles.

1 Pet. 2:9-10, 25 But you *are* a chosen generation, a royal priesthood, a holy nation, His own special people, that you may proclaim the praises of Him who called you out of darkness into His marvelous light; 10 who *once were not a people but are NOW the people of God, who had not obtained mercy but NOW have obtained mercy...* 25 For you were like sheep going astray, *but have NOW returned [or, lit. "have been returned" - IH] to the Shepherd and Overseer of your souls.*

Heb 8:6 But *NOW* He has obtained a more excellent ministry, inasmuch *as He is also Mediator of a better covenant*, which was established on better promises.

Oh, the wonder of God's grace, say the apostles, for the gospel of God, the day of his New Covenant salvation through the promised Messiah, is NOW !

CONCLUSION

The whole New Testament is full of similar teaching to that given in the sample collection of scriptures above, making it clear that the first pre-Parousia (pre-AD 70) Christians rejoiced that they were experiencing the New Covenant in Christ Jesus. They were glorying in the following new covenant blessings:

- the efficacy of the blood of Christ as the blood of the New Covenant
- the ministry of Jesus Christ as High Priest and Mediator of the New Covenant
- the gift of righteousness by faith in Christ Jesus
- the gift of redemption and remission of sins and reconciliation with God through the blood of Jesus
- the gift of new creation life and sonship, by the Spirit of God
- the deliverance from being under the law of the old covenant
- the ministry of Spirit-empowered preachers ministering the Spirit, not the letter
- the blessedness of having access to, fellowshipping with, and knowing God as loving Father
- the gospel of the grace of God, the New Covenant era, which is NOW.

However, as wonderful as the experience of these new covenant blessings was for the first Christians, it is clear from the epistles that all was *not yet total glory*. They were still painfully aware of the large degree of natural fallenness still present in their lives: selfish and sinful habits still persisted, problems with fellow believers arose, spiritual ignorance and insensitivity were not fully cured, many were tempted to be disheartened by the sufferings they had to endure for the sake of Christ, and the reality of physical death still confronted them and saddened them. The Christian life they faced was (to use a modern saying) one of blood, sweat and tears.

Total victory, *total perfection*, *total glory*, although *potentially* theirs in Christ, were not yet *experiential reality* for the first Christians. We find in the epistles a great many *expectation statements* regarding the Christians' hope for a consummate glory soon to come at the Parousia of Christ (which they expected in the near future). In coming chapters we will examine the relationship between what the first Christians already possessed in the way of new covenant blessings and what was still to come, and the nature of the blessings that the first Christians were expecting at Christ's Parousia.

Chapter 2

New Covenant Blessings — *Deposit and Fullness*

A Brief Study of the *Deposit Blessings* Experienced Prior to, and Corresponding Consummate Blessings Expected at, the Parousia of Christ, by the First Christians

---

As demonstrated in Chapter 1, "The New Covenant in the Days of The Apostles," the New Testament Scriptures clearly show that the first Christians were experiencing the blessings of the New Covenant since the Day of Pentecost. They rejoiced in the Gospel of God and of Jesus Christ, speaking of redemption through the blood of Christ and justification by faith in Christ, etc. They were glorying in the fact that Jesus was their great high priest and mediator, ministering the New Covenant into their lives.

Wonderful as this change was in their whole relationship with God, they knew, from the epistles of Paul and others, and from their own not-yet-perfected life experience, that a consummation of their salvation, when the FULL force of the new covenant would be manifested in them, was yet to come.

The all-encompassing hope of the first Christians, as the New Testament makes so clear, was the coming/appearance/revelation of the Lord Jesus Christ in his glorious kingdom (which the preterist view holds as having occurred circa AD 70). Within the compass of the Lord's coming, the Christians were taught to expect the full and glorious consummation of the partial or deposit experience and measure of new covenant blessings that they were already experiencing.

Let me make it clear that I am not saying that their justification or pardon was partial, or that the atonement made by Jesus on their behalf was incomplete. What I am saying is that the new covenant blessings *experienced* so far by the first Christians, such as a spiritually enlightened understanding, God's power and life in them, victory over sin and the flesh, experiential fellowship with God and knowledge of his love and guidance — i.e., the *effects* flowing into their lives from the completed atonement and their justified state before God — were far from perfected or fully manifested. This chapter aims to give a general overview of the multi-faceted eschatological hope of the first Christians, which they had in Christ Jesus, their soon-to-come Savior.

1. The Sustaining Power of Hope for the First Christians

"We were saved in hope" – Paul wrote to the Roman believers (Rom 8:24). By this he meant that while those first Christians had been saved and justified by God through Christ Jesus by faith and set apart by God as His own children, they were not yet able to enter into the fullness and consummation of the blessings comprising the new covenant salvation. Such fullness was still future. It was still a hope.

This required them to undergo a trial of great patience until that fullness or consummation of the new covenant would be experienced, when the Lord Jesus would come for them in His glory. Until then the believers would only know a "first fruits" or "deposit" measure of that fullness (Rom 8:23; Eph 1:14; 2 Cor. 1:22; 5:5). They were indeed saved, but were to reside in the sphere of hope for the time being, with perseverance. As Paul says:

> Rom. 8:24-25 For we were saved in this hope [i.e. the hope spoken of in vv. 17-23]; but [or, now] hope that is seen is not hope; for why does one still hope for what he sees? 25 But if we hope for what we do not see, then we eagerly wait for it with perseverance. (brackets mine - IH)

With their constant trials amidst persecution from Jews and gentiles, and waiting for years for the coming of the Lord, one can understand that disillusionment could easily sneak into their hearts. The Acts and Epistles (including the Revelation) plainly encourage the believers to keep in view the Lord's near coming, e.g., "For now our salvation is nearer than when we first believed. The night is far spent, the day is at hand." (Rom 13:11-12). NT writers constantly exhort them to hold fast their hope, be patient and not relax their faith in God's promises. Christ was about to come as He promised, within the lifetime of that generation. Prayer was made for God to keep them rejoicing in Him and His promises:

> Rom 15:13 Now may the God of the hope fill you with all joy and peace in believing, that you may abound in hope by the power of the Holy Spirit.

2. Promise, Hope and Inheritance

These first Christians were thus in a trial period of waiting, a period of hope, until the coming of the Lord. What they were waiting for is often called in the New Testament "the eternal inheritance." That which inspired their hope in the first place was the promise of God.

The three terms Promise, Hope and Inheritance are significant eschatological words used in the Bible to describe the ultimate new covenant blessings that God has for His people. It is helpful in our Bible study, especially in regard to eschatological matters, to understand that in the Scriptures the three terms — promise, inheritance, and hope — are related as three aspects or emphases of the one grand subject of God's final salvation and ultimate blessing for believers in Christ. The examination of these three concepts reveals the marvelous grace of God who has provided all spiritual blessings for us in Christ Jesus. The subject is in this chapter treated in a general overview. The actual nature of the many individual blessings comprising these three terms will be examined in further chapters. Here is the definition of these terms in respect to eschatological matters:

- *"the promise"* — the eschatological blessing as promised by God, originated in the will of God, expressed in the word of God, and backed by the power and faithfulness of God.
- *"the inheritance"* — the eschatological blessing itself, *the matter of the promise*, which belongs to believers by the grant of God, which they will receive and enjoy when the promise is fulfilled by God.
- *"the hope"* — the eschatological blessing *as a future expected certainty*, which will satisfy the believers' longings. The subjective heart-emotion of hope derives from a consideration of the objective hope presented in the Word of promise.

The *promise* of an *inheritance* inspires the emotion of *hope*. This hope is based on and supported by the reliability and the power of God who made the promise. In the many scriptures that will be given in this chapter, one will see the interrelatedness of the concepts of promise, inheritance and hope, as glowing facets of the one invaluable diamond of new covenant blessedness.

3. "Firstfruits" and "Deposit" Measures — Pentecost and Parousia

It bears repeating that the pre-Parousia believers were already experiencing God's New Covenant blessings in Christ in a measure which, as I will now show, was described as "the deposit and firstfruits of the Spirit," while they eagerly awaited the fullness, completion or consummation of their new covenant blessedness which could only as yet lie in the sphere of hope, until the time of the Lord's coming to give them their full inheritance.

Let us look at what is meant by the blessings experienced by the pre-Parousia Christians being called deposit and firstfruit blessings.

The Greek word *"arrabon"* (ἀρραβών) is translated in various Bible versions as "earnest," "guarantee," "pledge," "deposit," "deposit guaranteeing," etc. The general meaning of *arrabon* is a *deposit*, or a down-payment, which guarantees the full payment – partial payment on the total obligation. Several commentators also point out the *arrabon* (deposit) is of the same kind as the full payment to come. For example the following commentaries describe the meaning of the term *arrabon* (Gr. ἀρραβών), which comes from the Hebrew 'erabhon [עֵרָבוֹן] found in Gen. 38:17-20, where the LXX has ἀρραβῶνα, "arrabona"]

See the notes on 2 Cor. 1:22; and 5:5, in "The Second Epistle to the Corinthians" by Philip Hughes, in *The New International Commentary on the New Testament* series, (William B. Eerdmans Publishing Company, Grand Rapids, Michigan, 1980), pp. 41-43, 173-175.

The term earnest means a deposit which is in itself a guarantee that the full amount will be paid later. It is important to notice that, as Lightfoot observes, "the thing given is related to the thing assured - the present to the hereafter - as a part to the whole. It is the same in kind." Hence it is not simply a pledge, which may be different in kind, but a deposit, a first installment. The sense of "the earnest of the Spirit" is well illustrated in Rom. 8:23 where Paul speaks of the "firstfruits of the Spirit" — the Christian already possesses here and now the first of the fruits of the complete harvest which he is destined ultimately to enjoy. While, therefore, the word "earnest" denotes something given for the present, it also looks to the future and carries a strong eschatological overtone. (pp. 41-42)

Also see comments on Eph. 1:14 in the volume "The Epistles to the Ephesians and the Colossians" by E. K. Simpson and F. F. Bruce, in *The New International Commentary on the New Testament* series, (Eerdmans Publishing Company, Grand Rapids, Michigan, 1980), pp. 35-36.

The Hebrew word 'erabhon seems to have found its way into Greek through Phoenician traders. It conveys the meaning of a *token in kind*, viewed as the harbinger of future possession. The Spirit's agency affords a foretaste of bliss; for the life He implants in the saved soul partakes of the quality of that of heaven. (p. 36)

And also see the comments on Eph. 1:14 in the commentary on *Ephesians* by Charles Hodge (1797-1878), in the *Classic New Testament Commentary* series (pub. by Marshall Pickering, Britain, 1991), p. 40.

This Spirit is *the earnest of our inheritance*. It is at once the foretaste and the pledge of all that is laid up for the believer in heaven. 'Earnest' means a part of the price of anything purchased, paid as a security for the full payment, and, more generally, a pledge. ...In the same sense the Scriptures speak of 'the firstfruits of the Spirit' (Rom. 8.23). The influences of the Spirit which believers now enjoy are both a foretaste of future blessedness *(the same in kind though immeasurable less in degree)*, and a pledge of the certain enjoyment of that blessedness, just as the firstfruits were part of the harvest, and an earnest of its in-gathering. It is because the Spirit is an earnest of our inheritance, that his indwelling is a seal. It assures those in whom he dwells of their salvation, and makes that salvation certain. It is a very precious gift that should be carefully guarded. [Emphasis mine - IH]

This "arrabon" or "deposit" differs from a *pledge* which, while guaranteeing a future full payment, need not be of the same kind as the full payment. Thus the translation "deposit-guarantee" may adequately convey the meaning.

The Greek word *aparkee* (ἀπαρχὴ) translated "firstfruits" means the first part of a crop. In OT days the firstfruits were offered as a sacrifice to the Lord; the firstfruits, representing the entire harvest, were offered to the Lord as an acknowledgment that the whole harvest was a blessing from the Lord in the first place. The figurative use of firstfruits in the NT refers to the first part of something, and represents, forecasts and guarantees the full harvest of that something to come. E.g., Christ is the "firstfruits" of resurrection (1 Cor. 15:20, 23); i.e. He represents His people, and His resurrection is the first one which guarantees the resurrection of his many followers (i.e. the harvest) in due time.

Here are the relevant verses speaking of the "deposit-guarantee" (*arrabon*) and the "firstfruits" (*aparkee*) experienced by the first believers at the time of the NT letters (pre-AD 70). One will notice that the being sealed by the Holy Spirit is very closely related to the deposit of the Spirit, so I have also included verses alluding to the seal of the Spirit in the following:

> Rom 8:22-23 For we know that the whole creation groans and labors with birth pangs together until now. 23 Not only that, but *we also who have the firstfruits of the Spirit*, even we ourselves groan within ourselves, eagerly waiting for the adoption, the redemption of our body.
> 2 Cor. 1:21-22 Now He who establishes us with you in Christ and has anointed us is God, 22 *who also has sealed us and given us the deposit-guarantee of the Spirit in our hearts*.
> 2 Cor. 5:4-5 For we who are in this tent groan, being burdened, not because we want to be unclothed, but further clothed, that mortality may be swallowed up by life. 5 Now *He who has prepared us for this very thing is God, who also has given us the deposit-guarantee of the Spirit.*
> Eph 1:13-14; 4:30 In Him you also trusted, after you heard the word of truth, the gospel of your salvation; in whom also, having believed, *you were sealed with the Holy Spirit of promise, 14 who is the deposit-guarantee of our inheritance until the redemption of the purchased possession*, to the praise of His glory.... 4:30 And do not grieve *the Holy Spirit of God, by whom you were sealed for the day of redemption.*

The theme of these verses and their contexts is firstly, that there is a great future inheritance in store for the believers; and secondly, that they already have "the firstfruits and deposit-guarantee" of that inheritance now, by the presence and power of the Holy Spirit in them, which reassures them that God will surely bring them into that promised inheritance in His time.

In these verses, most commentators take the words "the Spirit" to be grammatically a 'genitive of apposition' to "the firstfruits" and "the deposit;" that is to say, that the Spirit himself is the firstfruits and the deposit. Assuming this grammatical interpretation is correct, there arises in my mind a query: "How can the Holy Spirit, who is almighty God, be called a firstfruits, or a deposit? For a firstfruits or a deposit implies that a greater blessing lies ahead, but truly, you cannot have anything greater than God himself!" The answer to this lies in the fact that while it is true that none other than the Holy Spirit – God Himself – already has come to dwell with his saints, yet His working in them and their ability to experience His working in them (such as His illumination and His transforming power and His enabling believers to truly know and fellowship with the Father and the Son), are limited in this earthly life.

The Holy Spirit is present as almighty God in Christians, but carries out his work of applying the new covenant blessings in a firstfruits and deposit measure, corresponding to the fact that the Christian has the capacity for only a firstfruit or deposit experience of God's new covenant salvation while in the mortal body.

This firstfruits and deposit measure of blessings, which the first Christians experienced, as described by the NT writings, is a very real and a great grant of God's grace, but the Scriptures encourage the Christians that it is but a down payment, forecasting and guaranteeing a far greater consummate measure of those blessings in the near future, at the Parousia of Christ.

4. **Helpful Comments on the Firstfruits and the Deposit of the Holy Spirit, from some Old Commentaries** *(See comments from other commentaries in Footnote 1).*

I recommend a thoughtful perusal of the comments below. They help me feel something of the majesty of God's wise method in bringing his people to glory.

On Rom. 8:23

"...they had the grace of God communicated to them in conversion, which they received *as the firstfruits, with respect to an after increase, or in regard to glory; like the firstfruits, grace is of the same kind with glory, and is a pledge and earnest of it*; saints judge by grace the firstfruits, what glory is, and therefore long after it;" (Dr John Gill's *Exposition on the New Testament*, in *Online Bible*, comments on Rom 8:23).

"The Spirit, given to believers as *the "firstfruits" of what awaits them in glory*, moulds the heart to a heavenly frame, and attempers it to its future element." (Jamieson, Fausset and Brown, *A Commentary on the Old and New Testaments*, 1871. [vol. 3, p. 242, in the full three-volume set, reprinted by Eerdmans in 1978].

Regarding the hope of glory in Rom 8:17f

"The grounds of this expectation in the saints. It is our having received the first fruits of the Spirit, which both quickens our desires and encourages our hopes, and both ways raises our expectations. *The first fruits did both sanctify and ensure the lump. Grace is the first fruits of glory, it is glory begun. We, having received such clusters in this wilderness, cannot but long for the full vintage in the heavenly Canaan.* Not only they—not only the creatures which are not capable of such a happiness as the firstfruits of the Spirit, but even we, who have such present rich receivings, cannot but long for something more and greater. *In having the first fruits of the Spirit we have that which is very precious, but we have not all we would have.*" (Matthew Henry's "Exposition of all the Books of the Old and New Testaments," from *Online Bible*, notes on Rom 8:17-25. Emphasis mine, IH).

On 2 Corinthians 1:22
"A *seal* assures the possession of property to one; "sealed" is the crowning assurance of the Spirit (1 Cor. 9:2). The *earnest of the Spirit* – i.e., the Spirit as the earnest (i.e., money given by a purchaser as a pledge for the full payment of the sum promised). *The Holy Spirit is to the believer now as a first installment to assure him his full inheritance as a son of God shall be his hereafter* (Eph. 1:13,14; Rom. 8:23): the pledge of the fulfillment of "all the promises" (v. 20)." (Jamieson, Fausset and Brown, *A Commentary on the Old and New Testaments*, 1871. Vol. 3, p. 340, in the full three-volume set, reprinted by Eerdmans in 1978).

"The giving unto believers the Holy Spirit, and those saving spiritual habits which are his effects in the soul, are both the firstfruits and an earnest; for as the firstfruits assured the harvest, and the earnest is a sure pledge of the bargain, when those who give it are honest and faithful; so the sanctifying habits, wrought in the soul by the Spirit of holiness, are a certain pledge of that glory which shall be the portion of believers." (Matthew Poole's "Annotations on the Holy Bible," from *Online Bible*, notes on 2 Cor. 1:22)

"The apostle, having mentioned the stability of the divine promises, makes a digression to illustrate this great and sweet truth, that all the promises of God are yea and amen. For,
1. They are the promises of the God of truth (2 Cor. 1:20), of him *that cannot lie,* whose truth as well as mercy endures forever.
2. They are made in Christ Jesus (2 Cor. 1:20), the Amen, the true and faithful witness; he hath purchased and ratified the covenant of promises, and is the *surety of the covenant,* Heb. 7:22.
3. They are confirmed by the Holy Spirit. He does establish Christians in the faith of the gospel; he has anointed them with his sanctifying grace, which in scripture is often compared to oil; *he has sealed them, for their security and*

confirmation; and he is given as an earnest in their hearts, 2 Cor. 1:21,22. *An earnest secures the promise, and is part of the payment. The illumination of the Spirit is an earnest of everlasting light; the quickening of the Spirit is an earnest of everlasting life; and the comforts of the Spirit are an earnest of everlasting joy.* Note, The veracity of God, the mediation of Christ, and the operation of the Spirit, are all engaged that the promises shall be sure to all the seed, and the accomplishment of them shall be to the *glory of God* (2 Cor. 1:20) for the glory of his rich and sovereign grace, and never-failing truth and faithfulness." (Matthew Henry's "Exposition of all the Books of the Old and New Testaments," from *Online Bible*, notes on 2 Cor. 1:15-24. Emphasis mine - IH).

On Ephesians 1:14

"The seal and earnest of the Spirit are of the number of these blessings [i.e. the blessings of Eph 1:3 - IH]. We are said to be *sealed* with that Holy Spirit of promise, Eph. 1:13. The blessed Spirit is holy himself, and he makes us holy. He is called *the Spirit of promise,* as he is the promised Spirit. By him believers are sealed; that is, separated and set apart for God, and distinguished and marked as belonging to him. *The Spirit is the earnest of our inheritance,* Eph. 1:14. *The earnest is part of payment, and it secures the full sum: so is the gift of the Holy Ghost; all his influences and operations, both as a sanctifier and a comforter, are heaven begun, glory in the seed and bud. The Spirit's illumination is an earnest of everlasting light; sanctification is an earnest of perfect holiness; and his comforts are earnests of everlasting joys.* He is said to be the earnest, until the redemption of the purchased possession. It may be called here the possession, because this earnest makes it as sure to the heirs as though they were already possessed of it; and it is purchased for them by the blood of Christ. The redemption of it is mentioned because it was mortgaged and forfeited by sin; and Christ restores it to us, and so is said to redeem it, in allusion to the law of redemption. Observe, from all this, what a gracious promise that is which secures the gift of the Holy Ghost to those who ask him." (Matthew Henry's "Exposition of all the Books of the Old and New Testaments," from *Online Bible*, notes on Eph 1:3-14. Emphasis mine - IH).

[The inheritance of Eph 1:14 is] "(t)he incorruptible and never fading one in heaven, or the heavenly kingdom; this is the Father's gift, his bequest, and belongs only to children; it comes to them through the death of the testator, Christ, and is for ever; and of this *the Spirit of God is the pledge and earnest: an earnest, is what confirms an agreement, and assures the right to the thing agreed to, and is a part of it, and lesser than it, and is never returned; so the Spirit of God certifies the right to the heavenly inheritance, as well as gives a meetness for it; he is the firstfruits of eternal glory and happiness, and of the same kind with it; and as he is enjoyed in measure by the saints now, is lesser than the communion which they shall have with him, and with the Father, and the Son, hereafter*, for the best things are reserved till last; and being once given into the heart as an earnest, he always continues, he never removes more, or is ever taken away." (Dr John Gill's *Exposition on the New Testament, in Online Bible*, comments on Eph 1:14. Emphasis mine - IH)

5. Occasion of the First Christians Receiving the Consummation

Under the preterist view, about AD 70 the Lord appeared the second time and took his waiting people to himself and granted them the consummate, full measure of New Covenant blessedness.

Suddenly for those first Christians, at that occasion, their firstfruits measure was overtaken by the full harvest of blessings; the deposit-guarantee which they had formerly experienced was honored by the full grant of their eternal inheritance in all its glory; their trial period of hope was replaced by perfect fulfillment. The first Christians living at that time, all deceased Christians prior to that time, and all deceased OT saints of all past history, all received at the Parousia of Christ the *full* effect of the great salvation of the New Covenant. This expectation will be enlarged upon in further chapters.

6. Deposit-Blessings and Corresponding Expected Fullness-Blessings

Here is a list of NT Scriptures about some of the firstfruits/deposit New Covenant blessings already possessed by those first Christians, alongside their corresponding hoped-for fullness or fulfillments which they were waiting to enter into at the soon-expected coming of the Lord.

Their all-consuming hope was the coming and revelation and manifestation of the Lord Jesus Christ himself. They were "looking for the blessed hope and glorious appearing of our great God and Savior Jesus Christ" (Tit. 2:13), for in Him was all fullness of blessing; in Him all promises were "Yes and Amen." All the blessings listed below are ones found in the all-sufficient Christ Jesus alone.

Note: In each section below, underneath the centered headings, there are both "A" and a "B" subheadings with Biblical texts. The contents of each of the "A" and "B" sections are arranged according to this pattern:

A = deposit-guarantee blessing, experienced prior to the Parousia
B = corresponding expected, hoped-for fullness at the Lord's coming

Salvation

It has been rightly said that salvation has past, present and future aspects: we who are believers into Christ Jesus the Lord, have been saved from the guilt of sin, are being saved (sanctification) from the power of sin, and shall be saved from the presence of sin.

A. Salvation already possessed (the deposit–guarantee):
Matt. 1:21 "And she will bring forth a Son, and you shall *call His name JESUS, for He will save His people from their sins.*"
Acts 2:21, 47 And it shall come to pass *that whoever calls on the name of the LORD shall be saved.'* 47 ...And the Lord added to the church daily *those who were being saved.*
Rom. 1:16 For I am not ashamed of *the gospel of Christ, for it is the power of God to salvation for everyone who believes*, for the Jew first and also for the Greek.
1 Cor. 1:18 For *the message of the cross* is foolishness to those who are perishing, but *to us who are being saved it is the power of God.*
1 Cor. 15:1 Moreover, brethren, I declare to you *the gospel* which I preached to you, which also you received and in which you stand, 2 *by which also you are saved*, if you hold fast that word which I preached to you——unless you believed in vain.
2 Cor. 6:1-2 We then, as workers together with Him also plead with you not to *receive the grace of God* in vain. 2 For He says: "In an acceptable time I have heard you, And in the day of salvation I have helped you." Behold, now is the accepted time; behold, *now is the day of salvation.*
Eph 2:4-5, 8 But God, who is rich in mercy, because of His great love with which He loved us, 5 even when we were dead in trespasses, made us alive together with Christ (*by grace you have been saved*),... 8 For *by grace you have been saved through faith....*
Phil. 2:12 Wherefore, my beloved, as ye have always obeyed, not as in my presence only, but now much more in my absence, *work out your own salvation with fear and trembling.*
Jam 1:19-21 So then, my beloved brethren, let every man be swift to hear, slow to speak, slow to wrath; 20 for the wrath of man does not produce the righteousness of God. 21 Therefore lay aside all filthiness and overflow of wickedness, and receive with meekness the implanted word, which *is able to save your souls.*
(Similar examples: Rom 8:24; 10:9, 13; Acts 16:30-32; 2 Cor. 2:14-15; 2 Tim 1:8-9; Tit. 3:4-5; 2 Cor. 1:6)

B. Salvation as an expected Fullness
Rom 13:11-12 And do this, knowing the time *[kairos = special period, season]*, that now it is high time to awake out of sleep; for *now our salvation is nearer* than when we first believed. 12 The night is far spent, the day is at hand. Therefore let us cast off the works of darkness, and...put on the armor of light.

1 Thess. 5:8-11 But let us who are of the day be sober, putting on the breastplate of faith and love, and as a helmet *the hope of salvation*. 9 *For God* did not appoint us to wrath, but *[appointed us] to obtain salvation through our Lord Jesus Christ*, 10 who died for us, that whether we wake or sleep, we should live together with Him. 11 Therefore comfort each other and edify one another, just as you also are doing.

Heb 1:14 Are they not all ministering spirits sent forth to minister for those *who will inherit [lit. who are about to inherit] salvation*?

Heb 9:28 so Christ was offered once to bear the sins of many. To those who eagerly wait for Him *He will appear a second time*, apart from sin, *for salvation*.

Heb 10:36-39 For you have need of endurance, so that after you have done the will of God, you may *receive the promise*: 37 "For yet a little while, And He who is coming will come and will not tarry. 38 Now the just shall live by faith; But if anyone draws back, My soul has no pleasure in him." 39 But we are not of those who draw back to perdition, but *of those who believe to the saving of the soul*.

1 Pet 1:3, 5, 8-10,13 Blessed be the God and Father of our Lord Jesus Christ, who according to His abundant mercy has begotten us again to *a living hope* through the resurrection of Jesus Christ from the dead... 5 who are kept by the power of God through faith *for salvation ready to be revealed in the last time*.... 8 ...Though now you do not see Him, yet believing, you rejoice with joy inexpressible and full of glory, 9 *receiving the end of your faith—the salvation of your souls*. 10 Of *this salvation* the prophets have inquired and searched carefully, who prophesied of *the grace that would come to you*... 13 Therefore gird up the loins of your mind, be sober, and *rest your hope fully upon the grace that is to be brought to you at the revelation of Jesus Christ;*

Righteousness

A. Righteousness already received and being manifested in the life

Rom 3:20-24 Therefore by the deeds of the law no flesh will be justified in His sight, for by the law is the knowledge of sin. 21 But now *the righteousness of God apart from the law is revealed*, being witnessed by the Law and the Prophets, 22 even *the righteousness of God, through faith in Jesus Christ, to all and on all who believe*. For there is no difference; 23 for all have sinned and fall short of the glory of God, 24 *being justified* [declared righteous] *freely by His grace* through the redemption that is in Christ Jesus,

Rom 5:1 Therefore, *having been justified by faith*, we have peace with God through our Lord Jesus Christ,

Rom 10:4 For Christ *is* the end of the law *for righteousness to everyone who believes.*

Rom 6:13, 19 And do not present your members *as* instruments of unrighteousness to sin, but present yourselves to God as being alive from the dead, *and your members as instruments of righteousness to God....* 19 *...now present your members as slaves of righteousness for holiness.*

Rom 8:3-4 For what the law could not do in that it was weak through the flesh, God did by sending His own Son in the likeness of sinful flesh, on account of sin: He condemned sin in the flesh, 4 that *the righteous requirement of the law might be fulfilled in us who do not walk according to the flesh but according to the Spirit.*

Rom 14:17 for *the kingdom of God is* not eating and drinking, but *righteousness and peace and joy in the Holy Spirit.*

Eph 4:21-24 if indeed you have... been taught by Him, as the truth is in Jesus: 22 that you put off, concerning your former conduct, the old man which grows corrupt according to the deceitful lusts, 23 and be renewed in the spirit of your mind, 24 and *that you put on the new man which was created according to God, in true righteousness and holiness.*

Eph 5:8-9 For you were once darkness, but now *you are* light in the Lord. Walk as children of light 9 (for *the fruit of the Spirit is in all goodness, righteousness, and truth*),

Phil. 1:9, 11 And this I pray, that your love may abound still more and more in knowledge and all discernment,... 11 *being filled with the fruits of righteousness* which *are* by Jesus Christ, to the glory and praise of God.

Psa. 23:1, 3 The LORD is my shepherd; I shall not want. 3 He restores my soul*; He leads me in the paths of righteousness For His name's sake.*

(Similar examples: Rom 5:9; 8:29-30; 1 Cor. 6:11; Acts 13:38-39; Tit. 3:4-6; 1 Tim 6:11; 2 Tim 2:22; 3:16; Jas. 3:18; 1 Jn. 3:7).

B. Righteousness as an expected Fullness
— when their fruits of righteousness will be wondrously manifested.

Gal 5:4-5 You have become estranged from Christ, you who attempt to be justified by law; you have fallen from grace. 5 For we through the Spirit *eagerly wait for the hope of righteousness by faith.*

2 Tim 4:7-8 I have fought the good fight, I have finished the race, I have kept the faith. 8 Finally, *there is laid up for me the crown of righteousness, which the Lord, the righteous Judge, will give to me on that Day,* and *not to me only but also to all who have loved His appearing.*

2 Pet. 3:13 Nevertheless we, according to His promise, look for new heavens and a new earth *in which righteousness dwells.*

Eternal Life

A. Eternal Life already received upon faith in Christ

Jn. 3:16, 18 "For God so loved the world that He gave His only begotten Son, that *whoever believes in Him should not perish but have eternal life.* 18 "He who believes in Him is not condemned;

Jn. 3:36 "*He who believes in the Son has eternal life*; and he who does not believe the Son shall not see life, but the wrath of God abides on him."

Jn. 5:24 "Most assuredly, I say to you, *he who hears My word and believes in Him who sent Me has eternal life,* and shall not come into judgment, *but has passed from death into life.*

Jn. 20:30-31 And truly Jesus did many other signs in the presence of His disciples, which are not written in this book; 31 but these are written that you may believe that Jesus is the Christ, the Son of God, and that *believing you may have life in His name.*

Acts 11:18 When they heard these things they... glorified God, saying, "Then God has also granted to the Gentiles *repentance to life.*"

Rom. 6:23 For the wages of sin *is* death, but *the gift of God is eternal life in Christ Jesus our Lord.*

Rom. 8:2 For *the law of the Spirit of life in Christ Jesus has made me free* from the law of sin and death.

1 Jn. 3:14-15 We know that *we have passed from death to life,* because we love the brethren. He who does not love his brother abides in death. 15 Whoever hates his brother is a murderer, and you know that no murderer has *eternal life* abiding in him.

1 Jn. 5:10-13 He who believes in the Son of God has the witness in himself; he who does not believe God has made Him a liar, because he has not believed the testimony that God has given of His Son. 11 And *this is the testimony: that God has given us eternal life, and this life is in His Son.* 12 He who has the Son has life; he who does not have the Son of God does not have life. 13 These things I have written to you who believe in the name of the Son of God, *that you may know that you have eternal life,* and that you may continue to believe in the name of the Son of God.

(Similar examples: Jn 6:47; 8:12; 10:27-28; 17:2-3; 1 Tim 1:16)

B. Eternal Life in its consummative manifestation

Matt 19:28-29 So Jesus said to them, "Assuredly I say to you, that in the regeneration, *when the Son of Man sits on the throne of*

His glory, you who have followed Me will also sit on twelve thrones, judging the twelve tribes of Israel. 29 "And everyone who has left houses or brothers or sisters or father or mother or wife or children or lands, for My name's sake, shall receive a hundredfold, *and inherit eternal life.*

Matt 25:31, 46 "*When the Son of Man comes in His glory*, and all the holy angels with Him, then He will sit on the throne of His glory.... And these [wicked people] will go away into everlasting punishment, but *the righteous into eternal life."*

Rom 2:5-7 ...in the day of wrath and revelation of the righteous judgment of God, 6 [God] "will render to each one according to his deeds": 7 *eternal life* to those who by patient continuance in doing good seek for glory, honor, and immortality;

Gal 6:7-8 Do not be deceived, God is not mocked; for whatever a man sows, that he will also reap. 8 For he who sows to his flesh will of the flesh reap corruption, but he who sows to the Spirit will of the Spirit *reap everlasting life.*

Tit. 1:1-3 Paul, a bondservant of God and an apostle of Jesus Christ, according to the faith of God's elect and the acknowledgment of the truth which accords with godliness, 2 *in hope of eternal life* which God, who cannot lie, promised before time began, 3 but has in due time manifested His word through preaching, which was committed to me according to the commandment of God our Savior;

Jas. 1:12 Blessed is the man who endures temptation; for *when he has been approved, he will receive the crown of life which the Lord has promised to those who love Him.*

Tit. 3:7 that having been justified by His grace we should become *heirs according to the hope of eternal life.*

Jude 21 keep yourselves in the love of God, *looking for the mercy of our Lord Jesus Christ unto eternal life.*

Rev. 2:10 ...Be faithful until death, and *I will give you the crown of life.*

Sonship, "Adoption as Sons"
Gr. υἱοθεσία, *huiothesia* = adoption as son,
from Gr. υἱός, *huios* = son, and from Gr. τίθημι, *titheemi* = to place

A. The Adoption as Sons Already Received/Experienced by Believers in Christ

Rom. 8:15-17 For you did not receive the spirit of bondage again to fear, but *you received the Spirit of adoption as sons [huiothesias]* by whom we cry out, "Abba, Father." 16 The Spirit Himself bears witness with our spirit that *we are children of God,* 17 and if children, then heirs – heirs of God and joint heirs with Christ, if indeed we suffer with Him, that we may also be glorified together.

Gal. 4:4-7 But when the fullness of the time had come, God sent forth

His Son, born of a woman, born under the law, 5 to redeem those who were under the law, *that we might receive the adoption as sons [huiothesia].* 6 And because *you are sons [huioi]*, God has sent forth the Spirit of His Son into your hearts, crying out, "Abba, Father!" 7 Therefore *you are no longer a slave but a son [huion]*, and if a son, then an heir of God through Christ.

Gal. 3:26 For *you are all sons [huioi] of God through faith in Christ Jesus.*

Eph. 1:3-5 Blessed be the God and Father of our Lord Jesus Christ, who has blessed us with every spiritual blessing in the heavenly places in Christ, 4 just as He chose us in Him before the foundation of the world, that we should be holy and without blame before Him in love, 5 having predestined us to *adoption as sons [huiothesian]* by Jesus Christ to Himself, according to the good pleasure of His will.

B. The Hoped-for Fullness of Manifestation of the Adoption as Sons

(The full realization of the dignity and function and happiness of sonship in relationship to and fellowship with God our Father in glory).

Rom. 8:18-23 For I consider that the sufferings of this present time are not worthy to be compared with the glory which shall be [Gr. μέλλω, *mello* = about to be] revealed in us. 19 For the earnest expectation of the creation *eagerly waits for the revealing of the sons of God.* 20 For the creation was subjected to futility, not willingly, but because of Him who subjected it in hope; 21 because the creation itself also will be delivered from the bondage of corruption into *the glorious liberty of the children of God.* 22 For we know that the whole creation groans and labors with birth pangs together until now. 23 Not only that, but we also who have the firstfruits of the Spirit, even we ourselves groan within ourselves, *eagerly waiting for the adoption as sons [huiothesian]*, the redemption of our body.

Rev. 21:5-8 Then He who sat on the throne said, "Behold, I make all things new." And He said to me, "Write, for these words are true and faithful." 6 And He said to me, "It is done! I am the Alpha and the Omega, the Beginning and the End. I will give of the fountain of the water of life freely to him who thirsts. 7 *"He who overcomes shall inherit all things, and I will be his God and he shall be My son.* 8 "But the cowardly, unbelieving, abominable, murderers, sexually immoral, sorcerers, idolaters, and all liars shall have their part in the lake which burns with fire and brimstone, which is the second death."

Redemption

A. Redemption possessed

Rom. 3:24 being justified freely by His grace through *the redemption that is in Christ Jesus,*

Eph. 1:7 *In Him we have redemption* through His blood, the forgiveness of sins, according to the riches of His grace

Col. 1:14 *in whom we have redemption* through His blood, the forgiveness of sins.

Heb. 9:12 Not with the blood of goats and calves, but with His own blood He entered the Most Holy Place once for all, *having obtained eternal redemption.*

Heb. 9:15 And for this reason He is the Mediator of the new covenant, by means of death, for *the redemption* of the transgressions under the first covenant, that those who are called may receive the promise of the eternal inheritance.

B. Fullness of Redemption hoped-for (full redemption implies resurrection from the dead)

The fullness of the saints' redemption (already received by title upon faith in Christ and experienced as yet in a firstfruits measure by the Holy Spirit's regeneration and sanctification) will be manifested and experienced in its full force and glory at the resurrection event.

Lk. 21:28 "Now when these things begin to happen *[the things forecasting the second coming of the Lord]*, look up and lift up your heads, *because your redemption draws near."*

Rom. 8:23 Not only that, but we also who have the firstfruits of the Spirit, even we ourselves groan within ourselves, *eagerly waiting for* the adoption, *the redemption of our body.*

1 Cor. 1:30 But of Him you are in Christ Jesus, who became for us wisdom from God, and righteousness and sanctification and *redemption...*

Eph. 1:14 you have been sealed by the Holy Spirit of promise who is the guarantee of our inheritance *until the redemption of the purchased possession*, to the praise of His glory.

Eph. 4:30 And do not grieve the Holy Spirit of God, by whom you were *sealed for the day of redemption.*

The Kingdom of God

A. The Kingdom of God already present and experienced upon faith in Christ.

Matt. 11:12 "And from the days of John the Baptist until now *the kingdom of heaven* suffers violence, and the violent take it by force.

Acts 8:12 But when they believed Philip as *he preached the things concerning the kingdom of God and the name of Jesus Christ*, both men and women were baptized.

Acts 19:8 And he went into the synagogue and spoke boldly for three months, reasoning and persuading concerning the things of *the kingdom of God.*

Acts 20:25 "And indeed, now I know that you all, among whom I have gone *preaching the kingdom of God*, will see my face no more.

Acts 28:23 So when they had appointed him a day, many came to him at his lodging, to whom he explained and solemnly testified of *the kingdom of God, persuading them concerning Jesus* from both the Law of Moses and the Prophets, from morning till evening.

Acts 28:31 preaching *the kingdom of God and teaching the things which concern the Lord Jesus Christ* with all confidence, no one forbidding him.

Rom 14:15-18 Yet if your brother is grieved because of your food, you are no longer walking in love. Do not destroy with your food the one for whom Christ died. 16 Therefore do not let your good be spoken of as evil; 17 for *the kingdom of God is not eating and drinking, but righteousness and peace and joy in the Holy Spirit.* 18 For he who serves Christ in these things is acceptable to God and approved by men.

1 Cor. 4:19-20 But I will come to you shortly, if the Lord wills, and I will know, not the word of those who are puffed up, but the power. 20 For *the kingdom of God is not in word but in power*.

Col. 1:13-14 He has delivered us from the power of darkness and *conveyed us into the kingdom of the Son of His love*, 14 in whom we have redemption through His blood, the forgiveness of sins.

Col. 4:10-11 Aristarchus my fellow prisoner greets you, with Mark the cousin of Barnabas (about whom you received instructions: if he comes to you, welcome him), 11 and Jesus who is called Justus. These are my only *fellow workers for the kingdom of God* who are of the circumcision; they have proved to be a comfort to me.

Rev. 1:9 I, John, both *your brother and companion in the tribulation and kingdom and patience of Jesus Christ*, was on the island that is called Patmos for the word of God and for the testimony of Jesus Christ.

B. **The Kingdom of God, expected in its fullness of power and glory, about to come at the Parousia of Jesus; and the disciples of Jesus about to enter that consummate phase of it.**

Matt 16:27-28 "For *the Son of Man will come in the glory of His Father* with His angels, and then He will reward each according to his works. 28 "Assuredly, I say to you, there are some standing here who shall not taste death till they see *the Son of Man coming in His kingdom.*"

Matt 25:31-34 "*When the Son of Man comes in His glory*, and all the holy angels with Him, then He will sit on the throne of His glory... 34 "Then *the King* will say to those on His right hand, 'Come, you blessed of My Father, *inherit the kingdom* prepared for you from the foundation of the world:

Lk. 21:29-32 Then He spoke to them a parable: "Look at the fig tree, and all the trees. 30 "When they are already budding, you see and know for yourselves that summer is now near. 31 "So you also, when you see these things happening *[i.e. the signs given in the Olivet discourse], know that the kingdom of God is near.* 32 "Assuredly, I say to you, this generation will by no means pass away till all things take place.

Lk. 22:28-30 "But you are those who have continued with Me in My trials. 29 *"And I bestow upon you a kingdom*, just as My Father bestowed one upon Me, 30 *"that you may eat and drink at My table in My kingdom, and sit on thrones* judging the twelve tribes of Israel."

Note the themes: The kingdom, fellowship of sharing the meal table, and ruling. The same themes occur in the following verses in the gospels: Matt. 8:11; Matt 19:28; Lk. 13:28-29.

Acts 14:21-22 And when they had preached the gospel to that city and made many disciples, they returned to Lystra, Iconium, and Antioch, 22 strengthening the souls of the disciples, exhorting them to continue in the faith, and saying, "We must *through many tribulations enter the kingdom of God*." [cf. 2 Pet 1:11]

2 Thess 1:4-5 so that we ourselves boast of you among the churches of God for your patience and faith in all your persecutions and tribulations that you endure, 5 which is manifest evidence of the righteous judgment of God, *that you may be counted worthy of the kingdom of God,* for which you also suffer;

1 Thess 2:11-12 as you know how we exhorted, and comforted, and charged every one of you, as a father does his own children, 12 *that you would walk worthy of God who calls you into His own kingdom and glory.*

2 Tim 4:1, 18 I charge you therefore before God and the Lord Jesus Christ, who will judge the living and the dead at His appearing and His kingdom:... 18 And the Lord will deliver me from every evil work and *preserve me for His heavenly kingdom.* To Him be glory forever and ever. Amen!

2 Pet. 1:10-11 Therefore, brethren, be even more diligent to make your call and election sure, for if you do these things you will never stumble; 11 for so *an entrance will be supplied to you abundantly into the everlasting kingdom of our Lord and Savior Jesus Christ.*

Christ our Light – The Light of Christ and Sons of Light

A. **The Light has come and believers are Sons of light already upon faith in Him.**

Jn. 8:12 Then Jesus spoke to them again, saying, *"I am the light of the world.* He who follows Me shall not walk in darkness, but *have the light of life."*

Jn. 12:36 "While you have the light, believe in the light, that you may become *sons of light."* These things Jesus spoke, and departed, and was hidden from them.

1 Thess. 5:5 You are all *sons of light* and *sons of the day.* We are *not of*

the night nor of darkness.

2 Cor. 4:6 For it is the *God* who commanded light to shine out of darkness, who *has shone in our hearts to give the light of the knowledge of the glory of God in the face of Jesus Christ.*

Eph. 5:8-11 For you were once darkness, but now *you are light in the Lord.* Walk *as children of light* 9 (for the fruit of the Spirit is in all goodness, righteousness, and truth), 10 finding out what is acceptable to the Lord. 11 And have no fellowship with the unfruitful works of darkness, but rather expose them.

1 Pet. 2:9 But you are a chosen generation, a royal priesthood, a holy nation, His own special people, that you may proclaim the praises of *Him who called you out of darkness into His marvelous light*;

B. An expected fullness of light, when the darkness/night has completely gone, and the sons of light will be completed and fully manifested in the light of God's eternal presence.

Rom. 13:11-14 And do this, knowing the time, that now it is high time to awake out of sleep; for now our salvation is nearer than when we first believed. 12 The *night is far spent, the day is at hand.* Therefore let us *cast off the works of darkness*, and let us *put on the armor of light.* 13 Let us walk properly, as in the day, not in revelry and drunkenness, not in lewdness and lust, not in strife and envy. 14 But put on the Lord Jesus Christ, and make no provision for the flesh, to fulfill its lusts.

2 Pet. 1:19 And so we have the prophetic word confirmed, which you do well to heed *as a light that shines in a dark place, until the day dawns and the morning star rises in your hearts*;

(Compare with Rev. 2:26-28 "And he who overcomes... I will give him *the morning star.*" Rev. 22:16 "I, Jesus, ... I am the Root and the Offspring of David, *the Bright and Morning Star.*")

1 Jn. 2:8 Again, a new commandment I write to you, which thing is true in Him and in you, because *the darkness is passing away,* and *the true light is already shining.*

[i.e. the true light was very soon to come in its fullness for believers. At present, says John, they were experiencing the firstfruits of the Light, as its initial rays were already shining over the horizon into their lives. Soon they would be out of the darkness, and living in God's light]

Rev. 21:9-11, 23-24 Then one of the seven angels who had the seven bowls filled with the seven last plagues came to me and talked with me, saying, "Come, I will show you the bride, the Lamb's wife." 10 And he carried me away in the Spirit to a great and high mountain, and showed me the great city, the holy Jerusalem, descending out of heaven from God, 11 having the glory of God. *Her light* was like a most precious stone... 23 The city had no need of the sun or of the moon to shine in it, for *the glory of God illuminated it. The Lamb is its light.* 24 And *the nations of those who are saved shall walk in its light*, and the kings of the earth bring their glory and honor into it.

Rev. 22:5 There shall be no night there: They need no lamp nor light of the sun, for *the Lord God gives them light*. And they shall reign forever and ever.

Participating in the New Jerusalem

A. **Participating in the life and Spirit of the New Jerusalem prior to the Parousia**

Gal 4:21- 5:2 Tell me, you who desire to be under the law, do you not hear the law? 22 For it is written that Abraham had two sons: the one by a bondwoman, the other by a freewoman. 23 But he *who was* of the bondwoman was born according to the flesh, and he of the freewoman through promise, 24 which things are symbolic. For these are *the two covenants*: the one from Mount Sinai which gives birth to bondage, which is Hagar——25 for this Hagar is Mount Sinai in Arabia, and corresponds to Jerusalem which now is, and is in bondage with her children——26 but *the Jerusalem above is free, which is the mother of us all*. 27 For it is written: "Rejoice, O barren, *You* who do not bear! Break forth and shout, You who are not in labor! For the desolate has many more children Than she who has a husband." *28 Now we, brethren, as Isaac was, are children of promise.* 29 But, as he who was born according to the flesh then persecuted him *who was born* according to the Spirit, even so *it is* now. 30 Nevertheless what does the Scripture say? "Cast out the bondwoman and her son, for the son of the bondwoman shall not be heir with the son of the freewoman." *31 So then, brethren, we are not children of the bondwoman but of the free*. 1 Stand fast therefore in the liberty by which Christ has made us free, and do not be entangled again with a yoke of bondage. 2 Indeed I, Paul, say to you that if you become circumcised, Christ will profit you nothing.

Heb 12:18-24 For you have not come to the mountain that may be touched and that burned with fire, and to blackness... 19 and the sound of a trumpet and the voice of words, so that those who heard *it* begged that the word should not be spoken to them anymore. 20 (For they could not endure what was commanded: "And if so much as a beast touches the mountain, it shall be stoned or shot with an arrow." 21 And so terrifying was the sight *that* Moses said, "I am exceedingly afraid and trembling.") But *you have come to Mount Zion and to the city of the living God, the heavenly Jerusalem*, to an innumerable company of angels, 23 to the general assembly and church of the firstborn *who are* registered in heaven, to God the Judge of all, to the spirits of just men made perfect, 24 to Jesus the Mediator of the new covenant, and to the blood of sprinkling that speaks better things than *that of* Abel.

Paul makes it very clear in the above two passages: There are two covenants: a Sinai, Mosaic one of law-works and a new covenant gospel, one of justification by faith in Christ, typified by Hagar and Sarai, corresponding to the earthly Jerusalem and the heavenly Jerusalem, the Jerusalem above, respectively. The believers in Christ are born of the Spirit and are children of the new gospel covenant, children of promise, children of the heavenly Jerusalem above, in contrast to the non-believing Jews who remain under the old covenant as children of bondage.

The first Christians were experiencing the heavenly Jerusalem reality or ideal in its firstfruits measure. They had come to it (Heb 12:21) and were experiencing it, just as really as they had come to, and were experiencing, Jesus and his ministry as the Mediator of the new covenant and the efficacy of his blood, (v.24).

B. An expected consummate manifestation of the New Jerusalem to enter and experience

Rev. 3:12 *Him that overcomes will I make a pillar in the temple of my God*, and he shall go no more out: and I will write upon him the name of my God, and *the name of the city of my God, which is new Jerusalem, which cometh down out of heaven from my God*: and *I will write upon him* my new name.

Rev. 2:7 "He who has an ear, let him hear what the Spirit says to the churches. *To him who overcomes I will give to eat from the tree of life, which is in the midst of the Paradise of God.*" [The tree of life is a central feature of the heavenly Jerusalem]

Rev. 21:1-7 Now I saw a new heaven and a new earth, for the first heaven and the first earth had passed away. Also there was no more sea. 2 Then *I, John, saw the holy city, New Jerusalem, coming down out of heaven from God, prepared as a bride adorned for her husband.* 3 And I heard a loud voice from heaven saying, "Behold, the tabernacle of God *is* with men, and He will dwell with them, and they shall be His people. God Himself will be with them *and be* their God. 4 "And God will wipe away every tear from their eyes; there shall be no more death, nor sorrow, nor crying. There shall be no more pain, for the former things have passed away." 5 Then He who sat on the throne said, "Behold, I make all things new." And He said to me, "Write, for these words are true and faithful." 6 And He said to me, "It is done! I am the Alpha and the Omega, the Beginning and the End. *I will give of the fountain of the water of life freely to him who thirsts. 7 "He who overcomes shall inherit all things, and I will be his God and he shall be My son.*

[vv. 6-7. The overcomers inherit a share in the new Jerusalem where the fountain of life is].

Rev. 21:10-11 And he carried me away in the Spirit to a great and high mountain, and *showed me the great city, the holy Jerusalem, de-*

scending out of heaven from God, 11 having the glory of God. Her light *was* like a most precious stone, like a jasper stone, clear as crystal.

Reigning with Christ

A. Reigning with Christ by faith, in this life on earth

Rom 5:17 For if by the one man's offense death reigned through the one, much more *those who receive abundance of grace and of the gift of righteousness will reign in life through the One, Jesus Christ.*

Rom 6:13-14 And do not present your members as instruments of unrighteousness to sin, *but present yourselves to God as being alive from the dead, and your members as instruments of righteousness to God.* 14 For *sin shall not have dominion over you, for you are not under law but under grace.*

Eph 2:4-6 But God, who is rich in mercy, because of His great love with which He loved us, 5 even when we were dead in trespasses, made us alive together with Christ (by grace you have been saved), 6 and raised us up together, and *made us sit together in the heavenly places in Christ Jesus,*

The ministry of prayer is virtually a reigning with Christ, and through the prayers of his people in harmony with Christ, God works on earth. For example: Matt 18:18-20; Eph 6:18-20; Jn 16:23-24.

B. Reigning with Christ in glory

Matt 19:28 So Jesus said to them, "Assuredly I say to you, that in the regeneration, *when the Son of Man sits on the throne of His glory, you who have followed Me will also sit on twelve thrones, judging the twelve tribes of Israel.*

Lk. 22:28-30 "But you are those who have continued with Me in My trials. 29 "And *I bestow upon you a kingdom,* just as My Father bestowed one upon Me, 30 "that you may eat and drink at My table in My kingdom, and *sit on thrones judging the twelve tribes of Israel.*"

Rom 8:17 and if children, then heirs – *heirs of God and joint heirs with Christ*, if indeed we suffer with Him, that we may also be glorified together.

1 Cor. 6:2-3 Do you not know that *the saints will judge the world*? And if the world will be judged by you, are you unworthy to judge the smallest matters? 3 Do you not know that *we shall judge angels*? How much more, things that pertain to this life?

2 Tim 2:12 If we endure, *we shall also reign with Him.*

Rev. 2:25-27 "But hold fast what you have till I come. 26 "And he who overcomes, and keeps My works until the end, *to him I will give power over the nations——* 27 *'He shall rule them with a rod of iron; They shall be dashed to pieces like the potter's vessels'* –

    as I also have received from My Father;
- Rev. 3:21 "To him who overcomes *I will grant to sit with Me on My throne, as I also overcame and sat down with My Father on His throne.*
- Rev. 20:4 And I saw *thrones, and they sat on them, and judgment was committed to them.* Then I saw the souls of those who had been beheaded for their witness to Jesus and for the word of God, who had not worshiped the beast or his image, and had not received his mark on their foreheads or on their hands. And *they lived and reigned with Christ* for a thousand years.

Rest and Comfort with God

A. Rest of soul in this life: a rest of peace and joy in fellowship with God upon faith in Christ

    Matt 11:28-30 "Come to Me, all you who labor and are heavy laden, and *I will give you rest.* 29 "Take My yoke upon you and learn from Me, for I am gentle and lowly in heart, and you will find *rest for your souls.* 30 "For My yoke is easy and My burden is light."

    Rom 14:17 for the kingdom of God is not eating and drinking, but righteousness and *peace and joy in the Holy Spirit.*

    Phil 4:6-7 Be anxious for nothing, but in everything by prayer and supplication, with thanksgiving, let your requests be made known to God; 7 and *the peace of God, which surpasses all understanding, will guard your hearts and minds through Christ Jesus.*

    2 Cor. 1:3-4 Blessed be the God and Father of our Lord Jesus Christ, *the Father of mercies and God of all comfort, 4 who comforts us in all our tribulation,* that we may be able to comfort those who are in any trouble, with the comfort with which we ourselves are comforted by God.

    1 Pet 5:7 *casting all your care upon Him, for He cares for you.*

B. An expected perfect rest and comfort about to be entered at the Lord's coming:

    This was a rest of soul and life from all that speaks of trial, persecution and spiritual imperfection; a rest in God's immediate presence.

    Rom 8:19-23 *[A deliverance and rest from the futility and bondage of corruption (humanity's fallen natural state) – a freedom that is only to be found in a glorified state, "glorified together with Christ"]* For the earnest expectation of the creation eagerly waits for the revealing of the sons of God. 20 For the creation was subjected to futility, not willingly, but because of Him who subjected it in hope; 21 because *the creation itself also will be delivered from the bondage of corruption into the glorious liberty of the children of God.* 22 For we know that the whole creation groans and labors with birth pangs together until now. 23 Not only that, but we also who have the firstfruits of the Spirit, even we ourselves groan within ourselves, eagerly waiting for the adoption, the redemption of our body.

[Note: the final redemption will involve freedom from groaning which the believers felt within themselves as flesh was at enmity with Spirit, etc.].

2 Thess 1:6-7 since it is a righteous thing with God to repay with tribulation those who trouble you, 7 and to *give you who are troubled rest with us when the Lord Jesus is revealed from heaven with His mighty angels,*

Heb. 3:17-19; 4:1, 9-11 Now with whom was He angry forty years? Was it not with those who sinned, whose corpses fell in the wilderness? 18 And to whom did He swear that they would not *enter His rest*, but to those who did not obey? 19 So we see that they could not enter in because of unbelief. 1 Therefore, since *a promise remains of entering His rest*, let us fear lest any of you seem to have come short of it..... 9 *There remains therefore a rest for the people of God.* 10 For he who has entered His rest has himself also ceased from his works as God did from His. 11 Let us therefore be diligent to enter that rest, lest anyone fall according to the same example of disobedience.

[In the context of the letter to the Hebrews the "rest" about to be entered, is the same concept as the eternal inheritance, the salvation, the reward, the heavenly city and country – all of which were consummate realities expected to soon come to the Hebrew Christians and which would be experienced at the Lord's appearing and coming].

Rev. 7:13-17 Then one of the elders answered, saying to me, "Who are these arrayed in white robes, and where did they come from?" 14 And I said to him, "Sir, you know." So he said to me, "These are the *ones who come out of the great tribulation*, and washed their robes and made them white in the blood of the Lamb. 15 "Therefore they are before the throne of God, and serve Him day and night in His temple. And *He who sits on the throne will dwell among them.* 16 *"They shall neither hunger anymore nor thirst anymore; the sun shall not strike them, nor any heat; 17 "for the Lamb who is in the midst of the throne will shepherd them and lead them to living fountains of waters. And God will wipe away every tear from their eyes."*

Rev. 14:13 Then I heard a voice from heaven saying to me, "Write: 'Blessed are the dead who die in the Lord from now on.'" "Yes," says the Spirit, "that they may *rest* from their labors, and their works follow them."

[Again this rest from their earthly labors and trials was to occur at the coming of Christ which is repeatedly spoken of in the Revelation as very shortly to occur, at which time Christ would reward the works of his people].

Rev. 21:3-5 And I heard a loud voice from heaven saying, "Behold, the tabernacle of God is with men, and He will dwell with them, and they shall be His people. God Himself will be with them and be their God. *4 "And God will wipe away every tear from their eyes; there shall be no more death, nor sorrow, nor crying. There shall be no more pain, for the former things have passed away."* 5 Then He who sat on the throne said, "Behold, *I make all things new.*" And He said to me, "Write, for these words are true and faithful."

God's Dwelling with His People

A. The deposit blessing of having God dwelling with/in his people.

Matt 28:19-20 "Go therefore and make disciples of all the nations, baptizing them... 20 "teaching them to observe all things that I have commanded you; *and lo, I am with you always, even* to the end of the age." Amen.

Jn. 14:16-17 "And I will pray the Father, and He will give you another Helper, *that He may abide with you forever*– 17 "*the Spirit of truth*, whom the world cannot receive, because it neither sees Him nor knows Him; but you know Him, for *He dwells with you and will be in you.*

Jn. 14:23 Jesus answered and said to him, "If anyone loves Me, he will keep My word; and My Father will love him, and *We will come to him and make Our home with him.*

1 Cor. 3:16 Do you not know that you are the temple of God and [that] *the Spirit of God dwells in you*?

1 Cor. 6:19 ...do you not know that your body is the temple of *the Holy Spirit [who is] in you*, whom you have from God, and you are not your own?

2 Cor. 6:16-17 And what agreement has the temple of God with idols? For you are the temple of the living God. *As God has said: "I will dwell in them And walk among [them].* I will be their God, And they shall be My people." 17 Therefore "Come out from among them And be separate, says the Lord. Do not touch what is unclean, And I will receive you."

Eph 3:19-20 Now, therefore, you are no longer strangers and foreigners, but fellow citizens with the saints and members of the household of God, 20 having been built on the foundation of the apostles and prophets, Jesus Christ Himself being the chief *cornerstone*, 21 in whom the whole building, being joined together, grows into a holy temple in the Lord, 22 in whom *you also are being built together for a dwelling place of God in the Spirit.*

Heb 13:5-6 *Let your* conduct *be* without covetousness; *be* content with such things as you have. For *He Himself has said, "I will never leave you nor forsake you."* 6 So we may boldly say: "The LORD *is* my helper; I will not fear. What can man do to me?"

B. **A hoped-for consummation of God's dwelling with his people at the Parousia of Christ**
   Rev. 7:9, 14-15 After these things I looked, and behold, a great multitude which no one could number, of all nations, tribes, peoples, and tongues, standing before the throne and before the Lamb, clothed with white robes,... 14 ...So he said to me, "These are the ones who come out of the great tribulation, and washed their robes and made them white in the blood of the Lamb. 15 *Therefore they are before the throne of God, and serve Him day and night in His temple. And He who sits on the throne will dwell among them.*
   Rev. 7:17 "for *the Lamb who is in the midst of the throne will shepherd them and lead them...*"
   Rev. 21:3 And I heard a loud voice from heaven saying, "*Behold, the tabernacle of God is with men, and He will dwell with them, and they shall be His people. God Himself will be with them and be their God.*
   Rev. 22:3 And there shall be no more curse, but *the throne of God and of the Lamb shall be in it* [i.e., in the New Jerusalem], *and his servants shall serve Him.*
   [His servants, the believers will have God and the Lamb in their regal majesty dwelling in their midst]

Access to and Fellowship with Father, Son, and Holy Spirit
(This is enlarged upon in the next section of knowing/seeing the Lord)

A. **The deposit blessing of a spiritual access to, and fellowship with God – but an access and fellowship greatly limited by the believers' fallen, natural bodies and minds.**
   Jn. 4:23-24 "But the hour is coming, and now is, when *the true worshippers will worship the Father in spirit and truth; for the Father is seeking such to worship Him.* 24 "God is Spirit, and those who worship Him must worship in spirit and truth."
   Phil 3:3 For *we are the circumcision, who worship God in the Spirit*, rejoice in Christ Jesus, and have no confidence in the flesh,
   1 Cor. 1:9 God is faithful, by whom you were called into *the fellowship of His Son, Jesus Christ our Lord.*
   2 Cor. 13:14 The grace of the Lord Jesus Christ, and the love of God, and *the communion* (fellowship) *of the Holy Spirit be with you all.* Amen.
   Eph 2:13, 17-18; 3:11-12 But now in Christ Jesus *you who once were far off have been brought near* by the blood of Christ. 17 And He came and preached peace to you who were afar off and to those who were near. 18 For *through Him we both have access by one Spirit to the Father....* 3:11 according to the eternal purpose which He accomplished in Christ Jesus our Lord, 12 *in whom we have boldness and access with confidence through faith in Him.*
   Phil 2:1 Therefore if there is any consolation in Christ, if any comfort

of love, if any *fellowship of the Spirit*, if any affection and mercy, 2 fulfill my joy by being like-minded, having the same love, being of one accord, of one mind.

Phil 4:6-7 Be anxious for nothing, but in everything *by prayer and supplication, with thanksgiving, let your requests be made known to God*; 7 and the peace of God, which surpasses all understanding, will guard your hearts and minds through Christ Jesus.

1 Jn. 1:3 that which we have seen and heard we declare to you, that you also may have fellowship with us; *and truly our fellowship is with the Father and with His Son Jesus Christ.*

B. A Fullness of access and fellowship in the immediate presence of God

A fellowship symbolized by sitting at meal with the Lord in the kingdom, gathered into God's Presence in the heavenly Holy of Holies.

Lk. 22:28-30 "But you are those who have continued with Me in My trials. 29 "And I bestow upon you a kingdom, just as My Father bestowed one upon Me, *30 "that you may eat and drink at My table in My kingdom*, and sit on thrones judging the twelve tribes of Israel." See Matt 8:11; Lk. 13:28-29

1 Thess 2:19 For what is our hope, or joy, or crown of rejoicing? Is it not even *you in the presence of our Lord Jesus Christ at His coming*?

1 Thess 4:16-17 ...And the dead in Christ will rise first. 17 Then we who are alive and remain shall be caught up together with them in the clouds *to meet the Lord* in the air. And *thus we shall always be with the Lord.*

2 Thess 2:1 Now, brethren, concerning *the coming of our Lord Jesus Christ and our gathering together to Him*,

[The last two texts imply an experiential "being with the Lord" in a manner far above what was experienced prior to the Parousia of Christ.]

Heb 6:19-20 This *hope* we have as an anchor of the soul, both sure and steadfast, and *which enters the Presence behind the veil*, 20 *where the forerunner has entered for us, even Jesus*, having become High Priest forever according to the order of Melchizedek.

Heb 9:24 For *Christ* has not entered the holy places made with hands, which are copies of the true, but *into heaven itself, now to appear in the presence of God for us*;

Heb 10:19-25 Therefore, brethren, *having boldness to enter the Holiest by the blood of Jesus,* 20 by a new and living way which He consecrated for us, through the veil, that is, His flesh, 21 and having a High Priest over the house of God, 22 let us draw near with a true heart in full assurance of faith, having our hearts sprinkled from an evil conscience and our bodies washed with pure water.

23 Let us *hold fast the confession of our hope* (note 6:19-20) without wavering, for He who promised is faithful. 24 And let us consider one another in order to stir up love and good works, 25 not forsaking the assembling of ourselves together, as is the manner of some, but exhorting one another, and so much the more as *you see the Day approaching.*

[The previous three quotes from Hebrews, declare that there is the hope of an entrance into the holiest, to be fulfilled at the Lord's coming (10:25, 36-37). This hope is for an access to and fellowship with God far exceeding what they already had, such as mentioned in Eph 2:18 and 1 Jn 1:3. The Christians are to have a confidence/boldness about their right of real entrance, for the blood of Jesus has cleared the way for them. They are to draw near or approach God (in their firstfruits/deposit measure of spiritual access to and fellowship with him), with faith in his faithfulness to keep his promise, and in the knowledge that the day is approaching, for their entrance into God's presence in the Holy of Holies. Then they will be with the glorified Jesus their forerunner, who had blazed the trail before them into God's presence in heaven in order for them to follow him there]

Rev. 7:9-10,15 After these things I looked, and behold, *a great multitude which no one could number, of all nations, tribes, peoples, and tongues, standing before the throne and before the Lamb*, clothed with white robes, with palm branches in their hands, 10 and crying out with a loud voice, saying, "Salvation belongs to our God who sits on the throne, and to the Lamb!"... 15 "Therefore *they are before the throne of God, and serve Him day and night in His temple. And He who sits on the throne will dwell among them.*

Rev. 21:3 And I heard a loud voice from heaven saying, *"Behold, the tabernacle of God is with men, and He will dwell with them, and they shall be His people. God Himself will be with them and be their God.*

Knowing and Seeing the Lord

A. A Present Spiritual Knowing and Seeing the Lord

Matt 11:25-28 At that time Jesus answered and said, "I thank You, Father, Lord of heaven and earth, that You have hidden these things from the wise and prudent and have revealed them to babes. 26 "Even so, Father, for so it seemed good in Your sight. 27 "All things have been delivered to Me by My Father, and no one knows the Son except the Father. *Nor does anyone know the Father except the Son, and the one to whom the Son wills to reveal Him.* 28 "Come to Me, all you who labor and are heavy laden, and I will give you rest.

Jn. 17:2-3 "as You have given Him authority over all flesh, that He should give eternal life to as many as You have given Him. 3 "And *this is eternal life, that they may know You*, the only true God, and Jesus Christ whom You have sent.

[Regarding eternal life, there was a present experience of it and an expected future fullness. Now eternal life means knowing the Lord: with a present experience and a future fullness yet to be experienced]

1 Cor. 13:12 For *now we see in a mirror, dimly*, but then face to face. *Now I know in part*, but then I shall know just as I also am known.

2 Cor. 3:18 But we all, with unveiled face, *beholding as in a mirror the glory of the Lord...*

Eph 1:15-17 Therefore I also, after I heard of your faith in the Lord Jesus and your love for all the saints, 16 do not cease to give thanks for you, making mention of you in my prayers: 17 that the God of our Lord Jesus Christ, the Father of glory, may give to you *the spirit of wisdom and revelation in the knowledge of Him*,

Phil 3:8 Yet indeed I also count all things loss for *the excellence of the knowledge of Christ Jesus my Lord*, for whom I have suffered the loss of all things, and count them as rubbish, that I may gain Christ

1 Jn. 2:12-13 I write to you, little children, Because your sins are forgiven you for His name's sake. 13 I write to you, fathers, Because *you have known Him who is from the beginning*. I write to you, young men, Because you have overcome the wicked one. I write to you, little children, Because *you have known the Father*.

1 Jn. 5:19-20 We know that we are of God, and the whole world lies under the sway of the wicked one. 20 And we know that the Son of God has come and *has given us an understanding, that we may know Him who is true*; and we are in Him who is true, in His Son Jesus Christ. This is the true God and eternal life.

B. An Expected Fullness Of Knowing And Seeing The Lord

Jn. 1:51 And He said to him, "Most assuredly, I say to you, hereafter *you shall see heaven open, and the angels of God ascending and descending upon the Son of Man."*

1 Cor. 13:9-12 For we know in part and we prophesy in part. 10 But *when that which is perfect has come, then that which is in part will be done away*. 11 When I was a child, I spoke as a child, I understood as a child, I thought as a child; but when I became a man, I put away childish things. 12 For now we see in a mirror, dimly, but *then* [we shall see] *face to face*. Now I know in part, but *then I shall know just as I also am known*.

Heb 12:14 Pursue peace with all people, and holiness, without which no one will *see the Lord*:

1 Jn. 3:2-3 Beloved, now we are children of God; and it has not yet been revealed what we shall be, but *we know that when He is revealed, we shall be like Him, for we shall see Him as He is*. 3 And everyone who has *this hope* in Him purifies himself....

Rev. 22:3-4 And there shall be no more curse, but the throne of God and of the Lamb shall be in it, and His servants shall serve Him. 4 *They shall see His face, and His name shall be on their foreheads.*

Marriage Union with to Christ

A. **Espoused to Christ upon faith in him**

Rom. 7:4-6 Therefore, my brethren, you also have become dead to the law through the body of Christ, that you may be *married to another——to Him who was raised from the dead*, that we should bear fruit to God. 5 For when we were in the flesh, the sinful passions which were aroused by the law were at work in our members to bear fruit to death. 6 But now we have been delivered from the law, having died to what we were held by, so that we should serve in the newness of the Spirit and not in the oldness of the letter.

1 Cor. 6:17 But *he who is joined to the Lord is one spirit with Him.*

2 Cor. 11:2-3 For I am jealous for you with godly jealousy. For *I have betrothed you to one husband,* that I may present you as a chaste virgin to Christ. 3 But I fear, lest somehow, as the serpent deceived Eve by his craftiness, so your minds may be corrupted from the simplicity that is in Christ.

Eph 5:28-32 So *husbands ought to love their own wives as their own bodies; he who loves his wife loves himself.* 29 For no one ever hated his own flesh, but nourishes and cherishes it, just as the Lord does the church. 30 For *we are members of His body, of His flesh and of His bones.* 31 "For this reason a man shall leave his father and mother and be joined to his wife, and the two shall become one flesh." 32 This is a great mystery, but *I speak concerning Christ and the church.*

B. **Full Marriage Union to Come**

Eph 5:25-27 *Husbands, love your wives, just as Christ also loved the church and gave Himself for her*, 26 that He might sanctify and cleanse her with the washing of water by the word, 27 *that He might present her to Himself a glorious church, not having spot or wrinkle or any such thing, but that she should be holy and without blemish.*

2 Cor. 11:2-3 For I am jealous for you with godly jealousy. For I have betrothed you to one husband, *that I may present you as a chaste virgin to Christ.* 3 But I fear, lest somehow, as the serpent deceived Eve by his craftiness, so your minds may be corrupted from the simplicity that is in Christ.

Rev. 19:5-9 Then a voice came from the throne, saying, "Praise our God, all you His servants and those who fear Him, both small and great!" 6 And I heard, as it were, the voice of a great multitude, as the sound of many waters and as the sound of mighty thunderings, saying, "Alleluia! For the Lord God Omnipotent reigns! 7 "Let us be glad and rejoice and give Him glory, *for the marriage of the Lamb has come, and His wife has made herself ready.*" 8 And to her it was granted to be arrayed in fine linen, clean and bright, for the fine linen is the righteous acts of the saints. 9 Then he said to me, "Write: 'Blessed are those who are called to *the marriage supper of the Lamb!*'" And he said to me, "These are the true sayings of God."

Rev. 21:1-2, 9-11 Now I saw a new heaven and a new earth, for the first heaven and the first earth had passed away. Also there was no more sea. 2 Then I, John, saw the *holy city, New Jerusalem, coming down out of heaven from God, prepared as a bride adorned for her husband*.... 9 Then one of the seven angels who had the seven bowls filled with the seven last plagues... talked with me, saying, "Come, *I will show you the bride, the Lamb's wife."* 10 And he carried me away in the Spirit to a great and high mountain, and showed me the great city, the holy Jerusalem, descending out of heaven from God, 11 having the glory of God.

Resurrection/New life

A. A present state of being spiritually risen to life with Christ upon faith in him

This is only experiencing the spiritual risenness in a limited measure, undergoing a constant renewing.

Rom 6:11 Likewise you also, reckon yourselves to be dead indeed to sin, *but alive to God in Christ Jesus our Lord*.

Rom 8:10-11 And if Christ is in you, the body is dead because of sin, but *the Spirit is life because of righteousness*. 11 But if the Spirit of Him who raised Jesus from the dead dwells in you, He who raised Christ from the dead will also give life to your mortal bodies through His Spirit who dwells in you.

2 Cor. 1:9; 4:8-11 Yes, we had the sentence of death in ourselves, *that we should not trust in ourselves but in God who raises the dead,...* 8 We are hard pressed on every side, yet not crushed; we are perplexed, but not in despair; 9 persecuted, but not forsaken; struck down, but not destroyed—10 *always carrying about in the body the dying of the Lord Jesus, that the life of Jesus also may be manifested in our body*. 11 *For we who live are always delivered to death for Jesus' sake, that the life of Jesus also may be manifested in our mortal flesh*.

Eph 2:4-6 But God, ...rich in mercy, because of His great love with which He loved us, even when we were dead in trespasses, *made us alive together with Christ* (by grace you have been saved), and *raised us up together*, and made us sit together in the heavenly places in Christ Jesus,

Phil 3:10 that I may know Him and *the power of His resurrection*, and the fellowship of His sufferings, being conformed to His death

Col. 2:11-13 In Him you were also circumcised with the circumcision made without hands, by putting off the body of the sins of the flesh, by the circumcision of Christ, 12 buried with Him in baptism, in which *you also were raised with Him through faith in the working of God*, who raised Him from the dead. 13 And you, being dead in your trespasses and the uncircumcision of your flesh, *He has made alive together with Him*, having forgiven you all trespasses,

Col. 3:1 If then *you were raised with Christ*, seek those things which are above, where Christ is, sitting at the right hand of God.

B. An expected fullness of resurrection life and glorification of body

Acts 23:6 But when Paul perceived that one part were Sadducees and the other Pharisees, he cried out in the council, "Men and brethren, I am a Pharisee, the son of a Pharisee; *concerning the hope and resurrection of the dead* I am being judged!" Also Acts 24:14-15 and Acts 26:6-8.

1 Cor. 6:14 14 *And God both raised up the Lord and will also raise us up by His power.*

1 Cor. 15:19-23 19 If we only have hope in Christ in this life, we are of all men most miserable. 20 But now Christ has been raised from the dead; He became the firstfruit of those having fallen asleep. 21 For since death *is* through man, also *through a Man is a resurrection of the dead*; 22 for as in Adam all die, so also *in Christ all will be made alive*. 23 But each in his own order: Christ, the firstfruit, *afterward those of Christ at His coming*. (Green's Literal Translation) Refer to all of 1 Cor. 15:35-57

1 Cor. 15:49-57 And as we have borne the image of the man of dust, *we shall also bear the image of the heavenly Man. 50 Now this I say, brethren, that flesh and blood cannot inherit the kingdom of God; nor does corruption inherit incorruption. 51 Behold, I tell you a mystery: We shall not all sleep, but we shall all be changed— — 52 in a moment, in the twinkling of an eye, at the last trumpet. For the trumpet will sound, and the dead will be raised incorruptible, and we shall be changed. 53 For this corruptible must put on incorruption, and this mortal must put on immortality.* 54 So when this corruptible has put on incorruption, and this mortal has put on immortality, then shall be brought to pass the saying that is written: "Death is swallowed up in victory... 57 But thanks be to God, who gives us the victory through our Lord Jesus Christ.

At the Parousia all pre-Parousia believers will then be totally changed into their glorified-body condition fully consisting of incorruption, honor, power and spirituality, where nothing of earthiness, fallenness, corruption, dishonor, weakness, earthly naturalness remains, (e.g., 1 Cor. 15:42-46).

2 Cor. 4:14-18; 5:1-5. knowing that *He who raised up the Lord Jesus will also raise us up through Jesus, and will present us with you....* 18 while we do not look at the things which are seen, but at the things which are not seen. For the things which are seen are temporary, but the things which are not seen are eternal. *5:1 For we know that if our earthly house, (that is) this tent, is destroyed, we have a building from God, a house not made with hands, eternal in the heavens. 2 For in this we groan, earnestly desiring to clothe ourselves over with our habitation which is from heaven,* 3 if indeed, having clothed ourselves, we shall not be found naked. 4 For we who are in this tent groan, being burdened, not because we want to unclothe ourselves, but to clothe ourselves over, that *the mortal* may *be swallowed up by life.* 5 Now He who has prepared us for this very thing is God, who also has *given us the Spirit as a guarantee.*

Phil 3:10-11 that I may know Him and the power of His resurrection, and the fellowship of His sufferings, being conformed to His death, 11 if, by any means, *I may attain to [or, arrive at] the resurrection from the dead.*

Phil 3:20-21 *For our citizenship is in heaven, from which we also eagerly wait for the Savior, the Lord Jesus Christ, 21 who will transform our lowly body for it to become conformed to His glorious body, according to the working by which He is able even to subdue all things to Himself.*

1 Thess 4:13-18 But I do not want you to be ignorant, brethren, *concerning those who have fallen asleep*, lest you sorrow as others who have no hope. *14 For if we believe that Jesus died and rose again, even so God will bring with Him those who sleep in Jesus.* 15 For this we say to you by the word of the Lord, that we who are alive and remain until the coming of the Lord will by no means precede those who are asleep. 16 For the Lord Himself will descend from heaven with a shout, with the voice of an archangel, and with the trumpet of God. *And the dead in Christ will rise first. 17 Then we who are alive and remain shall be caught up together with them in the clouds to meet the Lord in the air. And thus we shall always be with the Lord.* 18 Therefore comfort one another with these words.

Glory

A. The Deposit – Glory Begun in This Life on Earth

1 Cor. 1:30 But of Him you are in Christ Jesus, who became for us wisdom from God—and righteousness and *sanctification* and redemption—

[As Matthew Henry said: all the Holy Spirit's "influences and operations, both as a sanctifier and a comforter, are heaven begun, glory in the seed and bud." Sanctification is glory begun]

2 Cor. 3:18 But we all, with unveiled face, *beholding as in a mirror the glory of the Lord, are being transformed into the same image from glory to glory*, just as by the Spirit of the Lord.

2 Cor. 4:16-17 Therefore we do not lose heart. Even though our outward man is perishing, *yet the inward man is being renewed* day by day. 17 For our light affliction, which is but for a moment, is working for us a far more exceeding and *eternal weight of glory*. [i.e., the inward renewing is preparing for glory, and is glory in deposit form].

Eph. 1:6-7, 12 to the praise of *the glory* of His grace, by which He has made us accepted in the Beloved. 7 In Him we have redemption through His blood, the forgiveness of sins, according to the riches of His grace... 12 that we who first trusted in Christ should be to the praise of *His glory*.

[All of God's work in saving sinners in Christ is "to the praise of the glory of his grace" (Eph 1:6), and also "to the praise of his glory." (Eph 1:12). That is, believers are experiencing God's glory already, in a limited measure, in the form of his grace. Again, as old Matthew Henry said: "Grace is the firstfruits of glory, it is glory begun"]

1 Pet. 4:14 If you are reproached for the name of Christ, blessed are you, for *the Spirit of glory and of God rests upon you*. On their part He is blasphemed, but on your part He is glorified.

B. The Hoped-for Fullness of Glory

(Just a few of the many available verses)

Rom. 5:2 through whom also we have access by faith into this grace in which we stand, and *rejoice in hope of the glory of God*.

Rom. 8:17,18, 21 and if children, then heirs - heirs of God and joint heirs with Christ, if indeed we *suffer with Him, that we may also be glorified together*. 18 For I consider that *the sufferings of this present time* are not worthy to be compared *with the glory which is about to be revealed in us. [literal translation]...* 21 ...the creation itself also will be delivered from the bondage of corruption *into the glorious liberty [lit. the liberty of the glory] of the children of God*.

2 Cor. 4:17 For our light affliction, which is but for a moment, is working for us *a far more exceeding and eternal weight of glory*,

Eph. 1:18 the eyes of your understanding being enlightened; that you may know what is *the hope of His calling, what are the riches of the glory of His inheritance in the saints*,

Col. 1:27; 3:4 To them God willed to make known what are *the riches of the glory of this mystery among the Gentiles: which is Christ in you, the hope of glory*.... 3:4 When Christ who is our life appears, then *you also will appear with Him in glory*.

1 Pet. 5:1,4 The elders who are among you I exhort, I who am a fellow elder and a witness of the sufferings of Christ, and also *a partaker*

of the glory that is about to be revealed: *[literal translation]*... 4 and *when the Chief Shepherd appears*, you will receive *the crown of glory* that does not fade away

Jude 1:24 Now to Him who is able to keep you from stumbling, and to *present you faultless before the presence of His glory with exceeding joy*...

7. The Peculiarity of the Deposit-Fullness Language in the NT

It will be observed in reading the New Testament epistles, that one moment the writers speak as if they already have certain blessings, and the next moment they speak as if they don't have those same blessings, for they say they are still seeking them and hoping to obtain them at the Parousia of Christ.

This peculiarity of language is such that if a reader happened to only read the latter set of statements (i.e., ones expressing a hope of having certain blessings) one could easily assume that the first Christians did not yet have those stated blessings *at all*.

One might happen to read of the first Christians having a hope of salvation, and that they considered their salvation was drawing nearer (e.g., Rom 13:11; 1 Thess 5:8). Did that mean then that they were not yet saved or felt they were not yet saved, at all? In no way! As one reads elsewhere, (as I have shown in my list in Section 6 above), they were already experiencing the new covenant salvation of Jesus Christ — but in firstfruits measure.

Take other examples: One might happen to read of the first Christians hoping for their entrance into the eternal kingdom of God at Christ's Parousia, and hoping for the adoption as sons, and hoping for the heavenly city to come. Did that mean that they were not yet in the kingdom of God at all, and were not yet sons in fellowship with God at all, and that they did not yet have any association with the heavenly city at all? In no way! For elsewhere one reads of them already experiencing the kingdom of God, and already enjoying sonship with God, and already experiencing the spiritual blessings of the heavenly city — but, again, in firstfruits measure.

Just as a farmer of those days while expressing his eager hope of gathering in his full harvest of grain, was already enjoying the bread and porridge made from the firstfruits of that same crop, so also is the case with the NT writers: they express the eager hope of experientially entering into the full harvest or consummate manifestation of new covenant blessedness at the Parousia, but meanwhile they were already partaking of the firstfruits of that blessedness. It is just that as the greatness of the full harvest of salvation, the kingdom, eternal life, etc., is anticipated, the firstfruits tend to be forgotten as insignificant in comparison; and they tend to write as if the whole thing of salvation, the kingdom, eternal life, etc. was yet future in the sphere of hope.

The first Christians already possessed a firstfruits measure of new covenant blessedness prior to the Parousia, correlating to the fact that while they were in their mortal bodies, with imperfection in their souls, they only had a limited capacity to comprehend and receive God's revelation and new covenant blessings. Until their glorification with heavenly, spiritual bodies at the Parousia, they could experientially only cope with a deposit/firstfruits measure of new covenant blessedness. When saints, such as the apostles John and Paul, and prophets such as Ezekiel, Daniel and Isaiah, received a small vision into God's glory-realm, they fell down as dead men, depleted of all strength. While on this earth in earthly bodies and imperfect capacities, man can only cope with a deposit/firstfruits measure of the coming glory.

8. The Expectation of Consummation

I have listed above some examples to show how the first Christians were experiencing in their days the blessings of the new covenant in a firstfruits/deposit measure, while eagerly expecting a corresponding more-than-they-could-ask-or-imagine consummate, fullness measure of blessings — that we may collectively call the "eternal inheritance" or "glory." And the New Testament is clear that their expectation was to be fulfilled on the occasion of the soon-to-come Parousia of Christ.

O, the mind-staggering properties of the blessedness that the first Christians were anticipating! I believe that a thoughtful reading of the sixteen sections above describing the measure of blessings already experienced and the measure of blessings expected, will convince the reader that the first Christians were not expecting some merely figurative or objective change at the Parousia, but something absolutely experientially, gloriously, consummately real — a reality of life and light and holiness and righteousness in sinless, incorruptible, knowing, rejoicing union with the glorified Jesus in the heavenly Holy of Holies in the presence of their great Father in heaven.

Please note: The expectation of entrance into and full possession of this eternal inheritance and glory, consisting of the type and measure of blessings such as those described in the B sections above, was *an expectation of entrance into, and full possession of, a glorious, consummate, ultimate state and condition beyond which there was nothing higher or better described in the New Testament; because nothing higher or better could be promised.* The first Christians were expecting the salvation of their Lord and Savior Jesus Christ, at his Parousia, to lift them from their firstfruits/deposit measure of New Covenant Christian experience, into the *consummate* and *ultimate* state of *blessedness* of perfect holiness and fellowship in heaven with God.

From the scriptures referred to in this article, the first Christians were expecting *to possess and experience in a consummate, ultimate, perfect measure* the fully manifested eschatological blessings of God such as:

- *Full Salvation* - fully into God's will and purpose, where all presence of sin and fallenness and imperfection is gone.
- *The Crown of Righteousness* - fully conformed to the image of Jesus Christ the righteous.

- *The Crown of Eternal Life* - where all is life in union with God, experiencing the divine nature with no trace of death and fallenness.
- *Full Sonship* - full experience of living as God's glorified sons, no un-son-like aspects present at all.
- *Redemption* - total reclamation from every part of the legacy of death, fallenness and corruption and sin derived from the fall of Adam.
- *The Kingdom of God* - complete experience of the reign of God within, where all is of Christ, where all of his characteristics have full sway within, with no "flesh" warring against the Spirit.
- *Fullness of Light with Christ* - fullness of divine light within, no trace of darkness of mind or heart.
- *Participation in the New Jerusalem* - partaking of heavenly blessedness with all God's people in God's majestic presence.
- *Reigning with Christ* - the raised saints are completely taken up with Christ's interests in complete Christ-likeness, ruling in his name over all he gives them to rule over.
- *Rest and Comfort with God* - perfect joy and peace within the heaven of God's presence, with all evil influence no longer present.
- *God's Dwelling with His People* - enjoying His wonderful presence in ultimate reality.
- *Access and Fellowship with God* - full, clear fellowship, totally uncluttered by sin, the flesh, and mortality.
- *Knowing and Seeing God and his eternal realities* - undimmed knowing and appreciating Him.
- *Marriage-Union with Christ* - real life and happiness in heaven
- *Resurrection/Transformation and Glorification with Christ* - complete capacity to inhabit and experience the wonders of heaven with God in glorified-resurrection bodies.
- *The Crown of Glory* - full glorification together with the glorified Jesus where He dwells.

To repeat: there is nothing higher promised in the NT writings for man to partake of than these promised blessings in consummate measure. We must keep in mind the hermeneutic of audience relevance in our study. The teaching of the New Testament is that *for all believers who had existed up to the time of the Parousia, the Parousia of Christ would be the occasion of the fulfillment of these promises of consummate blessedness*.

In following chapters a closer examination will be made of relevant portions of Scripture and various aspects of the first Christians' expectations awaiting fulfillment at the Parousia of Christ, and *the nature* of the consummation will be clarified. It will be shown that:

- *Those believers who had died* before the time of the Parousia, expected to be gathered to Christ at the Parousia and to inherit fully their eternal inheritance as listed above.
- *Those believers who were alive* at the time of the Parousia, *also* expected to be gathered to Christ at the Parousia and to inherit fully

      the same eternal inheritance.
- Both deceased and living believers prior to AD 70, all, together, on the occasion of the Parousia, expected to receive the fulfillment of the promised consummate measure of new covenant blessings, (such as those mentioned above), which would see them totally delivered from remaining on earth in mortal bodies carrying a legacy of fallenness, and totally delivered into a permanent glorified state with the glorified Christ and the Father in heaven.

    At "his appearing the second time for salvation" (Heb 9:28) circa AD 70, the first Christians and all saints of prior history were completely saved by Him who has the ability to "save to the uttermost," i.e. "save to completion in every aspect," (expanded translation of the Greek of Heb 7:25).

    At this point, the reader may be asking: "What is the condition of those people on earth who have become Christians *following* the time of the Parousia c. AD 70? Do they have a deposit/firstfruits measure, or the consummate measure of new covenant blessedness?" I believe the answers to these two questions will become clearer as one reads the following chapters. However, you may wish to note that I deal explicitly with these ideas in the Appendix at the back of the book.

Chapter 3

The Good Things to Come

Some Eschatological Phrases in the Epistle to the Hebrews

The epistle to the Hebrews is an amazing letter, giving us an insight into the way the truth of Jesus Christ was conveyed to the Hebrew readers — the truth that He had fulfilled their Scriptures (i.e., what we now call the Old Testament) as the true and long-awaited Messiah. This letter gives insight into the great covenantal change that the first Christians were involved in, amidst much persecution.

The epistle to the Hebrews also sets out the great eschatological hope of the first Hebrew Christians. An understanding of the meaning of the some of the eschatological concepts and terms used in the epistle to the Hebrews will provide a solid basis for interpreting similar phrases and concepts in other New Testament writings. This chapter will attempt a brief examination of the following concepts in the epistle:

- These Last Days
- The End of the Ages
- The World to Come
- The Age to Come
- The Period of Reformation
- The Good Things to Come
- The City to Come
- The Approaching Day

To set the stage for this study, it would be helpful to remind ourselves of the main themes running through this epistle. I believe there are two main themes, with the second founded on the first. The two themes are:

(1) New Covenant Already Present and Operative In Jesus Christ

The writer spends much effort in restating and enlarging on gospel truths that his readers had been taught, and in which they ought to have attained a maturity, but were sadly tending to neglect due to the anti-Christian reactions and persecutions from the Jewish community. He emphasizes in an excellent manner *the superiority of Jesus' person and ministry as the Messiah of the New Covenant, in comparison to the typical and temporary Old Covenant personages and ministries.* Jesus is indeed God's appointed Messiah and Jesus has inaugurated the "better things" of the new covenant. The amazing blessing and privilege for the first Christians was that the new covenant age had broken in upon the Mosaic Jewish age that they had been living in.

The writer to the Hebrews alerts his readers to the fact that believers in Jesus Christ were present recipients of the Lord's ministry as the High Priest and Mediator of the new covenant founded on the Lord's sacrificial blood shed for them, and now sprinkled on them (signifying the application of the redemption gained by his cross). The new covenant, the gospel of grace, applied by the power of the Spirit of grace, was being preached by the apostles and experienced by all who believed. The believers were at peace with God, they knew him as "the God of peace" through the Lord Jesus. They were experiencing the new covenant shepherding of the Lord Jesus, that "great Shepherd of the sheep," and God's sanctifying work in their hearts. They now knew the blessing of sins forgiven; they knew the happiness of being able to serve and worship God in spirit and truth with a cleansed conscience, cleansed through the blood of Christ, the blood of the everlasting covenant.

In Chapter 1, *The New Covenant in the Days of the Apostles*, we perused some of the new covenant blessings that the first Christians were already experiencing. In that chapter a good number of passages from the epistle to the Hebrews were quoted, the writer of the epistle demonstrating that because Jesus was now the apostle and High Priest of their confession, and because his sacrifice of himself was the true sin offering for his people, it therefore followed that the first Christians were no longer under the strictures of the Mosaic system of Aaronic priests and animal sacrifices. The latter system was "weak and unprofitable" in the matter of salvation, but under the gospel ministry of the new covenant the believers were experiencing true forgiveness, new creation life, true spiritual fellowship with God in the Holy Spirit.

From God's point of view, the old covenant economy had ended and had been completed at the crucifixion and death of Jesus as the atoning sacrifice for sinners, the ending of which was symbolized by the tearing of the great veil in the temple at the time of the offering of the evening sacrifice by the Jewish priests — the great veil separating the holy place from the Holy of Holies where God's presence dwelt (Matt 27:50-51; old Matthew Henry's comments on this episode are illuminating). Jesus was indeed "the end of the law for righteousness for every one who believes," (Rom 10:4).

Nevertheless the old machinery of old covenant Judaism was still running, continuing in its majority rejection of Jesus as the Messiah. It would continue to limp along until God officially ended it at the destruction of Jerusalem and the temple in AD 70. It was the apparent continuance of old covenant Judaism, following the ascension of Jesus, that tempted the first Christians to fall away from the Way: they were pressured and persecuted by the many surrounding Jews, who warned them not to abandon the time-honored Mosaic system.

The writer to the Hebrews counters this temptation, by showing forcefully that the Messiah with his new covenant ministry had come, and was reigning in heaven and that he was the fulfillment, the "substance," of the Old Testament types and prophecies; therefore they must not fall into the trap of returning to the typical and shadowy old covenant forms. He made it clear to them that the worn out and obsolete system of Aaronic priesthood and animal sacrifices was soon to vanish away (Heb 8:13).

So there was this unusual state of things in those pre-Parousia years: The new covenant was present and proving a real blessing in the lives of Christians, coexisting alongside a corrupt, old covenant Judaism which was soon to be officially demolished.

(2) The hope of a consummation at the Parousia of Jesus.
On the basis of the firm truth of Jesus' superior ministry as the Messiah of the new covenant, the writer exhorts his Hebrew Christian readers to persevere in the hope of a wonderful consummation soon to come at the second appearing of the Lord Jesus. The epistle relates the expectation that would find fulfillment at the Parousia of Christ, a final salvation, a consummate experience of glory, the possession of their eternal inheritance in heaven, the entrance into the heavenly city and the heavenly Holy of Holies where their forerunner Jesus had gone ahead of them. Not only the first Christians had this exciting prospect but, as the writer shows, so also did all the deceased OT saints (which we examine in later chapters).

An understanding of this background and these twin themes aids in interpreting correctly the above-listed eschatological concepts that will be examined below. For whatever our interpretation is of these concepts, it must correlate with this background of firstly, the fact that new covenant was operating (in a deposit/firstfruits measure), through the matrix of the life, sacrificial death, resurrection, ascension and enthronement of the Lord Jesus; and secondly, that an expectation existed of a final salvation and consummate glorious measure of new covenant blessedness, that was to come at the Parousia of the Lord Jesus Christ.

Now let us look at several phrases used in the epistle to the Hebrews which have significant eschatological meaning, especially in regard to the expectations of the early pre-AD 70 Christians:

Phrases in the Epistle to the Hebrews
Which Have "Expectations" Significance:

1. "These Last Days"
God, who at various times and in various ways
spoke in time past to the fathers by the prophets,
has *in these last days* spoken to us
by His Son. [Heb 1:1-2]

The phrase "in these last days" in Heb. 1:2 in the Greek is, ἐπ' ἐσχάτου τῶν ἡμερῶν τούτων (lit. "upon these last days"). The earthly ministry of Jesus, the incarnate Son of God, occurred "in these last days," or, "at the end of these days," depending on one's translation of the Greek and its underlying equivalents in Old Testament Hebrew (בְּאַחֲרִית הַיָּמִים, "be-acharit ha-yamim," lit. "in the end of the days," cf. Gen. 49:1) and the Septuagint (LXX) (ἐπ' ἐσχάτων τῶν ἡμερῶν, "ep eschaton ton hemeron," lit. "in the last of the days"). The Greek phrase found here is a literal rendering of the Hebrew phrase (be'acharit ha'yamim, lit. "in the end of the days") which is used in the Old Testament to denote the epoch when the words of the prophets will be fulfilled," says OT scholar F. F. Bruce, "and its use here means that the appearance of [the Messiah Jesus] ... has inaugurated that time of fulfillment.[1] John Gill, expert on rabbinic writings also says: "It is a rule with the Jews [e.g. Kimchi and Aben Ezra in Isa. 2:2.], that wherever the phrase, "the last days," is mentioned, "the days of the Messiah" are designated: and they are to be understood not of the last days of the natural world, but of the Jewish world and state."[2]

The writer to this Hebrews epistle is thus saying the last days of the Mosaic-Jewish old covenant era was upon them. The Jews spoke of the present age of the law, and of a coming age of the Messiah; the Messiah was referred to as the One To Come or the Coming One. He was expected in the last days of the age of the law, or, more accurately, his coming to his people would signal that the last days of the age of the law were upon them. The Old Testament prophets prophesied of a coming time, called the latter/last days, when not only would the Messiah come but also, and importantly, through the Messiah a new covenant would be established. The coming of the Messiah Jesus into the world, preaching to the Jewish nation saying that the gospel of the kingdom of God was at hand, signaled the fact that the last days of the Jewish economy was upon them, that the time had now come when the words of the prophets were being fulfilled.

Jesus was alluding to this final stage of the Jewish old covenant era in his parable of the wicked vinedressers, in Matt 21:33-46; after the vinedressers had ill-treated every servant that the landowner had sent to them, "then, *last* of all, he [the landowner] sent his son to them," (v. 37). God had sent his servants, the prophets, to Israel, and now lastly God had sent His Son. In accordance with the parable, soon the nation of Israel would be judged by God for rejecting His Son whom he sent in "these last days." In his earthly ministry, Jesus said he had been sent specifically to the lost sheep of the house of Israel (Matt 15:24). For a time the apostles were not to go to the gentiles but were to preach to the lost sheep of Israel, (Matt 10:5-6). Following the crucifixion and resurrection and ascension of Jesus, the gospel ministry extended out to the world.

2. "The Consummation of the Ages"
For Christ has not entered the holy places made with hands,
which are copies of the true, but into heaven itself,
now to appear in the presence of God for us;
25 not that He should offer Himself often,

> as the high priest enters the Most Holy Place every year
> with blood of another– 26 He then would have had to
> suffer often since the foundation of the world; but now,
> once at the end of the ages, He has appeared to put away sin
> by the sacrifice of Himself. [Heb. 9:24-26]

The phrase "at the end of the ages" in the Greek is ἐπὶ συντελείᾳ τῶν αἰώνων = lit. "at [the] completion, consummation, or end of the ages"). The word "end" or "consummation" comes from Gr. συντελείᾳ, *sunteleia* which means "consummation, completion, or end." The word "age" comes from Gr. αἰώνων, *aionon* = ages, or periods of time. It is translated [inadequately] in the KJV as "in the end of the world"). *Young's Literal Translation* renders it, "at the full end of the ages." The ASV puts it, "at the end of the ages."

The writer refers to "the ages" that had passed since the creation of the world (9:26). There had been many ages (Gr. αἰώνων) down through biblical history since the foundation of the world – many periods characterized by various workings of God. For example: the times of the saints before Abraham, (i.e., before there was a specific called out nation of God's people); the times following Abraham until Moses, (wherein occurred the growth of a Hebrew people); the times of Moses, the exodus, the giving of the law to the people of Israel, and entry into the promised land, (i.e. the separation of a covenant people of God out from all other nations); the times under the kings until the deportations of northern and southern kingdoms of Israel, (times of God's warnings to, and later judgments upon, his people); the times of the return of many from captivity back to Israel under Ezra, and the building of the city walls under Nehemiah; the times following this, when there occurred attacks from Greeks and Romans, until the appearing of John the Baptizer who appeared about 400 years after the last prophet Malachi. There was especially the Mosaic-Jewish old covenant era, covering the time from the foundation of the nation of Israel at Sinai when the Mosaic covenant was given by God, to the time of the coming of the Messiah to Israel.

In all of these past ages God was working out his program for the world; preparing the stage for the coming of the Messiah and his atoning work of the new covenant. The age of the Mosaic economy of Aaronic priesthood and animal sacrifices and earthly temple had its unique preparatory value, while awaiting the manifestation of the reality or "substance" which it foreshadowed. Now, at the consummation of the ages, "when the fullness of the time had come, God sent forth His Son" (Gal 4:4).

Christ's appearing and sacrifice and ascension into heaven as High Priest for his people, marked the end or consummation of all previous preparatory ages from the foundation of the world. His great work signaled, and was performed in, the last days of the Jewish old covenant era (Heb 1:2). As the writer to the Hebrews demonstrates, Jesus was the fulfillment of all that which the Aaronic priesthood and animal sacrifices typified and he entered into the heavenly Holy of Holies, which was prefigured by the earthly tabernacle/temple.

3. "The World to Come"
"For not to angels has He subjected *the world to come,* of which we speak." [Heb. 2:5]

Look closely at the phrase, "the world to come," here in Heb. 2:5 – (Gr. τὴν οἰκουμένην τὴν μέλλουσαν, *teen oikoumeneen teen mellousan,* lit. means "the world the one about to be." The Gr. word *oikoumenee* = the world, or the habitable earth).

To the Jewish understanding, the Mosaic economy was introduced by angels from heaven at Sinai. When the Jews looked at the so-called leader of the new Christian "sect" all they could see was a man, Jesus, weak and crucified. Who was he, claiming to bring in a new kind of religion, compared to the heavenly angels with their divine commission? Surely, they reasoned, the Mosaic economy was superior to anything that the Christians could claim was introduced by the man Jesus. The suffering humanity of Jesus was a stumbling block to the Jews to their considering him the Messiah. In Heb. 1 the writer has shown from Scripture that the Son of God, the Lord Jesus, is superior to angels as to his person.

The theme of the section, Heb 2:5-18, is that it was the very humanity of Jesus that qualified him to accomplish a work that no angel could ever accomplish — the salvation of sinful mankind. He became for a little time lower than the angels, in his life on earth, in order to become the perfect Savior through sufferings, after which he was crowned, higher than the angels, with glory and honor.

The writer says in Heb 2:5 (following the original emphasis), "For not to angels has He [God] subjected *the world to come,* of which we speak." Note the implication: not to angels has he subjected it, but to someone else he has subjected it. As explained in Heb 2:6-9, the world to come has in fact been subjected to Jesus Christ as the representative Man, following his humiliation and subsequent exaltation. The fact of Jesus' having been crowned with glory and honor (v.9), means, to the writer, that Jesus has had all things put in subjection under him. The idea behind the Greek word translated subjected is to marshal under a commander, to subordinate under one's control. In and through the exalted Jesus, Christians were being renewed so as to fulfill God's ideal for man.

The "world to come of which [the writer is] speaking" (2:5) is the "world" that had been hoped for by the Jews and Old Testament saints, one which they had expected in their future. "The world to come" was a technical term used by the Jews to describe the period when the Messiah would come and rule.[3] The Messiah was called by the Jews, "the coming one," (e.g., Matt 11:3). The future sense of the phrase thus relates to the OT Jewish perspective, describing their hope for their future. The future tense does not relate in the same sense to the Christians' perspective, for to the first Christians the hoped-for Jewish "world to come" *had commenced* in the spiritual new covenant reign of Christ Jesus that commenced at Pentecost.

The writer to the Hebrews says he is [present tense] speaking about the world to come (2:5). What has he been speaking about already up to this point and what does he continue to speak about throughout the epistle? He speaks about the fact of Jesus Christ's intrinsic glory and his coming and purging his people's sins, of his being the great High Priest and the atoning sacrifice, and of his now sitting exalted at the Father's right hand, where he is greater than angels, and worshipped by angels. All this is to the purpose of demonstrating that Jesus has inaugurated and now rules over the "world to come," that promised great period of God's blessing — greater than the Mosaic old covenant "world" introduced by angels. The "world to come" concerns the gospel age with its "so great salvation" longed for by previous generations. And this is the theme the writer speaks about throughout the whole epistle — concerning great things that were prefigured in the old covenant law but now present and operative.

This is the "world to come": this new covenant gospel dispensation wherein true worshippers were now worshipping the Father in spirit and truth; this period of new covenant salvation, hoped for by past generations of Jews, and now commenced. It had been inaugurated by Jesus Christ's sacrifice of himself and by his enthronement as eternal High Priest at the Father's right hand in heaven, in the true heavenly tabernacle; and it had been subjected to the enthroned Jesus Christ as Lord and Mediator of it.

A deposit experience and future consummate experience of the world to come

It is important to realize, however, that this "world to come," this new covenant realm over which Jesus Christ now ruled, was only present and experienced by the first Christians in a deposit and firstfruits measure. They were eagerly looking for the Parousia of Christ at which time they would experience the unimaginable fullness encompassed in God's idea of the "world to come" — then they would enter and possess their ultimate glorification in the presence of the glorified Jesus in heaven. *At present they had only their big toe in the shallows of the ocean of life awaiting them in the world to come.*

> "The world to come, which is our theme" (Heb 2:5, NEB) is the new world-order inaugurated by the enthronement of Christ at the right hand of God, the world-order over which He reigns from that place of exaltation, the world of reality which replaces the preceding world of shadows. It has been *inaugurated* by Christ's enthronement, although it is not yet present in its fullness; its consummation awaits the time when Christ appears to bring His people into the final blessing of the salvation which He has procured for

them (cf. Ch 9:28); but here and now "the powers of the age to come" (Heb. 6:5), some of which have just been referred to in verse 4, are experienced by them. [F. F. Bruce[4]]

"The world to come" (Greek τὴν οἰκουμένην τὴν μέλλουσαν, lit. "the world, the about to be one" Heb. 2:5) – the new covenant empire of Jesus – is given this two-fold presentation in the letter to the Hebrews. The writer's argument to his readers, is that they should not apostatize under pressure and persecution from the Jews and Judaizers, but, undergirded by the sure testimony of Scripture and history that Jesus is the Messiah and that through Jesus the "world to come" which the Jews had hoped for has now commenced, they are to keep their hope firm regarding the coming consummate experience of the "world to come" that God has for them at the Parousia of Christ. There is the one "world to come" – the one new covenant age – but as the New Testament epistles reveal, there was for the first Christians the deposit and firstfruits measure and experience for the 40 years prior to the Parousia, which was a guarantee portion sealed to them by the presence of the Holy Spirit; then there was to be the eternal, consummate measure and experience to be given to the first Christians at the Parousia of Christ when with glorified, spiritual bodies and minds they would have the capacity to partake of the fullness.

That this is a correct interpretation of the phrase "the world to come" will be further confirmed by the examination of the meaning of the related terms "the good things to come" and "the age to come."

Terminology

The fact that the term, "to come," (Gr. μέλλουσαν, root μέλλω, or "mello"), qualifies the terms "world to come," "age to come," "good things to come," used in the Hebrews epistle, does not undermine the interpretation that I have given above which is based on the known Jewish idiomatic way of referring to the hoped-for times of the coming Messiah, and based on the exegesis of the New Testament epistles which shows that the new covenant of the Messiah had already commenced in the lives of the first Christians.

In regard to the Jewish idiomatic terms associated with the expected Messianic times, Gill and Brown[5] mention that the LXX (the Greek translation of the Hebrew Old Testament that was used by Jews at that time prior to and during Christ's day) refers to the Messiah in Isa. 9:6 as Πατὴρ τοῦ [μέλλοντος] αἰῶνος — "father of the age to come," where the verb *mello* is used. According to Calvin's commentary on Isaiah 9:6, "The Greek translator ... added μέλλοντος." The Hebrew word translated "Everlasting Father" is "abiy-ad" (אֲבִיעַד). The "abiy" means "father." The commentaries are not unanimous as to exactly what the "-ad" ending on that Hebrew word means. However, most of them believe that it has something to do with the future age of the Messiah, as if the Messiah will in some sense be the father, author, or source of the coming age. The

Brown-Driver-Briggs Lexicon says the Heb. word "ad" (עַד) means a "perpetuity" (or duration) of time, either of past time or future time, depending on how it is used in each context. The apostle Paul refers to Jesus in his letter to the Romans by a Jewish Messianic title when he speaks of "Adam who is a type/figure of 'the coming one,'" (Gr. τύτοῦ μέλλοντος, Rom 5:14). Similarly, using the pres. mid. ptc form of the Greek verb, ἐρχό μαι, translated "come," Jesus was asked by John the Baptizer, "Are you the coming one?" (Gr. σὺ εἶ ὁ ἐρχόμενος, Matt 11:3; Lk. 7:19). Some of the Jews wondered if Jesus was "the Prophet who is to come into the world." (Gr. ὁ προφήτης ὁ ἐρχόμενος εἰς τὸν κόσμον, Jn. 6:14). See also Heb. 10:37, "The coming one will arrive." (Gr. ὁ ἐρχόμενος ἥξει) The Messiah, the Coming One, the Prophet to come, had already come and had commenced his messianic rule. He was about to come again in a "very, very, little while" (Heb. 10:37, Gr. μικρὸν ὅσον ὅσον).

Also John the Baptizer is said by Jesus to be "Elijah who is to come" Matt 11:14, (Gr. Ἡλίας ὁ μέλλων ἔρχεσθαι, lit. "Elijah the one being about to be coming"). Such was the idiomatic title given to him. The Jews expected Elijah to reappear before the Messiah, based on the prophecy in Mal 4:5; he was called the "Elijah to come." Jesus says to his disciples: the 'Elijah to come,' expected by you Jews as the forerunner to the Messiah, has actually come; this prophecy has been fulfilled in John the Baptizer.

So the Jews had an expectation of several entities "to come" — an "Elijah to come"; the Messiah, "he who is to come," "the coming one," and "the prophet who is to come into the world;" and with him, "the age to come;" "the world to come;" and the "good things to come." The "Elijah to come" had come, "He who is to come" - the Messiah - had come (in his first appearing and incarnation). The New Testament epistles show that for the first Christians, the world, the age, and the good things to come, had all received fulfillment through the death and glorification of Jesus, albeit as yet in a deposit and firstfruits measure, with a consummative, harvest measure to be granted at the Parousia of Jesus. The Jews only had a very hazy idea that the mission of the Messiah might involve a two-phase manifestation, based on Isaiah's prophecy of both a "suffering servant" Messiah and a glorious, victorious, reigning Messiah.

4. "The Age to Come"
"...tasted the good word of God, and the powers of the age to come"
[Heb. 6:5]

"The age to come" (Gr. μέλλοντος αἰῶνος, *mellontos aionos*, lit. "about to be age") The Greek word αἰῶνος is properly "age, or a duration of time," and the word μέλλοντος comes from the Greek root "mello" which means "about to be." The KJV [mis]translates the phrase, "world to come.")

Like the phrase "the world to come" in Heb 2:5, the phrase, "the age to come" in Heb 6:5 was also an idiomatic phrase used by the Jews to describe the days when the Messiah would come and rule.[6] That "age to come," the age of the new covenant, was already present, having been inaugurated by Christ's atoning death and his subsequent enthronement as High Priest. The first Christians were experiencing "the powers" or, better, "the works of power" (Gr. δυνάμεις, *dunameis*) of the new covenant system. The powers among the first Christians were signs that the age to come, the new economy, had broken into the present age of the Mosaic economy. There was power in the new covenant ministry of the Messiah Jesus that could accomplish what the Mosaic old covenant could not, as it began to be seen on the Day of Pentecost with thousands being saved.

> "The ancient economy was comparatively weak as well as unprofitable, but the new economy is powerful. It has everything that can enlighten, and convince, and persuade, and alarm, and delight. It has the means of touching every spring of action - of stirring the human mind in its deepest recesses." [John Brown.[7]]

The apostle Paul gloried in the fact that now through Christ "what the law could not do" God is now doing in his believing Christians — giving victory over sin and empowering with new life in Christ, (see Rom 8:1-4). As well as the inward conscience-affecting, life-transforming "powers" of the new covenant ministry among the first Christians, the term "powers" can include the powerful works and signs worked through the apostles by the Holy Spirit, (e.g. Heb 2:3-4), witnessing to the truth that the "age to come" had broken in upon the present age of the law.

My comments previously regarding "the world to come" and its expected fullness, equally apply to this term: viz., the first Christians were experiencing a present deposit and firstfruits measure of the "powers of the age to come," while awaiting the coming expected fullness which was to be entered into at the Parousia of Jesus. As A. R. Fausset[8] rightly says,

> "The powers" of this new spiritual world, exhibited in outward miracles partly, and...especially consisting in the Spirit's inward influences are the fore*taste* of the coming inheritance.... "The world [age] to come,'" which, as to its "powers," exists already in the redeemed, will pass into a fully realized, manifested fact at Christ's coming (Col. 3:4).

The first Christians were already experiencing the saving power of Christ's new covenant ministry, but were not yet free from the experience of sin and the flesh and mortality. At the Parousia the first Christians expected to experience the "powers of the age to come" in full measure when the saving power of Christ, who is able to save to the uttermost degree, would be manifested in resurrecting the deceased saints and translating the living saints, bringing them all to heaven and giving them all resurrection-glorified-spiritual bodies.

Consider Jesus' remarks on "the age to come."
(a) On Mark 10:29-30 and Luke 18:29-30
> Mark 10:29-30 So Jesus answered and said, "Assuredly, I say to you, there is no one who has left house or brothers or sisters or father or mother or wife or children or lands, for My sake and the gospel's, 30 "who shall not receive a hundredfold *now in this time* [Gr. νῦν ἐν τῷ καιρῷ τούτῳ, in which καιρός, *kairos* = season, time] – houses and brothers and sisters and mothers and children and lands, with persecutions – and in *the age to come,* [Gr. ἐν τῷ αἰῶνι τῷ ἐρχομένῳ] eternal life.
>
> Lk. 18:29-30 So He said to them, "Assuredly, I say to you, there is no one who has left house or parents or brothers or wife or children, for the sake of the kingdom of God, 30 "who shall not receive many times more *in this present time* [lit. in this season/time (*kairos*)], and in *the age to come* eternal life."

Jesus said that then, in that present period of time, while they were preaching the gospel of the kingdom of God, there would be blessing mingled with trouble. There would be troubles such as loss of loved ones and persecutions. But there would be blessings of gaining a new family of fellow believers, (*cf. Mk.* 3:34-35). Such a mixture of experience – blessings together with troubles - is a characteristic of this present lifetime on earth, (not just the Mosaic age in Jesus' days). Jesus deliberately contrasts against this mixed condition of the present lifetime, the blessedness of eternal life that they will know in the age to come.

The "age to come," in general, is the age of the new covenant inaugurated by the sacrificial death and subsequent enthronement of Jesus in heaven as the Mediator of the new covenant. But, as has been demonstrated, the age to come has a deposit and firstfruits stage for the first Christians - experienced prior to the Parousia of Jesus - then the consummate, harvest stage and measure which they were expecting to enter fully at the Parousia of Jesus.

Corresponding to these two phases of the age to come, there are two phases to the first Christians' experience of the gift of eternal life. See the scriptures relating to this in my Chapter 2, Section 6 (iii). It must be recognized that during "this season" of life on this earth spent in preaching the gospel, from Pentecost until the Parousia, the apostles already had eternal life through their faith in Christ (as John's gospel promised to believers in numerous places, e.g. Jn. 3:16; 3:36; 5:24; 20:31; 1 Jn. 5:11-13), but only in a deposit-guarantee and firstfruits measure; they were looking for the full harvest of eternal life, at the Parousia of Christ.

When Jesus speaks of the reward of eternal life in the age to come, I believe he is speaking especially of that consummate eternal phase of the age to come, the consummate measure and experience of eternal life and the kingdom, which was expected by the first Christians at the Parousia. Jesus is referring to that consummate aspect of the age to come where there would be no more sufferings and persecutions, which are unhappy characteristics of "this present season" of life on earth. He is referring to the Christians' reward in the consummate phase of the new covenant "age to come" where all would be life and joy with the Lord in its fullest degree in heaven, with no tincture of sin and trouble. I understand Jesus to be saying to his disciples that the age to come (in this consummate phase) is not to be, cannot be, experienced in this troubled world in their present mortal condition that bears so much of the unhappy symptoms of the fall of man.

(b) Luke 20:33-36

"Therefore, in the resurrection, whose wife does she become? For all seven had her as wife." 34 And Jesus answered and said to them, "The sons of *this age* marry and are given in marriage. 35 "But those who are counted worthy to attain *that age*, and the resurrection from the dead, neither marry nor are given in marriage; 36 "nor can they die anymore, for they are equal to the angels and are sons of God, being sons of the resurrection. [Lk. 20:33-36]

Comments on Lk. 20:33-36

Jesus clearly says that "that age," (in contrast to "this age"), is an age of resurrection-life, of resurrection from the dead, where the characteristics of full sonship, as sons of God, are manifested. In "that age" they will have a spiritual body that will enable them to be fully suited to life in heaven with God just like the angels. This glorious liberty of the full revelation of sonship, free from corruption and suffering, with a redeemed body, is what the apostle Paul held as his expectation at the Parousia; see Rom 8:17-23. The term "sons of the resurrection," used by Jesus, is a combination of the hope expressed in Rom 8:23 (full sonship) and that expressed in 1 Cor. 15:42-50 (resurrection).

"This age" (v. 34) refers to our period of life on earth, subject to earthly responsibilities such as marriage, troubles, and mortality. As per the story of the Sadducees leading up to these words by Jesus, in "this age" people marry, and in this age married life is ended by death. (I do not believe that the context warrants "this age" to be limited to the "old covenant age," as some preterists define it). The term "age" (Gr. αἰών, *aion*) was in common use in those days, referring to any period of life on earth, e.g., Matt 13:22 - "the cares of this age (*aion*) and the deceitfulness of riches" can hinder the growth of the Word in one's heart.

"That age" of resurrection (v. 35) is, I believe, the equivalent to "the age to come" in its consummate, glory phase of the new covenant blessedness as used by Jesus in Mk. 10:29-30 and Lk. 18:29-30, and which was expected by the first Christians to be received at the Parousia of Christ.

Seen in this way there is no contradiction, but rather a lovely complement, in what Jesus said about "the age to come" and what the writer to the Hebrews said about "the age to come."

5. "The Period of Reformation"
"It [the old covenant tabernacle system] was symbolic for the present time in which both gifts and sacrifices are offered which cannot make him who performed the service perfect in regard to the conscience——10 concerned only with foods and drinks, various washings, and fleshly ordinances imposed until the time of reformation. (Gr. καιροῦ διορθώσεως, *kairou diorthoseos* = time/period/season of reformation; translated as "time of reformation" in KJV) [Heb. 9:9-10]

The writer to the Hebrews presents two systems or covenants in chapter 9; viz., the old Mosaic system which was unprofitable to save and reconcile to God and cleanse the conscience of the believer (9:9), and the new covenant system inaugurated by the blood of Christ, which could indeed save, reconcile and cleanse the conscience from dead works (9:1-14). Jesus is therefore called Mediator of the new covenant (9:15).

The first Christians were no longer under the old covenant system with its Levitical priesthood and animal sacrifices, which could never give people a cleansed conscience before the Lord (9:9). Rather, the first Christians were enjoying the new covenant system of justification, full pardon, and new creation life in Christ Jesus; they had peace with God through the Lord Jesus Christ and his blood sacrifice and rejoiced in their reconciliation (Rom 5:1, 9-11).

Heb 9:10 teaches that the "imposition" of, and the confinement under, the Mosaic law was only applicable until the time of reformation came. The same idea of an imposed confinement and a following time of liberty is taught by Paul in Gal 3:23-25; 4:1-7. The time of reformation spoken of in Heb 9:10 is that "time appointed by the father," the "fullness of time," spoken of in Gal 4, when law-confinement ended and liberty of sonship would be experienced. It is very clear then that "the season of reformation" is equivalent to the new covenant age that had now commenced and was being manifested in the lives of the first Christians. They were experiencing the effectiveness of the new covenant "season of reformation," which the previous, ineffectual Mosaic system had foreshadowed and prepared the ground for.

From the context-flow, the "season of reformation" of verse 10 is the season when "the good things to come" are brought in by the Messiah Jesus, mentioned in verse 11. The appointment of Christ Jesus as High Priest, enthroned in heaven, enabled him to commence his more excellent ministry of mediating the new covenant, (8:1, 6 and 9:15), called the season of reformation.

Once again, let me mention that, like "the world to come" and "the age to come," this "season of reformation" had been inaugurated and was already being experienced, much to the joy of the first Christians, (who were so relieved at having been rescued by Jesus their Savior out from under the yoke of bondage under the imposed old covenant), but was operative only in its deposit and firstfruits measure. (To be sure, this deposit measure was enough to ravish the heart and mind under the enlightenment and power of the Holy Spirit). The Parousia of Christ was the occasion when the first Christians would enter and experience the consummate blessedness of this "season of reformation."

The "re-forming" aimed at by God was firstly the spiritual re-creation, justification and reconciliation of men with God and their sanctification in this life, with that worship in spirit and truth that the Father desired in his people; and then at the Parousia of Christ, the completion of the re-forming process of these first Christians would occur by God's glorifying them in incorruptible spiritual bodies, sinless in heaven in union with their Lord. Only then would God's people be totally recovered from their fallenness from the glory of God (Rom 3:23) inherited from the first man; and only then would God's true ultimate desire for his creatures be brought to its fulfillment; (see further in Chapter 4, *The God of Glory and the Hope of Glory*).

6. "The Good Things to Come"

"But Christ has come forth as High Priest of the good things to come." [Heb 9:11, my translation, IH] *"1 For the law, having a shadow of the good things to come, and not the very image of the things, can never with these same sacrifices, which they offer continually year by year, make those who approach perfect." 12 But this Man, after He had offered one sacrifice for sins forever, sat down at the right hand of God, 14 For by one offering He has perfected forever those who are being sanctified.* [Heb 10:1, 12, 14]

Here are the Greek phrases found in these two verses, which are translated "good things to come": "γενομένων ἀγαθῶν" [lit. "good things to be," Heb. 9:11] and "μελλόντων ἀγαθῶν" [Lit. "good things *about to be*," Heb. 10:1]

Through the OT prophets the Lord promised he would in coming days perform the "Good Thing" (Jer 33:14) of bringing the Messiah, the Greater David, and through him work a new covenant of pardon and righteousness and new life and union with God. (e.g., Jer 33:14-16; 32; 31:31-33; 32:38-40; refer to my discussion of this in Chapter 1, *The New Covenant in the Days of the Apostles*).

The writer of Hebrews (10:1), says these promises were "now" being fulfilled: the promised Messiah has come, bringing with him the "good things" of his new covenant — things which the first Christians are already experiencing, such as full remission of sins and a cleansed conscience through the blood of Christ, justification and righteousness before God, and new creation life and ability to serve and worship God in the Holy Spirit. These promised things were known by the Jews as "good things to come," which "the One who is to come" (the Messiah) would introduce in the Messianic new covenant "age to come."

"Good things to come" is a descriptive appellation of that economy of which Jesus Christ is High Priest, and of which the law...was a "shadow." It receives this appellation as a salutary system, a system of blessings, not so much, if at all, because its best blessings are future blessings - blessings to be enjoyed in a future world, but, conformably to the Jewish mode of speaking on this subject, in which the state of things under the Messiah was termed "the coming world," or "the world to come," the peculiar benefits of that state are termed "the coming good things." The phrase describes that economy of which the two great characters are truth and grace, and which "came by Jesus Christ" - the "good things to come." [John Brown.[9]]

The old covenant could not impart the "good things," but only point to them. The animal sacrifices of the Mosaic law provided only a ceremonial cleansing, but could never deal with the moral guilt of sinners, and could never make those who desired to approach God, perfect and acceptable in his sight, (Heb 10:1). They merely foreshadowed what was to come under the Messiah.

The Hebrews writer says, "now we have such a High Priest" who is about to bring the good things to come, in the place of the Mosaic system which could not bring in the good things, but only foreshadow them, (Heb 8:1; 9:11; 10:1), who made the true atoning sacrifice for sin; "For by one offering He has perfected forever those who are being sanctified," (10:14). For the first Christians there was the fulfillment of that new covenant provision promised in Jeremiah, "Their sins and their lawless deeds I will remember no more," (Heb 10:17). "He [Christ] is the Mediator of the [Good Thing of the] new covenant [composed of many "good things"]," (9:15). Paul says the same thing about the reality of the good things being already present in Christ in his letter to the Colossians:

> Beware lest anyone cheat you through philosophy and empty deceit, according to the tradition of men, according to the basic principles of the world, and not according to Christ. 9 For in Him dwells all the fullness of the Godhead bodily; 10 and *you are complete* [or, made full] *in Him,* who is the head of all principality and power. 16 So let no one judge you in food or in drink, or regarding a festival or a new moon or Sabbaths, 17 *which are a shadow of things to come, but the substance is of Christ.* [Col. 2:8-10, 16-17]

That is, Christians already were experiencing "the substance," the reality, the good things in Christ Jesus of what the old covenant system (which the troublesome Judaizers were trying to bind on the Christians) foreshadowed. Christ Jesus was the fulfillment of the old covenant for the first Christians.

In Chapter 1, there are listed many of the good things of the new covenant already being experienced. These "good things to come" were already come to the first Christians, but in a deposit and firstfruits measure only. At the Parousia of the Lord Jesus, the first Christians would experience the full, consummate power and revelation of the "good things to come." The consummate measure of the good new covenant blessedness was ready for them in heaven (Heb 10:34).

7. "The City to Come"
For here we have no continuing city, but we seek the one to come. [Heb. 13:14]

The Greek phrase in Heb. 13:14 for "the one to come" is "τὴν μέλλουσαν" (lit. "the one about to be"). The concept of the city to come will be discussed more fully in a later chapter, so I will be brief here. The "city" of Heb 13:14 is clearly referring to the New Jerusalem, "the city of the living God, the heavenly Jerusalem" mentioned in Heb 12:22. It is "the city which has foundations, whose maker is God...[located in] a heavenly country," prepared by God for his people (Heb 11:10,16). The Jerusalem on earth represents the old covenant with children in bondage, while the Jerusalem above represents the new covenant with its Spirit-born children in liberty (Gal 4:21-31). The Old Testament saints were looking forward to entering this heavenly city. They were not looking for any inheritance on earth, but a heavenly inheritance, a city in a heavenly country, promised them by God. They had the promise of "the city to come."

Corresponding to the theme of firstfruits-consummation elsewhere, the same theme is present here. In a limited measure, "the city to come" (like the "age to come" and "the good things to come") had already come for the first Christians. And the first Christians had already come to, drawn near to, the heavenly city, (Heb 12:22). This city was, as it were, their mother, for they were partaking of its spirit and life and liberty, (Gal 4:26-28, 31). The believers in Christ were no longer at the old covenant scene of Mt Sinai (metaphorically speaking), (Gal 4:24-25,31; Heb 12:18-21), but had come to Mt Zion, into the new covenant grace of God in Christ, the Jerusalem above (Heb 12:22-24).

The first Christians' experience of the heavenly Jerusalem's blessings was in a firstfruits/deposit measure; far from complete; with more to come. They earnestly longed for that wonderful MORE. The writer to the Hebrews says, "we seek the city to come;" not implying that they had not already had *any* association with "the city to come," but meaning: "we seek to enter and experience the full glory of the heavenly city to come" — we have in our lives so far experienced the merest outskirts of blessedness of the city, but we seek to enter and experience the unimaginable fullness of blessedness that lies in the heart of that city.

8. "The Approaching Day"
"...not forsaking the assembling of ourselves together,

> *as is the manner of some, but exhorting one another,*
> *and so much the more as you see*
> *the Day approaching."* [Heb. 10:25]

"The Day approaching" in the Greek is "ἐγγίζουσαν τὴν ἡμέραν" (lit. "coming near the Day"). In relation to the time terminology reviewed in this article, it would seem clear to regard "the Day" as the period of ultimate fulfillment for all pre-AD 70 believers (i.e. the first Christians and all previous saints of history) at the Parousia of Christ.

The Day would be the time when the first Christians' hope would be fulfilled of experiencing the fullness, the consummation, the ultimate glory of that new covenant "world to come," "age to come" and "season of reformation," of which the first Christians were at present only experiencing in a deposit and firstfruits measure. The Day was to be the time when "the good things to come," which were already partially known and experienced, would be revealed and experienced in all their splendor and eternal blessedness.

The preterist Bible student believes that the Lord Jesus and the New Testament writers meant what they said, and were guided by the Holy Spirit to say it, when they said that "The Day" of the Lord's Parousia would be concurrent with the judgment and destruction of Jerusalem, and was expected before that messianic generation of Jews passed away. About AD 70 it *was fulfilled* for those waiting first Christians just as the Word said. The Day was a terrible one for Christ's enemies, but a glorious one for His people.

The first Christians could see The Day approaching, drawing near. (Heb 10:25):

- The Day of Christ's coming and appearing:
    Heb 10:37 (lit.) "For yet a very little while, *And* the coming one will come and will not tarry.
    Heb 9:28b To those who eagerly wait for Him He will appear a second time, apart from sin, for salvation.
- The Day of receiving their heavenly reward and inheritance and final salvation
    Heb 10:34b-36, 39 ...knowing that you have a better and an enduring possession for yourselves in heaven. 35 Therefore do not cast away your confidence, which has great reward. 36 For you have need of endurance, so that after you have done the will of God, you may receive [fulfillment of] the promise: ... 39 But we are not of those who draw back to perdition, but of those who believe to the saving of the soul.
    Heb 9:28b To those who eagerly wait for Him He will appear a second time, apart from sin, for salvation.

Paul elsewhere speaks of The Day of salvation for Christians as near:
> Rom. 13:11-12 And *do* this, knowing the time, that now *it is* high time to awake out of sleep; for now *our salvation is nearer* than when we *first* believed. 12 The night is far spent, *the day is at hand*. Therefore let us cast off the works of darkness, and let us put on the armor of light.
> 1 Thess 5:1-10 But concerning the times and the seasons, brethren, you have no need that I should write to you. 2 For you yourselves know perfectly that *the day of the Lord* so comes as a thief in the night. 3 For when they say, "Peace and safety!" then sudden destruction comes upon them, as labor pains upon a pregnant woman. And they shall not escape. 4 But you, brethren, are not in darkness, so that *this Day* should overtake you as a thief. 5 You are all sons of light and sons of the day. We are not of the night nor of darkness. 6 Therefore let us not sleep, as others *do*, but let us watch and be sober. 7 For those who sleep, sleep at night, and those who get drunk are drunk at night. 8 But let *us who are of the day* be sober, putting on the breastplate of faith and love, and *as* a helmet *the hope of salvation*. 9 For God did not appoint us to wrath, but *to obtain salvation through our Lord Jesus Christ*, 10 who died for us, that whether we wake or sleep, we should live together with Him.

Conclusion

The argument of the writer to the Hebrews may be summarized as follows:

Pay heed to the conclusive proof that Jesus is the Messiah of the New Covenant — his coming into the world signaled the last days of the old era; his high priestly sacrifice of himself for sins marked the consummation of the ages that have gone before, and the inauguration of the Messianic new covenant "world to come," "age to come," and "season of reformation" — the deposit-guarantee and firstfruits of which you who believe in Christ are experiencing now.

And upon this sure foundation, hold fast your hope and confidence as you wait for "the Day" of his second appearing with his final salvation that will raise you all to the consummate, harvest phase of the New Covenant blessedness – to the eternal inheritance of glory in the heavenly Holy of Holies with the Lord Jesus.

Footnotes

In my study above I have employed the comments of a number of well-respected Bible commentators. The fact that some of these commentators are futurists, having a mistaken view of the *timing* of the Lord's Parousia, does not detract from the fact that their comments on the verses that are examined in this article, are based on a sound exegesis of the relevant contexts, and have the effect of confirming my preterist understanding of New Testament eschatology. These commentators often very helpfully bring out the Jewish background of various phrases that Paul uses.

1. F. F. Bruce, The Epistle to the Hebrews, *The New International Commentary on the New Testament*, William B. Eerdmans Publishing Co., Grand Rapids, 1979, p. 3.
2. Dr John Gill, *Exposition on the Bible,* on the *Online Bible* CD, comments on Heb. 1:2.
3. Dr John Gill, *ibid.*, comments on Heb 2:5. "["the world to come"] seems therefore to intend the Gospel, and the Gospel dispensation and church state, in opposition to the Jewish state, and legal dispensation, *which was called a world*, and had in it a worldly sanctuary, and worldly ordinances, which is now at an end; and at the end of which Christ came, and then another world took place, here called "the world to come," *as the times of the Messiah are frequently called by the Jews Olam Haba, "the world to come,"* the Gospel dispensation, the apostle was treating of in the preceding verses, in distinction from the law, the word spoken by angels; for the Gospel was not spoken by them, but by the Lord: *the Gospel state is very properly the world to come, with respect to the Old Testament saints, who were looking for it, and in which old things are past away, and all things are become new*; angels desire to look into the mysteries of it, and learn from the church the manifold wisdom of God; but not they, but men, are the dispensers of the doctrines of it; and Christ, he is the Head, King, Governor, and Father of this new world. " (Emphasis mine - IH).
4. F. F. Bruce, op. cit., p. 33-34.
5. John Gill, op. cit., [comments on Heb 2:5); and John Brown, *Hebrews - Geneva Series of Commentaries*, Banner of Truth Trust, Edinburgh, 1994, pp. 287-288).
6. Dr John Owen [on Heb 6:5b] "Lastly, it is added, 'And the powers of the world [Gr. αἰών, *aion* - IH] to come;' the mighty miraculous operations of the Holy Ghost. *By 'the world to come' our apostle intends, the 'days of the Messiah,' that being the usual name of it in the [Israelite] church at that time, as the new world which God had promised to create....* [As to the meaning of the "powers"] Yet I would not fix on extraordinary gifts to the exclusion of those that are ordinary; they also are of 'the powers of the world to come;' so is every thing that belongs to the erection or preservation of the new world, or the kingdom of Christ." [John Owen, D.D., *An Exposition of the Epistle to the Hebrews*, Vol. 3, Revised and Abridged by the Rev. Edward Williams, D.D., in Four Volumes, James Black, London, 1815, pp. 133-134]. (Emphasis mine - IH)
7. John Brown, *Hebrews - Geneva Series of Commentaries*, Banner of Truth Trust, Edinburgh, 1994, p. 288.
8. A. R. Fausset, *A Commentary on the Old and New Testaments,* (In 3

volumes), by Robert Jamieson, A. R. Fausset and David Brown, Vol. 3, p. 542-543.
9. John Brown, op. cit., p. 391.

PART 2

In Which is Examined the
Nature of the Fullness
Of New Covenant Blessedness
Expected by the First Christians to be
received at the Parousia of Christ Jesus
Circa AD 70

Chapters 4 to 6

Chapter 4

The God of *Glory* and The Hope of *Glory*

The Meaning of *Glory* as the Christian Hope

In this chapter I hope to share some thoughts about the first Christians' hope of glory as found in the writings of the New Testament of the Bible. Before looking at this hope of an eschatological glory, I wish to establish the context in which this hope appears — the context of the God of Glory and the purpose of man's existence in God's universe. By proceeding in this order I believe it helps us to rightly keep God in the centre of things and helps us to appreciate more fully the wonder of the glory to which He has called his people.

The God of Glory
The living and true God, the Creator of heaven and earth, the God who has revealed himself in history as recorded in the Holy Bible, has been known by his followers down through the centuries as "the God of Glory." He is glorious as to his attributes and as to his deeds.

In Old Testament History
In his summary of Abraham's faith as father of the Israelites, the first Christian martyr, Stephen, said, "Brethren and fathers, listen: *The God of glory* appeared to our father Abraham when he was in Mesopotamia, before he dwelt in Haran." (Acts 7:2). It may be said that with Abraham, God began putting into action his plan of salvation through the Messiah to come. And God began this outworking of his plan by introducing himself as the God of glory!

The people of Israel were staggered at the Lord's visitation to them on Mt Sinai. "And *the glory of the LORD* abode upon mount Sinai, and the cloud covered it six days: and the seventh day he called unto Moses out of the midst of the cloud. And *the sight of the glory of the LORD was like devouring fire on the top of the mount* in the eyes of the children of Israel. (Ex. 24:16-17)

Moses, whose heart revered the Lord, knew there was more to the nature of God than just the outward fiery, thunderous display on Sinai. In holy daring he pleaded, " I beseech thee, *show me thy glory*." (Ex 33:18). Moses wanted to know more of the Lord's real nature, appearance, and inner moral glory. And the Lord graciously favored Moses' request, by saying that He would make *all his goodness pass before him* (Ex 33:19), and then He refers to it as an occasion when *his glory would pass by Moses* (v. 22). This signifies that the Lord's glory consists of his goodness. The Lord did cause his glory to be revealed to Moses in a display of his appearance (but not of the Lord's face, for no mortal man could see his face and live, Ex 33:20) and in the revelation of His name and nature as a merciful, gracious, longsuffering God, one who abounds in loving kindness and truth or faithfulness, (Ex 34:5-6). (See Ex. 33:12-34:9 for the full story).

The glory of the Lord filled the tabernacle of Moses, "And Moses was not able to enter into the tent of the congregation, because the cloud abode thereon, and *the glory of the LORD* filled the tabernacle," (Ex 40:35).

King David in his inspired reverence cried out: "Lift up your heads, O ye gates; and be ye lift up, ye everlasting doors; and *the King of glory* shall come in. *Who is this King of glory? The LORD strong and mighty, the LORD mighty in battle.* Lift up your heads, O ye gates; even lift *them* up, ye everlasting doors; and *the King of glory shall come in. Who is this King of glory? The LORD of hosts, he is the King of glory.* Selah." (Psa. 24:7-10). And David marveled at God's control of nature: "The voice of the LORD *is* upon the waters: *the God of glory thundereth: the LORD is upon many waters.*" (Psa. 29:3).

David was secure in the knowledge that "The *glory of the LORD shall endure for ever*: the LORD shall rejoice in his works. (Psa 104:1). And he just gloried in his God: "Thine, O LORD, *is* the greatness, and the power, and *the glory*, and the victory, and the majesty: for all *that is* in the heaven and in the earth *is thine*; thine *is* the kingdom, O LORD, and thou art exalted as head above all. (1 Chron. 29:11)

And later, the same glory of God filled the temple that David's son Solomon built for the Lord, "So that the priests could not stand to minister because of the cloud: for *the glory of the LORD* had filled the house of the LORD," (1 Kin. 8:11).

The prophet Isaiah was aware of the holiness and glory of the Lord God, e.g. Isaiah chapter 6. He realized that an essential aspect of God's glory was his holiness, his hatred of sin. He also said, "Jerusalem stumbled, and Judah is fallen, Because their tongue and their doings a*re* against the LORD, to provoke *the eyes of His glory*." (Isa. 3:8). Jesus said that Isaiah had seen his glory, (Jn. 12:41), which we believe refers to Isaiah's vision of the Lord in his holiness and glory in chapter 6 of his prophecies.

The commissioning of Ezekiel to prophesy in the Lord's name, was accompanied by an amazing vision of the Lord in his glory, of which I present just a few verses. (This reminds one of the vision that the apostle John had many years later of the glorified Christ in Revelation chapter 1).

> Ezek. 1:25 - 2:2; 3:12 A voice came from above the firmament that *was* over their heads; whenever they stood, they let down their wings. 26 And above the firmament over their heads *was* the likeness of *a throne*, in appearance like a sapphire stone; *on the likeness of the throne was a likeness with the appearance of a man high above it.* 27 Also from the appearance of His waist and upward I saw, as it were, the color of amber with the appearance of fire all around within it; and from the appearance of His waist and downward I saw, as it

were, the appearance of fire with brightness all around. 28 Like the appearance of a rainbow in a cloud on a rainy day, so *was* the appearance of the brightness all around it. *This was the appearance of the likeness of the glory of the LORD.* So *when I saw it, I fell on my face,* and I heard a voice of One speaking. 2:1 And He said to me, "Son of man, stand on your feet, and I will speak to you." 2 Then the Spirit entered me when He spoke to me, and set me on my feet; and I heard Him who spoke to me.... 3:12 Then the Spirit lifted me up, and I heard behind me *a great thunderous voice: "Blessed is the glory of the LORD from His place!"*

The prophet Habakkuk saw that sooner or later all enemies would fall, "For the earth will be filled with *the knowledge of the glory of the LORD,* As the waters cover the sea." (Hab. 2:14). Habakkuk was led to cry out the wonderful truth in the face of all opposition: "the LORD is in His holy temple. Let all the earth keep silence before Him." For he knew that "*in His temple everyone says, 'Glory!'* " (Hab. 2:20; Psa 29:9).

In New Testament History

As we move into the New Testament the same reality gripped the first Christians: they served the God of Glory. Indeed the herald of the birth of the Messiah involved the God of glory sending his angels to the shepherds: "And behold, an angel of the Lord stood before them, and *the glory of the Lord shone around them, and they were greatly afraid.*" (Lk. 2:9).

After Stephen had just finished relating how the "*God of glory*" had visited Abraham, that very same God of glory opened heaven to his servant Stephen as he became the first Christian martyr. "But he [Stephen], being full of the Holy Spirit, gazed into heaven and *saw the glory of God,* and Jesus standing at the right hand of God." (Acts 7:55). The Pharisee Saul who was assisting in Stephen's death was soon to be touched by that same glory of God that blessed Stephen.

The evil Saul was converted into the apostle Paul as he saw "a great light from heaven" on his journey to Damascus. It was the glory of the Lord Jesus shining around him. The "*glory of that [heavenly] light*" blinded him and humbled him to the dust. (See his testimony Acts 22:1-15). Paul understood from that time on that "*the Father of the glory,*" (Eph 1:17), the great LORD of the OT saints, was truly the God of the Lord Jesus Christ whom he had been opposing. Paul was glad that through the gospel of the Lord there would redound much *praise for His glory.* The *glory of God,* and the *glory of his grace* were displayed in the gospel of the Lord Jesus. (Eph 1:6, 12, 14).

It was the *glory of God* that raised Jesus from the dead. (Rom 6:4). Elsewhere it is said that it was by his power that God the Father raised Jesus. But Paul uses the word "glory" in Rom 6:4 to intimate that the power that operated in the Lord Jesus in his resurrection and his exaltation, was a manifestation of his glory, of supreme excellence, a glorious power, or rather the power of his glory.

Paul came to realize the greatness of the One whom Israel had rejected and whom he had formerly blasphemed: "But we speak the wisdom of God in a mystery, the hidden *wisdom* which God ordained before the ages for our glory, which none of the rulers of this age knew; for had they known, they would not have crucified *the Lord of glory*. (1 Cor. 2:7-8).

James, who also had once mocked his brother Jesus (according to his humanity through Mary), was aware of the greatness of the One whom Christians served. "My brethren, do not hold the faith of our Lord Jesus Christ, *the Lord of glory*, with partiality. (Jam 2:1).

John's vision of the Lord Jesus in his glory was more that he could bear. "And when I saw Him, I fell at His feet as dead." (Rev. 1:17). This same humbling to the dust upon seeing and hearing the Lord in his glory occurred to others in the past, such as to Moses, Isaiah, Ezekiel, Daniel and Paul.

And in Rev. 11:1-11 John relates his vision into heaven where he saw God on his throne in glorious appearance, with angelic beings describing how worthy He was to receive all glory and praise.

There are too many other cases throughout the Scriptures to mention them all here, but these are sufficient to reveal the fact that the true OT saints and the NT saints valued the Lord as the God of glory. There was none like him in glory, and they revered him as such. It is essential to catch something of the awesomeness and beauty and incomparableness of the God of glory and the glory of God so often referred to in the scriptures, in order to have a firm foundation for looking at the hope of the glory of God which the saints of God have through the gospel of the Lord Jesus Christ.

The Meaning of God being called "the God of Glory"

When the Scriptures speak of the God of glory and the glory of God, what do they mean? What does "glory" mean as it applies to the Lord? From my studies the best way I can describe God's glory is to say it is *His Excellence*:

God's Glory Is His Supreme, Incomparable Excellence

Everything about him is sheer unmixed *excellence* and *perfection*.

God's essential glory. There is firstly, the infinite excellence and fullness of God's own eternal essential nature which only God himself knows and comprehends, in which He ever rejoices in himself, and which was known and experienced amongst the trinity of Father, Son and Holy Spirit before there was any created universe, and which They will enjoy for eternity to come.

God's revealed glory. Secondly, there is God's revealed glory. It is God's good pleasure for His inner essential glory and fullness to be revealed in a created universe, and demonstrated in ways that his created beings can perceive. It is this revealed glory, flowing from his internal essential glory, that all his creatures, angelic and human, can know, appreciate, esteem, experience and rejoice in.

We can use the sun as an example. Light and warmth and gravitational power are external expressions, exhibitions, and manifestations of the inner mass and glory and fire of the sun. No creature can live at or experience the inner centre of the sun, but through all that emanates from the sun's essential glory and fullness, the whole solar system keeps in regular motion, and this earth with all its creatures, especially man, receive great benefit. It is through the external manifestations of the sun's inner glory that everything on earth receives its color, form and beauty, and every living thing receives light and life and warmth and comfort and joy and growth and health. But we must remember that the sun is a mere created thing, created by One whose nature pulses with infinite power and light. Indeed, the great sun of our solar system with its glory (1 Cor. 15:41), is but an emanation and display of the glory of God the Creator. "The heavens declare the glory of God; and the firmament show his handiwork," Psa. 19:1, (see rest of this Psalm for a description of the sun). [It is a sad and reprehensible fact that, because of sin, most of mankind fail to recognize that the wonderful design of the universe reveals the glory and handiwork of the master Designer].

Therefore, it is through the expressions, workings, manifestations of God's infinite inner essential glory and light into this world that God reveals himself and his ways to man. His holiness, his love, his power, his wisdom, his goodness, his judgments, his mercy, his salvation, his faithfulness, his sovereignty and providence over man and all nature and universe, are all characterized by glory, by an almighty excellence and perfection that lacks nothing, that can never be improved. Every attribute He has is excellent beyond comparison; everything He does is excellent in wisdom, righteousness, justice, mercy, power, etc.

One can understand then the constant calls of scripture for man to ascribe glory to God. It is so utterly reasonable and right, and absolutely vital, that mankind bows the knee to sincerely confess that God is the God of Glory, and that as such He is worthy of all praise, worship, love, reverence, obedience, trust.

The Basis And Goal Of All Things: God's Good Pleasure And Glory

Throughout the Scriptures there runs the high theme of the glory of God. The great end for which all the universe was created and exists is the glory of God. The great apostle Paul with his deep knowledge of the Scriptures and profound insight into God's government of the world and into his plan of salvation, admits he could not comprehend the fullness of God's glorious ways:

> Oh, the depth of the riches both of the wisdom and knowledge of God! How unsearchable *are* His judgments and His ways past finding out! 34 "For who has known the mind of the LORD? Or who has become His counselor?" 35 "Or who has first given to Him and it shall be repaid to him?" 36 *For of Him and through Him and to Him are all things, to him [is, or be] the glory forever. Amen.* (Rom. 11:33-36)

Weymouth's translation expresses this last verse well:

> For the universe owes its origin to Him, was created by Him, and has its aim and purpose in Him. To Him be the glory throughout the Ages! Amen. (Rom 11:36).

    Paul is saying here, firstly, that this fact of everything being of Him, through Him and to Him, is the fundamental reality of the universe. And secondly, this reality is a display and working of God's glory, which calls for all intelligent created beings to esteem and praise Him forever. In God's originating all out of himself, and working all by his own power, and causing all to work for his good pleasure, the glory of God is revealed, is manifested (for those with eyes to see) and is prospering, and is shown as the goal of all God's works.

Consider the following verses:
- Rev. 4:11 "You are worthy, O Lord, To receive glory and honor and power; For You created all things, And *for Your will* [or, *for your pleasure,* or *because of your will*] *they exist and were created.*" (from Rec. Greek text).
- Col. 1:16 For by Him all things were created that are in heaven and that are on earth, visible and invisible, whether thrones or dominions or principalities or powers. *All things were created through Him and for Him.*
- Eph 1:5b-6a, 9 [God's plan of salvation is] according to *the good pleasure of His will,* 6 to *the praise of the glory of His grace....* 9 having made known to us *the mystery of His will, according to His good pleasure which He purposed in Himself,*

    The central issue here is that all exists and was created *by God* and *for God*. The term "for God" means "for his glory and for his good pleasure." In creating the universe, in creating man, in creating and working out his wonderful plan of salvation through his beloved Son, in his gathering a family of redeemed men and angels to dwell with Him in heaven for eternity–in all of this it was and is God's good pleasure and will to manifest, exert, and fill all with his glory. For an enlightened believer, this knowledge that all is by and for God's glory, and that God wants to manifest his glory to and in his people for them to enjoy Him for ever, is purifying, humbling, awe-inspiring, and awakens a sense of profound wonder and gratitude. God is the centre of all things and man exists for him.

Mankind's Highest Privilege and Blessedness

From the Scriptures we find that God created man as his highest achievement, and was pleased to bestow upon him the highest privilege and blessedness that man could ever imagine.

> 1 Cor. 11:7b "...*[man] is the image and glory of God; but woman is the glory of man.*"

This verse at least means that God created man to be his representative (image) on earth in whom His glory was to be manifested: as such man was to be a class of being with whom God himself could fellowship and delight in as His workmanship. (Note that the woman was not made as the image of the man, but also is made in (or, as) the image of God, Gen. 1:26-27. But in the order of creation, the woman was to be the helper fully suited to the man, and was made as the glory of the man; all that characterized the man, was to be manifested in the woman, one in whom the man would glory and delight).

In Isaiah's prophesy, The Lord refers to "Everyone who is *called by My name*, Whom I have *created for My glory*; I have formed him, yes, I have made him." Isa. 43:7. What God, in the context, reveals as his purpose for His dispersed people, gives us an idea of what his original intention was in his creation of man. Here is man's high dignity, his highest privilege and calling. Those called by his name, those whom he had called and revealed himself or his name to, those whom he had claimed as his own to come under the care and protection of his great name, those are ones whom he had created for the most wonderful end; they were created for his glory. .

Apostle James in NT days recognized that God was visiting the gentiles and granting them repentance and faith in the Lord Jesus Christ and saving them. God's purpose was "to take out of them [the gentiles] *a people for His Name.*" To be a "people for His Name" (as in Isa. 43:7) signifies the same things as being a people for his glory. They would be a people whom he would have as his own special beloved ones in whom he would manifest his name, i.e. the wonderful qualities inherent in his name as God and Lord. In them his glory would be seen.

Also from the many verses, some of which I will list shortly, speaking of God's plan to have his glory be upon his redeemed people, and that through them his name would be glorified, we see that it has always been God's desire from the beginning of the world to have mankind in a unique relationship and fellowship with Him in the sphere of his glory — the glory of his revealed communicable attributes and the glory of his works of sanctification and providence. Man was designed to live in the knowledge, appreciation, and full esteem of the glory of God, to experience the glory of God as his refuge and light and life and happiness, and to manifest or exhibit the glory of God in his behavior and relationships and service toward God and fellow creatures. In this sphere of God's glory, man was to have conscious, living, intimate, fellowship with His Creator, the God of Glory. I like to think of man being created for the glory of God as meaning this:

> *Man was designed and created to be in an intimate, pure fellowship with his Creator, the God of Glory; wherein his life would consist of the ultimate blessedness of living in the sphere of the glory of God: viz., of continuously knowing and esteeming the glory of God; of continuously experiencing the glory of God; and continuously exhibiting the glory of God.*

Surely, no higher dignity or privilege or blessedness for man could ever be imagined than man in fellowship with God in the sphere of His glory. Yet...

Fallen Man - Fallen from Glory

Yet, tragically, the disobedience of the first people, Adam and Eve, to God's command, and their choosing not to trust and love God more their own faulty reason, sank the whole human race into a spiritual death, into a bondage to sin, into a separation from and enmity to, fellowship with God their Creator. In his letter to the Roman Christians the apostle Paul summarizes the corrupted, sinful, pathetic state of humanity in their natural condition:

> "There is none who understands; there is none who seeks after God. They have all gone out of the way; they have together become unprofitable; there is none who does good, no, not one...the way of peace they have not known. There is no fear of God before their eyes...all the world (is) guilty before God.... For all have sinned and *fall short of the glory of God*." [selected verses from Rom 3:10-23]

This last clause is truly a tragic one. It means that man has totally fallen short of his whole designed dignity, privilege and blessedness with the God of Glory. To fall short of the glory of God means:

- Man falls short of understanding and appreciating and esteeming with due reverence the glory of God his Maker ("There is none who understands; none who seeks after God; no fear of God before their eyes")
- Man falls short of experiencing the glory of God ("They have all gone out of the way; and the way of peace they have not known; guilty before God")

- Man falls short of exhibiting the glory of God as God's representative or image ("They have together become unprofitable; none who does good")

Indeed the scriptures state that man in his natural state is reduced to the level where his spiritual insight, intelligence, maturity and acquaintance with God are no better than a beast's, (Psa 49:20; Psa 73:22; Isa 1:3).

Consider the list of verses below that show how the prophets regarded the devastating fact of man losing the glory of God and of God withdrawing his glory away from them. Consistently God showed his desire to have a people who would honor him and whom he would bless, but the downward bias in man would not have it, and man even resorted to honoring idols instead of God.

> Psa. 106:20 Thus they changed *their glory* [i.e. their true God of glory] into the similitude of an ox that eateth grass.
> Jer. 2:11 Hath a nation changed *their* gods, which *are* yet no gods? But my people have changed *their glory* [i.e. their God of glory] for *that which* doth not profit
> Ezek. 10:18; 11:23 Then the glory of the LORD departed *from the threshold of the temple...And* the glory of the LORD went up from the midst of the city *and stood on the mountain. [God departed from Jerusalem because of the people's sin and idolatry]*.
> Rom. 1:18 For the wrath of God is revealed from heaven against all ungodliness and unrighteousness of men, who suppress the truth in unrighteousness, 19 because what may be known of God is manifest in them, for God has shown *it* to them. 20 For since the creation of the world His invisible *attributes* are clearly seen, being understood by the things that are made, *even* His eternal power and Godhead, so that they are without excuse, 21 because, *although they knew God, they did not glorify Him as God*, nor were thankful, but became futile in their thoughts, and their foolish hearts were darkened. 22 Professing to be wise, they became fools, 23 and *changed the glory of the incorruptible God* into an image made like corruptible man – and birds and four-footed animals and creeping things. 24 Therefore God also gave them up to uncleanness, in the lusts of their hearts, to dishonor their bodies among themselves, 25 who *exchanged the truth of God for the lie*, and *worshiped and served the creature rather than the Creator*, who is blessed forever. Amen.

Truly, as the Scriptures point out, there is nothing so horrible, criminal, blasphemous and pathetic as man glorying in his own pride of self-achievement, civilization, technical acumen, self-importance, while refusing to acknowledge, and honor and serve the Excellent One, the Creator, the God of Glory, who is infinitely above him in every respect.

> Rom 1:22 Professing to be wise, they became fools.
> Jer 8:9 Behold, they have rejected the word of the LORD; So what wisdom do they have?

While man self-proclaims his superiority, he is inadvertently giving evidence of his shameful inferiority. When man proclaims his integrity as one keen on upholding law and order in the world, combating terrorism, aiming to build a better world, etc., he is in fact inadvertently, criminally, trying to dethrone God, and is committing lawlessness against the Sovereign laws of the all-wise Creator, and is himself the problem, rather than a solution to society. Man is deceived and is deceiving his fellow man. Only the restraining grace of God keeps the world from falling into chaos and hell-on-earth (although in some places it is like that now for many victims of war, and those under evil dictatorship).

Is there any way to rescue man out of his fallenness, and restore him into the sphere of the glory of God? "Who then can be saved? With men this is impossible. But with God all things are possible." (Matt 19:25-26)

The Gospel Solution - The Glory of God's Grace Through Jesus Christ
Happily, there is a solution to man's tragic and evil fallenness! Of course the solution lies with God himself; it is the Glory of God's Grace — the sovereign grace of God!

It is perfectly reasonable that the only thing sufficiently qualified to recover fallen man and restore man into a fellowship with God in the sphere of His glory, is the glory of God itself.

God's sovereign grace is a quality or aspect of God's glory. And God chose to reveal to the world his glory in the form of his saving grace and mercy in and through the person of his beloved eternal Son incarnated as the Lord Jesus Christ. This whole salvation process by God's grace through the Lord Jesus Christ is called the New Covenant, established by the sacrifice and blood of Jesus, (e.g. Matt 26:28; Lk. 22:20; Heb 9:14-15; 13:20).

Grace means God's undeserved and unmerited loving kindness and favor going out in power to meet the needs of helpless man, on the basis of Christ's atonement. Some have anagrammed grace to mean *G*od's *R*iches *A*t *C*hrist's *E*xpense.

Only God's grace remedies the fallenness of man in the matter of his guilt before "the Judge of all the earth," bringing forgiveness, pardon and justification and peace with the holy God.

Only God's grace overcomes the enmity and darkness in man's heart, mind and will, and regenerates man so that he will sincerely seek and come to God in repentance and faith.

Only God's grace sanctifies the redeemed man by working in him the life of Christ and the fruit of the Spirit of God. Let us look at this grace of God and the glory of God in saving lost sinners.

The Glory of God Revealed in and through Christ Jesus
The apostle John wrote:

> And the Word became flesh and dwelt among us, and *we beheld His glory, the glory as of the only begotten of the Father, full of grace and truth....* 16 And *of His fullness we have all received, and grace for grace.* 17 For the law was given through Moses, *but grace and truth came through Jesus Christ.* 18 No one has seen God at any time. The only begotten Son, who is in the bosom of the Father, He has declared *Him.* (Jn. 1:14, 16-18).

John beheld and discerned the glory of God in Jesus, and this glory especially consisted of grace and truth or faithfulness. This is a most wonderfully pregnant statement. When God revealed his glory to Moses on the mount over 1000 years previously, God made all his goodness pass by Moses and he declared that his name, his glory, was especially in his attributes of graciousness and compassion, longsuffering, and loving kindness and truth or faithfulness, (see Exodus chs. 33 and 34). John, under the Holy Spirit's guidance, is declaring that the glory of God consisting of those wonderful qualities revealed to Moses was revealed in all its fullness in Jesus Christ in his life and death for lost sinners. The Son who dwelt on the bosom of the Father (i.e. in the most intimate, eternal fellowship, and union) declared/displayed/revealed what the glory of the Father was like in the form of His grace and faithfulness to save sinners.

There is a GLORY here that a natural man, sadly, can never see; but which the born-again Spirit-indwelt man can see – a glory which ever increases in appreciation and wonder, under the illumination of the Holy Spirit whose delight is to glorify Christ and the Father before the mind and spirit of the believer.

The Glory of God in the Gospel of Jesus Christ
Fallen man abides in spiritual darkness. He has, if left to himself, no sight or appreciation of, nor any desire for, the glory of God, especially the glory-qualities of his saving grace and truth. Notice what Paul says about this darkness and how it has been overcome.

> For it is the God who commanded light to shine out of darkness, *who has shone in our hearts to give the light of the knowledge of the glory of God in the face [or person] of Jesus Christ.* (2 Cor. 4:6).

The apostle Paul shares how God overcomes this darkness in man (for no man could overcome it!). It is by the knowledge of the glory of

God revealed in Jesus Christ.

Under the awakening light of God shining in a sinner's heart, (just like God sent his light out into the darkness of the original creation), the sinner is brought into a vital spiritual knowledge of the glorious things that God has done and provided in the person of Jesus Christ. This gripping knowledge moves him to faith and repentance; he comes to Jesus seeking his mercy and salvation. From the truth of the scriptures the enlightened sinner comes into a knowledge of his sinfulness, and of God's sending his Son to redeem him from his guilt and sin by Jesus' being the propitiation for sinners, and of the truth that through Jesus, through faith in Jesus, God graciously grants the gift of righteousness and reconciliation (see Rom. 3:21-26). This gospel solves the humanly impossible problem of man's fallenness and separation and guilt before God (as revealed in Rom 3:10-20).

The saving knowledge of God's blessing of salvation in Christ, is called in the above verse (2 Cor. 4:6), "the knowledge of *the glory of God* in the face/person of Christ;" that is, the glory of God as demonstrated in Christ Jesus in his whole work of saving sinners.

In a former verse, 2 Cor. 4:4, Paul refers to "the light of the glorious gospel of Christ," or literally, "the *light of the gospel of the glory of Christ.*" This gospel of salvation through Jesus Christ is also called, "the *gospel of the glory of the blessed God,*" (1 Tim 1:11). That is, the gospel of salvation flows from, is applied by, manifests, and results in, the glory of God and Christ.

The glory of God is Manifested in His Grace

Grace firstly enlightens a sinner and works faith in him, (sinners "believed through grace," Acts 18:27); then grace saves him as he puts his faith in Christ, "By grace you are saved through faith," (Eph. 2:8). Out of the fullness of the glory in Christ, a believer receives grace (Jn. 1:16), grace that saves him and makes him a child of God (Jn. 1:12).

All of God's work in saving sinners in Christ is "to the praise of *the glory of his grace,*" (Eph. 1:6), and also "to the praise of *his glory,*" (Eph. 1:12). That is, God's glory is revealed in, and accomplishes, this salvation work; and all who comprehend and appreciate this (including angels who observe with wonder) are led to esteem and praise that glory and excellence of God that flows from God's heart in the form of grace.

God manifests his glory in his Son Jesus Christ the Savior; and in the gospel of salvation; and in his saving grace. O, how indebted a redeemed man is to the glory of God for his salvation!

> Give to the LORD, O families of the peoples,
> Give to the LORD glory and strength.
> Give to the LORD the glory *due* His name; (Psa 96:7-8).

The Glory of Justifying Grace and Sanctifying Grace

The glory of justifying grace: As just discussed, "the gospel of the glory of God" involves the wonderful truth of fallen man experiencing the glory of God in the form of his justifying grace. By this glorious grace man is redeemed, justified, and reconciled to God through faith in the Lord Jesus Christ. The glory of God is manifested in this salvation. The following verses speak of His justifying grace, and grace that makes us accepted before God.

> Eph 1:6-7 to the praise of *the glory of His grace, by which He has made us accepted in the Beloved. 7 In Him we have redemption through His blood, the forgiveness of sins, according to the riches of His grace*
> Eph 2:8 *By grace you have been saved* through faith
> Rom 3:24-26 *being justified freely by His grace* through the redemption that is in Christ Jesus, 25 whom God set forth *as* a propitiation by His blood, through faith, to demonstrate His righteousness, because in His forbearance God had passed over the sins that were previously committed, 26 to demonstrate at the present time His righteousness, that He might be just and the justifier of the one who has faith in Jesus.
> Tit. 3:5, 7 ...according to His mercy He saved us... 7 that *having been justified by His grace* we should become heirs according to the hope of eternal life.

The glory of sanctifying grace: Also the newly born-from-above Christian receives sanctifying grace which works in him during his life on earth in which a believer grows in faith and knowledge of God and in which the life of Christ is more and more incorporated into him. The glory of God is the source of this sanctification. See the examples below, noting that the grace here is sanctifying grace, and that such blessing is to the praise of God's glory, i.e. God's glory is manifested in such gracious working.

> 2 Pet 1:2 *Grace and peace be multiplied to you in the knowledge of God and of Jesus our Lord,*
> 2 Cor. 12:9 And He said to me, "*My grace* is sufficient for you, for My strength is made perfect in weakness." Therefore most gladly I will rather boast in my infirmities, that the power of Christ may rest upon me.
> 2 Tim 2:1 You therefore, my son, *be strong in the grace that is in Christ Jesus.*
> Acts 20:32 "So now, brethren, I commend you to God and *to the word of His grace, which is able to build you up* and give you an inheritance among all those who are sanctified.

1 Cor. 1:30, 31 But of Him you are in Christ Jesus, who became for us wisdom from God — and righteousness and *sanctification* and redemption — 31 that, as it is written, "He who glories, *let him glory in the LORD.*"

2 Pet 3:18 but *grow in the grace and knowledge of our Lord and Savior Jesus Christ. To Him be the glory* both now and forever. Amen.

Eph 3:14-16 For this reason I bow my knees to the Father of our Lord Jesus Christ, 15 from whom the whole family in heaven and earth is named, 16 that He would grant you, *according to the riches of His glory, to be strengthened with might through His Spirit in the inner man*,

Heb 13:20-21 Now may the God of peace who brought up our Lord Jesus from the dead, that great Shepherd of the sheep, through *the blood of the everlasting covenant*, 21 *make you complete in every good work to do His will, working in you what is well pleasing in His sight, through Jesus Christ, to whom be the glory forever and ever.* Amen.

The Christians were constantly being renewed and transformed by this sanctifying grace of God. Paul's letters convey the following truths about the new creation lives of those first Christians, readers of the epistles:

The old is off. Believers in Christ already had "put off the old man with his deeds" Col. 3:9 (i.e. the unregenerate, without-God man that they were, before their being awakened and drawn to Christ and saved by God); their "old man was crucified with Christ, that the body of sin might be annulled, that [they] should no longer be slaves to sin" Rom 6:6. They were to therefore "reckon [themselves] dead indeed to sin." Rom 6:11.

The new is on. Believers in Christ already had "put on the new man," (Col. 3:10); in Christ they were a "new creation," (2 Cor. 5:17), and were God's "workmanship, created in Christ Jesus," (Eph 2:10). The wonderful fact is that "Christ lives in [them], (Gal 2:20); "Jesus Christ is in [them], who is not weak toward [them], but is powerful in [them]," (2 Cor. 13:5, 3); and since "Christ is in [them], the body indeed is dead because of sin, but the Spirit is life because of righteousness." (Rom 8:10). Indeed, "To them (to his saints, v. 26) God willed to make known what are the riches of the glory of this mystery among the Gentiles: which is Christ in you, the hope of glory." (Col. 1:27)

Constant renewing and transforming. Believers were being renewed by the power of Christ. They "have put on the *new* [Gr. νέος, *neos*] man who is being constantly renewed/remodeled/strengthened/given growth [Gr. ἀνακαινόω, pres pass ptc of *anakainoo*] in knowledge according to the image of Him who created him, (Col. 3:10). Their "inner man [was] *being renewed/given fresh growth* [Gr. pres pass indic of *anakainoo*] day by day," (2 Cor. 4:16). Paul exhorted, "I beseech you therefore, brethren, by the mercies of God, that you present your bodies a living sacrifice, holy, acceptable to God, *which is* your reasonable service. And do not be conformed [i.e., similar behavior] to this world, but *be transformed* [i.e. be changed in your behavior so that it matches your new-creation life within you, and matches your Christian profession] *by the renewing* [Gr. *anakainosis*] of your mind, that you may prove what *is* that good and acceptable and perfect will of God, (Rom 12:1-2). Those believers were taught that they were to "work out to its full conclusion your own salvation with fear and trembling; for it is God who works in you both to will and to do for *His* good pleasure," (Phil 2:12-13).

But Christians were only experiencing the deposit and firstfruits of the New Covenant.

The NT reveals the first Christians were not yet completed experientially despite their being the recipients of God's justifying and sanctifying grace.

As the New Testament epistles reveal, the Christian life is a battle, and fellowship with God and the esteeming, experiencing and exhibiting of the glory of God are far from perfect in the Christian's life. As every Christian is aware, the enmity of the flesh, and sin and the ungodly world are still in guerilla type warfare in the life of a Christian. Although his "inner man" is being renewed by the Spirit of God, there is still the legacy of the fallen state in him: his mind is still imperfect, limited in its capacity and ability to know and appreciate and fellowship with God the way he would wish; he is imperfect in discerning the will of God and serving God in the power of the Holy Spirit satisfactorily; he is lacking in fullness of the fruit of the Spirit; imperfect in his ability to love the Lord and fellow man perfectly; battling with lack of faith and dullness in prayer and praise; struggling to avoid fear, pride, despair, envy, discontentment with God's providence, self-dependence, selfishness, etc., etc. The apostle Paul himself confessed that he was groaning and laboring for a fullness of glory-life which he didn't yet possess; he was aware of the bondage of corruption within himself from which he desired to be freed (Rom 8:21-24; 2 Cor. 5:4). Constantly in his epistles, Paul exhorts, corrects, encourages and teaches, in the aim to help his Christian readers mature, to avoid sin and heresy, to walk in love, to keep trusting, etc., for he knew that they needed such teaching.

The Christians needed more than justifying grace and sanctifying grace (wonderful though these are) to solve their need, and to bring them fully and completely into the glory of God.

As demonstrated in my article, *The Hope of the First Christians - Deposit and Fullness*, prior to the Parousia the first Christians were limited to a deposit and firstfruits measure and experience of the New Covenant power and blessings, but it had been made clear to them in the epistles that their present measure was a down-payment guaranteeing a coming fullness. Therefore, while what they presently had was insufficient to perfect them experientially, they were not to feel disillusioned by that fact, for they had been taught that they were not able to be experientially perfected until the Parousia of Christ; and they had been taught to positively regard the measure of blessing that they had as an encouragement and assurance of the coming fullness.

The God of Glory planned more for his children than this incomplete or imperfect Christian condition. Wonderful as the blessings of knowing God were already, their happiness was incomplete while a legacy of fallenness was still in them. *The fact is that in the glorious gospel of Christ and God, there is more than justifying grace and sanctifying grace. There is glorifying grace!*

God's Glory Manifested in Glorifying Grace

The New Testament shows that the apostle Paul and the other apostles and the first Christians had a hope of an eschatological state of consummate glory that they believed was yet to come, and soon to come. And this state of glory for the believers would be brought about by the same way as every other spiritual blessing was brought about for them, by the glory of God's grace.

Glorifying Grace

We have looked at God's glory revealed in his justifying grace and sanctifying grace. But there is more! The epistles exhort believers to look forward to a coming grace, a *final, climactic revelation and working of God's grace that would bring the waiting believers into eternal glory at the revelation of Christ*:

> 1 Pet. 1:13 Therefore gird up the loins of your mind, be sober, and *rest your hope fully upon the grace that is to be brought to you at the revelation of Jesus Christ*;
> 1 Pet. 5:10 ...*the God of all grace, who called us to His eternal glory* by Christ Jesus...

The apostle Peter's epistle shows that *this expected, hoped-for grace would bring the believers into God's eternal glory, into their eternal inheritance*, into a participation of the glory that was to be revealed at the Parousia of Jesus, (see 1 Pet. 1:3-4, 10-11; 5:1-4).

A Glorifying Salvation

Just as there is a salvation associated with justifying grace ("By grace you have been saved through faith," Eph 2:8; and "being justified freely by His grace," Rom 3:24), so *there is a final, climactic salvation associated with this glorifying grace*. This final salvation is the last stage and completion of what was begun at the sinner's first call by God to faith and repentance.

> 1 Pet. 1:5 [You Christians] are kept by the power of God through faith for *salvation ready to be revealed in the last time.*
> 1 Thess 5:8 But let us who are of the day be sober, putting on the breastplate of faith and love, and as a helmet *the hope of salvation.*
> Heb 9:28 so Christ was offered once to bear the sins of many. To those who eagerly wait for Him He will appear a second time, apart from sin, *for salvation.*

And this hoped-for final salvation–the first Christians' portion at the Lord's Parousia–was a salvation into eternal glory. God's whole purpose in saving people was to eventually bring them into his eternal glory:

> 2 Thess. 2:13-14 But we are bound to give thanks to God always for you, brethren beloved by the Lord, because God from the beginning *chose you for salvation* through sanctification by the Spirit and belief in the truth, 14 *to which He called you by our gospel, for the obtaining of the glory of our Lord Jesus Christ.*
> 2 Tim. 2:10 Therefore I endure all things for the sake of the elect, that they also may obtain *the salvation which is in Christ Jesus with eternal glory.*
> Heb. 2:10 For it was fitting for Him, for whom are all things and by whom are all things, in bringing *many sons to glory*, to make the captain of *their salvation* perfect through sufferings.

This final salvation had to do with bringing many sons to glory, where they would experience a crown of glory (1 Pet 5:4).

The Glory of God manifested in this final climax

As always the glory of God would be the origin of, be manifested in, and be the power of, this final eschatological grace and final eschatological salvation. For example:

> Eph. 1:14 [the Holy Spirit] is the guarantee of our inheritance until *the redemption* of the purchased possession, *to the praise of His glory.*

In the NT the hope of a final phase of grace and salvation and of God's redemption-plan was expected to be fulfilled in the case of the first Christians at the Parousia. Eph 1:14 declares that this wonderful final phase of redemption and the resultant product would be "to the praise of His glory." This last phrase means that it is God's glory that would be the source of it all, and would be manifested in it all, and in their understanding and appreciating and experiencing it all, the fully redeemed, glorified saints would ever praise God for his glory.

The Nature of the Expected Glory
The process of sanctification had as its goal the state of consummate glory for believers. As the many verses soon to be listed will show, the first believers had the hope of an eschatological glory that they would enter into at the Parousia of Jesus Christ. The expectation of the first Christians expressed in the NT, is that at the Parousia of Christ, God's glorifying grace and associated glorifying salvation would bring them into the consummate experience of the glory of God. From all that has been mentioned above, I believe that the scriptures make it clear that this state of ultimate glory at the Parousia would involve for Christians the following:

In Consummate Glory **There Is** *No Trace of Fallenness*
From the negative point of view, the consummate glory expected by the believers meant the absence of all traces of fallenness. The trouble with mankind is that ever since the first man's "fall" away from God and into sin, mankind has "fallen short of the glory of God," (Rom 3:23,) as discussed previously. The ultimate aim in God's gospel plan in Christ Jesus is to recover his elect into the fullness of the glory that He designed them for. While there is any trace or symptoms of fallenness in his people they have not yet been glorified to the extent that God desires.

For example, the context of Rom 8:17-39 teaches that the hoped-for state of glory — that state of being glorified together with Christ — would at the Parousia deliver all believers who had existed up to the time of the Parousia from all that spoke of their fallenness. They were expecting to be delivered from futility and from the bondage of corruption, (which corruption, or corruptibility, as Paul demonstrates in 1 Cor. 15, especially applies to believers still in earthy, material bodies which are an image of Adam's fallen earthy body). They were expecting deliverance from a state of groaning and longing induced by the sense of imperfection and lack of conformation to the image of Christ and the warfare of sin and the flesh (which Paul has discussed in previous chapter 7 of his letter to the Romans).

They were expecting to leave behind the firstfruits stage of Christian experience, and to enter into the fullness of glory, with no admixture of fallenness, of sin, of mortality — where nothing in them fell short of the glory of God. Such a salvation (Rom 13:11) — viz., a salvation from the whole sad legacy of Adam's fall — was what they expected.

Take another example. The whole context of the apostle Peter's first epistle teaches that the final grace and final salvation that the Christians were hoping for at the Parousia of Jesus Christ would bring them into their eternal heavenly inheritance, which would consist of them participating fully in the glory of Christ, and of receiving the crown of glory. (See 1 Pet 1:3-13; 4:14-14; 5:1,4). This describes a state of experiential consummation, perfection, with no admixture of sin, or enmity of "the flesh." For Peter says that the inheritance that the first Christians were being kept for by God's power was to be "an inheritance *incorruptible* and *undefiled* and that does not fade away, reserved in heaven for you," (1 Pet 1:4). To me this means that in the expected consummate glory-state to be given to the first believers at the Parousia, there would be *no trace left of corruption or anything that is defiled* in the Christian. Spirit, soul and (resurrected/changed) body would have *no* "falling short" of God's glory about them.

Consummate Glory Means Everything is Glorious

From the positive point of view, this expected consummate glory would mean full, complete, experiential recovery into that glory and excellence of God that man was originally designed for by the God of Glory, (as discussed earlier in this chapter).

From the Romans epistle, chapter 8, this means the children/sons of God would be glorified together with Christ (v. 17). To receive the longed-for "adoption as sons" (i.e., in its consummate revelation), (v. 23), would mean that they would be revealed in the fullness of glory suited to persons of such rank and privilege, to enjoy a glorious liberty where the resurrected/changed body is in a fully redeemed state, and where the sons are fully conformed to the image of the glorified Son who sits at God's right hand, (v. 29).

The apostle Peter reminds his readers that the state of consummate glory which they, the early Christians, were expecting at the Parousia, was a heavenly inheritance where all would be incorruption, with no defilement and of unfading beauty (1 Pet 1:4). This was to be an inheritance, not existing just in name or legal entitlement, but an inheritance that they would actually possess and experience, where the saints would be crowned with an unfading crown of glory (1 Pet 5:4). There is nothing higher than this heavenly inheritance for them to inherit — it would mean nothing less than real heavenly perfection and blessedness.

The writer to the Hebrews teaches that "bringing many sons to glory" (Heb 2:10) meant bringing them into the sphere of glory that their Forerunner, Jesus, had previously entered (Heb 2:9; 6:19-20), that is, into that glorious sphere of the very presence of God the Father in the heavenly Holy of Holies. *There is nothing higher than this glory for the saints, just as it was the highest privilege and glory for Jesus himself.* And it would be at the Parousia that all saints who had existed up to that point of time would all together enter into the full reality of this glory in the Holy of Holies. It was for this blessed end that Jesus was to appear the second time with his salvation, (Heb 9:28). This was when they would actually and fully possess "the eternal inheritance" (Heb 9:15) and their "great reward" (Heb 10:35-36), receiving their "enduring possessions in heaven" (Heb 10:34). All of this would be at the coming of Christ, (Heb 10:37).

When Christ would be revealed in his glory, the saints would be revealed in glory with him (Col. 3:4). Everything for the saints would be new and heavenly and eternal and glorious at the Parousia of Jesus. They were to receive this great reward as the end of all their perseverance and suffering for the name of Christ, when the Coming One arrived.

The New Testament presents the case that, at the Parousia all saints up to that point in history would be glorified into the consummate, ultimate sphere of God's glory in heaven, where they would:

- perfectly appreciate and esteem the glory of God,
- fully experience the glory of God,
- fully exhibit the glory of God,

and where everything not conducive to glory, everything that even hints at fallenness of spirit, soul or body, will never more have any place in the glorified saints. Forevermore they would dwell with Christ in the presence of the God of glory with exceeding joy. This was the hope of glory that the NT saints held so dear.

Addendum – *Glory* and Post-Parousia Christians

One will have noticed, I hope, that I have been careful to point out in this article that the expectation of the first Christians (i.e. pre-Parousia Christians) was that *the Parousia would be the occasion* of their full, consummate, entry and possession of the eternal inheritance of the eternal glory of God. This means that the saints living on earth at the time of the Parousia had the unique privilege of bypassing death and being taken and glorified together with all deceased believers in heaven. (Such is the hope expressed throughout the whole New Testament writings, and will be demonstrated further in coming chapters).

In regard to all *post*-Parousia saints — those people who have become Christians after the AD 70 Parousia of Christ — the wonderful promise of the same glory (that the first Christians experienced fully at the Parousia of Christ) applies equally for post-Parousia Christians, however the timing of its fulfillment is of course different. The difference is that the hope of glory in the case of post-Parousia believers, finds its ultimate fulfillment at their physical death, as I will explain later.

The hermeneutic of *audience relevance* is a vital tool in correctly interpreting the Bible. For example, it was a consistent use of the hermeneutic of audience relevance in examining the time statements which led many Bible students to comprehend that the Lord's Parousia was indeed promised, expected and fulfilled in that first century, before the first generation had passed.

This same hermeneutic of audience relevance helps one to realize that the only saints who were ever promised glorification in all its fullness before they died, were that unique number of Christians who were alive at the coming of Christ circa AD 70. But they would not receive a glorification that left them in this life on earth in mortal bodies. For this unique company the Parousia was the occasion of concluding their allotted lifespan on earth, bypassing the normal process of physical death. The Parousia was the occasion of their glorification in heaven along with their deceased brethren.

The promised consummation events, of the resurrection and glorification of all the deceased pre-Parousia saints and the transformation and glorification, bypassing death, of all the living pre-Parousia, all took place at the Parousia of Christ as they were promised and as they expected.

Because the new covenant consummate state of glory is now fully instated in heaven since the Parousia, it can be said "Blessed are the dead who die in the Lord from now on" (Rev. 14:13). It was in the light of the Parousia of Jesus that this pronouncement was made. Before the time of the Parousia, all believers who died had to wait until the Parousia before the way into the holiest was manifest experientially and before they could enter glory with Christ. However since the Parousia those who die are blessed in that they don't have to wait for glorification like the pre-AD 70 believers and all old testament saints had to, but are immediately resurrected and glorified to be with Christ for ever. I will discuss the case of the post-Parousia saints in more detail at the close of Chapter 10, *The New Jerusalem – Consummation for the Saints*.

A remained-on-earth "glory"?

There exists a view among some preterists that teaches, (if I understand it correctly) that when a post-Parousia sinner comes to faith in the Lord Jesus Christ, that person receives the same consummation or perfection while living on earth, that the pre-Parousia saints received at the Parousia.

But I believe that to say that everything that was fulfilled to *pre-Parousia* Christians *at the Parousia* is fulfilled now to *post-Parousia* Christians *when they come to faith in Christ while they are living on earth*, is not sound exegesis, defeating all meaning of language, as I will demonstrate in greater detail in further chapters. From my discussion in this chapter, I trust that the reader will see *that a state of consummate glory (according to the true meaning of "glory" and "glorified with Christ" as used in the NT) cannot coexist with a life that is still mortal, and still with imperfections due to sin and immaturity.*

Some preterists say that the glorification promises were fulfilled at the Parousia in the living pre-Parousia Christians while they remained on earth, still living on earth in their mortal bodies. It is said that they underwent a covenantal change or covenantal resurrection at the Parousia. In view of the obvious fact that said Christians could by no means be said to be *experientially* perfected or glorified in either soul or body, this covenantal change and resurrection that they are said to have undergone, can only be viewed as a mere figurative thing with no real experiential change to show for it.

But surely the deceased pre-Parousia Christians were not looking for a non-experiential, figurative "change" at the Parousia, and neither were the living pre-Parousia Christians! They were not expecting and looking forward to something that had no *real, experiential* salvation in it.

This "remained-on-earth" view, it seems to me, takes away all meaning of language for it credits Paul, in his expectation of an exceeding weight of glory, and deliverance from all corruption and affliction, and salvation into the glory of God with Christ at the Parousia, as meaning no more by these great words than a figurative change that would offer no more real or higher experiential, spiritual advancement than the level of spirituality that is found in a modern-day preterist who claims to have now in this life the perfection, fullness of salvation and resurrection body that the pre-Parousia Christians expected to receive at the Parousia. May I politely suggest that I don't feel such remained-on-earth views really assist the preterist cause.

On the grounds of the hermeneutic of audience relevance and upon the grounds of true exegesis of various passages concerning the saints' expectation of glory at the Parousia, I believe that the pre-Parousia Christians were NOT at all expecting to inherit the fullness of their salvation while in their mortal bodies living on earth; that is, they were not expecting to remain on earth, in their imperfect, mortal condition after the Parousia of Christ when Christ brought his final salvation.

Chapter 5

Going to the Father and into His *Glory*

This chapter aims to examine the scriptural presentation of the expectation of the first Christians at the Parousia from the perspective of their hope of going home to the Father and into His glory. This hope of the first Christians is based, as we shall see, upon the prior example and experience of the Lord Jesus himself as their forerunner when He ascended as High Priest into the true Holy of Holies in heaven.

Regarding both Jesus and his disciples the scriptures speak firstly of a spiritual fellowship with God while they were on earth, and secondly of their expectation of rising to a higher and more glorious level of fellowship in heaven, termed "going to the Father." In Jesus' case, his going to the Father occurred at his ascension, while in the case of the disciples, their going to the Father occurred at the coming of Jesus for them about AD 70.

I believe the scriptures below clearly show the first Christians expected to go to the Father and into His glory at the Parousia, just as their Savior and Forerunner had previously gone to the Father and into His glory at his ascension.

1. Jesus' Fellowship with the Father

Let us consider two distinct aspects of Jesus' fellowship with the Father that are referred to in the Gospel records (especially that of John), and in the epistles (especially Hebrews):

(i) His fellowship and union with the Father while he lived on earth, and
(ii) His fellowship and union with the Father back in His glory in heaven after his earthly pilgrimage.

It is in regard to the second aspect that Jesus refers to his "going to the Father." Let us consider these two aspects in turn. (Of course there is the fellowship between Son and Father prior to the Son's incarnation, but that is not under examination in this article).

(i) Fellowship with the Father while Jesus was on earth

Jesus spoke of a vital union existing between the Father and himself during His life and ministry on earth, referring to the relationship as: the Father being with him, the Father being in him, his being with the Father, his being in the Father, living because of the Father, hearing the Father, seeing the Father, knowing the Father, doing the will of the Father, doing nothing but by the Father's working in him, etc.

Clearly Jesus was conscious of living in the Father's presence, having an intimate fellowship with Him, during his time on earth. Some relevant scripture passages will help us to gain a small insight into the inscrutable intimacy of that fellowship which was the key to Jesus' life and ministry:

- Matt. 11:27 "All things have been delivered to Me by My Father, and *no one knows the Son except the Father. Nor does anyone know the Father except the Son*, and the one to whom the Son wills to reveal Him."
- Jn. 4:31-34 In the meantime His disciples urged Him, saying, "Rabbi, eat." 32 But He said to them, "I have food to eat of which you do not know." 33 Therefore the disciples said to one another, "Has anyone brought Him anything to eat?" 34 Jesus said to them, "*My food is to do the will of Him who sent Me*, and to finish His work."
- Jn. 5:19-23 Then Jesus answered and said to them, "Most assuredly, I say to you, *the Son can do nothing of Himself, but what He sees the Father do*; for *whatever He does, the Son also does in like manner*. 20 "For *the Father loves the Son, and shows Him all things that He Himself does; and He will show Him greater works than these*, that you may marvel. 21 "For as the Father raises the dead and gives life to them, even so the Son gives life to whom He will. 22 "For the Father judges no one, but has committed all judgment to the Son, 23 "that all should honor the Son just as they honor the Father. He who does not honor the Son does not honor the Father who sent Him.
- Jn. 5:30 "*I can of Myself do nothing. As I hear, I judge*; and My judgment is righteous, because *I do not seek My own will but the will of the Father who sent Me.*
- Jn. 6:57 "As the living Father sent Me, and *I live because of the Father...*
- Jn. 8:16 "And yet if I do judge, My judgment is true; for *I am not alone, but I am with the Father who sent Me.* (literally: but I and the Father who sent me)
- Jn. 8:28-29 Then Jesus said to them, "When you lift up the Son of Man, then you will know that I am He, and that *I do nothing of Myself; but as My Father taught Me*, I speak these things. *And He who sent Me is* **with** [Gr. μετά, *meta,* "with"] *Me. The Father has not left Me alone*, for I always do those things that please Him."
- Jn. 8:38 "*I speak what I have seen with My Father*, and you do what you have seen with your father."
- Jn. 10:30 "*I and My Father are one.*"
- Jn. 10:38 "but if I do, though you do not believe Me, believe the works, that you may know and believe that *the Father is in Me, and I in Him.*"

Jn. 14:7-11 "If you had known Me, you would have known My Father also; and from now on you know Him and have seen Him."... 10 "Do you not believe that *I am in the Father, and the Father in Me*? The words that I speak to you I do not speak on My own authority; but *the Father who dwells in Me does the works.* 11 "Believe Me *that I am in the Father and the Father in Me*, or else believe Me for the sake of the works themselves.

Jn. 14:20 "At that day you will know that *I am in My Father*, and you in Me, and I in you.

Jn. 16:32 "Indeed the hour is coming, yes, has now come, that you will be scattered, each to his own, and will leave Me alone. And *yet I am not alone, because the Father is with* [Gr. μετά, *meta*, "with"] *Me*.

(ii) Jesus' going to the Father in heaven, and into His glory

Jesus spoke often (especially towards the end of his ministry on earth) of His future union or reunion with the Father that would come to pass after his death and resurrection. He mostly calls it a "going to the Father," and it would involve his being glorified. He spoke of a returning to heaven to share in the glory of the Father which he did not have during his earthly walk — a level of fellowship with the Father that he once knew before he came to earth, and one that he greatly desired to experience again.

The following scriptures speak of Jesus' going to the Father and into the Father's glory; where Jesus was himself glorified at the Father's right hand.

Jn. 13:1 Now before the feast of the Passover, when Jesus knew that His hour had come that *He should depart from this world to the Father*, having loved His own who were in the world, He loved them to the end.

Jn. 13:3 Jesus, knowing that the Father had given all things into His hands, and that *He had come from God and was going to God*,

Jn. 13:31-32 So, when he had gone out, Jesus said, "Now the Son of Man is glorified, and God is glorified in Him. If God is glorified in Him, *God will also glorify Him in Himself*, and glorify Him immediately."

Jn. 14:2 "In *My Father's house* are many mansions; if it were not so, I would have told you. *I go to prepare a place for you.*

Jn. 14:12 "Most assuredly, I say to you, he who believes in Me, the works that I do he will do also; and greater works than these he will do, *because I go to My Father.*

Jn. 14:28 "You have heard Me say to you, '*I am going away* and coming back to you.' If you loved Me, you would rejoice because I said, '*I am going to the Father,*' *for My Father is greater than I.*

Jn. 16:10 "of righteousness, because *I go to My Father* and you see Me no more [i.e. no more for "a little while," – see v. 16, for at Pentecost, Jesus would come to his followers by the Holy Spirit and indwell them, Jn 14:15-31];

Jn. 16:16 "A little while, and you will not see Me; and again a little while, and you will see Me, *because I go to the Father.*" 17 Then some of His disciples said among themselves, "What is this that He says to us, 'A little while, and you will not see Me; and again a little while, and you will see Me'; and, *'because I go to the Father'*?"

Jn. 16:28 "*I came forth from the Father* and have come into the world. Again*, I leave the world and go to the Father.*"

Jn. 17:4, 5 "I have glorified You on the earth. I have finished the work which You have given Me to do. 5 "And *now, O Father, glorify Me together with Yourself, with the glory which I had with You before the world was.*

Jn. 17:11 "Now I am no longer in the world [*the present tense implies his regarding his soon departure as if it were an already settled and present reality - IH*], but these are in the world, and *I come to You. Holy Father*, keep through Your name those whom You have given Me, that they may be one as We are.

Jn. 20:17 Jesus said to her, "Do not cling to Me, for I have not yet ascended to My Father; but go to My brethren and say to them, '*I am ascending to My Father* and your Father, and *to My God and your God.*'"

Lk. 24:26 "Ought not the Christ to have suffered these things and to *enter into His glory*?"

Lk. 24:50-51 And He led them out as far as Bethany, and He lifted up His hands and blessed them. 51 Now it came to pass, while He blessed them, that He was parted from them and *carried up into heaven.*

Acts 1:9,11,22 Now when He had spoken these things, while they watched, *He was taken up, and a cloud received Him out of their sight....* 11 [two men]...said, "Men of Galilee, why do you stand gazing up into heaven? This same *Jesus, who was taken up from you into heaven*, will so come in like manner as you saw Him go into heaven."... 22 "beginning from the baptism of John to that day when *He was taken up from us*, one of these must become a witness with us of His resurrection."

Acts 2:32-36 "This Jesus God has raised up, of which we are all witnesses. 33 Therefore *being exalted to the right hand of God*, and having received from the Father the promise of the Holy Spirit, He poured out this which you now see and hear. 34 For David did not ascend into the heavens, but he says himself: 'The LORD said to my Lord, "Sit at My right hand,

35 Till I make Your enemies Your footstool." ' [i.e., *Jesus did ascend into the heavens, cf. v. 34a - IH*] 36 Therefore let all the house of Israel know assuredly that God has made this Jesus, whom you crucified, both Lord and Christ."

Acts 3:12-13 So when Peter saw *it*, he responded to the people: "Men of Israel, why do you marvel at this? Or why look so intently at us, as though by our own power or godliness we had made this man walk? 13 "The God of Abraham, Isaac, and Jacob, *the God of our fathers, glorified His Servant Jesus* whom you delivered up and denied in the presence of Pilate, when he was determined to let *Him* go.

Col. 3:1 If then you were raised with Christ, seek those things which are *above, where Christ is, sitting at the right hand of God*.

1 Tim. 3:16 And without controversy great is the mystery of godliness: God was manifested in the flesh, Justified in the Spirit, Seen by angels, Preached among the Gentiles, Believed on in the world, *Received (or taken) up in glory*. (= "I am ascending, going up to my Father" Jn 20:17; and = "Jesus was taken up into heaven" Acts 1:11)

Heb 1:3, 13 when *He* had by Himself purged our sins, *sat down at the right hand of the Majesty on high*, . . 13 But to which of the angels has He ever said: "*Sit at My right hand*, Till I make Your enemies Your footstool"?

Heb 2:9 But we see Jesus, who was made a little lower than the angels, for the suffering of death *crowned with glory and honor*, that He, by the grace of God, might taste death for everyone.

Heb 6:19-20 This hope we have as an anchor of the soul, both sure and steadfast, and which enters into *the (place) within the veil, 20 where the forerunner has entered for us, even Jesus*, having become High Priest forever according to the order of Melchizedek.

Heb 8:1 Now this is the main point of the things we are saying: We have such *a High Priest, who is seated at the right hand of the throne of the Majesty in the heavens, 2 a Minister of the sanctuary and of the true tabernacle which the Lord erected, and not man.*

Heb 9:11-12 But Christ came as High Priest of the good things to come, with *the greater and more perfect tabernacle not made with hands*, that is, not of this creation. 12 Not with the blood of goats and calves, but with His own blood *He entered the Most Holy Place* once for all, having obtained eternal redemption.

Heb 9:24 For *Christ has not entered the holy places made with hands, which are copies of the true, but into heaven itself, now to appear in the presence of God for us*;

1 Pet. 1:20-21; 3:21 –22. 20 He [Christ] indeed was foreordained before the foundation of the world, but was manifest in these last times for you 21 who through Him believe *in God, who raised Him from the dead and gave Him glory*, so that your faith and hope are in God.... 3:21 There is also an antitype which now saves us—baptism (not the removal of the filth of the flesh, but the answer of a good conscience toward God), through the resurrection of *Jesus Christ, 22 who has gone into heaven and is at the right hand of God*, angels and authorities and powers having been made subject to Him.

Comments on Jesus' Relationship with the Father

Summarizing the two aspects described in the above list of scripture passages:

(1) During his earthly walk and ministry Jesus spoke of his being with the Father, in the Father's presence, and of the Father dwelling with him at all times and of having an intimate fellowship with His Father, yet -
(2) As shown in John's gospel, Jesus spoke of a going to the Father at the end of his earthly walk. He also spoke of this as a being glorified with the Father. The writer to the Hebrews refers to this as Jesus being crowned with glory, of his entering the Father's presence, of his entering the heavenly Holy of Holies. It was in this heavenly realm that his pre-incarnate glory was restored to him, and he was able to rule in his new covenant ministry to his saints. Other NT writers above also refer to Jesus being taken and carried up to heaven, and taken up in glory, and given glory.

We know that Jesus, in his resurrected, human body left earth and "went to the Father" in heaven, and in his glorified body sat down at the right hand of the Father. It was as the High Priest of his people that he presented his sacrificial atoning blood before the Father in the heavenly Holy of Holies (Heb 9:11-12).

Along with this redemptive reason for Jesus' return to the Father, there is also for Jesus a relational factor. His "going to the Father" was a return to a holy fellowship with the Father in a sphere of glory, to at a level and ministry that was not possible while He was on earth in his earthly body.

We see in Jesus' case a divine mystery: while he was with the Father in intimate fellowship already on earth, yet he desired to leave the world and "go to the Father" in heaven. While he rejoiced in the Father during his life on earth, he yet desired to be glorified, and crowned with glory, in order to experience a higher level of being with Him, and of serving Him in heaven at His throne.

The Father is spirit: Jesus was sinless and perfect in spirit; the Father and Jesus were one in life, purpose, nature and love, during Jesus earthly life. One might be excused for thinking that whether Jesus was on earth or in heaven, it would not make any difference to their spiritual fellowship, that it could not be improved upon. Yet, the facts are clear, there still remained a "going to the Father" and a being glorified, which to Jesus was a hope he rejoiced in, for the Father was greater than he (Jn 14:28), and he desired to share again in His glory. Of course Jesus also rejoiced that from that exalted position he would perform his new covenant ministry of giving eternal life to men (Jn 17:1-5). Jesus' return to the Father is described in the letter to the Hebrews as an entering the heavenly Holy of Holies, i.e. entering into the immediate presence of the glorious God.

All of this reveals that during his earthly walk Jesus was not in that Holy of Holies' degree of blessedness, or that glory-level of fellowship with the Father; it was only after his death, resurrection and ascension that he (in his perfect, spiritual, glorified human body) "went to the Father" - into that higher, more glorious, and heavenly, level of His presence.

2. The Disciples' Fellowship with the Father and Jesus.

Jesus' disciples, like Jesus, have two spheres of fellowship with the Father and with Jesus.

(i) A spiritual fellowship while the disciples are still on earth in their fallen bodies (which correlates with their deposit/firstfruits experience of the new covenant, as discussed in previous chapters); and,

(ii) A future, higher fellowship in glory in heaven when they, like Jesus, go to the Father and to Jesus at His right hand, (which correlates with the expected fullness, or consummation experience of the new covenant).

Consider firstly the following two passages referring to the disciples going to the Father:

Jn. 14:6 Jesus said to him, "I am the way, the truth, and the life. No one *comes* (*or* goes) *to the Father* except through Me.

1 Pet. 3 18 For Christ also suffered once for sins, the just for the unjust, that He might *bring us to God*.

The coming to the Father, also termed the being brought to God, referred to in these two verses can have two aspects:

1. These two passages of scripture are often used in referring to the spiritual reconciliation which occurs when a sinner puts their faith in Christ Jesus as Lord and Savior, when they are justified and have peace with God, and from that time know a

spiritual fellowship with God. They have then come to the Father through Jesus, and Christ has brought them to the Father – in this spiritual sense – while they are still on earth in their fallen bodies.

2. However, from the contexts surrounding both passages, and from Jesus own words about his going to the Father, and from references in other NT epistles depicting a future glory in heaven for the saints, I believe that the two verses above, Jn 14:6 and 1 Pet. 3:18, ought to be *also* considered in a consummative aspect, even as Jesus spoke of his "going to the Father" as a consummative event for him. That is, I believe both Jn 14:16 and 1 Pet 3:18 refer God's ultimate aim of the disciples coming to the Father in heaven like Jesus did, and of their being brought to God in his glory, even as Jesus ascended to God.

The following random selection of scriptures enlarge on this firstfruits/deposit measure of fellowship and then the expectation of a consummate level of fellowship, that the followers Jesus would experience with the Father and the Lord Jesus.

(i) Fellowship with God and Jesus while disciples were still on earth

Jn. 4:21, 23 Jesus said to her, "Woman, believe Me, the hour is coming when you will neither on this mountain, nor in Jerusalem, worship the Father.... 23 "But the hour is coming, and now is, when the *true worshipers will worship the Father in spirit and truth*; for the Father is seeking such to worship Him. *[And so the first Christians worshipped and communed with the Father after Pentecost - IH]*

Jn. 6:57 *"As the living Father sent Me, and I live because of the Father, so he who feeds on Me will live because of Me.*

Jn. 14:20 "At that day [Pentecost when the promised Holy Spirit comes - IH] you will know that I am in My Father, and *you in Me, and I in you.*

Jn. 14:23 Jesus answered and said to him, "If anyone loves Me, he will keep My word; and My Father will love him, and *We will come to him and make Our home with him.*

1 Cor. 1:9 God is faithful, by whom *you were called into the fellowship of His Son, Jesus Christ our Lord.*

Eph 3:17 And He came and preached peace to you who were afar off and to those who were near. 18 *For through Him we both have access by one Spirit to the Father.*

Eph 4:4-6 There is one body and one Spirit, just as you were called in one hope of your calling; 5 one Lord, one faith, one baptism; 6 one *God and Father of all, who is above all, and through all, and in you all.*

Phil 2:13 for it is *God who works in you* both to will and to do for His good pleasure.

Heb 7:19 for the law made nothing perfect; on the other hand, there is the bringing in of a better hope, through which *we are drawing near to God*.

Heb 7:24-25 But He, because He continues forever, has an unchangeable priesthood. 25 Therefore He is also able to save to the uttermost *those who come to God through Him*, since He always lives to make intercession for them.

Heb 13:5-6 Let your conduct be without covetousness; be content with such things as you have. For *He Himself has said, "I will never leave you nor forsake you." 6 So we may boldly say: "The LORD is my helper; I will not fear*. What can man do to me?"

1 Jn. 1:1-3 That which was from the beginning, which we have heard, which we have seen with our eyes, which we have looked upon, and our hands have handled, concerning the Word of life—— 2 the life was manifested, and we have seen, and bear witness, and declare to you that eternal life which was with the Father and was manifested to us—— 3 that which we have seen and heard we declare to you, that you also may have fellowship with us; and *truly our fellowship is with the Father and with His Son Jesus Christ*.

(ii) The future expectation of going to the Father and to Jesus in heaven, into their glory

Jn. 12:26 "If anyone serves Me, let him follow Me; and *where I am, there My servant will be also*. If anyone serves Me, him My Father will honor.

Jn. 14:2-3 "*In my Father's house* are many dwellings; if it were not so I would have told you. I go to prepare a place for you. 3 And *if I go and prepare a place for you, I will come again and receive you to myself: that where I am, there you may be also*."

Comments on John 14:1-6

When Jesus said, "I go to prepare a place for you," (Jn 14:2), I understand Jesus to mean that where he was about to go was where he would prepare a place for his disciples. Jesus was about to go to the Father. He alludes to this in verse 2, that he was going to the Father's house. But note that after Jesus had said to his disciples, "And *where I go you know*, and the way you know," (v. 4) and after Thomas' objection that they did not know where he was going nor did they know the way (v. 5), Jesus gives the clear answer in verse 6; "to the Father" was where he was going, and he, Jesus, was *their* way to the Father. Then Jesus says in the following discussion clearly that he was going to the Father (14:12, 28; 16:16, 28) and the disciples thought they understood this (vv. 29-30), but Jesus knew their faith and understanding were small at this stage (vv. 31-33).

Frequently, all through John's gospel, Jesus said he was soon to "go to the Father." *Jesus did go to the Father at his ascension; and that was where he said he would prepare a place for them.*

What is the natural meaning of Jesus' words in Jn. 14:3? How did the twelve understand it? They at least knew Jesus was going away somewhere to prepare a place for them. Their very question (v. 5) reveals that much: they wanted him to make it clear to them *where* he was going and the way to get there. As their spiritual understanding grew they would have understood about Jesus' destination being the Father, and that Jesus was their way to the Father (14:6).

From what I've shown in the above two paragraphs, consider now verse 3: "And if I go and prepare a place for you, I will come again and receive you to myself: that where I am, there you may be also." To me the following is obvious:

- When Jesus would come for his disciples, it would be to take them to the place prepared for them. Jesus had gone to the Father and the place prepared for them was with the Father; and Jesus was their way to the Father and to their prepared place.
- The very context then shows that Jesus' words, "where I am there will you be also" means, "where I am with the Father – which is where I have prepared a place for you – there you will be also." [Jesus spoke in the present tense – "that where I am" – because prophetically he saw himself there with the Father already, although historically he wasn't there yet when he spoke these words].

Just a few more words on Jn. 14:1-6. Jesus spoke these words to his chosen twelve. As explained above, the context and language demonstrates that Jesus' plan was to return and take his disciples to the place he had prepared for them in the spiritual realm, that they might be with him where he was with the Father. Now, I believe that historical records teach that many of the original apostles died or were martyred before AD 70. Jesus would have known that some of them would be deceased by the time of his Parousia (just as he prophesied that others of their number would not see death before he came in his glory and kingdom). Yet he gave this promise of Jn. 14:2-3 to them all. So whether they would be deceased or would still be living at the time of his Parousia, the disciples trusted that Jesus would fulfill his promise to them all: to take them to where he was (with the Father) and where he had prepared a place for them. To me, this can only mean that Jesus promised that all of them – deceased and living – would be taken, at the Parousia of Jesus, to be with the Father (with Jesus being their Way to the Father), just as Jesus had ascended years before. The Parousia would mean glorification of deceased and living disciples in the Father's presence.

> Jn. 17:24 "Father, I desire *that they also whom You gave Me may be with Me where I am [i.e. in heaven glorified with the Father; the present tense "I am" emphasizing the reality and certainty of his soon-coming ascension and glorification], that they may behold My glory* which You have given Me; for You loved Me before the foundation of the world.

Jesus' glory was his being enthroned at the Father's right hand in heaven. Jesus wanted his disciples to behold that wonderful reality, not just by faith, but really, experientially, by their being taken to the Father.

> Jn. 20:17 Jesus said to her, "Do not cling to Me, for I have not yet ascended to My Father; but go to My brethren and say to them, '*I am ascending to My Father and your Father, and to My God and your God.*'"

There appears to me to be the clear implication in Jesus' words that the Father and God who was welcoming Jesus home to His presence would be Father and God in the same sense to his brethren – that He would also welcome them into His presence just as He welcomed Jesus into His presence.

> Rom. 8:17 and if children, then heirs – heirs of God and *joint heirs with Christ*, if indeed we suffer with *Him, that we may also be glorified together with him.*

Epistle to the Hebrews
> But *we see Jesus*, who was made a little lower than the angels, for the suffering of death *crowned with glory and honor*, that He, by the grace of God, might taste death for everyone. 10 For it was fitting for Him, for whom *are* all things and by whom *are* all things, in *bringing many sons to glory,* to make the captain of their salvation perfect through sufferings. [Heb 2:9-10]

The context teaches that where man failed in his destiny to reign in God's name, (Heb 2:5-8), Jesus, as the representative man, has been victorious. In order to raise fallen man back to his true destiny as God's image, Jesus lived his victorious life and suffered for their sins, and was crowned with glory and honor after his atoning work was finished. It is in the victorious and glorified Christ that redeemed man is brought back to his designed place with God. Now what is the glory that God is bringing his many sons into (Heb 2:10)? Answer: the glory that Jesus the representative man, entered into and was crowned with (Heb 2:9; Jn. 17:1-5)! The first Christians were expecting that at the Parousia of Christ they would be glorified together with Christ, to be brought into the glory that Jesus their forerunner had been already brought into. They would be then be crowned with glory like Jesus (1 Pet. 5:4; Heb 2:9).

Heb. 4:14 Seeing then that we have a great High Priest who has passed through the heavens, Jesus the Son of God, let us hold fast *our* confession.

Hold fast: for we too will soon pass through the heavens to be with him; the high priest represents his people, and his going to the Father as high priest and forerunner is guarantee/surety of his peoples' soon going there too.

Heb. 6:19 *This hope* we have as an anchor of the soul, both sure and steadfast, and which *enters the Presence behind the veil, where the forerunner has entered for us, even Jesus,* having become High Priest forever according to the order of Melchizedek.

Heb 7:24-25 But He, because He continues forever, has an unchangeable priesthood. 25 Therefore He is also able to save to the uttermost *those who come to God through Him*, since He always lives to make intercession for them.

"Those who come to God through him." They come to God through him who had already come to God himself and who was in God's presence on their behalf interceding for them. He is able to save *to the uttermost* (Gr. εἰς τὸ παντελὲς, *eis to panteles*, "to the completed state," or "to perfection"). And what is a completed or consummated or perfected salvation? – to be glorified together with Christ in the Father's presence forever.

Heb 10:19-23 Therefore, brethren, *having boldness for the entrance into the Holiest by the blood of Jesus*, 20 by a new and living way which He consecrated for us, through the veil, that is, His flesh, 21 and having a High Priest over the house of God, 22 *let us draw near with a true heart in full assurance of faith*, having our hearts sprinkled from an evil conscience and our bodies washed with pure water. 23 *Let us hold fast the confession of our hope* without wavering, for He who promised is faithful.

Their hope had to do with entering the holiest where their high priest and forerunner, Jesus, had previously entered and was now dwelling at the right hand of the Father. At the time of this epistle the disciples could only draw near, approach, by faith and spiritual fellowship, this anticipated occasion which would occur at the second coming of Jesus. They had not yet entered the Holy of Holies (6:19) in the consummate sense, as Jesus had entered it; they were to have faith in the promise of it, and to keep their hope of it alive.

Heb 12:1-2 ...let us run with endurance the race that is set before us, 2 looking unto Jesus, the author and finisher of our faith, who for the joy that was set before Him endured the cross, despising the shame, and has sat down at the right hand of the throne of God.

The writer is saying: "We look away from everything else and look to Jesus; he is our Perfecter; knowing that the finishing point of our race is the same as it was for him – namely, the holy presence of the Father. We are running the race trusting in Jesus the high priest and forerunner who is already there, and who will bring us to be there with him; Jesus will perfect/complete our state and condition by bringing us to the Father, just as he was completed his own race and arrived at the Father and was glorified."

> 1 Pet. 5:1, 4 The elders who are among you I exhort, I who am a fellow elder and a witness of the sufferings of Christ, and also a partaker of the glory that will be revealed:... 4 and when the Chief Shepherd appears, *you will receive the crown of glory that does not fade away.*

Jesus was *crowned with glory* (Heb 2:9) on his ascension to the Father; so also the disciples would be crowned with glory; which can only mean sharing the glory of Jesus in the Father's presence. See comment on Heb 2:10 just above.

> Rev. 3:21-22 "To him who *overcomes I will grant to sit with Me on My throne, as I also overcame and sat down with My Father on His throne.* 22 "He who has an ear, let him hear what the Spirit says to the churches.""

Jesus' was glorified to sit on his throne at the right side of the Father; it was a very experiential reality. The promised blessing/privilege to the living and deceased saints' of sitting with Jesus on his throne cannot mean anything less experientially real than it was for Jesus – really being with Jesus in the Father's presence, where Jesus sat after his ascension and exaltation.

Comments on the Disciples' Fellowship with the Father and with Jesus
So the first Christians prior to the Parousia had a vibrant spiritual fellowship with the Father through the Lord Jesus in the power of the Holy Spirit. But they understood from the relevant eschatological passages above that the Parousia of Jesus would bring them into a perfection of fellowship and union with God, that they would be glorified together with Christ (just as Christ was glorified with the Father), and would go to the Father like Christ, and sit on thrones like Christ, in the heavenly Holy of Holies like Christ. And such was the great hope of all Christians whether living or deceased at the Parousia.

3. Summary of the teaching in the above Scriptures

From a consideration of all the above scripture verses, it is clear to me that the first Christians to whom the epistles were written had *an expectation that, at Christ's Parousia, they would be glorified and go to the Father — just as really and consciously as Jesus had done.*

Consider the two groups of saints immediately affected by the Parousia: the deceased saints, and the saints alive at the time of the Parousia. The same promises presented in the selection of scriptures above applied to *all* these saints. Many of the first Christians who had these scriptures would have died through persecutions, ill-health or old age before the time of the Parousia at about AD 70. These pre-Parousia deceased Christians would have "died in faith, not having received the promises, but having seen them [i.e. their fulfillment]...[as near]...were assured of them, embraced them" as the OT saints had done, (Heb 11:13). All Christians then, deceased and living, expected the fulfillment of the promises at the Parousia of Jesus, of their going to the Father and into his glory, through the Way of the Lord Jesus, their Perfecter. The letter to the Hebrews shows that all the past OT saints were also to be taken into the same glory.

Jesus was not with the Father in the ultimate reality of the heavenly Holy of Holies during his earthly walk, although his union with the Father while on earth was wonderful and perfect; Jesus had the hope of leaving this earth and being glorified and entering the Father's holy presence in the heavenly Holy of Holies. *For Jesus, being glorified meant going to the Father, entering the heavenly presence of the Father and sitting at his right hand.* Now Jesus is represented as the forerunner of his saints who entered the heavenly presence of the Father in advance of his saints following him. The letter to the Hebrews makes this especially clear.

For the pre-Parousia Christians (living and deceased), their expectation was to be glorified at the Parousia and to go into the Father's presence in heaven, in the same sense as Jesus had gone there, to enter into the Holy of Holies, the sphere of glory, and there they would be with Jesus their forerunner and perfecter, and sit with him on his throne. There, being with Jesus where he was, in the Father's presence, they would behold his glory — according to Jesus' prayer for them in Jn. 17. For the first Christians, living and deceased, being glorified at the Parousia meant being exalted to be with Jesus where he was, in the presence of the Father.

Nowhere do they express an understanding that the glorification and going to the Father (in the eschatological sense) involved a remaining on earth after the Lord's Parousia in their fallen, sin-harassed bodies and minds, with an imperfect, spiritual fellowship with God, as some preterists teach.

Since they understood that, in Jesus' case, glorification and going to the Father meant literally going to heaven into the heavenly presence of God the Father - something he could not experience while remaining in his earthly body on earth, surely it is only natural and logical that the first Christians understood that the scriptures which spoke of their own glorification and their own going to the Father referred to their entering the same wonderful reality that Jesus experienced. Also only in this way could the fact that Jesus was called their "forerunner" into the heavenly Holy of Holies (Heb 6:19) have valid meaning.

Conclusion

The first Christians (i.e. those prior to AD 70) expected the second coming of Jesus to occur within the lifetime of that generation (as Jesus had promised, Matt 24:34), and it was at that coming of Jesus that their expectation of going to the Father was to be fulfilled. Such is the theme running through the epistle to the Hebrews in particular, as well as the teaching in the other epistles quoted above in this article. They were not expecting to remain on earth after the Lord's coming but to go to the Father and into his glory and there be with the Lord Jesus forever.

Personally, I find it a great and exciting truth that at the Parousia of our Lord, both the deceased saints and the living saints were all taken up in glory, were glorified, went to the Father, just like their Lord before them did at his ascension, just as they were promised. I have the happy hope that when my allotted time on earth is completed I will be taken into the same glorious realm to be with my Savior and Lord in the presence of the Father, just like them.

Addendum – A further note on Jn. 14:1-6

As mentioned in a previous chapter, there is a preterist view concerning the lot of the Christians still alive at the time of the Lord's Parousia circa AD 70, that says that the disciples who were alive at Jesus' Parousia remained on earth after the Parousia in their same human bodies. But I submit that this view not only alters the plain meaning of Jn. 14:1-6 (where Jesus promised that he would come again and would take them to the Father where he was going to prepare a place for them), but also provides no feasible way of explaining how Jesus' promise applied to the deceased disciples.

Remember that a number of Jesus' disciples, to whom this promise was made, died before AD 70. If Jesus' promise didn't mean taking his living saints to heaven to be with the Father at his Parousia, like he himself had previously gone to heaven to be with the Father, then, logically, correspondingly, his promise didn't mean taking his deceased disciples to heaven to the Father either.

Or to put it another way. Jesus' promise was given to all his disciples, knowing that some would be deceased by the time of his Parousia. If, as some preterists say, the living Christians remained on earth following Christ's Parousia and retained their same earthy bodies, in a spiritual condition which involved a less-than-perfect holiness and less-than-perfect spiritual fellowship with God (like the condition we modern preterists are in), then that must be the same not-yet-consummated spiritual sphere that he brought his deceased saints into also at his Parousia! For did not

Jesus promise that he was going to prepare a spiritual place/spiritual condition for them *all*, and that he would come again and take them all there? And did he not say to them all, "where I am there shall you [all] be also"? But the accepted understanding by preterists is that at the Parousia all the deceased Christians were resurrected and glorified in heaven. The "remained-on-earth" view that I refer to just does not seem to have any support. Further chapters will even more clarify this.

My understanding of Rev. 7:9-17 is that it gives a preview of the happy end of the deceased, persecuted saints at the Parousia, appearing in heaven in glory before the throne of God, with Jesus their shepherd leading them in blessed ways, no longer subject to the evils of their previous fallen, earthy state. If this is the realm into which Jesus had brought his deceased saints, then in accordance with Jesus' promise to all his apostles in Jn. 14:1-6, this is the same place where the living saints would be brought to at his Parousia; for his promise was that he would bring all of them to the place he prepared for them with the Father, and he was their Way to that place. The Revelation was written to encourage persecuted saints, particularly those who would go through the Neronic persecutions. The saints (living and deceased) would understand that their hopes lay with Jesus at his Parousia taking them to heavenly realms to be with Jesus their Lord and with the angels in the presence of God.

Chapter 6

Crowned and Presented Before the Presence of God at the Parousia of the Lord

In this chapter we look at a threefold expectation the saints knew would be fulfilled at the Parousia of the Lord Jesus: namely:

1. To be crowned with righteousness, life and glory, and
2. To be presented blameless before the presence of the Lord, and then,
3. To have the blessed privilege of seeing the Lord's face.

We are on holy ground here, speaking of heavenly, spiritual things that we in this physical realm can only dimly imagine. For a greater insight into what the first Christians entered at the Parousia, and which post-Parousia Christians enter at death, let us examine some scriptures.

1. Crowned

"Do you not know that those who run in a race all run, but one *receives the prize*? Run in such a way that you may *obtain* [the prize]. And everyone who competes for the prize is temperate in all things. Now they do it to obtain a perishable crown, but we for *an imperishable crown*. Therefore I run thus: not with uncertainty. Thus I fight: not as one who beats the air." [1 Cor. 9:2ff]

" 'Behold, I am coming quickly! Hold fast what you have, that no one may take *your crown*.' " [Rev. 3:11]

The first Christians had the hope of receiving an imperishable crown, which they expected to be awarded to them at the Parousia of Christ — a crown of victory at the end of their Christian race and their fight of faith for the name of Christ. In a very real sense it would be a crown declaring the victory that the Lord had achieved in their lives, for what good can a Christian boast of but what the Lord has accomplished in him.

Now for the sake of the discussion below, we may figuratively think of the imperishable crown as composed of three separate crowns corresponding to three aspects of the Christians' hope in Christ as their soon-coming Savior and Lord. Here are the three aspects: righteousness, eternal life, and glory.

Hope of righteousness	Crown of righteousness
(Gal 5:5)	(2 Tim 4:8)
Hope of eternal life	Crown of life
(Tit 1:2; 3:7)	(Jas 1:12; Rev 2:10)
Hope of glory	Crown of glory
(Col 1:27; Rom 5:2)	(1 Pet 5:4)

To be crowned with a quality is an idiom used in the New Testament to figuratively describe the bestowment upon a person of the full blessing of that quality as a reward. To be crowned also signifies the fulfilling of the hope that the person had for obtaining the perfect experience of the quality.

In Chapter 2, we showed that the NT says the first Christians already had in their lives the new covenant qualities of righteousness, eternal life and glory – but only in a deposit/firstfruits measure. Those believers longed for the experience of the full measure of those blessings; and it is this hoped-for fullness that they are talking about when they refer to the hope of righteousness, the hope of eternal life and the hope of glory. And these three hopes would be respectively fulfilled when the saints received the corresponding crown of righteousness, crown of life and crown of glory, at the Parousia of Christ.

I wish to briefly look at the meaning or significance of these three crowns and identify the recipients of these crowns.

(i) The Crown of Righteousness

1 I charge *you* therefore before God and the Lord Jesus Christ, who is about to judge the living and the dead at His appearing and His kingdom:... 6 For I am already being poured out as a drink offering, and the time of my departure is at hand. 7 I have fought the good fight, I have finished the race, I have kept the faith. 8 Finally [or, as for what remains], there is laid up for me *the crown of righteousness*, which the Lord, the righteous Judge, will give to me on that Day, and not to me only but also to all who have loved His appearing. [2 Tim 4:1, 6- 8]

The Meaning of the Crown of Righteousness

Through faith in Christ as their Lord and Savior, Paul knew he and all other believers already had been justified through Christ, with all sins forgiven. They had been given the right to become children of God. Christ Jesus had become their *righteousness* (1 Cor. 1:30). Through their faith in Christ they had put off "the old man" and had put on "the new man which was created according to God, *in true righteousness* and holiness," (Eph 4:24). This "new man" or "new creation life" in them was being renewed and built up to make the Christians grow like "the image of Him who created [the new man]," (Col. 3:10). A genuine *life of righteousness*, by the working of the Spirit (e.g., Rom 6:18-19; 8:4), was taking place within them; they were bearing the *"fruits of righteousness."*

But while in their present mortal state, their condition could never reach the point of being fully conformed to the image of Christ, the Righteous One. There was the insidious presence of sin in their members, the enmity of the flesh and the natural limitations due to the legacy of their fallenness. Therefore the saints had a "hope of righteousness" (Gal 5:5). They eagerly looked forward to the Day of total deliverance from every aspect of unrighteousness and the consummate manifestation within them of the righteousness that was theirs in Christ – which was metaphorically called the Day of their being crowned with the crown of righteousness.

This crowning, when the full significance and manifestation of what the gift of righteousness meant for the saints, awaited the appearing of Christ. At his appearing he, the righteous Judge, would award the crown of righteousness to his saints. Then the full wonder of the meaning of righteousness in Christ would be experienced by the saints, when they would be fully conformed to the righteousness and holiness befitting the image of their righteous Creator, the image of the One who created the new man, (Col. 3:10; Eph 4:24; Rom 8:29-30).

The Recipients of the Crown of Righteousness

Note that in this letter to Timothy, Paul felt that his death was very imminent, that he was about to "depart" his earthly life [Gr. ὁ καιρὸς τῆς ἀναλύσεώς μου ἐφέστηκεν, "the time of my departure has come upon me"], having finished his race and fight. He felt he might die/be martyred before the occurrence of Parousia of Christ, (2 Tim 4:6). Nevertheless, as for what remains for him, he knew that at the Parousia the Lord would award him the crown of righteousness (v.7). For the encouragement of Timothy, and other believers, Paul reminds Timothy that this blessed crown is not just for him (Paul) or for apostles, but *it is for all Christians* who have come to love the Lord's appearing, whose appearing they expected *before that generation passed away* (as Jesus promised in Matt 24).

Paul clearly expected that he would receive the crown of righteousness at the Parousia, even if he died before that date. Paul clearly implies in these verses that this crown of righteousness which he, if he was a deceased Christian, expected to be awarded at the Parousia, is the same crown that those Christians who remained alive until the Parousia could also expect to receive. He says that Christ is "about to judge" [Gr. μέλλοντος κρίνειν, mellontos krinein] the *living and dead* at his appearing and kingdom. The sense of imminence is clearly indicated by the Greek word "mellontos" which means "about to" be, or "about to" occur. At Christ's appearing and kingdom the righteous Judge would reward his living and deceased saints with the crown of righteousness.

> Dr John Gill's comments on these verses are helpful. [While John Gill's timing of the Parousia is not preterist, yet his description of what the saints expected at the Parousia is still notable].
>
> 2 Tim. 4:8. *Henceforth there is laid up for me a crown of righteousness,...* The happiness of the future state of the saints is signified by a crown, on account of the glory and excellency of it; and in perfect agreement with the character of the saints, as kings; and who are raised to sit among princes, and to inherit the throne of glory, and have a kingdom prepared for them; and this is called a crown "of righteousness," because it comes through the righteousness of Christ; it is that which gives a right unto it, and without which it cannot be enjoyed; and because it is obtained and pos-

sessed in a righteous way, and not by force and usurpation, as crowns sometimes are: it is God the Father's free gift unto his children, what they are born heirs unto, and have a meetness for, through regenerating and sanctifying grace, and have a legal title to it through the righteousness of Christ. *Moreover, this [crown] may be expressive of the perfect holiness and righteousness of the heavenly state, and of the saints in it, wherein will dwell none but righteous persons, and who will be entirely without sin [Emphasis mine. This matches the meaning of the hope of righteousness in Gal 5:5* -IH)]. And this happiness, signified by a crown, is "laid up"; in the covenant of grace for the saints, which is ordered in all things and sure; and in Christ, in whose hands their persons are, and their grace is, and with him also is their life of glory hid and secured.

and not to me only, but unto all them also that love his appearing; that is, his appearing at his second coming; which is to be loved, and so looked for by the saints, not only because it will be glorious in itself, in its attendants and consequences, but will be of great advantage to the saints; Christ will appear unto salvation to them, and so to their joy; they will appear with him in glory, and be like him, and enjoy the everlasting vision of him. The devils believe this appearance of Christ, but tremble at it; wicked men will behold him, and fear; saints know, believe, and love both Christ and his appearing; and such will wear that crown: the Ethiopic version renders it, "who love him at his coming"; all that love him now, will love him then. (John Gill, *Exposition on the Bible* on *Online Bible* CD).

(ii) The Crown of Life
   Rev. 2:10; 22:12 – "Do not fear any of those things which you are about to suffer. Indeed, the devil is about to throw *some* of you into prison, that you may be tested, and you will have tribulation ten days. Be faithful until death, and I will give you *the crown of life*. 22:12 "And behold, I am coming quickly, and My reward *is* with Me, to give to every one according to his work. (NKJV)
   Jas. 1:12; 5:7-9 – 12 Blessed *is* the man who endures temptation; for when he has been approved, he will receive *the crown of life* which the Lord has promised to those who love Him. 5:7 Therefore be patient, brethren, until the coming of the Lord.... 8 You also be patient. Establish your hearts, for the coming of the Lord is at hand.... 9 ...Behold, the Judge is standing at the door! (NKJV)

The Meaning of the Crown of Life
   To be crowned with eternal life, as the fulfillment of the Christians' hope, symbolizes the receipt of the blessing of eternal life in its consummate form in two aspects: firstly, of eternal, glorious, sinless fellowship with, and knowledge of, God (cf. Jn 17:3); and secondly, of the believer's full transformation in spirit, soul and body, filled with the life

and nature of God, with no trace of all that is associated with death and sin and corruption (the opposites of life).

The same idea to being crowned with life is expressed in Rev. 2:7 "To him who overcomes *I will give to eat from the tree of life*, which is in the midst of the Paradise of God." To eat from the tree of life in the heavenly paradise of God means that at the Lord's Parousia the saints would receive that fullness of eternal life which the Lord promised. The tree of life reminds of the paradisiacal Edenic fellowship of man with his God. Now death and sin are associated with the fall of man in the original Garden of Eden, the earthly paradise of God, where mankind lost their right and ability to enjoy the physical tree of life, which signified mankind's loss of intimate life and fellowship with their Creator. So the promise that believers would partake of the tree of life at the Lord's coming was metaphorically teaching the restoration of the full life of blessed fellowship with God, with all fallenness gone. This is eternal life.

The Recipients of the Crown of Life

Note that James and John (in the Revelation) refer to the blessing of the crown of life, at the soon-expected Parousia of Christ, as the reward for the Christians who endured and loved the Lord. In Rev. 2:10, the Lord warns the church that it is clear that a number of saints may lose their lives in their fight of faith; (see later in 20:4). Antipas in the church at Pergamos (Rev. 3:13) had already been martyred at the time John wrote. But these first Christians were to be encouraged by the thought that even if they died before the time of the Parousia, they were nevertheless promised that they all would receive the crown of life at the Parousia of the Lord. And that great Day was not far away. Both James and John refer to the fact that the saints expected, as a near event, the Lord's coming as Judge to reward his saints and give them the crown of life.

From the above verses we gather that both living and deceased Christians up to the time of the Parousia (about AD 70) – including those "overcomers" (i.e. the faithful Christians referred to in each of the letters to the seven churches in Revelation chapters 2-3) who endured and remained alive until the Lord's Parousia and those overcomers who lost their lives before the Parousia–all would receive their reward of the crown of eternal life at the Lord's Parousia.

(iii) The Crown of Glory

1 The elders who are among you I exhort, I who am a fellow elder and a witness of the sufferings of Christ, and *also a partaker of the glory that is about to be revealed*: 2 Shepherd the flock of God which is among you, serving as overseers, not by compulsion but willingly, not for dishonest gain but eagerly; 3 nor as being lords over those entrusted to you, but being examples to the flock; 4 and *when the Chief Shepherd appears, you will receive the unfading crown of glory*.... 10 ...the God of all grace...called *us to His eternal glory* by Christ Jesus... [1 Pet 5:1-4, 10]

The Meaning of the Crown of Glory

From other parts of his epistle we gather that Peter was well acquainted with OT prophets. He knew that OT prophets had prophesied of the grace of God which was to come to those who believed in the Christ (1:10), and of "the sufferings of Christ and the glories that would follow;" i.e. the glories for Christ (at his ascension) and the glories for the Christians (expected by the first Christians at the Lord's Parousia).

Peter's terminology in 1 Pet 5:4, strongly suggests that he was adopting ideas from Isa. 28:1-5, in which the Lord condemned the crown of pride of Ephraim and promised to give a crown of glory to Judah:

> "Woe to the crown of pride, to the drunkards of Ephraim, whose glorious beauty *is a fading* flower...In that day the LORD of hosts will be for *a crown of glory* and a diadem of beauty to the remnant of His people." Isa. 28:1,5.

The Lord's gracious promise of *a crown of glory* to his people of Judah was in vivid contrast to the punishment God would issue to the northern tribes, for he would cause their *crown of pride* to become like a *fading flower* that would be trampled underfoot (Is 28:1-4). Man's boasting and confidence in his highest achievements amount to a crown of pride that will end up like a fading, withering flower.

It seems that Peter is using Isaiah's imagery when he refers to the Christians' highest privilege of receiving *the unfading crown of glory*, at the Parousia of Christ (1 Pet. 5:4). The Greek word translated "unfading" is ἀμαράντινος *(amarantinos)* and is derived from "amaranth," a flower that never faded and which came to be used metaphorically of the quality of everlastingness. The crown of glory, which the Lord will grant to his people will be an everlasting, unfading crown, speaking of an unfading glory, unlike all the best, earthly glories that are as fading flowers.

Peter counsels his readers to rest their hope fully on the grace that would be brought to them at the revelation of Jesus Christ (1 Pet. 1:13). This grace would impart a consummative salvation that was ready to be revealed in the last time (1 Pet. 1:5). This salvation would involve the saints' receiving *"the unfading crown of the glory"* of the Lord (1 Pet. 5:4), that is, the *eternal glory* (1 Pet. 5:10) to which they were called by the grace of God in the gospel. The glory of God would be upon them; they would live in the realm of His eternal, unfading glory; no greater privilege or experience could exist. In chapter 4, we looked at something of the nature of this consummate state of glory. To be crowned with glory, means to receive the blessedness of glory in its fullness. The mind of mortal man cannot possibly imagine what such terms really mean – only when delivered from this mortal realm into the realm of heaven will a man know it.

In 1 Pet. 1:4 Peter refers to the hope of the eternal, heavenly inheritance, reserved for the saints in heaven. He says that this inheritance is incorruptible and undefiled and *unfading* (Gr. ἀμάραντος, *amarantos*, similar to its use in 5:4), for it is not of man, nor of this fallen world, but is of heavenly quality. So when Peter says the saints expected to receive the "unfading" crown of glory (1 Pet. 5:4) he is referring to the saints entering into, possessing and experiencing the unfading, eternal, incorruptible inheritance, the ultimate glorified state of the saints — where all that spoke of corruptibility, dishonor, weakness, and the natural state and image of the earthly man of dust, (as per 1 Cor. 15, where corruptibility is the characteristic of fallen, mortal man), would be replaced by all that was glorious, eternal, spiritual, incorruptible and *unfading*.

While in the earthly state in their mortal bodies, in the case of the living saints, or in their disembodied spirit-state, in the case of the deceased saints, all the saints still had in them or upon them to some degree the legacy of the sin and the fallenness that characterize fallen, separated mankind; their condition of life and body still displayed a falling short of the glory of God (Rom 3:23), even though they had already been justified by, and reconciled to, God. Therefore the saints, both living and deceased rejoiced in the hope of the glory of God (Rom 5:1-2), which would be fulfilled at the appearing of their Chief Shepherd.

The Recipients of the Crown of Glory

This hope of the unfading crown of glory sustained the early Christians amidst all persecutions and "fiery trials" that Peter said in his epistles that they would suffer. As the history books tell us, many Christians were killed under Nero's persecutions. But death for the sake of Christ was bearable when one knew he would soon be crowned with eternal glory at the Parousia. And O, we marvel as we learn from history how the grace of God sustained his people with this hope of glory as they faced martyrdom in those days. The flame of hope in their hearts gave a stronger blaze than the fires of the Romans which burnt them alive as human torches, and they could sing hymns of praise while facing being torn to bits by lions. However, Peter knew he would die before the Parousia of Christ:

> *[Jesus speaking to Peter after His resurrection:]* "Most assuredly, I say to you, when you were younger, you girded yourself and walked where you wished; but when you are old, you will stretch out your hands, and another will gird you and carry *you* where you do not wish." This He spoke, signifying by what death he [Peter] would glorify God. Jn. 21:18-19.

> Yes, *[says Peter,]* I think it is right, as long as I am in this tent, to stir you up by reminding *you*, knowing that shortly I *must* put off my tent, just as our Lord Jesus Christ showed me. 2 Pet 1:13-14.

Even though he knew he would die before the Parousia Peter still expected to partake of the glory that was about to be revealed at the Parousia. And he expected the living saints to whom he was writing to partake of the same glory at the Parousia. Peter says: "the God of all grace called *US* to his eternal glory by Christ Jesus." Peter here refers to "us" as called to glory - the "us" meaning himself and his Christian readers. He knew some of his readers as well as himself would die under the persecutions about to come, while others would remain alive until the Parousia. He therefore teaches that whether deceased or living at the time of the Parousia, all saints had the same expectation of being glorified and of possessing the eternal inheritance and eternal glory at the revelation and appearing of the Lord Jesus. Read again 1 Pet. 5:1,4,10 with this understanding in mind. We could paraphrase the substance of these verses like this:

> "God called *US* to his eternal glory, which we all will experience at Christ's Parousia. I say *US* - meaning *you* my Christian readers — some of whom will remain alive until the Parousia, but others of whom I know will die under the fiery trials soon to come — and *myself* who will be among the deceased saints by the time of the Parousia. Even though I know I will be deceased by the time of the Parousia, as my Lord Jesus told me, I know I will partake with you all in the glory which is about to be revealed at the appearing of the Chief Shepherd, and we all, deceased and living, will receive the crown of glory that will never fade away, and fully possess and experience the eternal, incorruptible, undefiled, unfading inheritance in our Lord's presence."

Comment regarding the Crowning at the Parousia

The above scripture portions reveal the fact that it was the universal hope of the early church that at the soon-expected Parousia/revelation/appearing of Christ, all believers in Christ who had existed up to that point in time — both deceased and living — would receive their promised reward from the Judge, the Lord Jesus. Deceased and living saints were taught by the apostles to expect to receive the crown of righteousness, the crown of life and the crown of glory. All scriptural evidence shows that the early church's understanding was that the living believers' experience of these blessed realities at the Parousia would be just as real, experiential, and consummative as it would be for the deceased believers. These scriptures above, focusing on the crowns of righteousness, life and glory, confirm the view that the saints living at the time of the Parousia were raised into the same state of glory as the deceased saints were; that both groups were totally saved from all traces of sin and corruption into a spiritual, incorruptible, and glorious state, forever being at home with the Lord.

A note regarding post-Parousia (post-AD 70) Christians.

The same crowns discussed above, signifying the ultimate, consummative, eternal state in the Lord's presence remain the hope of all believers who have arisen since the AD 70 Parousia of Christ, a hope that would be fulfilled upon physical death.

The crowns that all the pre-Parousia saints experienced *at the Parousia*, are experienced by all post-Parousia saints when they physically die, (not at their conversion, as is taught by some preterists). The promise to the saints who remained alive until the Parousia, viz., that they would be crowned and consummated *at the Parousia*, was a promise unique to *them*, the messianic generation. To them it was promised that they would bypass physical death and be crowned and glorified along with, and together with, the deceased saints *at the Parousia*.

Clearly, all those believers who have arisen since the Parousia in about AD 70, *did not, do not,* receive their crowns of righteousness, life and glory, at the time of their conversion to Christ, for they remained/ remain in their mortal, earthly bodies after their conversion. But their hope is that on their "departure" from this life they then enter into their glorious, heavenly inheritance that was brought into place at the Parousia of Christ. It is true for all believers since AD 70 – "Blessed are the dead who die in the Lord from this time on." (Rev. 14:13)

2. Presented Before the Presence of God

As well as the expectation of being crowned with righteousness, life and glory, the New Testament scriptures show that there was also in the early church of the first Christians an expectation of the saints being presented to God and to the Lord Jesus, so as to stand in Their presence and glory — a presentation that would occur at the coming of the Lord Jesus, whose coming was viewed by them as a soon-to-happen event.

As the scripture passages below will demonstrate, this presentation of the saints before God in the presence of his glory, was expected to be a very real, experiential event – a heavenly event. It involved both deceased and living saints together at the time of the Lord's coming.

This study of the expectation of a presentation of the saints before God, confirms the scriptural evidence already given, that the early Christian hope was that at Christ's Parousia the saints living at the time of the Lord's coming would be changed and glorified *along with* the risen deceased saints, resulting in all saints up to that point in history — deceased and living — being glorified together with the glorified Christ, and commencing to reign with Christ (as promised) in heaven in the presence of the Father.

Some Terminology

Knowing the following terminology will be helpful. (Taken from: *Online Bible* Greek Lexicon; *Bagster's Analytical Greek Lexicon*)

A presentation, a being caused to stand

Some Greek words used to describe a standing and a presentation of the saints at the Lord's coming are:

- *histeemi* (ἵστημι) (as transitive) = to cause to stand, to set up, to place, to confirm, to establish; or, (as intransitive) = to stand, to be confirmed
- *paristeemi* (παρίστημι) (as transitive) = to place near, to present, to dedicate; (as intransitive) = to stand by

In the presence of God, before God

Greek words used to describe "before" God and "in the presence" of God are:

- *katenopion* (κατενώπιον) = before the face of, in the presence of, in the sight of
- *enopion* (ἐνώπιον) = before, in the presence of
- *emprosthen* (ἔμπροσθεν) = before, in the presence of, in the face of, in the sight of

These words are used frequently in *non-eschatological* contexts; but it is their use in *eschatological* contexts that is examined here.

Passages describing an eschatological *presentation* and *standing* of the saints *before God* and *in the presence* of God, at the Parousia:

> Matt 25:31-32, 34 *When the Son of Man comes in His glory*, and all the holy angels with Him, then He will sit on the throne of His glory. 32 *All the nations will be gathered before* (*emprosthen*) *Him*, and He will separate them one from another, as a shepherd divides his sheep from the goats.... 34 "Then the King will say to those on His right hand, 'Come, you blessed of My Father, *inherit the kingdom* [i.e., *in its consummate phase* - IH] prepared for you from the foundation of the world
>
> Lk. 21:31-36 "So you also, *when you see these things happening, know that the kingdom of God is near*. 32 "Assuredly, I say to you, this generation will by no means pass away till all things take place. 33 "Heaven and earth will pass away, but My words will by no means pass away. 34 "But take heed to yourselves, lest your hearts be weighed down with carousing, drunkenness, and cares of this life, and that Day come on you unexpectedly. 35 "For it will come as a snare on all those who dwell on the face of the whole earth. 36 "Watch therefore, and pray always that you may be counted worthy to escape all these things that will come to pass, and *to stand* (*histeemi*) *before* (*emprosthen*) *the Son of Man*."
>
> Rom 14:10-12 But why do you judge your brother? Or why do you show contempt for your brother? For *we shall all stand before* (*paristeemi*) *the judgment seat of Christ*. 11 For it is written: "As I live, says the LORD, Every knee shall bow to Me, And every tongue shall confess to God." 12 So then each of us shall give account of himself to God.
>
> 2 Cor. 4:11-14 For we who live are always delivered to death for Jesus' sake, that the life of Jesus...may be manifested in our mortal flesh. 12 So then death is working in us, but life in you. 13 And since we have the same spirit of faith, according to what is written, "I believed and therefore I spoke," we also believe and therefore speak, 14 knowing that *He who raised up the Lord Jesus will also raise us up with Jesus, and will present (paristeemi) us with you*.

2 Cor. 5:6-10 6 So *we are* always confident, knowing that while we are at home in the body we are absent from home away from the Lord. 7 For we walk by faith, not by sight. 8 We are confident, yes, well pleased rather to be absent from home out of the body and to be at home with the Lord. 9 Therefore we make it our aim, whether being at home [*in the body - still alive at the time of the Parousia - IH*] or absent from home [*out of the body - deceased by the time of the Parousia - IH*], to be well pleasing to Him. For *we must all* [*i.e., both living and deceased*] *appear* (lit. be manifested) *before (emprosthen) the judgment seat of Christ*, that each one may receive the things done in the body, according to what he has done, whether good or bad.

Paul said in 2 Tim 4:1 that the Lord Jesus Christ "is about to judge the living and the dead at his appearing and kingdom." The early church expected their appearing before the judgment seat of Christ to occur soon.

2 Cor. 11:2-3 For I am jealous for you with godly jealousy. For I have betrothed you to one husband, *that I may present (paristeemi) you as a chaste virgin to Christ*. 3 But I fear, lest somehow, as the serpent deceived Eve by his craftiness, so your minds may be corrupted from the simplicity that is in Christ.

Eph 5:25-27 Husbands, love your wives, just as Christ also loved the church and gave Himself for her, 26 that He might sanctify and cleanse her with the washing of water by the word, 27 *that He might present (paristeemi) her to Himself a glorious church*, not having spot or wrinkle or any such thing, but that she should be holy and without blemish (Gr. ἄμωμος, *amomos*).

Col. 1:21-23 And you, who once were alienated and enemies in your mind by wicked works, yet now He has reconciled 22 in the body of His flesh through death, *to present (paristeemi) you holy, and blameless (amomos), and above reproach in His sight (katenopion)* – 23 if indeed you continue in the faith, grounded and steadfast, and are not moved away from the hope of the gospel which you heard, which was preached to every creature under heaven, of which I, Paul, became a minister.

Col. 1:24-28 I now rejoice in my sufferings for you, and fill up in my flesh what is lacking in the afflictions of Christ, for the sake of His body, which is the church, 25 of which I became a minister according to the stewardship from God which was given to me for you, to fulfill the word of God, 26 the mystery which has been hidden from ages and from generations, but now has been revealed to His saints. 27 To them God willed to make known what are the riches of the glory of this mystery among the Gentiles: which is Christ in you, the hope of glory. 28 Him we preach, warning every man and teaching every man in all wisdom, *that we may present (paristeemi) every man perfect in Christ Jesus*.

> 1 Thess 2:19-20 For what is our hope, or joy, or crown of rejoicing? Is it not even *you in the presence of (emprosthen) our Lord Jesus Christ at His coming?* 20 For you are our glory and joy.
> 1 Thess 3:12-13 And may the Lord make you increase and abound in love to one another and to all, just as we do to you, 13 so *that He may establish your hearts blameless in holiness before (emprosthen) our God and Father at the coming of our Lord Jesus Christ with all His saints.*
> Jude 20-21, 24-25 But you, beloved, building yourselves up on your most holy faith, praying in the Holy Spirit, 21 keep yourselves in the love of God, looking for the mercy of our Lord Jesus Christ unto eternal life.... 24 Now to Him who is able to keep you from stumbling, and *to present* (or cause to stand, to place, *histeemi*) *you faultless (amomos) before the presence (katenopion) of His glory* with exceeding joy, 25 To God our Savior, Who alone is wise, Be glory and majesty, Dominion and power, Both now and forever. Amen.

Just a few thoughts on Jude 20-21, 24-25 –

> Jude 24 expresses the same hope of being *presented faultless in God's presence* as Eph 5:27 and Col. 1:22.
> Eph 5:27 *that He might present (paristeemi) her to Himself a glorious church*, not having spot or wrinkle or any such thing, but that she should be holy and *without blemish (amomos)*.
> Col. 1:22 *to present (paristeemi) you holy, and blameless (amomos), and above reproach in His sight (katenopion)*.

Note the theme of "keeping" in Jude vv. 20-21. The saints were to be *keeping* themselves in faith and prayer and in the love of God while "looking for" (Gr. προσδέχομαι, *prosdekomai*) the mercy of our Lord Jesus Christ resulting in eternal life," (v. 21). Verse 24 continues the same theme of keeping, but from God's side: the saints were *being kept* by God so as to be presented to God in the presence of his glory. The correspondence of the theme of keeping/being kept in vv. 20-21 and 24 implies that the goal for which the saints were keeping themselves corresponds with the goal for which the Lord was keeping them.

The goal of the saints in keeping themselves was to experience the "mercy" or "merciful and kind blessing" [Gr. τὸ ἔλεος, *to eleos*] of the Lord and eternal life (v. 21). For this the saints were keeping themselves and looking expectantly. This corresponds with the Father's goal in keeping them, viz., of presenting them faultless before His glory with exceeding joy. For this God was keeping them (v. 24).

The correspondence implies that in that time of being presented before the presence of the glory of God (v. 24) the saints would enter and experience the consummate fullness of eternal life (v. 21).

Interestingly, in 1 Peter chapter 1, there is the same theme as in

Jude 20-21, 24-25 of God's keeping the saints by his power while the saints fully set their hope on the grace being brought to them at the revelation of Jesus Christ, (1 Pet. 1:5,13).

The saints in Paul's letter to Titus were "looking for" the same wonderful event as the saints in Jude's letter: Tit. 2:13, "looking for (*prosdekomai*) the blessed hope and glorious appearing of our great God and Savior Jesus Christ." In Jude 21 they were "looking for (*prosdekomai*) the mercy of our Lord Jesus Christ into eternal life," (v. 21).

The Vision of the Saints in the Revelation

This expectation of the saints, of being presented, or being caused to stand, before the presence of God, at the Parousia, is foreseen in vision by John in the Revelation; wherein the Christians are seen as raised at his Parousia of Christ to stand before the very presence of God, to appear before his throne. (Regarding the following verses from the Revelation, also refer to my Further Note below).

> Rev. 3:5 "He who overcomes shall be clothed in white garments, and I will not blot out his name from the Book of Life; but I will confess his name *before* (Gr. ἐνώπιον, *enopion*) My Father and before (*enopion*) His angels.
> [As the saints appear before God, as mentioned in scriptures above, the Lord Jesus confesses their names before God, as ones belonging to him and for whom he is mediator.]
> Rev. 7:9 After these things I looked, and behold, a great multitude which no one could number, of all nations, tribes, peoples, and tongues, *standing* (*histeemi*) *before* (*enopion*) *the throne and before* (*enopion*) *the Lamb*, clothed with white robes, with palm branches in their hands, 10 and crying out with a loud voice, saying, "Salvation belongs to our God who sits on the throne, and to the Lamb!" 11 All the angels stood around the throne and the elders and the four living creatures, and fell on their faces *before* (*enopion*) the throne and worshiped God, 12 saying: "Amen! Blessing and glory and wisdom, Thanksgiving and honor and power and might, Be to our God forever and ever. Amen." 13 Then one of the elders answered, saying to me, "Who are these arrayed in white robes, and where did they come from?" 14 And I said to him, "Sir, you know." So he said to me, "These are the ones who come out of the great tribulation, and washed their robes and made them white in the blood of the Lamb. 15 "Therefore they are *before* (*enopion*) *the throne of God*, and serve Him day and night in His temple. And He who sits on the throne will dwell among them.
> [This standing before God in these verses, is something beyond the general meaning that we speak of, of us all on earth being in his presence. Rather the context shows that it is a real, experiential, consummative happening in heaven, where the fallenness of the saints' earthly lives is not present.]

Rev. 14:1-5 Then I looked, and behold, a Lamb standing on Mount Zion, and with Him one hundred and forty-four thousand, having His Father's name written on their foreheads. 2 And I heard a voice from heaven, like the voice of many waters, and like the voice of loud thunder. And I heard the sound of harpists playing their harps. 3 They sang as it were a new song *before* (*enopion*) the throne, before the four living creatures, and the elders; and no one could learn that song except the hundred [and] forty-four thousand who were *redeemed* from (Gr. ἀπὸ, *apo*) the earth. 4 These are the ones who were not defiled with women, for they are virgins. These are the ones who follow the Lamb wherever He goes. These were redeemed from among (Gr. *apo*) men, being firstfruits to God and to the Lamb. 5 And in their mouth was found no deceit, for they are without fault (*amomos*) *before* (*enopion*) *the throne of God*.

Compare Rev. 14:5 with Jude 24
- "Now to Him who is able to...present you *faultless* (*amomos*) *before the presence (katenopion) of His glory* with exceeding joy...."
- "they are *without fault* (*amomos*) *before* (*enopion*) *the throne of God*.

Rev. 14:5 pictures the hope in Eph 5:27 and Col. 1:22 of the saints being presented faultless/blameless (*amomos*) before God].

Rev. 20:12 And I saw the dead, small and great, *standing* (*histeemi*) *before* (*enopion*) God, and books were opened. And another book was opened, which is [the Book] of Life. And the dead were judged according to their works, by the things which were written in the books.

Noteworthy Themes from the above scriptures

From the group of Scriptures given above we can note some consistent themes associated with the expected presentation and standing of the saints before God, in the presence of God, at the coming (Parousia) of the Lord Jesus Christ:

- Both living and deceased believers were to experience this presentation before God and the Lord Jesus.
- It was the time when the saints would come before the Lord Jesus, the Judge, at his Parousia, to receive their rewards.
- The saints would be presented before God without fault or blemish.
- At this time of presentation the saints would experience God's glory.
- It would be the time for experiencing the consummate phase of the kingdom of God.
- It would be the time when eternal life in its consummate measure would be fully bestowed upon the saints.
- There would be the consummation of union (marriage) of saints with Christ.

- It would occur in the immediate presence of God in heaven, before His throne, where the Lord Jesus and the angels dwell.
- This presentation was to be just as real, conscious, and transforming for the living saints at the Parousia as for the deceased brethren at the Parousia. It was to involve just as real an appearing before the throne of God in heaven for the living saints as for the deceased saints. It was to involve just as real a receiving of eternal rewards from Christ for the living saints as for the deceased saints. It was to be the occasion of the same entering into the fullness of eternal life, with complete absence of sin, for both living saints and deceased saints.

To me it is an exciting thought that circa AD 70 when the Lord Jesus Christ appeared the second time for salvation to those who were eagerly awaiting him (Heb 9:28) – to both deceased saints and those saints then living – all those true disciples who existed up to that point in history were presented before the presence of God and his glory and in the presence of the Lord Jesus, with exceeding joy, as a glorious church, perfected in Christ Jesus, in the consummate fullness of eternal life.

Having been presented before the presence of God and the Lord Jesus at the Parousia of Christ, all the saints were to continue to live in the presence of God and the Lord Jesus in the New Jerusalem, which the first Christians and all previous deceased saints were to enter fully at the Parousia of Christ. In the Revelation we have the wonderful vision of the saints living in the presence of God and the Lord Jesus in the New Jerusalem. They will experience ultimate, consummate blessedness because:

- the Lord God Almighty and the Lamb are its temple, (Rev. 21:22)
- the throne of God and of the Lamb are in it, (Rev. 22:3)
- a pure river of water of life, clear as crystal, proceed[s] from the throne of God and of the Lamb, (Rev. 22:1).
- the glory of God illuminates it. The Lamb is its light, (Rev. 21:23).

For all of us Christians who have arisen since the Parousia of Christ, we all, upon our departure from this life, individually enter this same glorious reality of appearing before the presence of the Lord in heaven, of full union with Christ Jesus, of entering the consummate fullness of eternal life, and living in the presence of God in the New Jerusalem–the same glorious reality that the pre-Parousia saints entered as one great company at the Parousia of Christ.

More about the expectation of appearing in the presence of God.

Frequently throughout the Revelation the focus is on the throne of God, and events and personnel are said to be "*before* (*enopion*) the throne," i.e. in the very presence of God. One can be sure that the apostle John's vision of what was soon to come, particularly of the persecuted saints appearing before the throne in the presence of God and the Lord Jesus and the angels at the Parousia of Christ, would have greatly encouraged the early Christians as they faced persecutions, especially those under Nero. For *the place where the persecuted Christians of John's day were soon to appear–namely, before the throne of God and the Lamb–was in fact the control centre of heaven and earth*, the very place where the angels dwelt, and from where sovereign power and justice were being administered to a wicked world. What an awesome thought this is; what an encouraging and sobering thought amidst an environment when their lives were under threat, and the temptation to be afraid was very great.

Consider the following examples of where action centers on the throne, remembering that this was the very sphere that the first Christians were taught they would soon be taken:

> Rev. 1:4 John, to the seven churches which are in Asia: Grace to you and peace from Him who is and who was and who is to come, and from the seven Spirits who are *before* (*enopion*) *His throne*,
> Rev. 4:5 And *from the throne* proceeded lightnings, thunderings, and voices. Seven lamps of fire [were] burning *before* (*enopion) the throne*, which are the seven Spirits of God.
> Rev. 4:6 *Before* (*enopion*) *the throne* [there was] a sea of glass, like crystal. And in *the midst of the throne*, and *around the throne*, [were] four living creatures full of eyes in front and in back.
> Rev. 4:10 the twenty-four elders fall down *before* (*enopion*) *Him who sits on the throne* and worship Him who lives forever and ever, and cast their crowns *before* (*enopion) the throne*, saying:
> Rev. 5:8 Now when He had taken the scroll, the four living creatures and the twenty-four elders fell down *before* (*enopion*) *the Lamb*, each having a harp, and golden bowls full of incense, which are the prayers of the saints.
> Rev. 7:11 All the angels stood around the throne and the elders and the four living creatures, and fell on their faces *before* (*enopion*) *the throne* and worshiped God,
> Rev. 8:2 And I saw the seven angels who stand *before* (*enopion*) *God*, and to them were given seven trumpets.

3. The Face of God and the Presence of God

In Section 2, many of the quoted portions of scripture referred to an expectation of being presented, or having standing, before God, in his presence, in his sight – at the Parousia of Christ. In this section we will briefly note some references to a similar concept, that of the believers being before and seeing the face of God, or the presence of God.

For this brief study we look at another Greek word, *prosopon* (Gr. πρόσωπον), which basically means the face or countenance. This word is used in the phrase, "the face of God," which phrase is often used in the Scriptures to signify the very presence of God, and the source of all Sovereign power and blessing and justice.

Consider the use of *prosopon* in each of the following cases; following which I will draw a few conclusions. In each of the following verses, the word in bold type is the translation of *prosopon*.

> Matt. 18:10 "Take heed that you do not despise one of these little ones, for I say to you that *in heaven their angels always see the **face** of My Father who is in heaven.*
>
> Acts 3:19 "Repent therefore and be converted, that your sins may be blotted out, so that *times of refreshing may come from the **presence** of the Lord,*
>
> 2 Thess. 1:9 These shall be punished with everlasting destruction from *the **presence** of the Lord and from the glory of His power,*
>
> Heb. 9:24 For Christ has not entered the holy places made with hands, [which are] copies of the true, but *into heaven itself, now to appear in the **presence** of God for us*; [or, ...now to appear or be manifested before the *face* of God for us].
>
> Rev. 6:16 and [they] said to the mountains and rocks, "Fall on us and hide us from *the **face** of Him who sits on the throne* and from the wrath of the Lamb!
>
> Rev. 20:11 Then I saw a great white throne and Him who sat on it, from whose ***face*** the earth and the heaven fled away. And there was found no place for them.
>
> Rev. 22:3-4 And there shall be no more curse, but the throne of God and of the Lamb shall be in it, and *His servants shall serve Him. They shall see His **face**, and His name [shall be] on their foreheads.*

Comments

From the above Scripture passages referring to the face (*prosopon*) of God, consider the following conclusions:

1. For his enemies, painful justice can be expected from God's face or presence. For this reason they wish to be hidden from his face.
2. For other personalities, being before the face, or seeing the face of God in heaven describes the sphere of their consummate blessing:
    - *The Angels*: The angels *in heaven see God's face*; i.e. they behold Him and are in his very presence in heaven. As mentioned in Section 2 above, the angels are before (*enopion*) Him, in his presence, before His throne in heaven.
    - *The Lord Jesus Christ*: The Lord Jesus *in heaven appears before the face of God the Father*. In the letter to the Hebrews Jesus is said to be in heaven, in the true, heavenly Holy of Holies, in the presence of God, sitting at his right hand. The Lord Jesus, the Word, is ever facing, is ever towards (Gr. πρὸς, *pros*) God the Father (Jn 1:1), He sees God as the One who is in the bosom of God, (Jn 1:18). As the Creator of the angels, the Lord Jesus sees God's face.
    - *The Saints*: The first Christians were expecting to be brought to a

state, at the Lord's coming, where they too would see God's face; which must mean that they too, like the angels and the Lord Jesus, would experience God's immediate presence *in heaven*. Compare with Jude 1:24 "Now to Him who is able to keep you from stumbling, and to *present you faultless before the presence of His glory with exceeding joy...*" The saints were expecting to "*see his face and [have] His name on their foreheads*," (Rev. 22:3-4) which can mean no less than that they were expecting to come before Him into his immediate glorious presence, where the glorified Lord Jesus and the angels dwell; and there to experience God's ownership and love of them, and His divine nature in them, as His special people, manifested in wonderful, consummate fullness.

Conclusion

To me the study presented in this chapter clearly shows, and further confirms the conclusions drawn from previous chapters, that it was the expectation of the early church that at the coming of Christ all the Christians who had existed up to that point in history (deceased and living) would enter the realm of glory with the Lord in heaven, in the presence of the Father; that at the Parousia, they would not remain on earth in their fallen, mortal bodies and with their earthy, imperfect minds.

For all his people born anew by the Spirit since the Parousia, (including modern Christians), to be glorified in God's presence and to see his face has been their highest desire and happiness too. At their physical death every post-Parousia Christian has joined the glorified pre-Parousia saints in that most blessed situation.

> Rev. 14:13 Then I heard a voice from heaven saying to me, "Write: 'Blessed *are* the dead who die in the Lord from now on.'" "Yes," says the Spirit, "that they may rest from their labors, and their works follow them."

Unlike the saints who died before the Parousia, and who had to wait in a disembodied state until the time of the Parousia of Christ, (at which time they were resurrected and glorified), the post-Parousia saints are upon their death instantly resurrected and glorified, (i.e., they don't have to wait for any future coming of Christ).

And for us twenty-first century Christians living on earth, our expectation is nothing less. It will not be long before each of us reaches our allotted life-span, and we too will join the mighty host of saints and angels who worship before the loving face of Him who sits on the throne — to the praise of the glory of His grace.

PART 3

In Which is Examined a
Number of Relevant New Testament Scriptures
which reveal the *Expectation of Consummation*
held by the First Christians, that was about to be
fulfilled at the Parousia of Jesus Christ, circa AD 70

Chapters 7 to 8

Chapter 7

Relevant Scriptures Regarding The First Christians' *Hope of Consummation* at the Parousia of Jesus Christ, circa AD 70

The New Testament is abundantly clear on the fact that the first Christians were with eagerness looking for the second coming of Christ from heaven. This expectation was based, firstly, on the promises of Jesus himself, who stated that his coming would occur within the lifetime of that current generation, and secondly, on the Holy Spirit inspired apostolic teaching in the epistles, which said that the coming of Jesus was very near, "at hand," "at the very doors," "about to come," in their days.

As we have seen, the Parousia was felt to be so near that it was taught in the epistles that some of the readers would still be alive when it occurred. I believe the second coming of Jesus occurred within that first century just as promised in the gospels and epistles of the New Testament.

In former chapters we have examined many passages of Scripture regarding the expectation of a harvest measure of new covenant blessing at the Parousia – a measure that involved consummation of their salvation, the bringing of them into the glory of heaven. In this chapter and the next I wish to examine some further relevant passages of Scripture that clearly show the hope of the first Christians at the Parousia of Christ. It is an exciting study to find out what they were expecting to happen to them at the time of the Parousia of the Lord Jesus; that is, into what new state or condition they expected the Savior (Phil. 3:20) to save them into, when he came with his salvation (Heb 9:28).

The Saints directly affected by the Parousia

Before studying some further relevant scriptures on this subject, let us be reminded of the two groups of saints immediately affected by the Lord's coming circa AD 70. The first group is the *deceased saints* of all previous ages, from creation to AD 70 — composed of deceased OT saints and deceased NT Christians. The second group is the *Christians who were alive* at the time of the Lord's coming in AD 70.

In accord with the conclusions of previous chapters, the relevant scriptures to be examined below also show clearly, I believe, that the first Christians actually held a hope concerning the deceased and living-remaining believers that may be summarized as:

1. *The deceased saints*: At the soon coming of Christ the already deceased saints would be raised with heavenly, spiritual bodies to be with Christ in heaven, and
2. *The living saints*: Those still alive at Christ's coming would, at the time of his coming, be changed/transformed, and bypassing death, would be glorified in their heavenly, spiritual bodies to join with

the risen deceased saints into the presence of the Lord, with whom they all would live forever. Let me call this view the "taken-to-heaven" view. (Some call it the literal rapture view, but actually the rapture is just one component of the taken-to-heaven view).

This taken-to-heaven preterist view differs from another popular preterist view which basically holds that the Christians who were alive at the time of the Parousia remained on earth following the Parousia, still in their mortal bodies, with the legacy of mankind's fallenness still present in them. Let me call this the "remained-on-earth" view, for convenience.

The scriptural evidence we have considered so far, consistently testifies that the living Christians were *not* expecting to remain on earth in their earthly bodies limited by sin and weakness, after the Lord's Parousia, but rather were expecting a completion of their redemption, just as in the case of the deceased believers – nothing less than glorification in heaven in new immortal spiritual bodies with the Lord. Let us now look at some additional scriptural evidence to confirm and clarify this.

Further Relevant Scriptures Regarding the First Christians' Expectations of Glory at the Parousia

As best we can, let us put ourselves in the shoes of the first Christians, and try to appreciate what these Scriptures would have signified to them, to whom the letters containing these scriptures were originally sent.

(1) Heb. 11:39 – 12:2

> And all these [OT saints], having obtained a good testimony through faith, did not receive the promise, God having provided something better for us, that they should not be made perfect apart from us. Therefore we also, since we are surrounded by so great a cloud of witnesses, let us lay aside every weight, and the sin which so easily ensnares us, and let us run with endurance the race that is set before us, looking unto Jesus, the author and finisher of our faith, who for the joy that was set before Him endured the cross, despising the shame, and has sat down at the right hand of the throne of God. [Heb. 11:39–12:2]

Prior to this passage, the writer to the Hebrews explained to his Hebrew readers that with the incarnation of Christ Jesus and his sacrifice for their sins, true and full atonement was made for all the saints who had been under the old covenant – an atonement which legally qualified them to enter into the long-awaited inheritance:

> And for this reason He is the Mediator of the new covenant, by means of death, for the redemption of the transgressions under the first covenant, that those who are called may receive the promise of the eternal inheritance. [Heb 9:15]

However, the writer to the Hebrews also made it clear to his readers that at the time of this epistle the deceased saints of the ages before

Christ had not yet entered their eternal inheritance. They were to enter the perfection of the eternal inheritance at the same time as the first Christians would–at the Parousia of Christ (c. AD 70).

(i) The Promise of Perfection – Heb 11:39-40

Let us consider the promise of the perfection of entering the eternal inheritance, by firstly considering Heb 11:39-40.

> Heb 11:39-40 And all these [old testament saints], having obtained a good testimony through faith, did not receive *the promise* [i.e. the fulfillment of the promise], 40 God having provided *something better for us*, that they should not *be made perfect* apart from us.

A note on correct punctuation of this passage:

The clause "God having provided something better for us" (v. 40a) in the Greek text is a genitive absolute (refer to *Robertson's Word Pictures in the NT*), which means it is not part of the main sentence, although it is an important addition. This means that the purpose clause, "in order that they should not be made perfect apart from us," qualifies the main sentence verb "did not receive," (v.39), and *not* the clause, "God having provided," as our English version has it. The main idea then is : "And all these...did not receive the promise [i.e., in their days] in order that they should not be made perfect apart from us." The secondary idea is "God having provided something better for us." In other words:

> Heb 11:39-40 [expanded]: "39 And all these [OT saints], having obtained a good testimony through faith, did not receive *the [fulfillment of the] promise* [in their days] 40 in order that they should not *be made perfect* apart from us – God having provided *something better for us*."

Let us look at this short, interesting passage under the headings of "The Promise," "They and us" and "Something Better for Us,"

(a) The Promise

The promise referred to here, whose fulfillment had not been received by the OT saints in their lifetime, has been referred to previously in Hebrews 11 under various phrases all coming under the umbrella of the one eternal inheritance: The OT saints were looking for the "homeland," (v. 14), consisting of the "better, that is, a *heavenly* country," a city prepared for them by God, (v. 16), "the city which has foundations, whose builder and maker is God," (v. 10); they desired to *enter this heavenly realm* of "the reward," (v. 26), by means of "a better resurrection," (v. 36), (i.e., *better* than a rising again to life in this fallen world, or an earthly Canaan).

The promise of God for all his people was/is bound up in the Christ; all salvation and blessing is in him. These aspects of a heavenly inheritance were all pictures of a perfection under the new covenant in Christ Jesus. How definitely the OT saints looked forward to their heavenly inheritance, is seen in the writer's use of graphic Greek words: Heb. 11:14 "They are seeking, seeking diligently for, searching for, are in quest of (Gr. ἐπιζητέω, *epizeteo*) a homeland, or a land of their own." Heb. 11:16 "But now they are stretching themselves out in order to obtain (Gr. ὀρέγω, *orego*) a better, that is, a heavenly country." (v. 16).

Jesus said Abraham rejoiced to see His day – i.e. Abraham saw with the eye of faith the promised day of the Christ; but he did not receive the fulfillment of that promise in his lifetime, he did not live to physically see the Christ on earth, nor did he or his generation experience the glorious, consummation the Christ had prepared for them.

In Heb 11:39-40 it says that the occasion of the OT saints receiving the fulfillment of the promise/s (v. 39), involves the same thing as the being made perfect or complete (v. 40). The saints were still awaiting the fulfillment of these wonderful promises of a resurrection and heavenly dwelling – to be fully perfected or completed in glory. As the whole letter expects the soon appearing of Jesus Christ to give his final consummative salvation and fulfill the promises, so then, to the writer of Hebrews, the perfecting of the OT deceased saints was an imminent event.

(b) "They" and "Us."

"And all these [OT saints]...did not receive the [fulfillment of the] promise 40 *in order that they should not be made perfect apart from us....*" [Heb 11:39-40]

God, in his administration of the ages, did not arrange for the promise to be fulfilled in the lifetimes of "these" previously mentioned OT saints. While they believed God's faithfulness to His promises, they "did not receive [the fulfillment of] the promise." The purpose for God's withholding such blessing was, "in order that they should not be made perfect apart from us." God was waiting for his specific time in history when those saints designated "us" should be born and come to faith, before He would fulfill his promise to them (i.e. the saints of the OT). Keeping in mind "audience relevance," the "us" are the Christians of that first century generation including the author of Hebrews and his readers who were already experiencing the firstfruit blessings of the new covenant in Christ..

God did not wish to make the Old Testament saints perfect/complete by fulfilling the promises to them, without including the Christians of the messianic generation of the writer of Hebrews.

So what is to happen now that the "us" have arrived? The implication of the writer is clear: *the time for the perfecting has now come for both the deceased OT saints and the first Christians of that first century (pre-AD 70) church* (the "us" of v. 40).

The first Christians, like their OT counterparts, were waiting for the fulfillment of the promise of a consummate salvation, and their entering the city of God in a consummate sense. (Heb 13:14) They had already drawn near to that city [Heb 12:22], but were partaking of its spiritual life and liberty only in a firstfruits measure [Gal 4:21-31].

They were also seeking the promised rest, not in the earthly land of Canaan, but a place of spiritual rest in the presence of God. Heb. 3 and 4 speak of a promised "rest of God," an inheritance awaiting the believers for them to enter under their greater leader Jesus, as typified by the land of Canaan given to the Israelites under Moses and Joshua. The warning is that apostates will fail to enter God's rest which is soon to be manifested (at the expected soon-coming of Jesus, 10:34-39), just as unbelieving Israelites failed to enter the physical Canaan-rest centuries before. For the true believers there remains the promise of the rest of God to inspire their hope in their present trials. This is not to say they didn't already know a kind of spiritual rest and peace of God in their hearts (in a firstfruits measure), for since their coming to Jesus as their Lord and Savior they were experiencing his promise of rest for their souls (Matt 11:28-30). But they were still in their mortal frames, subject to the flesh, and sin and the world, and were looking to the fulfillment of a glory-rest at Christ's coming.

The first Christians, like the OT saints referred to earlier, didn't need to cling to earthly possessions, for they had the hope of "a better and an enduring possession for [themselves] in heaven" (Heb 10:34). This was the "great reward" (10:35) that awaited them. They were to persevere in order to "receive the promise" (10:36) of all these wonderful things.

The greatest thing of all, which all of these things involved, was the hope of entering, through the mediation of Christ, into the very presence of God into the heavenly Holy of Holies presence of the God of Glory. That was where Jesus their Savior and forerunner had gone, in order to bring them all there into that same glory (which I have spoken of in previous chapters); (e.g. Heb 6:19-20; 2:10; Heb 10:19-25). This wonderful event was also a promise of God that the first Christians were to hold onto until the end, until the Day of Christ (see Heb 10:23, 25b).

So with all these exciting, similar promises, pertaining to both OT saints and NT Christians, the writer views the situation as that *both the OT saints and all the first NT Christians were eagerly looking for the same consummative fulfillment at the very soon-coming of the Lord Jesus.* "For yet a very little while, and the Coming One will have arrived" (Heb 10:37).

(c) Something Better Provided by God for Us

"God has provided something better for us," (v. 40), says the author (the "us" referring to his contemporary first century generation of first Christians). What is this "something better for us"?

It is *not* the coming of the new covenant, as such; for the blessing of the new covenant is something that the OT saints as well as the NT saints would experience together, whereas the writer is implying that God had something better that was just "for us" [the first Christians], which the OT saints did not, would not, have.

The "something better for us" clearly indicates that the first Christians would *in their lifetime and generation* experience the Messiah and his promised new covenant – something which none of the past OT saints ever experienced, for they died in faith not having received the fulfillment of the promise within their lifetime or generation.

This answer has been hinted at in (b) just above. I believe a first century believer might have expressed it like this:

> "Unlike prior generations of saints who died without seeing the eschatological promises of God fulfilled in their lifetime or generation, we of this present generation have "something better" provided for us — the privilege of having God fulfill His multifaceted promise through Christ Jesus, *within the lifetime of our generation*:
>
> "Our generation has already seen fulfilled (in a firstfruits and deposit measure only) the Scripture promises of a new covenant through the Messiah, the Lord Jesus Christ. Ours is the generation that has witnessed the Messiah's incarnation and his atoning work on the cross for sinners, his resurrection, his promotion to sit at the right hand of the Father in heaven, and the outpouring of the Holy Spirit. We are born anew of the Spirit, and have experienced already the peace of forgiveness and justification with God through the cross of Jesus; we know His love poured out in our hearts; we have the firstfruits of the Spirit; we have fellowship with Father and Son by the Holy Spirit. What a privileged generation we are!
>
> *"But that it not all. Ours is also the generation that will see the fulfillment of the promise of the Christ's second appearing (for did he not say it would be before this generation passes away, Matt 24:34) in his glory and kingdom with his angels and with his final phase of his great salvation, to bring all his people into their eternal inheritance, into the full experience of his unshakable kingdom and the heavenly city and country. (The soon coming of these latter events "in a very little while" is a constant theme in the book of Hebrews). Before our generation passes, all will be fulfilled.*
>
> *"In all of the aforementioned, one can see that God has provided something better for us, the first Christians of this messianic generation — viz., fulfillment in our lifetime or generation — something better than the portion of past saints who all died waiting in faith and hope without seeing fulfillment in their generation.*
>
> "But the OT saints will not miss out on the blessings we are expecting. For within the current generation, the faithfully waiting *old testament saints, along with us - the first Christians* - who also eagerly await Him, will all experience the second appearing of Jesus and the complete fulfillment of God's promises."

Scripture speaks of a special generation that would have the blessing of the things of Christ being fulfilled in their lifetime - Lk. 10:23-24; 1 Pet 1:10-12, 20-21 (note the use of "to you" and "to us").

(ii) Perfection with the Perfecter   Heb 12:1-2

Therefore we also, since we are surrounded by so great a cloud of witnesses, let us lay aside every weight, and the sin which so easily ensnares us, and let us run with endurance the race that is set before us, 2 looking unto Jesus, the author and finisher of our faith, who for the joy that was set before Him endured the cross, despising the shame, and has sat down at the right hand of the throne of God. [Heb. 12:1-2]

"Therefore we [Christians] *also*, like the aforementioned Old Testament saints who endured in faith and hope, grounded on the promise of God, are to carry on with our assigned course." Life on earth is an endurance course, faced with many trials. A good contestant keeps his eye on the goal line. Those first Christians who were awaiting the Parousia, were to imitate Jesus who had already run his course and reached the joyful finish of sitting down at the right hand of God.

The destination (where they would be perfected/completed - Gr. τελειόω, *teleioo*, Heb 11:40) of both the dead and living was to be with Christ in the Holy of Holies in heaven. To him they were to be eagerly looking, disregarding all else–to him who was the *Perfecter*/Finisher/Completer (Gr. τελειωτής, *teleiotees*) of their faith (Heb 12:2) – the finish line of their race, which was in God's presence in the heavenly Holy of Holies. Jesus the forerunner was already there; and soon he would bring all his saints to perfection and glory there to be with him. The day of this salvation was approaching at the time of the epistle to the Hebrews (9:28).

Perfection or completion (as defined by the Greek word) for the deceased OT saints and for deceased Christians who died before the Parousia (circa AD 70) meant *passing into heaven itself*, into God's presence where Jesus dwelt, to actually experience the eternal, heavenly homeland, the city built by God, the better resurrection in its fullness, having, as 1 Cor. 15 shows, new spiritual bodies fit for such heavenly living. The hope of the living Christians, to whom the Hebrews letter was sent, was no different from that of the deceased saints–perfection in heaven.

The state of the Christians alive at the time of the Parousia was expected to be no less glorious than the state of their deceased brethren, (i.e., OT brethren and NT brethren), following the Parousia. They all expected the same ultimate blessing of being made perfect. Such was the one great "promise" whose fulfillment was awaited by both the OT saints (Heb 11:39-40), and the NT Christians, (Heb 10:36).

We mentioned above "the reward" that both OT saints and NT Christians were looking for at the Parousia. When Christ would come in his glory to reward his saints (both deceased and living) (Matt 16:27, Rev. 22:12), there is nothing to distinguish both groups–the one and only "reward" of being brought to glory (Heb 2:10) was the expectation of all, regardless of whether one was still alive or dead by the time of the Parousia.

To say, as some preterists do, that the Christians who were alive at the time of the Parousia were left on earth after the Parousia, still in their earthy bodies with its legacy of fallenness, is to deny the clear expectation of glory urged upon the saints in the letter to the Hebrews–an expectation of glory in heaven that they were taught would be shared with all the deceased OT saints; an expectation of entering the Holy of Holies in heaven, where their forerunner Jesus had gone before.

To say that the living Christians at the Parousia did not enter into the same heavenly glory as their deceased brethren did, denies Heb 11:40, and necessitates an absurd dichotomy of meanings be given to the eschatological terms in Hebrews describing the first Christians' hope. There would have to be two kinds of the one eschatological blessing granted at the Parousia: viz., two kinds of final salvation, two kinds of "reward," two kinds of "perfection," two kinds of "the rest of God," two kinds of "eternal inheritance," two kinds of "better resurrection," and two kinds of "heavenly Holy of Holies" existence. One kind–a lower, partial meaning–would describe the (glorious?) state of the living Christians who were left on earth in their earthy bodies, still subject to suffering and persecution, and the enmity within themselves of the flesh versus the Spirit, with imperfect minds limited in their ability to know, appreciate and reverence God. Which of us modern preterists would deny that we still feel *our* own imperfection? And another kind of meaning of those same eschatological terms–an exalted, complete and true meaning–would describe the truly heavenly, spiritual, exalted, glorified state/condition of the deceased believers at the Parousia, in heaven where they have no more sorrow or death, and all is light and life and glory in intimate communion with God.

Such a strange dichotomy of meaning is never hinted at in the letter to the Hebrews or in any other NT epistle. *There is only one meaning ever assigned to these eschatological terms, a real, experiential consummation. And both deceased and living saints, were expecting to enter together into that same blessedness at the Parousia.*

Note the idea of the race in Heb 12:1-2. There is only one finish line to a race; a runner has either finished or he has not finished. We know the deceased saints were perfected in God's heavenly presence at the Parousia. The living saints were taught to expect the same finish at the Parousia! If the living saints were not at the same finish line in God's heavenly presence with the resurrected saints, and did not experience the same glory as those resurrected brethren, but remained in earthly bodies on earth, then it can only be said that the living saints did not reach their finish at the Parousia as promised! They still had more race to run!

Scripture says that God, through Jesus the Captain of their salvation, would bring many sons to glory at Jesus' Parousia (e.g. Heb 2:10). The sons included both deceased and living saints. Their Captain had been glorified, crowned with glory (Heb 2:9), as the first fruits, as the forerunner (6:20), waiting in the presence of the Father for his brethren to be crowned with glory also (1 Pet 5:4), to be with him where he is. The word says, "...many sons to *glory*"–the one and only glory in heaven– *not* a lower, partial glory on earth for the living saints at AD 70, and a higher, heavenly glory for the resurrected saints– but the same glory for all.

There is in the NT writings only one all-encompassing hope which *all* believers were taught (and they believed) to be fulfilled at the Parousia: only one salvation, one perfection, one eternal inheritance to be entered into; and both deceased and living believers were expecting that same great consummation. There is nothing in the letter to the Hebrews that even remotely hints that the living saints expected to remain on earth after the Parousia. Rather there is clear teaching that the living saints' hope of salvation at the coming of the Lord Jesus involved receiving fully their eternal inheritance in glory, along with Abraham, Isaac, Jacob, Moses and the great cloud of witnesses of past history.

(2) 1 Cor. 15:12-23

12 Now if Christ is preached that He has been raised from the dead, how do some among you say that there is no resurrection of the dead?... *19 If in this life only we have hope in Christ, we are of all men the most pitiable.* 20 But now Christ is risen from the dead, *and* has become the firstfruits of those who have fallen asleep. ...as in Adam all die, even so in Christ all shall be made alive. 23 But each one in his own order: *Christ the firstfruits, afterward those who are Christ's at His coming.*

In 1 Cor. 15:12-34, Paul writes against those who denied the resurrection of the dead. By arguing the fact of the real resurrection of Jesus, Paul shows that it is sheer logic to expect a real resurrection of the dead followers of Jesus at His Parousia. But let us focus on 1 Cor. 15:19 in particular. Paul says,

"If in this life only we have hope...we are of all men the most pitiable."

That is to say, if the believers' hope in Christ gains them no more than what can be had in this life –which would be the case if there was not a resurrection from the dead, as some were saying, – then his followers are to be pitied!

Why would they be pitiable? Because it would mean that their God was either too weak and/or too unloving to give them a greater, higher life in fellowship with himself after they died; which would mean that he wasn't a God worth following and worshipping after all. It would mean that all their devotion during this life, all their endurance of persecution for the name of Christ, and all their self-denial of many worldly pleasures would all make no sense because they would receive no recognition and blessing from God after their death, if there was no resurrection. Their lot after death would be no better than the lot of the heathen after death, if God showed no blessing of resurrection for his people.

But Paul, rejoicing in the true God who is worthy of the name, says, 'Such is not the case at all, for the expected resurrection of his people at the Parousia *is* a real experiential event and Christ's followers *do* have a glorious hope of eternal blessing after "this life." The Christian's God is all-loving and all-powerful, and he desires his people to be freed from the fallenness of this life and to be with him forever.

Let us note the important implication here in verse 19. We can, I believe, make the following application from v. 19: If the eschatological hope that believers have in Christ is something that goes no further than a blessedness that is compatible with, and can be realized in, "this life" – if the fulfillment of his best promises still leaves a Christian in the corruption and imperfection of "this life" – if Christ can not provide living believers a hope of something far greater, that can actually raise them out of the confines and fallenness of this life into a heavenly blessedness after and beyond "this life" – then believers are to be pitied.

Paul also speaks of "this life" in 1 Cor. 6:3, referring to life in the physical realm on earth. *A hope that can be realized by believers while they are "in this life," is far too low a hope, and is no real hope at all. It is, in effect, an insult to God's glorious hope that can only be realized in heaven after this earthly life is over.* I challenge the idea of some preterists that the great eschatological hope of the first Christians, expected at the Parousia, was realized by those living saints if they remained "in this life" on earth, after the Parousia, still imperfect in soul and body.

This clearly means that *the final resurrection of which Paul speaks to the Corinthian Christians, expected through Christ at the Parousia, is not something that is to be manifested or possessed or realized in "this life," that is, in this earthly life in this fallen world* (as described in vv. 42-44, a life which involves Christians in what is corruption, weakness, dishonor, naturalness or materiality). A figurative or covenantal resurrection of the dead which can be experienced by men "in this life" while remaining in mortal bodies, bothered by sin, would be inglorious and unworthy of their hope. A worthwhile hope, a worthwhile resurrection, has to pertain to something greater than leaving believers in this life.

The expected resurrection through Jesus at the Parousia, the hope of the believers, the subject of chapter 15 in Paul's letter to the Corinthians (1 Cor. 15:42-58), has to do with a resurrection into a glorified existence in a realm not of this life; it is beyond this life on earth; greater than what can be manifested in this life. Paul argues that the dead, as well as the living, had a hope of resurrection and change, (grounded on the fact of the real resurrection of Christ and his real ascension and real glorification in real heaven), a hope that was concerned with an end to and deliverance from this life, and full participation in the heavenly realm where Christ is.

To me this is an instance showing that *Paul did not expect those believers who were living at the time of the Parousia to receive their eternal reward in "this life."* The resurrection and change expected was not something that could be obtained and enjoyed "in this life" on earth.

1 Cor. 15:20-23 show that Paul was looking forward to the Parousia when, in the case of all pre-Parousia believers in Christ, all the "death" inherited through Adam, would be overcome fully by their being made "alive" in Christ. The death through the first man, Adam, consisted of spiritual death in the spirit and physical death in the body. Man is, since Adam, born spiritually dead with a corruptible body. Those who belong to Jesus, receive a complete new life through Him. Firstly, while "in this life," they are made spiritually alive (e.g. Eph 2:5-6), receiving the new

covenant blessings in a deposit/firstfruits measure – a measure compatible with their limited capacity while they are still in an imperfect condition – something that the first pre-Parousia Christians already had received; but while "in this life" the "body is dead because of sin," (Rom 8:10). The subject of 1 Cor. 15 is that through Jesus, the second and heavenly Man, they would, at his Parousia, receive the completion of Christ's new creation work in them, i.e., they would be made fully restored and alive spiritually, and made fully alive bodily, so that they would have a new spiritual, heavenly body to match their new-creation soul and spirit, and so would be fitted out for living in the consummated kingdom of God (that flesh and blood cannot inherit), as discussed in Section (2) above.

In the case of us post-Parousia Christians, the principle of God's new creation work is the same — the firstfruits/deposit while in "this life" and then the consummation after this life, when we physically die. Our hope of glory and resurrection beyond this life, is every bit as real as for the pre-Parousia saints. The difference being that for the pre-Parousia saints the change happened at the time of the Parousia to them all at once, whereas for us post-Parousia saints, the change happens at the time of our death to each of us individually. We then enter into the glory realm that was established at the Parousia.

(3) 1 Corinthians 15:35-57

35 But someone will say, "How are the dead raised up? And with what body do they come?" 36 Foolish one, what you sow is not made alive unless it dies. 37 And what you sow, you do not sow that body that shall be, but mere grain, perhaps wheat or some other grain. 38 But God gives it a body as He pleases, and to each seed its own body. 39 All flesh is not the same flesh, but there is one kind of flesh of men, another flesh of animals, another of fish, and another of birds. 40 There are also celestial bodies and terrestrial bodies; but the glory of the celestial is one, and the glory of the terrestrial is another. 41 There is one glory of the sun, another glory of the moon, and another glory of the stars; for one star differs from another star in glory. So also is the resurrection of the dead. 42 The body is sown in corruption, it is raised in incorruption. 43 It is sown in dishonor, it is raised in glory. It is sown in weakness, it is raised in power. 44 It is sown a natural body, it is raised a spiritual body. There is a natural body, and there is a spiritual body. 45 And so it is written, "The first man Adam became a living being." The last Adam became a life-giving spirit. 46 However, the spiritual is not first, but the natural, and afterward the spiritual. 47 The first man *was* of the earth, *made* of dust; the second Man *is* the Lord from heaven. 48 As *was* the *man* of dust, [i.e. subject to dishonor, weakness, naturalness and earthliness - IH] so also *are* those *who are made* of dust; and as *is* the heavenly *Man*, [i.e. incorruptible, glorious, powerful, spiritual, heavenly - IH] so also [*will be* (no verb here in the Greek)] those *who are* heavenly. 49 And as we have borne the image of the man of dust, we shall also bear the image of the heavenly Man. 50

> Now this I say, brethren, that flesh and blood cannot inherit the kingdom of God; nor does corruption inherit incorruption. 51 Behold, I tell you a mystery: We shall not all sleep, but we shall all be changed — 52 in a moment, in the twinkling of an eye, at the last trumpet. For the trumpet will sound, and the dead will be raised incorruptible, and we shall be changed. 53 For this corruptible must put on incorruption, and this mortal must put on immortality. 54 So when this corruptible has put on incorruption, and this mortal has put on immortality, then shall be brought to pass the saying that is written: "Death is swallowed up in victory." 55 "O Death, where is your sting? O Hades, where is your victory?" 56 The sting of death is sin, and the strength of sin is the law. 57 But thanks be to God, who gives us the victory ....

In Paul's famous teaching about the resurrection here, we will notice the exact correspondence of the destinies of the deceased saints and living saints at the Lord's coming. They receive the same blessings.

Natural Versus Spiritual

1 Cor. 15:35 suggests that some among the Corinthians were denying the resurrection because they felt it to be impossible for the dead believers to be raised since they no longer had bodies to live in; their bodies had decomposed and gone. Paul counters this in vv. 36-38 by explaining that they are familiar with the everyday natural fact that seed that is sown loses its first form, but that "death" does not rule out the coming up of new life. Paul argues that similarly the natural body of a believer passes away in order that a new form may appear.

Paul lists several entities in this universe which have special bodies or forms that make them suited to the position and function assigned to them (vv. 39-41). Similarly, the body which man is born with as he comes into this world, that body which is "sown" on this earth, is one that is suited to this material, fallen world; this body is "natural," "made of dust (earthy, KJV)," "corruptible," "dishonorable," "weak," "mortal," (vv. 42-44, 48, 53). Paul is not using these terms to describe the body in its dead or decomposing state once buried, but rather the body belonging to fallen man as it is sown or brought into existence in this fallen world. (M. S. Terry clarifies this, *Biblical Dogmatics Part 1, Section 3, Chapter 10, The Doctrine of the Resurrection* via the website www.preteristarchive.com. See also Dr John Gill on this section in his *Exposition on the Bible*). While man in his natural state is suited to this material, fallen world, he is definitely not suited for God's kingdom. In keeping with this theme of correspondence or suitedness, it follows then that for a man to live and serve in heaven before God, he must have a body or form suited to that spiritual environment and function.

So how can fallen man ever fully enter God's perfect kingdom? The answer: God exerts his creative, resurrection power! The original, natural form passes away, and God raises his people into a new type of body or form, different from what is sown in this material and fallen world;

he gives a body which is "spiritual," "heavenly," "incorruptible," "glorious," "powerful," "immortal." (vv. 42-44, 49, 53). One cannot bear both forms: a man bears the natural form first and then, after death, it is replaced by the spiritual. In the case of the Lord's people, the image which they bore of the fallen man of dust, Adam, is to be replaced by the image of the perfect Man of heaven, the Lord. Paul includes the body as part of the overall image which a person bears.

A matter of image

1 Cor. 15:47-49 The first man *was* out of earth, earthy. The second Man *was* the Lord out of Heaven. 48 Of what kind [Gr. οἷος, *oios*] *is* the earthy *man*, of this kind [Gr. τοιοῦτος, *toioutos*] also *are* the earthy ones. And of what kind *is* the heavenly *Man*, of this kind also *are* the heavenly ones. 49 And as we bore the image of the earthy *man*, we shall also bear the image of the heavenly *Man*. (My literal translation. Words in italics are not in the original Greek but are added to make sense of the sentences. In the Greek verbs-to-be are often not inserted, but are understood).

"The earthy ones" refer to all humans descended from "the earthy man," Adam. "The heavenly ones" are those out of the human race who are joined to "the heavenly Man," Christ Jesus. The earthy ones (which includes all men as they come into this world) bear the image of the man of dust — viz., corruptibleness, dishonor, weakness, naturalness or materiality (vv. 42-44). The heavenly ones (i.e. regenerated humans whose citizenship is in heaven) will bear the image of the man of heaven — viz., incorruption, glory, power, spiritualness, (vv. 45-49). Paul had already mentioned this identity of representative and those joined to that representative in 15:21-23,

21 For since by man *came* death, by Man also *came* the resurrection of the dead. 22 For as in Adam all die, even so in Christ all shall be made alive. 23 But each one in his own order: Christ the firstfruits, afterward those *who are* Christ's at His coming.

The being made alive in Christ (v. 22) involves not just the being made spiritually alive (which the Christians Corinthians had already experienced), but also being made bodily fully alive, being resurrected, which will occur at Christ's Parousia. Being made alive at the Parousia means receiving the image completely of the heavenly Man, receiving a body of incorruption, of glory, of power, of spiritual life — just like Jesus' heavenly body.

Paul affirms his view of natural man in stating: "Flesh and blood cannot inherit the kingdom of God; nor does corruption inherit incorruption" (v.50). That is, man in his present material, earthy condition ("flesh and blood") cannot participate in God's heavenly and spiritual realm (the consummate form of the kingdom of heaven). Man's whole natural makeup is corruptible, and corruptible man ("incorruption") cannot inherit or possess and participate in the heavenly "incorruption" of God's spiritual realm or kingdom. Spiritually and physically man's natural condition is totally unsuited to life in God's presence. As to man's inner soul/spirit: "Unless one is born anew of the Spirit he cannot see or enter the kingdom of heaven," (Jn. 3); and as to man's body, which is the special subject Paul is addressing in this chapter, only with a spiritual, heavenly body, (as well as a regenerated spirit), can a man in totality participate in the fullness of the kingdom of God "Here it is important to observe the representation of the true nature of 'the kingdom of God.' It is not 'the gospel;' nor 'the Christian dispensation;' nor any earthly state of things at all, but a heavenly state, into which flesh and blood are incapable of entering." (J S Russell).

The Change at the Parousia

In 1 Cor. 15:35-50 Paul has spoken in general answering the question, "How are the dead raised up? And with what body do they come?" (v. 35). He has responded by stating that the dead will be raised with spiritual, heavenly, etc. bodies. It is known that this will occur at the Parousia of Christ. All along so far Paul has been describing the great change coming for the deceased at the Parousia. How fortunate and privileged this makes the deceased believers at the Parousia! But what of the living saints? One couldn't blame them for being envious of the deceased. What have they, the living, got to look forward to at the Parousia? Paul anticipates this concern. Now Paul shares a special revelation from the Lord regarding those saints who would be still living at his Parousia. Notice especially verses 51-53 –

> 51 Behold, I tell you a secret; we indeed shall not all sleep, but we all shall be changed, 52 in a moment, in the twinkling of an eye, in the last trumpet...it shall sound, and the dead shall be raised incorruptible, and we shall be changed: 53 for it behoveth this corruptible to put on incorruption, and this mortal to put on immortality.

To catch more clearly Paul's meaning consider the following paraphrase of vv. 51-53:

> 51 "In regard to us who are alive now as I write, it is true indeed that not all of us will have died before the Lord comes; but that doesn't mean, because some of us haven't died, that we will miss out on the blessings that the dead will receive (as discussed already in vv. 42-49). I tell you a secret: all of us – those of our number who will have died by the time of the Parousia as well as those of our number who still be living at that time – all of us shall be changed, in a moment, in the twinkling of an eye, in the last trumpet; for it shall sound, and the dead shall be raised incorruptible, and we (the ones still living) – we shall be changed: 53 for it is necessary for this corruptible image of the earthy Adam that we

living ones presently bear, to put on the incorruption (and associated glory, power, spirituality) that characterizes the image of the heavenly Lord (remember vv. 48-49); and this mortal form shall put on immortality."

Note the context of Paul's use of "all" and "we" in vv. 51-53. *Both deceased and living believers shall be changed at the Lord's coming. And that change results in the same end-product for both groups – an incorruptible, immortal existence with spiritual, heavenly, glorious bodies.* For brevity's sake Paul has not included, when he uses the words "incorruptible" and "incorruption" in verses 52 and 53, all the other associated new qualities previously mentioned (in vv. 42-44, etc.) which would also apply at that time: heavenly, spiritual, glorious, powerful, etc; these new qualities are implied and included in the use of the words "incorruptible" and "incorruption." In the case of the living believers, to emphasize the wonder of the change, he adds: "mortal" shall put on "immortality."

Paul then says, "We shall not all sleep but *we shall all be changed*."

- The Change in the case of the dead believers is described as : "The dead shall be raised incorruptible," (1 Cor. 15:52); that is with incorruptible, glorious, spiritual, heavenly, powerful bodies, (vv. 42-44, 49).
- The Change in the case of the living saints is described as: "and we *[the living]* - we shall be changed *[emphasis on "we" is in the Greek]*. For it is necessary for this corruptible to put on incorruption, and this mortal to put on immortality," (vv. 52-53). Note that the living saints are to be changed to a condition called "incorruption" (Gr. ἀφθαρσία, *aphtharsia*), which is the same condition that the deceased saints are to be changed into, called "incorruptible" (Gr. ἄφθαρτος, *aphthartos*, adjective of *aphtharsia*).

There is some difference in the way the change affects each of the two groups, but no difference in the end result and nature of the change: the dead saints would be raised from their disembodied state into glory and given their new heavenly, spiritual bodies, while the still-living saints would bypass the normal procedure of death and its disembodiment and would be changed instantaneously into the same glorious, heavenly, spiritual condition as the raised deceased brethren; the living ones will "put on" incorruptibility and immortality. "For it is necessary for this corruptible to put on incorruption, and this mortal to put on immortality" (v. 53). This "putting on" (from Gr. ἐνδύω, *enduo*) of the heavenly, glorified body without having to pass through the normal experience of physical death is also the subject of Paul's longing in 2 Cor. 5:2-4. His longing was "to clothe ourselves over [or "super-invest ourselves," from Gr. ἐπενδύομαι, *ependuomai*] with the dwelling from heaven, that what is mortal may be swallowed up by life (2 Cor. 5:4). This was a "putting on" of their heavenly body "over the top of" their present earthly body, without being stripped of their earthly body first (a "change" or "exchange" of bodies without disembodiment, "taking off," or "nakedness" having to take place). The dead were raised and given their new bodies to put on, but the living were "changed" without taking off their old bodies.

In 1 Cor. 15:53 the terms, "this corruptible" and "this mortal," both refer to the state of the bodies of the living saints who were still dwelling in their corruptible and mortal bodies on earth. One can imagine Paul considering his trial-worn body as he essentially says: *"this,* present, *corruptible body*, still affected by the fall of Adam and bearing his earthy image." The "change" that the living will undergo at the Lord's coming refers to the change of their bodies that will enable to them to meet with the resurrected dead saints before the Lord in his consummated heavenly kingdom. (Remember verse 50, implying that corruptible flesh and blood cannot inherit the kingdom of God in heaven). Remember that *all through this passage, the context shows that "corruption" is a description of the natural, material, fallen human body, as a legacy of the fall of Adam, the earthy man. "Incorruption" is mentioned as the glorious portion of both deceased and living believers at the coming of Christ, something that separates them from the image of earthy Adam and fully conforms them to the image of the heavenly Man, the glorified Jesus — an incorruption that includes the ideas of glory, power, spirituality and heavenly quality.* Partaking of this realm and nature of incorruption and glory is the "crown" consummating a believer's life of faith:

1 Cor. 9:25 And every man that striveth for the mastery is temperate in all things. Now they do it to obtain a corruptible crown; but we *an incorruptible crown.*
1 Pet. 5:4 And when the chief shepherd has been manifested you shall receive *the unfading crown of glory.*

Note the uses of incorruption and unfadingness of glory, characterize the expectation of the first Christians. I have expounded on these two latter verses in Chapter 6.

The term "mortal" (Gr. θνητός, *thneetos*), used twice in 1 Cor. 15:53,54, is used numerous times by Paul, and in all cases he is referring to the fallen, imperfect, subject-to-death state of man's natural, earthy body.

"Therefore do not let sin reign in your *mortal* body..." [Rom 6:12]
"...He will also give life to your *mortal* bodies because of His Spirit who dwells in you." [Rom 8:11]
"For we who live are always delivered to death for Jesus' sake, that the life of Jesus also may be manifested in our *mortal* flesh." [2 Cor. 4:11]
"For we who are in this tent [i.e. earthly tent – physical body] groan, being burdened, not because we want to be unclothed, but clothed over, that the *mortal* may be swallowed up by life." [2 Cor. 5:4]

Prior to the Parousia the deceased were not in their mortal bodies (because they had died), but the living saints were still in their mortal bodies. Paul was expecting that at Christ's Parousia the living saints would be changed by having their mortal, corruptible state clothed over, transformed into an incorruptible, immortal state. The mortal bodies of the living saints would be changed by God's power into incorruptible, immortal ones.

The context implies that the change to be undergone by both the deceased and the living saints, would perfectly enable them all - both deceased and living ones - in their heavenly bodies, to enter fully the heavenly kingdom of God (v. 50). Paul looked forward to the victory over death that would be manifested in fact, not just in principle, at the Parousia (vv. 54-57). Such a manifested victory over death is the portion for all the pre-Parousia saints - the deceased and the living saints - on the occasion of the Parousia. *For the victory over death to be truly manifested it meant that both deceased and living believers were to be glorified together into the same heavenly state at the Parousia, such that all in them or about them that once spoke of death and fallenness would be totally gone.*

> "The revelation, then, which the apostle here communicates, the secret concerning their future destiny, is this: That they would not all have to pass through the ordeal of death, but that such of them as were privileged to live until the Parousia would undergo a change by which they would be qualified to enter into the kingdom of God, without experiencing the pangs of dissolution. He had just before (v. 50) been explaining that material and corruptible bodies of flesh and blood could not, in the nature of things, be fit for a spiritual and heavenly state of existence: 'Flesh and blood cannot inherit the kingdom of God.' Hence the necessity for a transformation of the material and corruptible into that which is immaterial and incorruptible." (J. S. Russell, *The Parousia*, p. 209)

This understanding of the above verses in 1 Cor. 15 demonstrates a conformity with the passages in the epistle to the Hebrews already discussed above; and with all the conclusions of previous chapters.

"All" means *All*; "Incorruption" means *Incorruption*

In this whole context in 1 Cor. 15 concerning resurrection and change and entering a heavenly state after this earthly one, for deceased believers and for still-living believers at the Lord's coming, I see nothing to suggest that the believers living at Christ's Parousia expected to remain in the same fallen bodies after the Parousia. To the contrary, I believe a straightforward reading of Paul's words clearly reveals an excited hope of glorification for the living saints as well as for the deceased at the Lord's Parousia. That is the exciting thing behind Paul's "Behold" in v. 40 - that is the happy "secret" or mystery revealed to him by the Lord – that "*all*," both deceased and living, at the Parousia will be changed and pass into the spiritual, heavenly state, taking on the image of the heavenly Man, leaving behind all of the old natural and earthy image of the man of dust.

The terms immortality and incorruption in this whole context refer to the bodies of the saints. Note that Paul applies the term "incorruption" to both the deceased saints and to the living saints at the Lord's coming. Paul is quite clear here: What the term "incorruption" means for the former at the coming of Christ, it means for the latter at the coming of Christ. This is the hope that excites Paul in this section: Incorruption with all that term implies (the glory, the power, the spirituality, the heavenliness) was to be the portion of both deceased and living at the Parousia.

Paul makes no intimation whatsoever that the assuming of incorruption in the case of the living saints is some different version from the incorruption to be assumed by the deceased at the Parousia. To think that the living Christians would remain on earth after the Parousia, (as many preterists believe) would necessitate the invention of two kinds of incorruption — a lower version of incorruption that the living would possess which would leave them compatible with corruptible bodies, (which would really be a misnomer), and a higher, true version of incorruption for the deceased that would be the real thing–giving them glorious, spiritual bodies. But of course this is a totally unacceptable idea. There is no place that any expectation of remaining on earth with incorruption still present in them, still carrying the image of fallen Adam, can be found in this whole discussion by Paul the apostle.

Paul envisaged that death would be just as truly vanquished in the case of the living saints as it was in the case of the deceased believers at the Parousia of Christ. He looked for a real victory - not just in principle or figuratively - but a victory in fact; manifested; in full; experiential.

I cannot see that Paul is saying anywhere that the kind of resurrection of the dead that Paul is defending in the whole of 1 Cor. 15 is a mere covenantal concept without real, experiential change, wherein pre-Parousia Christians would remain living on earth in mortal, corruptible bodies after the Parousia. Rather, the whole context is about the Corinthians' questions concerning a real, literal resurrection of the dead, out of the realm of corruption and fallenness inherited from fallen Adam and into the presence of their resurrected, glorified Lord Jesus Christ.

(4) 1 Corinthians 6:13-15
Foods for the stomach and the stomach for foods, but God will destroy both it and them. Now the body is not for sexual immorality but for the Lord, and the Lord for the body. 14 *And God both raised up the Lord and will also raise us up by His power.* 15 Do you not know that your bodies are members of Christ? Shall I then take the members of Christ and make them members of a harlot? Certainly not!

It appears that some of the Corinthian brethren were assuming their freedom in Christ meant they could be lax about their eating and sexual lifestyles. In 1 Cor. 6:12-20, Paul corrects this licentious idea. In particular he points out the need to "glorify God in your body and in your spirit, which are God's," (v. 20). The point of Paul's teaching in this passage is that the body is of particular importance to the Lord. The body of the believer is for the Lord, for His glory, for His service. And the Lord is for the body, i.e. He will rule in it, empower it, protect it, will change it (in the case of those still alive at the Parousia) out of corruption into incorruption (as discussed in 1 Cor. 15:49-53, and 2 Cor. 5:1-4, and Phil 3:20-21), and through the new spiritual, heavenly body of the saints he will display his glory. That is why the body cannot be used for immoral purposes. The Lord's purpose is for his children to have a body in which their soul would dwell, and through which the life of Christ would be manifested. First there is the natural earthy body in which they are to glorify Christ, then there is the spiritual heavenly body (see 1 Cor. 15) in which they are to glorify God forever.

Within the background of the first Christians' expectation of the coming of Christ eventuating very soon, 1 Cor. 6:14 is intriguing. Elsewhere, when Paul refers to the resurrection of saints at the Parousia, he clearly speaks of the dead saints as the ones to be "raised." Here, in 1 Cor. 6:14, he refers to "us," i.e., *his readers and himself*, as ones to be "raised" by God's power. Now from 1 Cor. 15:51, as we have seen, the "us" who would be benefited by the Parousia would include that portion of Paul's Corinthian brethren who would still be alive at the time of the Parousia, and the other portion of his brethren who will have died by that time. So when under the Spirit's inspiration Paul says in 6:14, "God will raise *US* up by his power," he says in effect: "God will raise us up, all of us–those of us who remain alive until the Parousia and those of us who will have died before the Parousia–God will raise all of us by his power just as he raised the Lord."

We tend to think of being raised as applicable only to deceased saints. Often when we hear of the saints being "raised" we automatically tend to think of what they are raised *from*. But there is the other side, of viewing what they are raised *to*. Now both deceased saints and living saints required God by his power to raise them *into* the glorious state of incorruptibility at the Parousia, with glorified, spiritual bodies, to be conformed to the image of the heavenly Man, the Lord Jesus, (see 1 Cor. 15). The difference is that the deceased needed to be raised from their disembodied state into that glorious state, while the living saints needed to be raised from their mortal state into that same glorious state. The rising into a state of glory was just as humanly impossible to the deceased as it was to the living saints. *The power of God would raise both groups of saints into their glorious inheritance.*

To me, 1 Cor. 6:14 reveals that in Paul's mind the expectation and destiny of the dead believers - to be raised by God's power - was the same as the expectation and destiny of the living believers at the Parousia - to also be raised by the power of God. Both groups expected to be raised up by God's power at the Parousia.

(5) Romans 8:15-25

For you did not receive the spirit of bondage again to fear, but you received the Spirit of adoption by whom we cry out, "Abba, Father." 16 The Spirit Himself bears witness with our spirit that we are children of God, 17 and if children, then heirs – heirs of God and joint heirs with Christ, if indeed we suffer with Him, that we may also be glorified together. 18 For I consider that the sufferings of this present time are not worthy to be compared with the glory which *shall be* [Gr. μέλλω, *mello*, "is about to be"] revealed to us. 19 For the earnest expectation of the creation eagerly waits for the revealing of the sons of God. 20 For the creation was subjected to futility, not willingly, but because of Him who subjected it in hope; 21 because the creation itself also will be delivered from the bondage of corruption into the glorious liberty of the children of God. 22 For we know that the whole creation groans and labors with birth pangs together until now. 23 Not only that, but we also who have the firstfruits of the Spirit, even we ourselves groan within ourselves, eagerly waiting for the adoption as sons, the redemption of our body. 24 For we were saved in this hope, but hope that is seen is not hope; for why does one still hope for what he sees? 25 But if we hope for what we do not see, we eagerly wait for it with perseverance.

Glorified together with Christ

In Rom 5:2 Paul joyfully proclaimed the fact that through grace the Christians now had a hope of experiencing the glory of God, a hope which could not be diminished by trials. In Rom. 8:17ff Paul returns to this theme of the hope of glory. In this passage Paul expresses his hope of soon being glorified with Christ (v. 17) after the present time of suffering. This hoped-for-glory is "about to be revealed" [*literal translation*] to the believers, (v. 18). The apostle Peter also refers to this near event: "I...am...also a partaker of the glory which is about to be revealed," [literal *translation*], (1 Pet 5:1).

Rom. 8:17 contains three aspects of a believer's togetherness with Christ. In the Greek text each aspect is from a word with the prefix *sun* (with, together with) attached to it. The believers are "joint-heirs with Christ," they are to "jointly-suffer" (with Christ) and they are to be "jointly-glorified" (with Christ). The various Bible translations express this verse in different ways. To express the believers' togetherness with Christ verse 17 could be translated: "[We are]...heirs indeed of God, and heirs together with Christ, if so be we suffer together (with him), that we may be glorified together (with him)."

The NT epistles regard Christ Jesus as glorified in heaven, having been resurrected from the dead and having ascended to the right hand of the Father. As M. S. Terry says: "The resurrection and ascension are looked upon as essential parts in the one great fact of the glorification of the Son of God, so that the resurrection apart from the ascension was not an end or complete consummation in itself, but required the exaltation to the right hand of God to perfect the glorification...." (Milton S. Terry, *Biblical Dogmatics*, Chapter 10, "The Doctrine of the Resurrection," p. 222)

To be glorified together with Christ, which meant a glorification with him in heaven, was the hope expressed by Paul, which the first Christians believed would soon be fulfilled at the Parousia of Christ. Paul elsewhere says they were called by the gospel "with the view to obtaining the glory of our Lord Jesus Christ," (2 Thess 2:14). Such a thought is beyond human imagination! No wonder that Paul says it would be an incomparable glory, (v. 18). Together with Christ in his glory, the believers would enter a state of glory – "the glory of the children of God," (v. 21).

The Whole Creation Expectant

I agree with William Bell (see his article *The Illusion of the Conclusion* in www.preteristarchive.com) in holding that "the creation" spoken of in this passage is not the physical, material creation (e.g. trees, animals) of this earth – such an interpretation cannot do justice to the context or linguistics – but the term refers to an intelligence that has a hope, that eagerly waits, that groans, that has a will, that can experience a spiritual liberty in God. I feel that "the creation" (at least) refers to the great family of saints who had lived and died in faith down through the centuries - from Adam to those of Paul's day, including all the believers from among the Israelites down through the centuries. From the Lord's first promise of a Savior to fallen Adam (Gen 3:15), all true believers in the Lord, feeling their fallenness, (having fallen short of the glory of God - Rom 3:23) had held to a hope of full salvation and resurrection into the glory that was lost by Adam. Paul refers to this hope of the fathers, of resurrection from the dead, in the book of Acts, claiming that it was near (Acts 26:6,8; 24:14,15; 23:6). This understanding of the term "the creation" does justice to the context; (see further detail in footnotes after this section).

Paul was overwhelmed by his awareness of and contemplation of the surpassing greatness of the soon-coming glorious blessing that would vastly more than compensate for all suffering presently endured (Rom. 8:18; also 2 Cor. 4:17). He says in effect, 'The reason I am excited is that what is about to come upon us, the present generation of Christians, is nothing less than what the whole body of God's people have been waiting for ever since the fall of Adam; it will be a climactic, awesome occasion and it is coming in our generation. The thought of it makes the sadness of present suffering seem as nothing in comparison!'

This interpretation concurs with the teaching of the writer to the Hebrews that I have explained in Section (1) of this chapter, namely, that the OT saints were longing for a perfection, as were the present generation of first Christians, and that the time was very soon when all the past numbers of saints along with the present first Christians would pass into glorious perfection on the occasion of the Lord's Parousia.

Longing for Full Revelation of Sonship

The Romans passage clearly says that all the creation (past saints) as well as that first generation of Christians - both groups together (Rom. 8:22, 23) - were groaning and eagerly waiting the time of their glorification with Christ.

Both the dead saints of the past waiting in Hades, and the still living Christians of that first generation were "eagerly waiting" for the revelation of the sons of God, also called the full adoption as sons (Rom. 8:19, 23). At the Parousia both groups would enter the fullness of what it means to be an adopted son of God; they would all (not just the Christians from the time of Christ but all previous saints) be revealed as sons of God in glory. This adoption and revelation as sons would consist of their being clothed with the glory that goes with the title of sons of God. Earlier in this letter to the Romans Paul had mentioned the sad state of man in his natural state: "All sinned and fall short of the glory of God" (Rom. 3:23). Christ's incarnation, his atoning death and subsequent resurrection and ascension were God's way of saving and restoring a multitude of fallen human beings to a glorious state where they were no longer be falling short of the glory of God, but would experience his glory and manifest his glory fully without any admixture of sin or fallenness. (See my Chapter 4). While in their mortal, corruptible bodies - although they were "sons" by faith in Christ - the full glory of the sonship state into which they had been saved by grace was not revealed; and likewise the greatness of Christ's salvation and redemption provided for them was not revealed, and he did not as yet have the full satisfaction of seeing the full fruit of the travail of his soul. The revelation of the sons of God in glory meant the full display of Christ's victory.

At this revelation of sonship, all past and present saints would experience the glorious liberty that belongs to the sons of God, literally "the liberty of the glory of the children of God," (Rom. 8:21). This "liberty of the glory" which would characterize the children and sons of God consisted of freedom from the bondage of corruption (v. 21), and the redemption of the body (v. 23). This "liberty of the glory" of the children of God is a state where they are free from the realm of corruption, free from the groaning as with birth pangs for their deliverance from the presence of sin, and when they experience that salvation (Rom 13:11f) which involves redemption of their body, where the Savior gives them a glorious body like the Lord's glorious body, (Phil 3:21 - to be discussed later). In Rom 2:6, 7, 10 Paul implies that "reward" of eternal life, which the believers sought for at the righteous judgment of Christ in that Day of his Parousia, consisted of glory, honor and incorruption.

From our study in 1 Cor. 15, we saw that corruption is a characteristic of man in his natural, earthy, fallen body; it is part of the "image of the man of dust." This "liberty of the glory" of Rom 8 is the same state of resurrection and change expressed in 1 Cor. 15: of having their new spiritual, heavenly bodies, characterized by incorruption, glory, power, and immortality (1 Cor. 15:42-44, etc.). This was the hope they were eagerly waiting for with perseverance (Rom 8:25), when the things previously unseen and eternal, would be experiential and visible realities.

This passage Rom 8:16-25 presents the whole family of God – all the dead saints of all past human history waiting in Hades, and that first generation of living Christians of Paul's day – as together grounded in the same hope of glory; together groaning; together waiting for the revelation and adoption of the sons of God; together waiting for the liberty, the deliverance from corruption, the redemption of the body.

Christ was glorified in heaven in the presence of the Father at his ascension. Paul's hope and that of the living believers of his day was that at the coming of Christ they would finish their time in the earthly sphere ("this life," 1 Cor. 15:19) where there was suffering, corruption and groaning in their present body and, along with "the whole creation" of all past believers, be glorified together with, in company with, Christ; which can only mean living with him in heaven in glorified, resurrection bodies like His, in an eternal life of glory, honor and incorruption. It was at the soon expected Parousia of Christ that God the Father would bring his many sons to glory (Heb 2:10). The Lord's people, deceased and living, who had shared in the sufferings of Christ on earth, were expecting to be glorified brethren in company with Jesus the captain of their salvation, who as their forerunner had been crowned with glory and honor in heaven following his time of humiliation on earth (Heb 2:9).

Footnote on "The Creation" in Rom 8:19-22

Some commentators make a point of the fact that Paul uses the word "also" at v. 23, saying that this "also" means that Paul contrasts himself and his fellow Christians with "the creation," so that "the creation" cannot mean mankind or all past believers down through the ages, and therefore must have some other meaning. Here again is vv. 22 and 23, where I have underlined the relevant "also."

Rom 8:22-23 "For we know that the whole creation groans and labors with birth pangs together until now. 23 Not only that, but we *also* who have the firstfruits of the Spirit, even we ourselves groan within ourselves..."

The Greek word translated "also" (*kai* = and, even, also) can faithfully be rendered "even," and is in fact translated as "even" (in the KJV and NKJV, at least) in the next clause. Look at Rom. 8:23 again: "And not only so, but even [*kai*] ourselves, having the first fruits of the Spirit, even [*kai*] we ourselves groan in ourselves..." Paul is saying that the whole creation, the whole mass of God's people of all past history prior to Christ, is awaiting with groaning the very soon coming of the Lord with glory; and even that privileged section of God's people, the first Christians who have the first fruits of the Holy Spirit, are not exempt from this longing and groaning for the liberty that glorification with Christ will bring.

In the OT writings Israel is referred to as the Lord's created people; not primarily meaning their physical existence as humans, for all heathen nations were created in that sense; but rather meaning their creation as a covenant people under the Lord's protection and care, a people made and formed for his glory. (See e.g. Isa 43:1, 6-7; 44:1-2). Strictly speaking it was the true believers in Israel, who were his creation, the true Israel within Israel (Rom 9:6). This idea is carried into the NT where believers are described as "God's workmanship, created in Christ Jesus," (Eph 2:10), and those in Christ are a "new creation," (2 Cor. 5:17).

So it is, I believe, in Rom. 8:18-23. The "whole creation," the whole family of God's special creation of believing humans down through the centuries was waiting and groaning for the experience of the glory of God. The first Christians with the first fruits of the Holy Spirit, are actually part of this whole creation; their separate mention is merely to emphasize their privileged position above previous O T saints who died before the Christ came.

(6) Romans 8:26-39

26 Likewise the Spirit also helps in our weaknesses. For we do not know what we should pray for as we ought, but the Spirit Himself makes intercession for us with groanings which cannot be uttered. 27 Now He who searches the hearts knows what the mind of the Spirit is, because He makes intercession for the saints according to the will of God. 28 And we know that all things work together for good to those who love God, to those who are the called according to His purpose. 29 For whom He foreknew, He also predestined to be conformed to the image of His Son, that He might be the firstborn among many brethren. 30 Moreover whom He predestined, these He also called; whom He called, these He also justified; and whom He justified, these He also glorified. 31 What then shall we say to these things? If God is for us, who can be against us?...
35 Who shall separate us from the love of Christ? Shall tribulation, or distress, or persecution, or famine, or nakedness, or peril, or sword? 36 As it is written: "For Your sake we are killed all day long; we are accounted as sheep for the slaughter." 37 Yet in all these things we are more than conquerors through Him who loved us. 38 For I am persuaded that neither death nor life, nor angels nor principalities nor powers, nor things present nor things to come, 39 nor height nor depth, nor any other created thing, shall be able to separate us from the love of God which is in Christ Jesus our Lord.

The remainder of Romans chapter 8 (i.e. vv. 26-39) confirms my analysis just above for Rom 8:16-25. Rom 8:26-39 continues the same theme as Rom 8:16-25 of God's faithfully bringing his people to glory. Paul says that the climax of the chain of blessings which God applies to his foreknown people is glorification, (v. 30). Commentators suggest it is expressed in the past tense as a thing done - "these He also glorified" - because of the certainty of it in the counsel and purpose of God. But what does this glorification involve?

The Destiny of Glorification and Conformation

God foreknew a people (v. 29), his elect, before time began, (He chose them in Christ before the foundation of the world, Eph 1:4), and those whom He foreknew He predestined to a certain destiny. The purpose of God spoken of in verse 28 is the purpose of bringing his elect to their predestined destiny. There are two mentions of predestination in this passage, pointing out two aspects of the destiny of God's people. Verse 30 shows that the predestination of God leads to the destiny of glorification. Verse 29 speaks of the predestination of God leading to the destiny of conformation to the image of God's son, that he might be the firstborn among many brethren. Now God's Son here is referring to the glorified Christ reigning at the right hand of the Father. Joining these two aspects of God's predestined destiny we see that *glorification involves conformation to the image of the glorified Christ, as fully revealed brethren of Christ and sons of God.*

Therefore, here we have the same themes as in Rom 8:17-23 - glorification and the revealing of the sons of God (or, their official placement as sons). To bring many glorified brethren into conformity to the image of Christ is another way of describing the revealing of the sons of God and their full adoption as sons. Conformation is the object and substance of their glorification. There is nothing higher than this: - being glorified together with Christ as his many glorified brethren, and Christ and them being joint heirs under their God and Father, (8:17 with 8:29).

God's son referred to in 8:29 is the glorified Christ. Conforming his people to the image of Christ is God's purpose, the goal of God's predestination. What does this conformity to the image of Christ involve?

Conformation to the Image of the Glorified Christ

Remember the context of 1 Cor. 15 discussed above. From Adam - the first man, the man from the earth - all his descendants took on a natural, earthy body subject to corruption, etc. In this natural state of flesh and blood man can never inherit the kingdom of God. Christ is called the second man, the Lord from heaven, who became a life-giving spirit, who alone can raise his people out of their natural earthy state into a spiritual, heavenly state. The believers had borne *the image* of Adam; their hope was to soon bear *the image of Christ* at his Parousia. Christ is the heavenly Man whose heavenly image the believers would bear at their change and resurrection (1 Cor. 15:47-53). *This image meant having incorruptible, glorious, powerful, spiritual, heavenly bodies.* Only those who bore such an image could possess the spiritual and heavenly kingdom of God. Such was the lesson from 1 Cor. 15.

Rom. 8:29-30 expresses the same thing as in 1 Cor. 15. Glorification means conformation to *the image of the heavenly, glorified Christ*, that he might be the firstborn among many glorified brethren. Being conformed to the image of Christ means leaving behind the image of the natural, earthy Adam, (that "flesh and blood" condition that cannot inherit the consummated kingdom of God, 1 Cor. 15:50), and being changed to "put on" or bear the spiritual, heavenly image of the spiritual, heavenly Christ, and so be enabled to fully participate in his heavenly kingdom.

Rom. 8:29 is speaking of the climax of sanctification: full conformity of spirit, soul and body to the image of Christ. Rom. 8:29 is not to be limited to only a moral or spiritual transformation in this life while the saints remain in their natural, earthy, fallen bodies; that is not the destiny for which God predestined them. Rom 8:29 is about glorification, it is about the arriving at the predestined destiny of full conformation to Christ. The Greek word translated "conformed" (σύμμορφος) implies that the outward form fully expresses the inner essence of a Christ-filled new-creation life.

Overcomers – Dead or Alive
Paul exults in the love of God for His children:

> Rom. 8:35 Who shall separate us from the love of Christ?
> Rom. 8:39 [Absolutely nothing] shall be able to separate us from the love of God which is in Christ Jesus our Lord.

In speaking of the love of God and Christ here, he is not speaking of love as a sentimental feeling, but of a powerful force flowing from the heart and will of God. This love refers to an active, powerful, accomplishing love which will achieve His purpose upon His foreknown and beloved elect – the purpose of bringing them to the glorification and conformation mentioned in vv. 29–30. Already, Paul says, this love has been working all things together for the good of the called ones of God – even difficult things like tribulations and persecutions, (v. 28). This love will further bring them to glory. And nothing can separate the saints from this love; i.e. nothing can separate the saints from this powerful, purpose-achieving, love. All the evils of this world cannot stop this love.

Not even death can separate a saint from this purpose-achieving love of God. Paul admits that some will feel the sword cutting down their earthly life; and persecution may reach the point where it seems as if the saints of God are like sheep ready for slaughter, being killed all day long, (vv. 35-36). But love's purpose of bringing the saints of God to glory will not one bit fail, but will triumph, despite all the appearances to the contrary. So we have Paul's triumphant confession:

> "Yet in all these things [including death], we [*whether dead or alive*] are more than conquerors, abundantly victorious, prevailing mightily, supremely overcoming [Gr. verb ὑπερνικάω, *hupernikao* conveys all these meanings] through him who loved us," (Rom. 8:37).

The victory is decreed and settled in God's mind for all the pre-Parousia saints, whether they would be dead or alive at the time of Christ's Parousia — their expected glorification and conformation to the image of the glorified Christ would be accomplished.

Paul's declaration here means that the victory for a living saint who remained alive until the Parousia of Christ is the same as for a saint who would die under Nero's evil persecutions prior to the Parousia of Christ in AD 70. He who predestined his elect is He who will bring his saints to their glorious destiny. This whole passage is clear on the fact that the expectation of the living saints of Paul's day was glorification and conformation to the image of Christ. And if under some evil circumstances some of the saints died before the Parousia of Christ — well, that death could not thwart the love and power and purpose of God: alive or dead the saints were "more than conquerors."

This point needs extreme emphasis: the expectation of the deceased saints was exactly the same as the expectation of the living saints – that God would bring them both to glorification and conformation at the same time, at the Parousia of Christ.

This theme of ultimate victory for both living and deceased believers at the Parousia of Christ is echoed in 1 Cor. 15:54-57, where the victory of incorruption and glory, which would swallow up all that speaks of death, is the portion of both deceased and living believers at the Parousia. The phrase: "we are more than victors through him who loved us," in Rom 8:37, is paralleled by the phrase: "But thanks be to God who is giving us the victory through our Lord Jesus Christ," in 1 Cor. 15:57.

We post-Parousia Christians have this same wonderful hope of being glorified together with Christ, when our allotted time on earth is finished, with the difference that we will not escape the experience of physical death like the living saints did at the Parousia.

(7) 2 Cor. 4:13 – 5:10

In this passage which I quote below, I have endeavored to help the reader more fully grasp the meaning of some of the significant words in this context (according to the original Greek meaning and verb tense). Here is the definition of those significant words that are found in this section of scripture. In order for the reader to perceive the different shades of meaning in the Greek, I have noted in brackets the following Greek words where relevant:

oikia = a house, dwelling, abode;
skeenos = a tent;
oikeeteerion = a dwelling place, habitation;
oikodomee = a building (with emphasis on something built, in this case by God)
enduo = to put on, to clothe oneself;
ekduo = to put off, to strip off one's clothes;
ependuomai = to put on over (as an upper garment);
endeemeo = to be or stay at home, in one's own country;
ekdeemeo = to go abroad, to be absent from home.

13 And since we have the same spirit of faith, according to what is written, "I believed and therefore I spoke," we also believe and therefore speak, 14 knowing that He who raised up the Lord Jesus will also raise us up through Jesus, and will present us with you. 15 For all things are for your sakes, that grace, having spread through the many, may cause thanksgiving to abound to the glory of God. 16 Therefore we do not lose heart. Even though our outward man is perishing, yet the inward man is being renewed day by day. 17 For our light affliction, which is but for a moment, *is working for us a far more exceeding and eternal weight of glory*, 18 while we do not look at the things which are seen, but at the things which are not seen. For the things which are seen are temporary, but the things which are not seen are eternal. 1 For we know that if our earthly house [*oikia*], (that is) this tent [*skeenos*], is destroyed, we have a building [*oikodomee*] from God, a house [*oikia*] not made with hands, eternal in the heavens. 2 For in this we groan, earnestly desiring to clothe ourselves over [*ependuomai*] with our habitation [*oikeeteerion*] which is from heaven, 3 if indeed, having clothed ourselves [*enduo*], we shall not be found naked. 4 For we who are in this tent [*skeenos*] groan, being burdened, not because we want to unclothe ourselves [*ekduo*], but to clothe ourselves over [*ependuomai*], that the mortal [*thneetos*] may be swallowed up by life. 5 Now He who has prepared us for this very thing is God, who also has given us the Spirit as a guarantee. 6 Therefore we are always confident, even [*kai*] knowing that while we remain at home [*endeemeo*] in the body we are absent [*ekdeemeo*] away from [*apo*] the Lord. 7 For we walk by faith, not by sight. 8 We are confident, yes, well pleased rather to be absent [*ekdeemeo*] out from [*ek*] the body and to be at home [*endeemeo*] with [*pros*] the Lord. 9 Therefore we make it our aim, whether we are at home [*endeemeo, i.e., at home in the body – remain alive on earth*] or we are absent from home [*ekdeemeo, i.e., away from the body – deceased*], to be well pleasing to Him. 10 For we must all appear before the judgment seat of Christ, that each one may receive the things done in the body, according to what he has done, whether good or bad.

Raised by God and a Hope of Glory (2 Cor. 4:13-18)

In the immediately preceding context Paul had been explaining his constant touch with death as an apostle of Christ. However his confidence in the Lord was undiminished even faced with the prospect of death at the hand of his persecutors, *for he believed that if it came to his actually dying then the Lord would raise him up (with the other deceased saints) and present him with the living saints before the Lord, at the Lord's Parousia*, (4:14). (See details on this eschatological "presentation" theme in Chapter 6 of my book. Refer to Rom 14:10-12; 2 Cor. 5:10; 2 Cor. 11:2-3; Eph 5:25-27 and Jude 24 for the same teaching of the saints being presented and caused to stand before the Lord at his Parousia, there to receive their rewards from the glorified Christ). As in passages previously discussed we see again Paul's understanding that at the Lord's coming *both* deceased saints and living saints would be presented before the Lord in His glory.

Just as in Romans 8 Paul here also expresses his hope of experiencing an incomparable, exceeding, eternal weight of glory in exchange for his present earthly, suffering condition, (2 Cor. 4:16-18). In 2 Cor. 3:1-17 Paul's theme was his confident hope that the super-excelling glory of the new covenant (which was at present only revealed in its deposit and firstfruits measure) would soon be manifested, while the inferior glory of the old covenant was being brought to an end. The glory Paul refers to in 2 Cor. 4:16-18 is the consummative glory of the new covenant fully manifested in the saints who would be fully transformed into the glorious image of Christ, glorified together with Christ. This glory, as we know from Paul's letter to the Romans, was about to be revealed (Rom 8:18; 13:11-12). The Parousia was near when the saints would appear at the judgment seat of Christ (2 Cor. 5:9-10) and receive an eternal reward of glory with Christ. Paul speaks of an *eternal* weight of glory because he was expecting to enter the eternal realm that could not be seen or entered while in his earthly state, (vv. 17-18. cf. 1 Cor. 15:50).

A Heavenly Body (2 Cor. 5:1-10)

In 2 Cor. 5:1-10 Paul discusses his belief that if he physically dies – if his "earthly house is destroyed, taken down" – he has another body, a heavenly one reserved for him from God — a "house not made with (human) hands," (5:1).

However rather than die before the Lord's Parousia and be "unclothed" (v. 4) and "naked" (v. 3), i.e. body-less (like the deceased saints), and have to wait in that disembodied state for the Parousia when he (with all the deceased saints) would receive his new spiritual, heavenly body, Paul desired to remain alive until the Parousia when, bypassing the process and experience of death, he could just clothe himself (lit. clothe upon or over) with his heavenly body or "house, " such that his mortal frame would be swallowed up by life, (5:2-4).

This privilege of bypassing death, and being "clothed upon, swallowed up by life" is exactly the same belief expressed in 1 Cor. 15:50-53 where he said that at the Parousia those who were not "asleep," i.e. the living saints, would be "changed," and their incorruptible and mortal bodies would "put on" incorruption and immortality, taking on the image of the heavenly Man, Christ Jesus.

That Paul is looking forward to a new heavenly, glorified condition, at the coming of the Lord, in exchange for his earthly, burdened condition is clearly expressed. While he remained at home in his present body or "tent" – the term "tent" emphasizing a temporary dwelling – which was perishing and in which he "groaned" (same Greek verb translated "groan" as in Rom 8:22,23), he was away from his heavenly home with the Lord

(2 Cor. 5:6-8 - note the meaning of the Greek verbs here in my translation above). Because he was absent from home in the Lord's immediate presence while he remained in his present body he had to walk by faith, not sight, for while in his earthly body he could not see the eternal things (4:18; 5:7); they were unseen; he walked by faith in the Lord's promises of glory. He clearly implies that once he has departed from his present mortal body and has come to that permanent home in company with the Lord, in his heavenly body (5:8), he will then be able to walk by a heavenly, spiritual sight, seeing the eternal things of the Lord, like the angels do.

Paul clearly expected that if he were still alive at the Lord's Parousia (which he preferred, rather than die before the Parousia), he would be taken out of his earthly trial and brought into an eternal weight of glory, and that his mortal frame would be overclothed with life and that he would put on his heavenly body. But if he died before the Parousia He expected to be raised by the power of God at the Parousia and presented with the living saints before God into His glory and receive a heavenly, eternal body. He expected that with his new heavenly body he would then be able to be home in the Lord's presence and have full sight and experience of heavenly realities.

Sealed by the Holy Spirit for inheritance of a heavenly body and life

Paul was confident that this expectation of a heavenly, glorified body in Christ's presence would be fulfilled because he had been sealed by the Holy Spirit as a deposit-guarantee of such consummative blessing, (2 Cor. 5:5). Corresponding ideas of sealing and deposit-guarantee in view of the ultimate fulfillment in glory occur in other NT epistles. Consider Rom 8:17-23. The Roman saints had "the firstfruits of the Holy Spirit," the firstfruits being a guarantee and foretaste of the fullness to come. In the Romans passage the expected fullness is called "the adoption as sons, the redemption of our body," (v.23), and also called being glorified together with Christ and conformed to the image of the glorified Christ. The Romans also were groaning within themselves in their present fallen state like the Corinthians were, and longing for that time of glory. Similarly in Eph 1:13-14 Paul says the Ephesian saints were "sealed with the Holy Spirit as a deposit-guarantee of their inheritance, until the redemption of the purchased possession." And Eph 4:30 - "And grieve not the Holy Spirit by whom you were sealed for the day of redemption." A comparison of these verses would suggest that the "redemption of the purchased possession" of Eph 1:14 is the same blessing discussed in Rom 8:23 "the adoption as sons, the redemption of the body," i.e. the receiving of their glorified bodies and the full revelation of their sonship. Thus the idea of saints having been sealed for a glorious fulfillment of their redemption is a common theme in the NT.

Those Christians who died before the Parousia had been sealed, while they were alive, by the Holy Spirit upon their faith in Christ; sealed for the same hope that Paul expressed here in 2 Cor. 5:1-8.

Note the significance of this sealing: All Christians — whether they had died before the Parousia of Christ or were still alive at the Parousia — ALL had received the SAME sealing as guarantee of the SAME glorious fulfillment to be received on the SAME occasion of the coming of Christ as Judge to give the rewards to his saints. Therefore ALL Christians, whether dead or alive, had the SAME expectation of the same destiny to be given to both of them at the Parousia, the same destiny of a heavenly, incorruptible body and eternal life.

As Paul said, it was only with a new heavenly, spiritual body that the saints could be "at home with the Lord," inheriting the kingdom of God, at his Parousia, (2 Cor. 5:6-8; also note 1 Cor. 15:49-50). All saints (both living and dead) were expecting this same reward. The truth and significance of the sealing cannot permit the view that the saints living at the time of the Parousia would get a different fulfillment from the deceased believers at the Parousia. Whether deceased or living, the sealing signified the same, one and only fulfillment for all pre-Parousia believers at the Parousia.

Appearing at the Judgment Seat

2 Cor. 5:9-11 Therefore we make it our aim, whether present or absent, to be well pleasing to Him. 10 For we must all appear before the judgment seat of Christ, that each one may receive the things *done* in the body, according to what he has done, whether good or bad. 11 Knowing, therefore, the terror of the Lord, we persuade men; but we are well known to God, and I also trust are well known in your consciences.

Paul states that whether he be found still alive ("present" in his earthly body) or deceased ("absent" from his earthly body) at the time of the Parousia, his aim and ambition now was to be well pleasing to the Lord (v.9). For he was acutely aware that all saints - living *and* deceased - would appear before the judgment seat of Christ when Christ came, to be rewarded according to their work done while in the body. This is in accord with the Lord's own words:

> Matt 16:27-28 "For *the Son of Man will come in the glory of His Father* with His angels, and *then He will reward* each according to his works. 28 Assuredly, I say to you, there are some standing here who shall not taste death till they see the Son of Man coming in His kingdom."
>
> Matt 25:31-34 "When *the Son of Man comes in His glory*, and all the holy angels with Him, then *He will sit on the throne of His glory*. 32 All the nations will be gathered before Him, and He will separate them one from another, as a shepherd divides his sheep from the goats. 33 And He will set the sheep on His right hand, but the goats on the left. 34 "Then the King will say to those on His right hand, 'Come, you blessed of My Father, in-

> *herit the kingdom* prepared for you from the foundation of the world.
> Rev. 22:12 And, behold, *I come quickly*; and *my reward is with me, to give every man* according as his work shall be.

Jesus, in the verses above implied that all disciples would receive their rewards at his Parousia. Whether the disciples would be living or deceased at the time of the Parousia - all would meet the Lord and receive their rewards. And the reward for both living and deceased saints would be the actual inheritance of the glorious kingdom of God (i.e. in its consummate reality; the first Christians already had the deposit/firstfruits measure of the kingdom).

Paul knew that whether he remained alive until the Parousia or died before the Parousia, he would nevertheless appear at the judgment throne of Christ, and that at the judgment seat of Christ, at the Parousia, the rewards for all the saints, both dead and alive, according to what they had done in the body would be given, and the saints would fully enter the consummated kingdom of God, partaking of glorified, changed, resurrected, spiritual, heavenly bodies, at home in the immediate presence of the Lord Jesus.

Paul expressed his hope, that he would be rewarded by the Lord as Judge of living and dead in his letter to Timothy, (and note Paul's feeling that he is about to die):

> 2 Tim 4:1, 6-8, 18 I charge *you* therefore before God and the Lord Jesus Christ, *who is about to judge the living and the dead at His appearing and His kingdom*... 6 For I am already being poured out as a drink offering, and the time of my departure is at hand. 7 I have fought the good fight, I have finished the race, I have kept the faith. 8 Finally, there is laid up for me the crown of righteousness, which *the Lord, the righteous Judge, will give to me on that Day, and not to me only but also to all who have loved His appearing*.... 18 And the Lord will deliver me from every evil work and *preserve me for His heavenly kingdom*. To Him *be* glory forever and ever. Amen!

The point I wish to draw attention to here is that Paul expected that the eschatological, consummative reward involving the final glorious destiny for the living *and* the dead believers of all prior history up to that time, would be decided and issued at the Parousia, at the judgment seat of Christ. This was the time when the deceased and living believers were to be presented before God, (2 Cor. 4:14), and when they would inherit the kingdom of God in its fullness. Now Paul taught that "flesh and blood," that is, men in their fallen, earthy bodies, could not inherit the kingdom of God in its consummate form (1 Cor. 15:50), but that all saints needed to put on incorruption and the spiritual body to enter the kingdom. It was at this judgment seat session that the changing of the living saints into their heavenly bodies and the raising of the deceased saints into their heavenly bodies would occur - as discussed by Paul earlier in 2 Cor. 4:14; 5:1-8. Paul's expectation (as given in the 2 Timothy verses just quoted) was that ALL - both deceased and living saints - who had loved and looked forward to the Lord's appearing, would along with himself (and he felt that he would be deceased by that time), be rewarded with the crown of righteousness on that Day when the Judge would reward his living and deceased saints.

There is in this whole section of 2 Cor. 4:13 - 5:10 the clear impression that Paul's expectation was that whether believers were alive or deceased at the time of the Parousia, they would all get their rewards from the Lord and enter the same eternal weight of glory and receive or put on their glorious, heavenly bodies and thereby enter the new realm of being home with the Lord.

Further Note:

Some preterist commentators interpret Paul's use of the terms "heavenly house" and "earthly house" as meaning the heavenly house of the New Covenant system, replacing the earthly tent of the Old Covenant system. But, to me, Paul's frequent mention of the physical body in the chapters 4 and 5 — e.g. the treasure in *earthen vessels* (4:1), carrying about in the *body* the dying of the Lord Jesus that the life of Jesus also may be manifested in our *body* (4:10), delivered to death...life of Jesus in his *mortal flesh* (4:11), *raise us up*, implying his body and soul (4:14), the *outward man* perishing (4:16), at home in the *body*, absent from the Lord (5:6), absent from the *body*, present with the Lord (5:8), rewarded according to deeds done in *the body* (5:10) — make it clear and natural that the terms "tent" and "house" are just figurative terms for the human body.

Peter (no doubt familiar with Paul's writings) used a similar, related term, Greek *skeenoma* (= tent, tabernacle), to describe his failing human body which he was soon to put off, lay aside (2 Pet 1:13, 14). The Lord Jesus' human body is also called a tent or tabernacle – a temporary dwelling: "the Word became flesh and tabernacled (*skeenoo*) among us, (Jn. 1:14). So I see no reason to diverge from what seems a logical and natural flow of thought by Paul in 2 Cor. 5 as referring to the leaving his earthly body behind and taking on a heavenly body in glory at the Lord's Parousia. The theme in 2 Cor. 5:1-8 is the same as in 1 Cor. 15 where the natural, earthy body is to replaced by a spiritual, heavenly body; where the image of the man of dust is to be replaced by the image of the Man from heaven. And it is only with a heavenly body that a man can fully inherit the kingdom of heaven, for flesh and blood (man in his earthy body) cannot so inherit the kingdom.

Note that in all the references to the sealing of the saints by the Holy Spirit and having the Holy Spirit as a guarantee, Paul expects the fullness of blessing for which the saints were sealed to be manifested at the Parousia of Christ. This leaves no place for the theory that the living saints still remained in their earthy bodies amidst the fallenness of earth at the Parousia, while only the deceased entered the fullness of glorification with Christ at the Parousia. All Christians were sealed for the one and the same fullness promised to be revealed at the Parousia. Nowhere in all of this discussion in 2 Cor. 3-5 is there any suggestion that I can see that Paul and his fellow Christians expected at the Parousia to remain on earth in their fallen bodies.

Paul's language of receiving an eternal weight of glory and a heavenly body and being present with the Lord, having received their eternal rewards from the glorified Jesus, is describing the ultimate, the consummation of a believer's hopes and longings — of glorification with Christ, beyond which there is no higher experience or privilege. Nowhere does Paul imply an intermediate stage expected by the living saints at the Parousia, of a glory commingled with the continued earthy experience of corruption, weakness and dishonor of their mortal bodies, the enmity of the flesh, the imperfectness of minds still needing renewing, the groaning for release, and the hostility of the fallen world around them. Rather, the passages studied above reveal that all saints were expecting at the Parousia complete redemption, perfect glorification, release from all that spoke of mortality or corruption, and the glory of being present with Christ in a way that just was not possible while on earth in a natural, mortal condition.

Continued in Chapter 8

Chapter 8

Relevant Scriptures Regarding The First Christians' Hope of Consummation at the Parousia of Jesus Christ, circa AD 70

(Continued from Chapter 7)

This chapter continues the examination of the first Christians' expectations of glorification that they would receive on the occasion of the Parousia of Christ.

(8) Philippians 3:17 - 4:1

17 Brethren, join in following my example, and note those who so walk, as you have us for a pattern. 18 For many walk, of whom I have told you often, and now tell you even weeping, that they are the enemies of the cross of Christ: 19 whose end is destruction, whose god is their belly, and whose glory is in their shame —who set their mind on earthly things. 20 For our citizenship is in heaven, from which we also eagerly wait for the Savior, the Lord Jesus Christ, 21 who will transform our lowly body for it to become [*so reads the Greek*] conformed to His glorious body, according to the working by which He is able even to subdue all things to Himself. 1 Therefore, my beloved and longed-for brethren, my joy and crown, so stand fast in the Lord, beloved.

In this passage Paul seems to be especially focusing on the lot of the living believers at the Parousia of Christ.

Citizenship in heaven

Paul says that the home country of Christians in which they hold citizenship is heaven. "For our citizenship exists in heaven." (Gr. ὑπάρχει, *huparchei* = exists, is established; which is a stronger translation than "is" in the KJV). This citizenship is far more important and impressive than the earthly Roman citizenship of which the people of the Roman colony of Philippi could boast.

> The Greek word (πολίτευμα) translated "conversation" in the KJV has the ideas of "our state or country; *our citizenship: our life as citizens*. We are but pilgrims on earth; how then should we mind earthly things?" (*Jamieson, Fausset and Brown*, Commentary).

This idea of the believers having their true citizenship and home in heaven is also a theme in the letter to the Hebrews. The Old Testament saints knew that they had no lasting homeland on earth, but "waited for the city which has foundations, whose builder and maker *is* God," (Heb 11:10). They "confessed that they were strangers and pilgrims on the earth. For those who say such things declare plainly that they seek a homeland. And truly if they had called to mind that *country* from which they had come out, they would have had opportunity to return. But now they desire a better, that is, a heavenly *country*. Therefore God ...has prepared a city for them," (Heb 11:13-16). New Testament saints were waiting to enter that same heavenly city/ homeland: they had drawn near "to Mount Zion and to the city of the living God, the heavenly Jerusalem," (Heb 12:22), and were seeking the full experience of that city, "For here we have no continuing city, but we seek the one to come (Heb 13:14)."

Our lowly estate (v. 21)

Paul refers to the saints' present bodily state as "our lowly body," or "the body of our humiliation." The *Online Bible* Greek Lexicon gives the meaning of the word describing "our body" as:

1) lowness, low estate;
2) metaphorically: spiritual abasement, leading one to perceive and lament his (moral) littleness and guilt."

"The body of our humiliation, and low estate" refers to the fallen natural body, vividly described in 1 Cor. 15:42-54 as natural, corruptible, dishonorable, weak, earthy, mortal. The same thought is in Rom 8:20-21, where "the creation" is described as "subjected to vanity, futility, inappropriateness," and enduring a "bondage of corruption." It is while in this earthy body that God's people groan for release and redemption of the body, groan to have their mortality swallowed up by life and immortality (Rom 8:23; 2 Cor. 5:4; 1 Cor. 15:53). While a believer still bears the image of the man of dust, in a fallen, earthy, natural body there exists an inappropriateness for full participation in the perfections of the kingdom of God in the presence of God.

Paul was grieved that all around were nominal believers who were losing their focus on Christ by indulging wrongfully in earthly things (Phil 3:18-19); sadly the earthy, natural body and mind have a natural affinity with things of sense in this world, not with spiritual, invisible things of heaven. That is why believers are in a constant battle and groaning within themselves until they can change the body of their lowly estate for a glorious, spiritual body.

The Savior from heaven

While on earth, away from the homeland in heaven, and while having earthly bodies and not their heavenly ones, (remember that "flesh and blood cannot inherit the kingdom of God" see 1 Cor. 15:47-50 and 2 Cor. 5:6-8 discussed above), Christians are not able to enjoy the fulfillment of their entitlement to the inheritance of heaven purchased by the Lord Jesus for them. So the saints of Paul's day were eagerly waiting for the Savior from heaven, the Lord Jesus Christ, who had promised to take them to where he is with the Father. The term "Savior" seems deliberately used to convey the sense that the saints expected the Lord Jesus to work a great deliverance for them at his coming: a saving them completely from the fallenness of this earthly life, and from their humiliated bodies and imperfect minds with their sin and weakness, and a bringing them into the glory of their homeland, the "heavenly country," and "the city which has foundations," (along with all the deceased believers, including those of Heb. 11), into heaven itself, with glorified, spiritual bodies fit to inhabit that place and to fully enjoy fellowship with God. Jesus is Lord, and he had the power and authority to fulfill his will.

Salvation to Glory

Paul describes the salvation expected from the Savior: He "will transform our lowly body for it to become conformed to His glorious body." The verb "will transform" is from the Greek verb *metaschematizo* = to change the appearance, fashion, shape; (a derivative of Gr. *schema* = the habitus, as comprising everything in a person which strikes the senses, the figure, bearing, discourse, actions, manner of life, etc (*TDNT*); shape, fashion, mode, (external) condition; [cf. Gr. *morphee*, discussed next paragraph]).

The use of *metaschematizo* in this context implies that the Lord requires the saints to have a body new in fashion or condition, and that the new state of body is not derived from any powers or qualities inherent in the old body, nor does the old body have any expression in the new fashion. The Lord will apply his effective working in this situation, he will come with a power outside of the old body, a power impossible to the old body, and will change it into a different condition or quality.

The change or transformation done by the Lord results in the old, lowly body becoming something different: "The Lord Jesus Christ will transform [Gr. *metaschematizo*] our lowly body for it to become [Gr. *ginomai*] conformed [Gr. *summorphos*] to his glorious body."

"Conformed" is the translation of the Greek adjective *summorphos* = having the same form as another, conformed to. *Summorphos* is from *sun* = with, and *morphee* = form. *Morphee* refers to the form of an entity: not merely to the outward appearance or *schema*, but to where the outward appearance or quality is the expression of the inner essence of that entity. "Conformed to his glorious body (or, the body of his glory)" means that the saints will have the same form (*sun* + *morphee*) as the Lord's glorious body which he has in heaven; that is, where the appearance and condition of the saints' new body is an expression of the same inner power and essence that abides in the Lord and expresses itself in the Lord's glorious body.

We can put it this way: The Lord changes the *schema* of the present body by the process called *metaschematizo*. The present *schema* of the Christians is earthy and corruptible. The Lord changes this present earthly *schema* for it to become a body with a *schema* that is spiritual, heavenly, incorruptible, honorable, powerful (see 1 Cor. 15:42ff), having perfect affinity with and giving true expression to the new spiritual, eternal life within the believer. The old fallen, earthly body could never express the inner heavenly life commenced in a recreated, born-from-above believer. So the Lord gives a heavenly body that expresses perfectly the heavenly life within, a body that is able to inhabit heaven. Where there is a *schema* that fully expresses the inner essence, then it is called a *morphee*. The believer's form (*morphee*) thus becomes like the Lord's form (*morphee*).

Paul says, in expanded form: "We eagerly wait for the Savior, the Lord Jesus Christ who will remodel the whole outward appearance and fashion and condition of the body of our humiliation for it to become a form just like the Lord's body of glory, i.e. where the schema of our glorified body has perfect affinity with, and is an expression of, the inner life and power of God just like in the case of the Lord's glorified body."

The saints awaited the Savior, for they needed his final salvation to bring them to glory. Elsewhere Paul expresses this: "Therefore I endure all things for the sake of the elect, that they also may obtain *the salvation which is in Christ Jesus with eternal glory*." 2 Tim. 2:10

Consistent expectations:
- The "body of humiliation" of Phil 3:21 is the "flesh and blood" body, "natural, mortal, corruptible, dishonorable, weak, earthy" discussed in 1 Cor. 15:42-53; it is the "earthly house," "tent," "the mortal" of 2 Cor. 5:1-8, and is subject to "vanity, futility" and "corruption" as in Rom 8:20-21. It is the "image of the man of dust" of 1 Cor. 15:48-49.
- The "transformation" of Phil 3:21 is the same as the "change" of 1 Cor. 15:52 and the "being clothed upon/over" of 2 Cor. 5:2,4, and the "redemption of our body" of Rom 8:23.
- The new body which is "conformed to the Lord's glorious body," spoken of in Phil 3:21, is the "spiritual, immortal, incorruptible, honorable, powerful, heavenly" body discussed in 1 Cor. 15:42-53, and the "house not made with hands, eternal in the heavens," "the house from heaven," that which is full of "life," as in 2 Cor. 5:1-8.
- This transformation and conformation to the Lord's body of glory in Phil 3:21 is the same occasion as "be(ing) glorified together [with Christ]," and "the revealing of the sons of God...the liberty of the glory of the children of God...the adoption, the redemption of the body" of Rom. 8:17-23; it is being glorified so as to be conformed to the image of God's Son, as in Rom 8:29-30. This is exactly what Paul said to the Corinthians in 1 Cor. 15:42-49 - the saints, the heavenly ones united to the Lord of heaven, would, at the Parousia, bear the image of the heavenly Man, instead of the image of the earthy man of dust (vv. 47-49). Such was the hope for living and deceased saints at the Parousia.

Such an understanding of Phil 3:20-21 is perfectly consistent with the teachings in all the other passages already studied.

Just a few extra thoughts on this passage:

Where is Christ's citizenship? This letter to the Philippians (in chapter 2) answers this: His homeland, His citizenship is with the Father, glorified and exalted in his presence. He left that heavenly sphere to be incarnated and accomplish his atoning work for his elect, and he returned to that sphere as his eternal reward, (see Phil 2:5-11). During his time on earth Jesus was acutely aware that his citizenship was in heaven with the Father. Repeatedly he said he had come from the Father in heaven, and was going back to his Father in heaven (see Gospel of John). The Hebrews epistle also especially makes it clear where Jesus' homeland is: it is at throne of his Father in the heavenly Holy of Holies; and he is there as the forerunner for his people who will follow him.

As in the case of Jesus, the citizenship of the saints is in heaven; their homeland, their citizenship, is in the heavenly country (as the writer to the Hebrews calls it, and where, he says, Abraham, etc., were all expecting to enter at the Parousia). Paul was expecting the Savior to come — what for? To take His people home, just as He returned home when His time on earth was accomplished! At the Parousia of Christ the lifespan on earth of the Christians living at that time would be accomplished. The Lord, the Savior would take them home to glory. And to suit them for their true homeland he would transform them to have spiritual, heavenly, glorified bodies, like his. In this way the saints would be glorified together with Christ, sharing the same citizenship in heaven with him.

Regarding us post-Parousia Christians, our citizenship is also in heaven. At the end of our allotted time on earth, when we die, the great Savior will likewise grant us glorious bodies like his glorified body so that we can join all the saints who have gone before us, in the beauties of the heavenly realm where Christ and the Father live.

Footnote on Greek transformation words

For those interested, here are some further thoughts on the relationship between *schema* and *morphee*, and *metaschematizo* and *metamorphoo*.

Where entity 1 is said to have the same *morphee* (form) as entity 2, it automatically follows that the *schema* of entity 1 is the same as entity 2, as well as their inner essences being the same. Or to say it the other way round, where the *schema* of entity 1 is the same as entity 2, and entity 1 has the same essence and spirit as entity 2, then it is true to say that entity 1 has the same *morphee* as entity 2, and that entity 1 is conformed (*summorphos*) to entity 2.

If there occurs, in a case where initially the *schema* does not match the inner life and essence of an entity, a change (*metaschematizo*) in the *schema* to the point where the *schema* comes to truly express the inner life, it is called a *metamorphoo*. This is what happened in Jesus transfiguration (*metamorphoo*) on the mount, (e.g. Matt 17:2, Lk. 9:29); his outward schema changed from an earthly one to a glorious one which expressed more fully his inner deity.

Rom 12:2 deals with behavioral *schema*, not bodily, but the same idea holds. In Rom 12:2 the born-from-above believer is told not to adopt the same behavioral *schema* (*suschematizo*) as that which characterizes the world, for such a *schema* is not in accord with the new spiritual life implanted in him; therefore he is to be transformed (*metamorphoo*), i.e. he is to have his behavioral *schema* changed such that it becomes a Christ-like behavioral *schema* matching and expressing his new life within. The deceitfulness of Satan and his false workers in 2 Cor. 11:13,14,15 is that they transform themselves (*metaschematizo*), that is, they change their behavioral schema, into what appears to be good when in reality such behavior does not come from a good inner nature at all.

The saints in Phil 3:21 were to undergo bodily what the saints in Rom 12:2 were to undergo behaviorally; the saints in Phil 3:21 were to undergo a *metamorphoo*, i.e. a change (*metaschematizo*) in their bodily *schema* resulting in its truly corresponding to the perfected divine life within, such that the new body had the same form (*summorphee*) as the Lord's glorious body.

So *metamorphoo* = the process of changing the *schema*, *metaschematizo*, so as to give a resultant *schema* which truly corresponds with the inner essence of the entity involved; thereby producing a true *morphee*.

Morphee = the case where the schema of an entity corresponds with the inner essence of that entity.

(9) Colossians 3:1-4

If then you were raised with Christ, seek those things which are above, where Christ is, sitting at the right hand of God. 2 Set your mind on things above, not on things on the earth. 3 For you died, and your life is hidden with Christ in God. 4 When Christ who is our life *appears*, then you also *will appear* with Him in glory. [Col. 3:1-4]

The Christians' Hope of Glory and Life.

Paul had earlier in this epistle remarked on the Colossian Christians' hope, "the hope which is laid up for you in heaven," (1:5). It was a "hope of glory" secured by the fact that Christ was already in them, (1:27). Paul then further elaborates on this hope in Col. 3:4. The hope laid up in heaven consisted in the appearing of the Lord Jesus for them, and in their appearing or being manifested with him in glory.

The verb translated "appear/s" in Col. 3:4 is from the Greek verb *phaneroo* = to make manifest or visible or known what has been hidden or unknown, to manifest, whether by words, or deeds, or in any other way, (from *Online Bible* Greek Dictionary). See the following translations of Col. 3:4–

- Whenever Christ our life is revealed, then also you will be revealed with Him in glory. (*Green's Literal Translation*)
- When the Christ—our life—may be manifested, then also you with him shall be manifested in glory. (*Young's Literal Translation*)

This manifestation or appearing or revealing of Christ is referring to the Lord's Parousia which the first Christians expected to occur soon. Gr. *phaneroo* is also used in 1 Pet. 5:4 and in 1 Jn. 2:28; 3:3 referring to the second coming of Christ. See also 1 Tim 4:1 "I charge you therefore before God and the Lord Jesus Christ, who is about to judge the living and the dead according to his *appearing* (Gr. *epiphaneia*) and his kingdom."

Paul understood that when Jesus was manifested at his second coming, the saints (living and deceased) would be manifested in glory with him.

The Christians already had new spiritual life in Christ, and indeed had Christ as their life. ("For me, to live is Christ." " Christ lives in me; and the life which I now live in the flesh I live by faith in the Son of God." Phil 1:21; Gal 2:20). However, what they had before the Parousia was a deposit measure of life. Their true life in its consummative fullness was hidden securely for them with Christ in God awaiting the Parousia. At Christ's Parousia eternal life in its fullness would be revealed and experienced by them; their union with Christ, which was now only experienced in its deposit measure, would be fully manifested.

Glory with Christ.

When one compares Col. 3:4 with Rom. 8:17-23, 2 Cor. 4:16 – 5:10, and Phil 3:20-21 we see the similar themes of the saints being glorified with the Lord at his coming, and the revealing/manifestation of the sons of God in glory. The statement of Col. 3:4b, "you will be manifested with him in glory," is surely equivalent to Rom 8:17, 19, 21 "glorified together [with Christ]...the revealing of the sons of God...the liberty of the glory of the children of God." It was God's purpose to "bring many sons to [or, into] glory," (Heb 2:10) when the Lord Jesus would appear to those eagerly waiting for him (Heb 9:28).

For the saints to "appear/be manifested...in glory" means to appear or be manifested in incorruptible, glorious, spiritual, heavenly bodies like the body of the glorified Lord Jesus, (1 Cor. 15:42ff; Phil 3:21). Passages of scripture already studied make it clear that the state of glory is the opposite to man's fallen, earthy, corruptible, dishonorable state. There is nothing higher than "glorified together with Christ" and "be(ing) manifested with him in glory." This is what is meant by Christians being co-heirs with Christ (Rom 8:17) - to be with him in his glory, the saints sharing his glory and appearing in glory.

The image of the glorified Lord
Let us consider the mention of the image of God and Christ in Col. 3:9-11–

(Y)ou have put off the old man with his deeds; 10 and have put on the new man, which is being renewed in knowledge *according to the image of Him that created him*: 11 Where...Christ is all, and in all.

The purpose of God is to bring his saints to the point where they are conformed fully to the image of Christ, when Christ will really (not just potentially) be all in all, when the new life of Christ which is in them, in which the saints are being renewed now, will totally fill them, and the Christians will have no portion of the legacy of Adam's fall in them at all in spirit, soul or body. To be fully conformed to the image of the Creator, and having Christ filling all in all, is the same thing as saying that the saints will appear with him in glory. In 1 Cor. 15 we have already studied the goal of God — to totally deliver his people from the earthy image of Adam the man of dust, and totally conform them to the image of the heavenly Man, Jesus Christ. To appear with Christ in glory at the Parousia is the same thing as appearing fully conformed to the image of the glorified Jesus.

The phrase "with him" in Col. 3:4 - "you shall be manifested *with him* in glory"- is used in eschatological contexts (see "forever with the Lord" in 1 Thess 4; and "at home with the Lord," 2 Cor. 5:8) to refer to a being with the Lord in a manner not possible on earth, a being with him in a perfected and glorified state.

From the time that Paul gave this wonderful encouragement to the saints at Colossae to the time of the Lord's appearing, we must remember that many Christians were killed under the Neronic persecutions. No doubt, the Christians would have held such a hope of glory with Christ at his appearing very dear to their troubled hearts as they braved the constant threat of death.

For us post-Parousia Christians, "Christ is our life," and we "seek the things above where Christ is." We have the wonderful hope of also appearing with Christ in glory when we die.

(10) 1 Jn. 2:28; 3:1-3
And now, little children, abide in Him, that when He *appears*, we may have confidence and not be ashamed before Him at His coming.... 3:1 Behold what manner of love the Father has bestowed on us, that we should be called children of God! Therefore the world does not know us, because it did not know Him. 2 Beloved, now we are children of God; and it has not yet *been revealed* what we shall be, but we know that when He *is revealed*, we shall be like Him, for we shall see Him as He is. 3 And everyone who has this hope in Him purifies himself, just as He is pure.

The manifestation of the Lord and the children of God.
In these verses John is referring to the same expected event as Paul in Col. 3:4, in almost identical language. The verbs translated "ap-

pear" in 1 Jn 2:28, and "revealed" in 1 Jn 3:2 (in NKJV) are from the same Greek verb as in Col. 3:4, *phaneroo* (φανερόω) which means to make manifest or visible or known what has been hidden or unknown, to manifest, whether by words, or deeds, or in any other way (from *Online Bible Greek Dictionary*). Like Paul, John is saying that the hope of the saints is that at the appearing/manifestation of the Lord Jesus [in glory] the saints would be manifested in their glorified state.

Note the emphasis on the manifestation/appearing of the Lord and the saints at his Parousia:

"...when He appears/is manifested [Greek φανερόω, *phaneroo*]...and it has not yet been manifested [*phaneroo*] what we shall be, but we know that when He is manifested [*phaneroo*], we shall be like Him, for we shall see Him as He is."

It is not yet manifested what we shall be, says John, but when Christ is manifested then we shall be manifested in our true full nature as children of God; we shall be manifested in his likeness.

The following passages are clearly speaking of the same great occasion of the Lord's Parousia, when the Lord Jesus would appear/be manifested/revealed in his glory and his saints would be manifested in glory with him:

Jn. 3:2 "...it has not yet *been revealed* (*phaneroo*) what we shall be, but we know that when He *is revealed* (*phaneroo*), we shall be like Him, for we shall see Him as He is."
Col. 3:4 "When Christ who is our life *appears* (*phaneroo*), then you *will be manifested* (*phaneroo*) with him in glory."
2 Tim. 4:1 I charge *you* therefore before God and the Lord Jesus Christ, who will judge the living and the dead at *His appearing* [*epiphaneia*] and His kingdom...
1 Pet 5:1,4 The elders who are among you I exhort, I who am a fellow ...partaker of the glory that is about to be (*mello*) revealed (*apokalupto*)...and when the Chief Shepherd *appears* (*phaneroo*), you will receive the crown of glory that does not fade away.

"We shall be like him." (v. 2)

John says, "It has not yet been manifested what we [the children of God, v. 1] shall be;" but when Christ is manifested, "like him we shall be" (word order in the Greek). "Like" Christ, or "resembling" Christ (Greek ὅμοιος, *homoios*) - that is the form the manifestation of the saints would take. John is clearly expecting a new mode of being for the children. In saying, "we shall be like him," John is describing the nature of the revealing or manifestation of the saints.

At present the saints are not seen or known for whom they really are — the beloved children of God; just as the Lord was not seen or known in the glory of whom he really was by the world when he walked the earth. At present, although they are already children of God, it had not yet been revealed or manifested what they would be in their consummated saved state. The fullness of blessings purchased for them by Christ as his children (Eph 1:3) had not yet been fully manifested. The "all things" which the Father had prepared to give them with His Son (Rom 8:32) – and the context shows that the "all things" have to do with blessings bringing them to glorification with Christ – were still to be granted and worked out for them. When that fullness would be revealed or manifested, the children would appear in the glory that perfectly accorded with the fact that they were the redeemed children of the living and true God, just as Jesus was vindicated as the obedient Son of God in his exaltation and glorification following his resurrection (e.g. Phil 2:9-11). Then they would appear free from all that would remind them of their previous fallenness and lack of intimacy with their heavenly Father. I believe that John's reference to the manifestation of "being like him" can only refer to being like the Lord in his glorious mode of existence in heaven, as referred to by Paul in Phil 3:21, etc.

> "We shall be like him" in body, fashioned like to his glorious body, in immortality and incorruption, in power, in glory, and spirituality, in a freedom from all imperfections, sorrows, afflictions, and death; and in soul, which likeness will lie in perfect knowledge of divine things, and in complete holiness; (John Gill, *Exposition on the Bible*, on 1 Jn. 3:2, *Online Bible* CD).

I believe the following are all *parallel descriptions of the glorified state "like him"* that the saints would experience and be manifested in at the Parousia:

> Jn. 3:2 we know that when He is revealed, *we shall be like Him*
> Phil 3:21 who will transform our lowly body that it may be *conformed to His glorious body*, according to the working by which He is able even to subdue all things to Himself.
> 1 Cor. 15:49 And as we have borne the image of the man of dust, *we shall also bear the image of the heavenly Man*.
> Rom 8:29 For whom He foreknew, He also predestined to be *conformed to the image of His Son*, that He might be the firstborn among many brethren.

"For we shall see him as he is." (v. 2)

Qualifying the statement, "we shall be like him," there follows an explanation: "for we shall see him as he is." The clear implication of the explanatory clause "for we shall see him as he is" is that while in their present fallen body and mind Christians do not have the capacity or ability to see the Lord as he is, so they necessarily have to walk by faith, not by sight. But as Paul further says the time was soon to come when the saints would be transformed with an immortal body and would be at home with the Lord in heaven, and then they would be able to walk by sight viewing the glory of the Lord and the eternal things of heaven with a new spiritual vision. "We shall be like him, [*and how can we know this?*] Because we shall see him as he is; for the only way anyone can have the capacity or ability to see him, is for them to be like him in spiritual, heavenly soul and body like him."

To see the Lord as he is — such was their hope. At the time the apostles wrote they obviously did not yet see the Lord "as he is," but it was their hope to so see him when he appeared.

> 1 Pet. 1:8 whom *having not seen* you love. Though *now you do not see Him*, yet believing, you rejoice with joy inexpressible and full of glory. *[the implication is that while "now" you don't see him, the time is soon coming when you will].*
> 2 Cor. 5:6-8 So we are always confident, (even) knowing that while we remain at home in the body we are away from home from the Lord. 7 For *we walk by faith, not by sight.* 8 We are confident, yes, well pleased rather to be away from home from the body and to be at home with the Lord. *[Again the implication is that when the saints change their old body for the new heavenly body and they are at home then with the Lord, they will have true sight of the Lord].*
> 1 Cor. 13:12 For *now we see in a mirror, dimly, but then face to face. Now I know in part, but then I shall know just as I also am known. [Then, no dim seeing by faith, but clear seeing the Lord].*

John says, "When He is revealed...we shall *see* him as he is" when he appears. The Greek word for "see" is a form of *horao* (ὁράω), which *Strong's Greek Dictionary* (#3708) says has the meaning: "to stare at." Compare #3700 – [optomai] a closely related alternate form which means: "to gaze (that is, with wide open eyes, as at something remarkable)" differing from a normal, casual voluntary seeing of things. The Christians were expecting to have a remarkable vision of the glorious Lord at his coming.

This is confirmed by Heb 9:28–

Christ was offered once to bear the sins of many. To those who eagerly wait for Him *He will appear* a second time, apart from sin, for salvation. [Heb 9:28]

The words in Heb 9:28, "he will appear," are actually from the same Greek verb as used in 1 Jn. 3:2. "He will appear" is the 3rd person future *passive* indicative of the verb *horao* (or its closely related form, *optanomai*). Now the passive form of a Greek verb usually means the action described by the verb is received, rather than done, by the subject. (E.g. "he will see or gaze" is third person, future *active* of the verb "to gaze;" while "he will be seen and gazed upon" is the third person future *passive* of the verb "to gaze" - the action is received by the subject). The writer to the Hebrews says that at his second coming Jesus' intention was to be seen, beheld, gazed upon, by his waiting followers. In the passive Greek *horao/optanomai* means "to be seen, gazed upon," "to appear so as to be seen," or "to reveal oneself." What Heb 9:28 is actually saying is that Christ "will be seen, beheld, gazed upon, will reveal himself so as to be seen, a second time." (See my Further Note at the end of this section).

Note the correspondence of ideas between Heb 9:28 and 1 Jn. 3:2. Both speak of the occasion of the Lord's second coming; both speak of the Christians seeing Jesus in his glory; and both speak of this seeing him as correlative to a wonderful change in the Christians' lives, called "salvation" in Heb 9:28, and called "being like him," in 1 Jn 3:2. In this course of studies we have seen that the great salvation promised to the first Christians at the Parousia was expected to consist of being conformed to the image of the glorified Christ.

I think John's reference to "seeing" the Lord, has not to with any materialistic seeing with the physical eyesight of their mortal bodies, but to a "seeing" the Lord in his glory with an ability given by the Holy Spirit, an ability of the new heavenly, spiritual body that will have a capacity for heavenly vision; an ability and capacity of seeing the Lord like the angels in heaven see him. The Christian's sight of the Lord will no longer be dim, and by faith, as it is while in these mortal, earthy bodies; it will involve a clear and intimate, seeing face-to-face. Christians will be in that sense like angels: "in heaven their angels always *see* the face of My Father who is in heaven," (Matt 18:10); for in their glorified state, "they [the saints] shall *see* His face, and His name [shall be] on their foreheads," Rev. 22:4.

The psalmist prophesied in a similar vein to the apostle John, with a desire to have the Lord's likeness, and to see him as he is:

Psa. 17:15 As for me, *I will see Your face* in righteousness; I shall be satisfied *when I awake in Your likeness.*

Our hope, as post-Parousia Christians, is that when we die, we will immediately be resurrected to be like him and we too will see the Lord as he is; and the glory of our being children of God, which in this life is only manifested in a partial, firstfruits measure, will then be manifested in full measure.

A further note on the text of 1 Jn. 3:2

In view of the Greek of 1 Jn. 3:2 – which is literally, "If (Greek *ean*) He is manifested, we shall be like Him, for we shall see Him as He is," – one "remained-on-earth" preterist has focused on the Greek word *ean* ("if") and has suggested that John, by using the word *"if"* here, was expressing a doubt as to whether any of his readers would actually see the Lord at his appearing. Let me make a few comments on this.

1. All other references to the Lord's appearing or manifestation in the NT give the clear teaching that *all saints were expecting and eagerly looking for the Lord's appearing and to the great changes that his appearing would bring them.* (I have given some passages above). There is not a hint elsewhere that the manifestation or appearing of Christ was only a doubtful possibility, an "if." (See the following, all containing the Greek words to do with Christ's appearing/manifestation; Col. 3:4; 2 Tim 4:1; 1 Tim 6:14; Tit. 2:13; Heb 9:28). Surely John in 1 Jn 3:2 is *not* teaching a different idea; John would not mean that Christ's manifestation to the saints is only a possibility and that their seeing him was only a possibility.

2. John often uses the Greek conjunction *"ean"* in situations where it does *not* carry an idea of "if" in the sense of uncertainty, or mere possibility. John often uses *"ean"* with a meaning of: "when," or "in the case that," where a case is proposed and then a response to that case is stated. Several of the standard translations render it "when."

    Consider the several examples below, in each of which John uses *"ean"* in proposing a case, preparatory to, or following on from, a main statement that emphasizes a particular fact. In each of the verses below one may substitute for "if" the words *"in the case that"* or "when" in order to gain the true sense. The "ean" as used here is not introducing an uncertainty or contingency, but rather a focus on a particular case.

    Jn. 8:36 If [*ean* - "In the case that"] the Son therefore shall make you free, ye shall be free indeed.
    Jn. 12:32-34 And I, if [*ean* - "in the case that"] I be lifted up from the earth, will draw all *men* unto me. 33 This he said, signifying by what death he was about to die. 34 ...how can you say 'The son of man must be lifted up?'
    Jn. 14:3 And if [*ean*] I go and prepare a place for you, I will come again, and receive you unto myself; that where I am, *there* ye may be also.
    Jn. 16:7 Nevertheless I tell you the truth; It is expedient for you that I go away: for if I go not away, the Comforter will not come unto you; but if [*ean*] I depart, I will send him unto you.
    1 Jn. 2:1 My little children, these things write I unto you, that ye sin not. And if [*ean*] any man sin, we have an advocate with the Father, Jesus Christ the righteous:
    1 Jn. 2:3 And hereby we do know that we know him, if [*ean*] we keep his commandments.

1 Jn. 2:24 Let that therefore abide in you, which ye have heard from the beginning. If [*ean*] that which ye have heard from the beginning shall remain in you, ye also shall continue in the Son, and in the Father.

In the same way, the "if" in 1 Jn. 3:2 is not introducing a clause of uncertainty or possibility such as: He may be revealed or he may not be revealed; but it is the "if" of proposing a case, preparatory to emphasizing the main fact: "In the case that (or "when") he is manifested, we know that the children shall be like him." The context of 1 Jn. 3:2 speaks of the privilege of the children of God. John says the world does not appreciate their significance, just as the world did not appreciate Jesus' significance. But the saints knew that "in the case that He is manifested" they would be like him, they would be manifested in their true glory with Him (as said in Col. 3:4), for they would see him as he is. In this case the King James Version, "We know that *when* he is manifested, we shall be like him," is a satisfactory translation.

3. The suggestion that John is presenting an uncertainty regarding Jesus being manifested and only a possibility that the saints would see him as he is, just does not make sense of the passage. John says, "We know..." (1 Jn 3:2). What real encouragement or sense is there in the paradoxical saying: "We *know* a possibility; we *know* something that may be or may not be?" Note also that 1 Jn. 3:3 says that "this hope" in a Christian, viz., the hope of becoming like the Lord when he is revealed, has a purifying force. Now in the NT the Christian hope is always based on the certainty and imminency of the final events as promised by the Lord. True biblical hope is never grounded in just possibilities. The saints *knew* that when Christ was manifested in glory, they would be like him, manifested in glory with him, for they would see him as he is, would see his face. This was a certain hope.

(11) 1 Peter
1 Pet 1:3-5; 13 Blessed be the God and Father of our Lord Jesus Christ, who according to His abundant mercy has begotten us again to *a living hope* through the resurrection of Jesus Christ from the dead, 4 to *an inheritance incorruptible and undefiled and that does not fade away, reserved in heaven for you,* 5 who are kept by the power of God through faith *for salvation ready to be revealed* in the last time.... 13 Therefore gird up the loins of your mind, be sober, and *rest your hope fully upon the grace that is to be brought to you at the revelation of Jesus Christ*;

1 Pet 4:5, 7 They will give an account to Him who is ready to judge the living and the dead. 7 But the end of all things is at hand; therefore be serious and watchful in your prayers.

1 Pet 4:12-13 Beloved, do not think it strange concerning the fiery trial which is to try you, as though some strange thing happened to

you; 13 but rejoice to the extent that you partake of Christ's sufferings, that *when His glory is revealed, you may also be glad with exceeding joy*. 14 If you are reproached for the name of Christ, blessed *are you*, for *the Spirit of glory and of God rests upon you*.
1 Pet 5:1-4, 10. 1 The elders who are among you I exhort, I who am a fellow elder and a witness of the sufferings of Christ, and *also a partaker of the glory that is about to be revealed*: 2 Shepherd the flock of God which is among you, serving as overseers, not by compulsion but willingly, not for dishonest gain but eagerly; 3 nor as being lords over those entrusted to you, but being examples to the flock; 4 and *when the Chief Shepherd appears* (Greek *phaneroo*), *you will receive the crown of glory that does not fade away*.... 10 ...the God of all grace, ...*called us to His eternal glory* by Christ Jesus...

These texts in 1 Peter speak of the same exciting themes we noticed throughout the New Testament: viz., the soon-expected coming of Christ, the revealing of his glory, the concurrent receiving of glory by the saints, the salvation ready to be revealed, and the eternal inheritance about to be inherited.

A living hope through the resurrection of Christ

Peter refers to the living hope of an eternal inheritance reserved in heaven for the saints. This hope is secured and sustained by the fact of the resurrection of Jesus Christ. The clear implication behind these statements of Peter is that the inheritance reserved in heaven is of such a nature that no natural, earthy man can inherit or attain to it. A man needs to be the recipient of resurrection power - in his spirit and in his body - before he can partake of this heavenly inheritance. The resurrected Jesus is the firstfruits of a resurrected family of saints (1 Cor. 15:20-23). The resurrection of Jesus is the guarantee and power source for raising fallen man into a heavenly inheritance. By the grace and mercy of God and through the resurrection of Christ, fallen men are firstly made alive in their spirit together with Christ, raised from their spiritual death, "begotten again," as Peter calls it, born of the Spirit. Secondly, through the resurrection of Christ (and his subsequent exaltation which is the climax of his resurrection, see 3:21c-22), there is guaranteed to the believer the raising of a new heavenly body that corresponds with his already renewed spirit, and participation in the eternal realm of the kingdom of God. This is the living hope of these already born again saints: to be raised with glorified bodies and to share in heavenly, sinless, fellowship with their Lord in glory.

An eternal, heavenly inheritance

It would be at the coming of Christ that the saints would experience that perfect inheritance reserved in heaven for them (1:4), an inheritance which involved sharing in the Lord's "eternal glory" (1 Pet 5:10).

Paul also refers to "the hope which is laid up for you in heaven, of which you heard before in the word of the truth of the gospel," (Col. 1:5).

What Peter calls the "inheritance reserved in heaven," the writer to the Hebrews calls the "eternal inheritance" (Heb 9:15), which in the context of Hebrews means entering the "heavenly country," of sharing with Jesus and God the Father in the heavenly Holy of Holies — which both living and deceased saints were expecting to enter at the Parousia.

Peter refers to the expected heavenly inheritance as "an inheritance incorruptible and undefiled and that does not fade away." The description is of an "incorruptible" inheritance. This reminds one of Paul's words in 1 Cor. 15 and 2 Cor. 5 where it is said that the saints hope to put on "incorruptibility," and immortality, at the Parousia, and also reminds one of the words in Phil 3:21 where the "body of our humiliation" will become like the Lord's glorious body.

Peter's expectation matches the expectation expressed in all the other passages discussed above — the expectation that at the coming of Christ the living saints (along with the deceased saints) would fully enter their heavenly inheritance with Christ, where there is no corruption, but all is of heavenly quality. I believe that the eternal inheritance is an all-encompassing term composed of all the various consummate blessings listed in section 8 of Chapter 2, *New Covenant Blessings – Deposit and Fullness*. The eternal inheritance is equivalent to what Peter elsewhere calls "the everlasting kingdom of our Lord and Savior Jesus Christ," (2 Pet 1:11), that the saints were to seek to enter.

A Revelation of Christ, of Salvation, and of Glory - for all Christians (whether living or dead) to partake of, at the Parousia.

While with Jesus in his earthly ministry, Peter learned the special nature of God's *revelation* [Gr. *apokalupto* (verb) and *apokalupsis* (noun)]. He had heard Jesus say that it was only by the spiritual revealing work of the Father and the Son that anyone would come to truly know both the Father and the Son (Matt 11:25, 27). Then Jesus confirmed to Peter that it was the Father who had revealed in Peter's heart the truth of who Jesus really was (Matt 16:16-17). Such inner revelation is the foundation of a sinner's coming to faith in Christ and crying "Jesus is Lord."

And now Peter, knowing that the Parousia is near (such knowledge was from the Holy Spirit, assuring Peter that the signs foretelling the Parousia were upon them), now writes about his conviction that all living and remaining (pre-Parousia) Christians were about to partake of a great consummative revelation from God. Various aspects include (using the Greek *apokalupto* and *apokalupsis*):

- The revelation of the Lord Jesus, wherein there would be praise, honor and glory, (1 Pet 1:7, 13).
- The revealing of a final salvation, leading all his people into the eternal inheritance, (1 Pet 1:5, 9).

- A revealing of the Lord's glory, making his people "glad with exceeding joy," (1 Pet 4:13).
- A revealing of glory of which the Lord's people would partake; and not only partake of it, but be crowned with it, (1 Pet 5:1, 4)

Both deceased and living saints were expecting to be glorified and possess the eternal inheritance and eternal glory at the revelation and appearing of the Lord Jesus. Peter was aware that the end of all things was at hand, and that the Lord was ready to come and judge the living and the dead, (1 Pet 4:5, 7). As discussed in the section above on 2 Cor. 5, the Parousia would be the occasion when the Lord would judge living and dead, and impart the ultimate rewards for living and dead saints up to that point in history. The fullness of eternal life and the crown of glory would be the reward for living and dead saints. Peter himself knew that he would die before the Parousia and so would be among the number of the deceased saints expecting to be glorified at that Day (see details on this in Chapter 6 of this book).

Yet even though he knew he would die before the Parousia, Peter still expected to partake of the same glory (about to be revealed at the Parousia) that the living saints to whom he was writing would partake of. See 1 Pet. 5:1,4,10.

Consummation of hope at the Parousia of Christ

From Peter's eschatology we gain the understanding that all saints up to that point in history, those living until the time of the Parousia and those deceased saints who may have died under the fiery trials of Nero, etc., had *the one and the same hope, to be fulfilled at the Parousia of the Lord Jesus.*

Peter advise his readers to "rest their hope *fully* on the grace being brought to them *at the revelation of Christ,*" because this coming grace would bring them fully into glory. Peter urged all his readers, whether dead or alive at the time of the Parousia, to understand that full salvation would occur for them all - whether deceased or living. It is simple, pure logic that by Peter's counsel, the living Christians knew they would partake of the promised glory and eternal inheritance the same as their deceased brethren. Peter nowhere suggests that the lot of the living Christians would be different from the deceased brethren after the Parousia. *All* would be crowned with *the one promised glory*.

All saints – deceased and living – had the one and the same living hope –
A hope resting fully on the one and only grace being brought to them at the revelation of the Lord Jesus;
A grace giving the one and only promised consummative salvation;
A salvation introducing them into possession of the one and only promised eternal inheritance;

An inheritance consisting of the one and only promised eternal glory of the Lord Jesus.

We modern living-on-earth Christians have the wonderful hope that when we die we will graduate from the deposit/firstfruits measure of new covenant experience that we enjoy now into the same eternal inheritance, into the same eternal glory, that Peter and his readers entered into at the Parousia of Christ.

Further Note

If, according to the "remained-on-earth" theory held by some preterists, it happened that the Parousia of Christ actually left the living pre-Parousia Christians still on earth after the Parousia – *if* the expected glory was only to do with a covenantal or figurative glorification that still left them with the legacy of sin and spiritual imperfection like we see in all of us modern preterists – *then* Peter was wrong in urging the first Christians to set their hope *fully* on the grace coming to them at the Parousia. For, by this remained-on-earth theory, the Parousia did *not* impart the necessary grace to deliver them *fully* from their fallenness or save them *fully* into their final glorified state, but left them still in only a deposit state of blessing, awaiting a real and final glorification sometime later, when they later physically died. (*But all the promises have to do with the fact that the Parousia would be the occasion of their full glorification*).

If the remained-on-earth theory were true, Peter should have been honest enough to say, "Rest your hope only *partially* on what you'll receive at the Parousia, because the Parousia won't fully save you; you'll still be left hoping for *a further and real consummation* after the Parousia — a real, experiential consummation that will occur later, presumably when you physically die." I know it's a hypothetical question, but let me ask it: Can it really be imagined that Peter's readers would understand from Peter's letter to them, that many of them would be *left on earth after the Parousia in basically the same physical conditions they were experientially in before the Parousia*, no more spiritual than we modern preterists?

Under the remained on earth theory, the promised coming grace at the Parousia would only bring a *non-consummative salvation* to the living Christians. There would be a strange dichotomy: The deceased brethren would have their hope in Christ fully satisfied for they would experience at the Parousia the full fulfillment of all Peter's inspired wonderful promises, and following the Parousia be enjoying the bliss of a fully consummative salvation in glory in heaven in real resurrection, glorified bodies in Christ's immediate presence. Sadly, the living brethren would only know a far inferior type of fulfillment (if one could call it that) of their hope of glory, for, unlike their deceased brethren, their hope would only be partially (if I can even call it that) satisfied for, remaining on earth in their same earthy bodies, they would at best only have a partial salvation, only a partial experience of their eternal, heavenly inheritance, only a partial taste of glory; they would be left after the Parousia in semi-corruption still hoping for, still awaiting, a yet-to-come consummative experience of grace, salvation, eternal inheritance and eternal glory, which would come at their death, whenever that would occur, and then they would join their glorified brethren, those who were formerly deceased at the time of the Parousia. *In other words they would still be left in a deposit/firstfruits stage of new covenant experience.*

But in all the previous chapters we have seen that the hope of ALL Christians was that at the Parousia of their Lord, they would ALL receive the real experiential final salvation. There are *not* two types of crowns of glory in the NT: one type for the living saints at the Parousia who remain on earth in fallen bodies, and another type for the deceased saints at the Parousia who are raised in glory to be with the Lord! For in such a proposed case, "glory" would cease to have any definable, ultimate meaning. Glory would cease to mean "glory." Peter, however did not go along with this theory in question. He believed that, although he would die before the Parousia, he would partake of the same glory at the appearing of the Lord as those saints who would be alive at the Parousia would, and vice versa. But enough of this illogical theory which twists all meaning of words. Of course there is no hint at all of such a dichotomy of meaning in Peter's eschatological passages discussed above.

Let me repeat: From Peter's eschatology we gain the understanding that all saints up to that point in history, those living at the time of the Parousia and those deceased prior to the Parousia, had the one and the same hope of eternal glory, to be fulfilled at the Parousia of the Lord Jesus. There is no hint of any expectation by the pre-AD 70 saints that they would remain in a mortal, corruptible state after the Parousia.

(12) 1 Corinthians 6:1-3 – The saints reigning and judging with Christ

> 1 Dare any of you, having a matter against another, go to law before the unrighteous, and not before the saints? 2 Do you not know that the saints will judge the world? And if the world will be judged by you, are you unworthy to judge the smallest matters? 3 Do you not know that we shall judge angels? How much more, things that pertain to this life?

Note the theme of the saints judging the world and the angels in 1 Cor. 6:2-3; something that will occur at the Parousia of Christ. *"the saints will judge the world,"* (v. 2); *"the world will be judged by you,"* (v. 2); *"we shall judge angels,"* (v. 3).

Consider firstly the words of Jesus in regard to the disciples' reigning and judging with him when he would come.

> Matt. 19:28 So Jesus said to them, "Assuredly I say to you, that in the regeneration, when the Son of Man sits on the throne of His glory, you who have followed Me will also sit on twelve thrones, judging the twelve tribes of Israel.

It is historically known that a number of the original apostles died or were martyred before AD 70. Jesus knew that some of them would die before his Parousia, yet he still made this promise to them. Therefore we believe that the Lord's words of Matt 19:28 regarding their reigning with him and judging the nations were fulfilled in the case of all his apostles (minus Judas Iscariot, of course), whether they were deceased or living at the time of his Parousia.

Consider also the Revelation to John, where he saw the near-future event of the saints reigning and judging with Christ. Jesus refers to the "overcomers" in his messages to the churches in Rev. 2 and 3. Note that the "overcomers" are composed of those faithful saints who would be still alive at the time of the Parousia, and those saints who would be martyred for their faith before the Parousia. (Who are the overcomers? Just true believers in Christ Jesus the Lord. 1 Jn. 5:4-5 "For whatever is born of God overcomes the world. And this is the victory that has overcome the world—our faith. Who is he who overcomes the world, but he who believes that Jesus is the Son of God?")

The overcomers - regardless of whether they would be living or deceased by the time of the Parousia - were given the promise of reigning and judging with Christ at his second coming.

> Rev. 2:25-27 "But hold fast what you have till I come. 26 "And he who overcomes, and keeps My works until the end, to him I will give power over the nations — 27 'He shall rule them with a rod of iron; They shall be dashed to pieces like the potter's vessels' — as I also have received from My Father;
>
> Rev. 3:20-21 "Behold, I stand at the door and knock. If anyone hears My voice and opens the door, I will come in to him and dine with him, and he with Me. 21 "To him who overcomes I will grant to sit with Me on My throne, as I also overcame and sat down with My Father on His throne.
>
> Rev. 20:4 And I saw thrones, and they sat on them, and judgment was committed to them. Then I saw the souls of those who had been beheaded for their witness to Jesus and for the word of God, who had not worshiped the beast or his image, and had not received his mark on their foreheads or on their hands. And they lived and reigned with Christ for a thousand years.

Paul also said to Timothy: "If we endure, we shall also reign with Him." 2 Tim 2:12. No one would doubt, especially as this letter was written when Paul knew he was facing death, that the "we" in this verse applies to "we - whether living or deceased at the time of the Parousia." *So by Jesus' words and by the revelation given to John and to Paul we know that the deceased saints and the living saints would all be involved in reigning with Christ and judging the world at the Lord's Parousia.*

Getting back to 1 Cor. 6:2-3, Paul says, "*the saints* will judge the world," and "the world will be judged by *you*," and "*we* shall judge angels." Paul used three expressions: "the saints" - meaning the saints in general; "you" - meaning the Corinthian Christians; and "we" - meaning perhaps Paul and the Corinthians. Paul did die, and some of the Corinthians no doubt died before the Parousia, (from Neronian persecutions, or illness, etc.), and yet Paul taught that at the Parousia of Christ the saints, including the Corinthians and himself (the "we"), would reign with Christ and judge the world and the angels. I believe that Paul meant all saints - whether living or deceased at the time of Parousia of Christ - would together be involved in this awesome activity. This is in conformity to the teaching of Jesus and the apostle John.

This is just another aspect of that theme of reunion and togetherness which Paul expected for living and deceased believers at the Parousia, a theme which consistently runs through his epistles. Surely the natural conclusion from this teaching of all saints together reigning with Christ at his throne at his Parousia and with him judging the world, is that the saints still alive at the Parousia expected to be raised into a spiritual sphere beyond the mortal at the Parousia, where they would have the same place with Jesus at his throne and the same glorious power, that the deceased saints would have, in order for all saints to be able to carry out such a holy work.

(13) 1 Thess. 4:13-18

> 1 Thess 4:13-18 But I do not want you to be ignorant, brethren, concerning those who have fallen asleep, lest you sorrow as others who have no hope. 14 For if we believe that Jesus died and rose again, even so God will bring with Him those who sleep in Jesus. 15 For this we say to you by the word of the Lord, that we who are alive and remain until the coming of the Lord will by no means precede those who are asleep. 16 For the Lord Himself will descend from heaven with a shout, with the voice of an archangel, and with the trumpet of God. And the dead in Christ will rise first. 17 Then we who are alive and remain shall be caught up together with them in the clouds to meet the Lord in the air. And thus we shall always be with the Lord. 18 Therefore comfort one another with these words.

[**Note**: for ease of identification in the following writings, I have called the saints of verse 17, who were alive at the time of Paul's letter and who would remain alive until the Parousia, the "living saints."]

I realize this is a controversial passage, but my fears about putting down some thoughts on it were lessened as I came to see that what it appeared to speak about in figurative language, was quite consistent with the theme of both living and deceased believers being glorified together with Christ at the Parousia that is clearly taught in all the previous scripture passages examined in this chapter and in all previous chapters.

Of the preterists who teach that the living saints stayed in their same bodies on earth after the second coming of Christ, I have read of two interpretations of verse 17 above ("Then we who are alive and remain shall be caught up together with them in the clouds to meet the Lord in the air. And thus we shall always be with the Lord ") that perhaps I should mention.

One interpretation says that verse 17 does speak of the living saints being glorified in heaven like the deceased brethren, but not at the same time. This interpretation says that the word "then" (– "*then* we who are alive and remain shall be caught up with them....") means "thereafter;" referring to a considerable gap in time between the rising of the deceased brethren to heaven and the rising of the living saints to heaven. This interpretation says that only the deceased believers would rise to heaven and be glorified at the Lord's coming in AD 70. The living saints at AD 70 would, says this interpretation, stay on earth in their same bodies until they died, and *then* verse 17 would be fulfilled; *then* (possibly years after AD 70) they would be raised to meet the Lord together with the previously deceased brethren who were raised in AD 70.

A second interpretation is that verse 17 refers to a rising and meeting of the Lord at AD 70 by the living believers together with the deceased believers, but for the living believers it would be while still in their earthly bodies; it would be for them a non-experiential, covenantal matter only, transferring them into Christ's consummated kingdom, but leaving them to stay on earth afterwards. For the deceased saints, however, the rising to meet the Lord involved their receiving resurrection bodies and being glorified to be with the Lord in heaven.

But does the context and words favor either of these two interpretations which both leave the living believers on earth in their earthly bodies after the Lord's coming, separated from the risen, deceased brethren in glory with God? From all the passages previously examined in this chapter and previous chapters, my answer is a definite NO. It seems clear to me that the "remained-on-earth" theory does not fit in with the many scriptures we have examined.

Please consider the following exegesis of 1 Thess 4:13-18 that I believe is clearly in accord with consistent theme in all of the passages examined in this whole series: viz., that the living believers expected to be actually raised to heaven and glorified there along with the deceased brethren at the Lord's Parousia.

1. Unfounded Sorrow. 1 Thess 4:13-15

Paul was concerned that the ignorance of the Thessalonian believers regarding the fate of their deceased brethren left them vulnerable to hopelessness just like the pagans around them. It seems that the Thessalonians feared that their deceased brethren would not be reunited with them, the living believers, at the Parousia of Christ, and so would miss out on the blessing that was to come to those who were still living at the time of the Lord's Parousia. That something like this was the case can be gauged by the way in which Paul rectified their ignorance — by relating how the deceased believers would be right there with the living saints at the Lord's Parousia and share in the blessing of meeting the Lord and ever being with him. They were to comfort themselves with this truth.

Ignorance Means Sorrow

One wonders why the Thessalonian believers had this faulty understanding regarding their deceased brethren, as one can be sure that Paul preached the hope of the resurrection of the dead where ever he went (See in Acts). Although they had a genuine hope following their conversion, being determined "to wait for His [God's] Son from heaven," (1:10) and knew Paul's previous teaching that God had called them to His own kingdom and glory (2:10-12), they had somehow failed to understand about the prospects of the deceased brethren at the Parousia.

One can appreciate that if the living saints thought that their deceased brethren and loved ones were somehow hindered from participating with the living saints in the glories associated with the Lord's Parousia they could easily become unsettled or fearful. No doubt there were some living at the time Paul wrote whose lives were drawing to a close through old age or ill-health and knew that soon they would join the ranks of the deceased before the Lord came. Also the church could expect that some of their living brethren would be killed by persecuting Jews or Romans before the Lord came. Imagine their sadness then, if in their ignorance they feared that death would rob them of sharing with their loved ones at the blessing of meeting the Lord together. In this letter Paul reassured the Christians that there would be no separation at the Lord's coming, rather there would be a true and fulfilling reunion in the Lord's presence.

Living Saints to be reunited with the Deceased Saints at the Parousia

"For if we believe that Jesus died and rose again, [then we are to believe that] even so God will bring with him those who sleep in Jesus." [1 Thess. 4:14]

Paul could have said in the second clause: "God will raise with Him those who sleep," to connect it with Jesus' rising; but Paul uses the verb "bring," as a reassurance, implying that God will not only raise those who sleep [the deceased], but bring them with Jesus into reunion with the living saints at his coming. To me, the word "bring" implies that the deceased brethren were already with Jesus in some manner. Paul refers to this idea in Phil 1:22-23, "But if *I* live on in the flesh, this *will mean* fruit from *my* labor; yet what I shall choose I cannot tell. 23 For I am hard pressed between the two, *having a desire to depart and be with Christ, which is far better.*" So in pre-Parousia times Paul knew that deceased believers were in some happy state with Christ in heaven, but not yet having their consummate glory (which was "far better").

"For this we say by the word of the Lord, that we who are [now] alive and remain until the coming of the Lord will by no means precede those who are asleep." [1 Thess. 4:15]

Paul strongly denies (with a double negative in the Greek "οὐ μὴ" lit. "not not") the thought that the living saints would enter their blessing at the Lord's coming before the deceased. The deceased would absolutely "not not" be left behind or miss out on the Parousia's blessings that the living would experience. The living would "not not" precede the resurrected dead into the presence of Christ. The dead would be raised first, before the living were changed.

2. Reunion of saints and their union with Christ – 1 Thess 4:16-17

For the Lord Himself will descend from heaven with a shout, with the voice of an archangel, and with the trumpet of God. And the dead in Christ will rise first. 17 Then we who are alive *and* remain shall be caught up together with them in the clouds to meet the Lord in the air. And thus we shall always be with the Lord. 18 Therefore comfort one another with these words. [1 Thess 4:16-17]

The section 4:16-17 commences with "for" or "because" — "For the Lord will descend, etc." Paul gives in vv. 16-17 his reason for affirming in verses 14-15 that both living and deceased saints would be together at the Parousia. Any sorrow based on a fear that death could hinder the fulfillment of the hope of the deceased saints of meeting the Lord in his glory at his coming together with the living saints is unfounded. Why? Because of how things will occur at the Parousia (vv. 16-17). Therefore comfort one another with these words, he says.

This section presents the two groups – the deceased and living believers – being caught away together to meet the Lord at his coming. The sentence does *not* convey any thought that at the coming of Christ only the deceased believers will be caught away to meet the Lord leaving the living believers to wait until they die in some future time before they can be together with the deceased to meet the Lord and ever be with him. Neither does this passage say anything about a meeting with the Lord for all believers that subsequently differentiates the believers, equipping the deceased for immediate entry to the presence of God in heaven, while leaving the living believers to continue in their fallen bodies amidst future suffering on earth. Rather the whole context of these relevant verses is that a reunion will take place at the time of the Lord's coming with all believers being caught away together and meeting the Lord, and together commencing a new experience of ever being with the Lord. Let us examine these verses.

"Then..." (1 Thess. 4:17)

15 For this we say to you by the word of the Lord, that we who are alive and remain until the coming of the Lord will by no means

precede those who are asleep. 16 For the Lord Himself will descend from heaven with a shout, with the voice of an archangel, and with the trumpet of God. And the dead in Christ will rise *first*. 17 *Then* (*epeita*) we who are alive and remain shall together with them be caught away... [1 Thess. 4:15-17]

The Greek word *epeita* (ἔπειτα) found here at the beginning of v. 17 is an adverb marking succession of time or order. In v. 17 *epeita* is translated by "then" and emphasizes succession of order, and relates to the word "first" of v. 16: "16 ...And the dead in Christ will rise *first*, 17 *next, then in order,* (*epeita*) we who are alive and remain shall together with them be caught up to meet the Lord...." First - next: such is the order at the Lord's Parousia. While time may be involved, the emphasis is on order. Any time difference is not the issue here, it is the order of events that is the issue. This focus on succession of order among deceased and living believers in v. 16b and 17a follows the mention about succession of order in v. 15 where the living believers are said not to precede those who are asleep.

However, we are not to read an indefinite time delay into that *epeita*. We are *not* to read this "then" (*epeita*) as implying that at the Parousia only the deceased would be raised to glory, while the living remained on earth for some time after the Parousia (e.g., until their physical death), and that "then" they would be taken into the same glory that their deceased brethren entered into years before at the Parousia. This is not a grammatically nor contextually validated interpretation, for everywhere in the NT it is clear that all pre-Parousia saints expected to enter the consummate glory at the same time as the resurrected saints – *on the occasion of the Lord's Parousia*, not some years after it at their individual deaths. Such an idea of delay (in the timing of their reunion) defeats Paul's whole purpose of solving the issue of a sorrow due to the mistaken understanding amongst the church that deceased and living brethren would be separated and not together in experiencing the blessings of the Parousia. (See *epeita* used in the sense of "then, in order" in 1 Cor. 12:28; Jas. 3:17).

"...And the dead in Christ will rise *first,* then/next we who are alive and remain together with them shall be caught away." And all of this happens on the occasion of the Parousia of Christ. (See my Excursion a couple of paragraphs down for more information on the "rise first").

"Together" (1 Thess. 4:17)
The sentence structure emphasizes the togetherness of deceased and living believers at the critical time of the Lord's coming. The Greek order is: "16 The Lord himself shall descend from heaven...and the dead in Christ shall rise up first, 17 then, we who are alive and remain, *together with them,* shall be caught away in clouds to meet the Lord into the air." The emphasis is on the togetherness of both groups of believers enjoying God's blessing at the Parousia. They are "caught away" together as one group, and they meet with Christ together as one group. Paul is emphasiz-

ing the togetherness of deceased and living believers in order to allay the fears of some Christians that the deceased saints would not share with them in the blessings associated with the Parousia of Christ.

> "We, the living ones who remain [until the Parousia], *together with* [Greek ἅμα σὺν, *hama sun*] them [the deceased believers] shall be caught away to meet the Lord..." [1 Thess. 4:17]

Paul uses not only the preposition "*sun*" which means "together with, in company with," but also the word "*hama*" which may be used as an adverb meaning "at the same time," and as a preposition meaning "with, together with." So Paul seems to be deliberately emphasizing the fact that *the living believers together with, in company with and at the same time as, the deceased believers*, will be caught away to meet the Lord. The living saints and the deceased saints are caught away to the Lord *together*, at the same time.

An Excursion (relevant, but not crucial to my main theme):

I am intrigued as to why Paul used the word "first" in the position he did at the end of verse 16, "And the dead in Christ will rise *first*." The word in its position immediately after "rise"— "[they]...shall *rise first*" - naturally implies that there are others who will rise next or second in order after the first ones have risen. The way in which this sentence in vv. 16-17 is usually explained however doesn't really explain the use of "first" in its present position. The usual interpretation of vv. 16-17 is that the Lord will descend with accompanying phenomena and the deceased will rise and then the living and the deceased will be caught up together to meet the Lord — which, while correct, does not take into account Paul's use and positioning of "first," and makes the presence of "first" seem superfluous.

If Paul merely meant to say that first, before the living and deceased together would be caught away the deceased would rise, then one would have thought that "first" should have been positioned before the whole clause, such that the sentence would read: "First [i.e. as the first event], the dead will rise, then [i.e. as the next event] we who are alive and remain shall together with them be caught away to meet the Lord."

Or, as I tend to think, did Paul insert "first" where he did, in order to make some particular point?

Although I have not seen it mentioned anywhere, I think the original Greek could legitimately and easily be translated as follows — remembering that in Greek there are no punctuation marks, and that it is not uncommon for the verb in a related second clause in a sentence to be omitted where it can be readily supplied by ellipsis through noting the flow of the first clause. Here is my suggested translation from the Greek:

> "...and the dead in Christ will rise first, then we [will be changed] who are alive and remain. Together with them we shall be caught away in

clouds to meet the Lord in the air. And thus (in this manner) we shall always be with the Lord."

In this translation, the word "first" is taken as qualifying the verb "rise," which seems to me to be Paul's intention. The deceased will rise first; then/next the living will be raised/changed. After the rising/change of each group in their order, they both together as one group shall be caught away to meet the Lord. This agrees with v. 15 where Paul says that the living believers shall not precede the deceased; which I take to mean that the living shall not precede the deceased in meeting the Lord in his glory. The deceased believers shall rise first, then the living believers will be raised/changed; and the living believers together with, and at the same time as the deceased believers shall be caught away in clouds into the air to meet the Lord. In 1 Cor. 6:14 Paul says, "And God both raised up the Lord and will also raise us up by his power." Paul says "God will raise *us* up," referring to "us" as a collective group, making no distinction between the ones who remained living until the Parousia and the ones who died before the Parousia. He knew that not all of them would die before the Parousia, that some of their group would still be alive at the Parousia (1 Cor. 15:51), yet he still said "God will *raise us* up." That "raising up" for the living was a "change" of their mortal bodies. So Paul seems to say that, in a very real sense, both living and deceased would be raised up, would rise, at the Parousia. (See my comments on 1 Cor. 6:14 in Chapter 7, section (4)).

This small excursion of mine is just a suggestion. My argument for the glorification of the living believers to heaven at the Lord's Parousia does not depend on this excursion being accepted, but is based on the normal translation in our Bibles.

"Caught away" (v. 17)

"We, the living who remain, together with them [the deceased believers] shall be *caught away* [Gr. ἁρπαγησόμεθα] in clouds into the air to meet the Lord. And thus always with the Lord we shall be."

The Greek word here for "caught away" (ἁρπαγησόμεθα, from the root *"harpazo"*) is used elsewhere of Philip being "caught away" by the Spirit (Acts 8:39), of Paul's being "caught up" to the third heaven (2 Cor. 12:2), of the man-child being "caught up" to God out of the devil's reach (Rev. 12:5). In other places the word is used of seizing eagerly or forcibly (Matt 11:12 "the violent *take* it *by force*"), of taking away forcibly (Jn. 10:28,29 "none *can pluck* them out of my hand"). The *Online Bible* Greek Lexicon defines the meaning of *harpazo* as 1) to seize, carry off by force; 2) to seize on, claim for one's self eagerly; 3) to snatch out or away.

There would be a powerful working of God which would forcefully claim, seize or carry away together all the deceased and living believers that the Lord's coming. Without stretching the meaning, it would seem that the *harpazo* seizing is such that it takes the seized person or thing away from its present condition or whereabouts. It is not a seizing that keeps the seized one or thing where or how it originally was. This powerful carrying away of deceased and living saints would bring them (away from their original condition or realm) into a realm where the meeting with the Lord would take place. "Together," both the deceased believers and the living believers were to experience the powerful action of God taking them to meet the Lord. Together! So often only the living saints are focused on. But the deceased saints were just as really expecting the catching away.

Just how this powerful seizing and claiming by God would take place in the believers is not described; indeed such details are a side issue, for Paul's main concern is to allay the Thessalonians' fears of separation by emphasizing the togetherness of deceased and living at the Parousia. What matters is that there would be a common experience together of God's powerfully seizing them at the Parousia. *[Note: Let us preterists not shy away from this natural meaning of what the scripture says because of an aversion we may have to a futurist caricature of bodies rising into the air. Let us beware of unwisely and prejudicially "throwing the baby out with the {futurist} bath water."]*

"In clouds" (v. 17)

"We, the living who remain, together with them [the deceased believers] shall be seized/caught away *in clouds* into the air to meet the Lord. And thus always with the Lord we shall be."

We need to consider the meaning of being caught away "in clouds" as it applies to the deceased and living believers together. Mention of the Lord's coming with clouds in the OT is symbolically referring to His deity and power and heavenly position. We understand the Lord's coming in clouds to be figuratively referring to his coming in power, deliverance or judgment. But what of the deceased and living believers together (not just the living) being seized "in clouds" into the air to meet the Lord?

See the references to "clouds" associated with the Lord Jesus and the disciples in passages such as Matt 17:5 at Jesus transfiguration and the presence of God in the cloud; Rev. 11:12, the witnesses called to heaven and ascending to heaven "in the cloud;" Acts 1:9, at his ascension the Lord Jesus was "taken up, and a cloud withdrew him from their eyes;" other places in the Revelation referring to the Lord Jesus and cloud/s Rev. 1:7; 10:1; 14:14,15,16). All of these give the notion that in 1 Thess 4:17 Paul is using *the symbolism of clouds* to teach that the deceased and living believers together will be seized/caught away *in and by the supernatural power and presence of God*.

There is an interesting parallel between the case in Rev. 11:12 of the two witnesses/martyrs who as deceased believers were called up by a great voice from heaven, and who ascended to heaven in the cloud; and the case in 1 Thess 4:16-17 where the Lord descending from heaven gives a loud command (Gr. κέλευσμα, *keleusma*) and the deceased rise and the living and deceased believers are then seized/caught away together in clouds into the air to meet with Christ.

The living believers in company with the deceased believers were to experience at the same time the same seizing in "clouds" of divine power.

"Into the air" (v. 17)

"We, the living who remain, together with them [the deceased believers] shall be seized/caught away in clouds *into the air* to meet the Lord. And thus always with the Lord we shall be." [1 Thess. 4:17]

The Greek says "*into* the air;" (*eis aera*). As Vincent in his Word Studies points out, the Greek here cannot be translated as "*in* the air," as is popularly done, (which would require the Greek *en* = in), but should be translated as "into the air;" (Greek *eis* = into, implying direction). Vincent therefore connects this directional phrase with the verb, to catch, seize (*harpazo*). The movement of the sentence is: "we...together with them shall be seized...into the air to meet the Lord."

The LXX (Gr. translation of Hebrew scripture used by both Jews and Christians in the first century) uses the word *aer* (Gr. ἀήρ) to refer to the sky where the clouds are: In 2 Sam. 22:12 and Psa. 18:11, it says the Lord had his dwelling in "clouds of the sky/skies (*aer*)." In the Greek NT *aer* is used of the atmosphere above ground and the air around man. The word is used in a figurative sense in Eph 2:2, where unsaved men are referred to as walking according to the prince of the authority of the *air* (*aer*), the spirit that works in the disobedient. *Aer* here in Eph 2:2 is referring (in OT and NT cosmology) to the space between heaven and earth (in the spiritual realm) where Satan and his demons had their activity.

The words "into the air" of 1 Thess 4:17 seemingly refer to something like: "into the spiritual realm" - the invisible spiritual realm where angels and demons had their activity, where Satan was the ruler of the demons at that time (Eph. 2:2), and into which the Lord Jesus descended from heaven (1 Thess. 4:15) at His Parousia to crush Satan (Rom. 16:20). Note that *both* the living and the deceased believers together, at the same time, were to be seized into this spiritual realm, figuratively called "the air," at the Parousia. It was clearly a realm that neither living nor deceased believers were in before the Parousia, for they were to be brought *into* it at the Parousia, and was clearly a realm that was not possible for the Christians to attain to by their own powers, for it would take the Lord's descending from heaven and a seizing of them in and by the power and presence of God ("in/with clouds") to bring them into this realm of "the air."

While *aer* does sometimes refer to the material air or atmosphere in which men live and breathe on earth, the picture language that Paul uses of clouds and a seizing directed into the air, certainly suggests that Paul is using *aer* here as the spiritual realm which temporarily becomes visible (theophany) in the sky where birds fly and the clouds congregate. Paul is thus using theophany language to explain how the saints will be supernaturally taken up in clouds into the sky (the same way Christ ascended in a cloud, Acts 1:9). He is no doubt figuratively referring to the power and presence of God (always veiled in clouds) seizing believers, living and deceased, into the spiritual realm (in the air between heaven and earth) where they could meet the Lord "face to face." Since it would require superhuman power for a human to rise in a material cloud and ascend into the material air/sky above this planet (like Christ did at His ascension), Paul uses this theophany or "ascension" language to emphasize that the spiritual reality the saints were to be taken to at the Parousia was just as impossible for mortal "man who walks" to enter while still in his mortal body (Jer 10:23). They would have to be changed and receive a new body. But, what is impossible for man is possible with God, and the saints of God could expect, at the Parousia of Christ, to be seized away by the divine power of God from their present mortal body (if still alive) or disembodied state into the heights of a heavenly fellowship with Christ that they had not experienced before.

The disembodied dead saints and living believers on earth were *together* (as one group) caught up and seized by God "into the air." In other words, "the air" has the same meaning when applied to the deceased as when applied to the living believers. Wherever the dead were taken, the living were taken also, "together" as one group – a place where neither dead nor living saints had dwelt before. Both deceased and living believers together as one group would be seized into the spiritual realm visible above the earth "in the air" to meet the Lord Jesus at His descent from heaven at the Parousia.

"The Meeting" (v.17)

"We, the living who remain, *together with* them (the deceased believers) shall be seized/caught away in clouds into the air *to meet* the Lord." [1 Thess. 4:17]

The Greek for "to meet" is *eis apanteesin* which literally means "for a meeting," (eis = for, *apanteesin* is accusative singular of noun *apanteesis* = a meeting, an encounter). *Eis apanteesin*, is rightly translated idiomatically as "to meet." (Refer to the *Analytical Greek Lexicon*). The associated verb simply means "to meet."

The Greek noun *apanteesis*, has the simple everyday meaning of "a meeting," or "an encounter." *Eis apanteesin* is said by some to also have a somewhat technical usage in some of the Greek papyri of that age, describing the official welcome given to a visiting magistrate, (refer e.g. to *Vines Expository Dictionary*). *Apanteesis* is used in three other places in the NT – Acts 28:15; Matt 25:1 (acc. to Received Text); and Matt 25:6.

This technical meaning can easily be applied to the Parousia when we remember that visiting dignitaries did not stay long at the place where they came to visit. And they quite often took some of the townspeople back with them to their palace when they finished their visit. This is exactly what Christ promised to do at His return (John 14:1-3). Jesus told his disciples that He would soon ascend to heaven, and that they could not go with Him at this time, but they would go later. Jesus said that He would prepare places for them to dwell in heaven with him, and that He would return to "receive them to himself, that where He was (in the heavenly realm), there they would be taken also."

As for the usage of this term "meeting" in Matt 25:1 and 6, it is a matter of the Jewish wedding customs that the lady friends of the bride would watch for the approaching groom as he came in a jubilant procession from his own (or his father's) house to fetch the bride and take her back to his house that he had prepared for her. The lady friends would run out *to meet* the groom and join his procession and accompany him to the groom's house for the wedding feast. The groom would take his bride away from her home, amidst jubilant procession, back to his own (or his parent's house) for the final ceremonies or festivities.

Some commentators take up the supposed technical sense of *apanteesis* and apply it so as to give a particular interpretation to 1 Thess 4:17; viz. that the raptured saints will go up to meet the coming Lord as an official welcoming party and they will then escort him to earth as they return to live back on earth, and thus the Lord will dwell with them on earth. But, as I explained above, none of the other NT occurrences of *apanteesis* can be pressed to favor such a meaning of the word. So it is best not to press it here in 1 Thess 4:17.

The Matt. 25 parable of the ten virgins (which uses the same word "meet" in Matt. 25:1,6) could just as well be used to counter this suggested earthbound interpretation of the meeting in 1 Thess 4:17 by pointing out that *the bridegroom's visit to his bride's house was only preparatory to his taking her away from her own house back to his own home*, where the marriage ceremonies/celebrations were completed and the marriage consummated. Surely the original going out of the virgin friends of the bride to "meet" the groom was followed by their joining the procession as *the bridegroom took his bride to his own home for the final festivities.* The bride left her father's house with the groom and went in procession to the groom's home, where she would stay forever. For Christians, the Groom's home, where the marriage would be consummated, is heaven. Now the point must be made also that the believers in 1 Thess 4:17 who were to be caught away to "meet" the Lord were not friends or attendants to the bride; they were the bride. *If we keep to the marriage custom analogy, just as the bridegroom comes to the bride's home to claim her and take her back to his home, even so the believers (the bride) were to be caught away, claimed by the power of God to meet the Lord who would take them to his home, i.e. heaven.* This is in accordance with Jesus' words, "Where I am [with the Father] there shall you be also." [Jn. 14:3] And with the words of the prophetic Psa. 45:10-15 –

> Hearken, O daughter, and consider, and incline thine ear; *forget also thine own people, and thy father's house*; *so shall the king greatly desire thy beauty*: for he is thy Lord; and worship thou him. And the daughter of Tyre shall be there with a gift; even the rich among the people shall entreat thy favor. The king's daughter is all-glorious within: her clothing is of wrought gold. *She shall be brought unto the king* in raiment of needlework: the virgins her companions that follow her shall be brought unto thee. With gladness and rejoicing *shall they be brought: they shall enter into the king's palace.* [Psa 45:13-15]

For those wishing to exploit a supposed implication in the word Greek *apanteesis* of the welcomers going out to officially welcome a visiting dignitary and then returning and escorting him to their city, (in order to favor their interpretation that the living saints rise to meet the Lord at his coming and then return with him to reign on earth), please consider this: In 1 Thess 4:17 *both* the deceased believers *and* the living believers *together* are caught away to meet the Lord. If the resurrected dead stayed together with the living in the presence of Christ ("thus we shall always be") from that meeting onwards, then the resurrected saints were still with the living ones when they went back to earth with Christ. That means the resurrected dead are still here on earth living among us forever. And there is another problem with the "return to earth" theory: There would be far more deceased believers in number than living believers meeting the Lord at AD 70 at his coming (consider the innumerable multitude in Rev. 7:9, 13-14). Which group does the Lord accompany after the meeting if, according to the supposed technical meaning of *apanteesis*, he is to be escorted by his welcomers back to where they came out from? If he was to go with the majority, then the Lord would have gone with the risen deceased back to where they were waiting before they were caught away to meet the Lord (in Hades). Why do some commentators focus their energies on the meeting of the living with the Lord, when the presence of the deceased at that meeting is just as significant? Reading such a particular technical meaning into *apanteesis* creates more difficulties than its adherents would want to face.

But it is illogical, according to the context of reunion at the Parousia and *together* being carried away by the Lord's power to meet the Lord, to say that after the meeting with the Lord the raised deceased brethren would go one direction or into one condition and the living brethren would go in a different direction or into a different condition - and all the while the scriptures saying that they (i.e. all believers - see relevant discussion above) would forever be with the Lord. If one wishes to talk of direction, then keep the idea of reunion in context and either say both groups go to earth after the powerful meeting with the Lord in the air, or say that both groups go together into the place where the deceased were waiting before being caught away. But if neither of these options is satisfactory then, based on the normal meaning of *apanteesis* ("a meeting"), there is a third option, that is so clear and which I have presented above, that both the changed living saints and the risen deceased saints – all together as one group – accompany the Lord to a realm new to both groups, and more wonderful and glorious than either could imagine. The innumerable multitude of out-of-the-great-tribulation saints in Rev. 7:9-17, waving palm branches of triumph, and rejoicing in the salvation of God, are certainly in a wonderful state and condition before the throne of God with the Lord Jesus, the Lamb, there to shepherd them.

Any idea of separation after the "meeting" with the Lord would flounder Paul's whole effort of comforting the Thessalonian saints. Divergent destinies of deceased and living believers at the Parousia is just not taught here. The Groom does not stay at the Bride's house forever afterwards. He "meets" the wedding party there at the bride's home, and then takes the bride back to his house to live with her forever. It is just a temporary "meeting" before they form a procession and proceed back to the Groom's house for the wedding feast and marriage consummation. It is no surprise that *apanteesin* is used in Matt. 25:1,6 of this "meeting."

In 1 Thess 4:17 the 'forceful carrying away in clouds into the air" of the believers and their "meeting" with the Lord – the Lord who had come in his glory and kingdom – surely describe events that were to be an amazing, tangible, experiential reality to both deceased and living believers. There is no merit to the suggestion that the "meeting" in the air for the "living and remaining ones" was only a non-experiential, "covenantal" change or "positional-only" meeting with the Lord while still on earth in their physical bodies, but for the deceased believers the meeting with the Lord in the air was a literal, fully-experiential, conscious reality. *This meeting was to be as real, powerful, subjective, glorious, transforming, and as much in the presence of Christ in the case of the living saints as it was to be in the case of the deceased saints.* At this meeting with the Lord they both (living and dead) would "see him as he is" (1 Jn 3:2), and be "changed" to "be like Him."

The "powerful catching away" was to be the same reality for both deceased and living saints; the meeting with the Lord was to be the same glorious reality for both deceased and living saints. Only then could Paul's comforting words concerning the togetherness or reunion of deceased and living at the Parousia have any real validity.

I believe that this meeting of all the saints with the Lord refers to the "gathering together to him" of the saints at the coming of the Lord spoken of in 2 Thess 2:1, and where Paul would be crowned with joy in seeing the Thessalonians in the presence of the Lord Jesus at his coming, 1 Thess 2:19, (among whom would be deceased Thessalonian Christians); also the gathering together of the elect in Matt 24:31.

"Always With the Lord." (v. 17)

"And thus [Gr. *houtos*, lit. in this manner] always with the Lord we shall be." [1 Thess. 4:17b]

I don't feel it is being pedantic to point out that verse 17b says, "And in this manner always *we shall be with the Lord*" and *not*, "And in this manner always *the Lord shall be with us*." To me, the scripture wording, "we shall be with the Lord," implies that the believers go to be where the Lord is and so be with him there, (as the Lord says in Jn. 14:3); while the latter wording, "the Lord shall be with us," would imply the Lord comes to be where the believers are and so becomes with them there. Those preterists who claim the living believers at AD 70 stayed in their earthly bodies on earth are obliged to interpret v. 17b in the second sense, as meaning that the Lord came to dwell with or in those earthly believers *on earth* in a special way at his Parousia in AD 70. But in so doing, perhaps they inadvertently give a different sense from the scriptural sense of the words.

I believe that *the "we" in verse 17b has to mean "we, both the deceased brethren and the living brethren - we all together."* The whole context of relieving the Christians' fears about the lot of their loved ones has to do with the togetherness of deceased and living believers at the Parousia — together in their rising and being caught away in clouds and in their meeting the Lord. Here after the reunion together in meeting the Lord, it is: "we [undefined, implying all of us, as a reunited whole] shall always be with the Lord."

V. 17b "And thus [Gr. *houtos*, lit. in this manner] always with the Lord we shall be."

"In this manner — i.e. through together being caught away powerfully and meeting the Lord in the air — we shall always be with the Lord." The same powerful catching away, in the same clouds of divine power, into the same air of the spiritual realms, for the same meeting, the one and the same together being with the Lord forever - would be experienced by deceased believers and living believers together. "And in this manner we [all of us together] shall always be with the Lord." I believe this catches the context flow of this whole section of Paul's words of comfort.

The meaning of "always we shall be with the Lord" clearly means entering a new, permanent and perfect existence in company with the Lord, which they did not have before. It would be through the power of God in catching/seizing the believers away to meet the Lord who had come in his glory, that they would enter this new and perfect realm of being with the Lord.

The meaning of "always being with the Lord," as it relates to the deceased brethren, clearly implies their receiving glorified, spiritual bodies, and dwelling with the Lord where he is in heaven - at the right hand of the Father. I don't think anyone would disagree with this. 1 Cor. 15 also clearly refers to the deceased believers rising to a glorified, heavenly state at the Lord's Parousia.

Now the passage places the living believers together with the deceased believers in their being caught up and meeting the Lord. In keeping with the context of reunion of deceased and living believers with the

Lord at his Parousia, the language seems to naturally and logically imply that the living believers would also be together with the deceased brethren in their always being with the Lord. That is, the living believers would enter the same heavenly kind of "being with the Lord" following the meeting with the Lord that the deceased believers enter, the same glorified state in heaven with the Lord Jesus. 1 Thess 5:10 would seem to confirm this; "... whether we wake or sleep [i.e. whether we are alive or dead], *we should live together with him* [the Lord Jesus]." Paul regards both the deceased and living as having the same hope of union together in a permanent dwelling with the Lord.

With this lovely ending Paul concludes his comforting talk. The fears of separation have been addressed and resolved — "his point being established, that the dead in Christ shall be on terms of equal advantage with those found alive at Christ's coming," (Jamieson, Fausset and Brown). At the coming of Christ there is the wonderful picture of the reunion of deceased believers and the living believers and their union together with the Lord Jesus.

Glory Together (A summary)

Let me just summarize what I believe is the natural, straightforward meaning of 1 Thess 4:13-18. True comfort was intended to be given by clearing the ignorance about the lot of the deceased believers at the coming of Christ. A tendency to sadness was present because of fears that the deceased brethren would not be there with the living brethren to meet the Lord at his coming. Paul deliberately met their need by showing how all the events surrounding the coming of the Lord would see the deceased and living believers sharing together in experiencing God's power carrying them away to meet the Lord and ever being with the Lord — no more separation from each other nor any separation from the Lord — forever. This interpretation is further confirmed by Paul in 1 Thess 5:8-11, discussed in the next section.

It is worth noting that the "remained-on-earth" preterist view that separates the destinies of the deceased and the living Christians at the Parousia – by saying that the church expected the deceased to go to heaven, but expected the living to remain on earth – actually creates a reversed situation compared to what is presented here in 1 Thessalonians.

A straightforward reading of the above passage gives the understanding that the living are expectant of great blessing at the Parousia but are nervous about whether their deceased brethren will be there with them to enter the kingdom blessings at the Parousia. And Paul comforts them by asserting that the living will not precede the deceased but all would be caught away together to meet the Lord and be with Him forever. However, the remained-on-earth view creates a reversed situation in which, instead of the living believers having a possible reason for being sad for the sake of their loved ones who may miss out at the Parousia, in actual fact it is the living believers who should be sad that they themselves would miss out on blessings, while only their deceased brethren would experience glory in heaven. Under the remained-on-earth view the deceased would enter the promised glory in all its consummation at the Parousia, while the living would not, but would remain on earth still in a deposit stage of Christian experience in comparison to the fulfillment stage of the glorified deceased. *Instead of Paul's comfort that the living saints can be happy knowing that they were not to precede the deceased at the Parousia, the living saints would have the very sad knowledge that the deceased were to precede them at the Parousia.* Indeed, if the deceased were taught this remained-on-earth view, they would have been sad that the living were not to be with them to share with them in their fullness at the Parousia.

If the earthbound interpretation were true, Paul's recorded manner of comforting the fears of the living Thessalonians regarding their deceased brethren would be totally misleading and false.

(14) 1 Thess. 5:8-11
> 8 But let us, who are of the day, be sober, putting on the breastplate of faith and love; and for an helmet, the hope of salvation. For God did not appoint us to wrath, but to obtain salvation through our Lord Jesus Christ, 10 who died for us, that whether we are awake or sleep, we should live together with Him. 11 Therefore comfort each other and edify one another, just as you also are doing.

As in 1 Thess 4:13-18 so also in this passage Paul wanted the Thessalonian Christians to be comforted by knowing the truth about the destinies of the deceased believers [those who "sleep" in Jesus] and the living believers [those "awake"] who remain until the Lord's Parousia. The truth is that at the Parousia they all would experience the one promised salvation and live together with the Lord Jesus.

Hope of Salvation at the Parousia - whether living or deceased.
The preceding context 5:1-8 concerns the coming of the Day of the Lord and its unexpected destruction upon the wicked. Paul uses a picturesque play on words to show that God's people are people of light to whom the Day will be no unwelcome surprise as it will be to the people of darkness. In vv. 9-11 Paul encourages the Christians that "God did not appoint us to wrath," to face God's judgment, to share the fate of non-Christians and apostate Jews around them; "but to obtain salvation through our Lord Jesus Christ." They were to put on the helmet of the hope of salvation (v. 8).

Remembering the Thessalonian Christians' concern for their deceased brethren, as discussed in 4:13-18, Paul inserts another reminder to them that the intrusion of death upon some of their brethren in no way means God has forsaken his care and promises of salvation to the ones who have died. He affirms that this salvation which would be manifested at the coming of Christ would ensure "that *whether we are awake or sleep* [i.e. alive or dead], we should live together with him," (5:10). This last clause echoes his words in 4:17 that all the believers would be caught away by God's power and so always be with the Lord, as the result of his Parousia. Note that the phrase "whether we are awake or sleep" applies to verse 9 as well as verse 10. "For God did not appoint us [- whether we are awake or sleep - living or deceased] to wrath, but [he appointed us - whether we wake or sleep] to obtain salvation through our Lord Jesus Christ, 10 who died for us, that whether we are awake or sleep, we should live together with Him."

It may seem to be stating the obvious, but I note that Paul made no distinction here between the kind of salvation that the living saints expected and would experience at the Parousia and the kind of salvation that the deceased saints expected and would experience at the Parousia, nor did he make any distinction between the kind of living together with the Lord Jesus that the salvation through the Lord Jesus would introduce the living believers into at his Parousia and the kind of living together with the Lord Jesus that the salvation of the Lord would introduce the deceased brethren into upon at his Parousia. Both deceased and living believers would experience the one and the same final salvation and the one and the same bliss of then living together with the Lord.

The context and language is clear and beautiful: there is no fear of wrath for *all* the believers; rather there is for all the one hope of salvation, the "one hope of [their] calling " (Eph 4:4), to be experienced at the Parousia of Christ; "whether we wake or sleep," i.e. whether living believers or dead believers. And this great salvation would bring all believers - whether dead or alive - into a new heavenly, glorious, consummated life of living together with the Lord Jesus at his Parousia.

This salvation expected by the believers – whether alive or deceased – at the Parousia of Christ would be a consummative salvation that had to do with entering and experiencing *Christ's kingdom and eternal glory*.

> 1 Thess. 2:12 ...walk worthy of *God who calls you [or who is calling you] into His own kingdom and glory*.
> 2 Thess. 2:13-14 But we are bound to give thanks to God always for you, brethren beloved by the Lord, because God from the beginning *chose you for salvation* through sanctification by the Spirit and belief in the truth, 14 to which *He called you by our gospel, for the obtaining of the glory of our Lord Jesus Christ*.
> 2 Tim. 2:10 Therefore I endure all things for the sake of the elect, that they also may obtain *the salvation which is in Christ Jesus with eternal glory*.

There would not be a lesser form and a greater form of this expected salvation - only the one great final salvation into eternal glory for all believers, deceased and alive.

Imagine the case of one of the Thessalonian Christians alive at the time Paul wrote his letters and who had put on his helmet of the hope of salvation (1 Thess 5:8). What if he died before the Parousia? Would the salvation he now hoped for as a deceased believer be any different from the salvation he had hoped for as a living believer? Of course not. The clear implication in Paul's words is that whether alive or dead, there was the expectation that at the Lord's Parousia all believers would experience the same, one great salvation - a salvation that would enable all, whether dead or alive, to live together with the Lord in his glory. This is of edifying comfort for these Thessalonians who were concerned for the lot of their deceased loved ones. Paul nowhere differentiates between the destinies of the living and the deceased believers at the Parousia. There is the one and the same great destiny for them all at the Parousia.

PART 4

In Which is Examined
The Significance of
the *New Jerusalem* in the Book of Revelation,
and the *Victory of the Lord Jesus Christ*
as the Heir of the Nations

Chapters 9 to 11

Chapter 9

The *New Jerusalem* and *Consummation for the Saints*

There are many preterist articles that clearly demonstrate from Scripture that the first church, as depicted in the New Testament, was promised, and so expected, the imminent Parousia of the Lord Jesus Christ – before that messianic generation passed away, circa AD 70. In previous chapters we have looked at the fact that the first Christians were partaking of the new covenant in a deposit and firstfruits measure – in accordance with their limited capacity for the things of God due to the legacy of fallenness in their humanity. The great hope of the first Christians was to partake of the new covenant blessedness in full, consummate measure at the Parousia of Christ. According to the NT Scriptures and as we have seen in previous chapters, the kind of fullness that they expected to receive at the Parousia is as follows:

- *The deceased saints of all past history.* The deceased OT saints and deceased NT Christians would be raised/resurrected with incorruptible, glorious, heavenly, spiritual bodies, and they would be glorified together with Christ, and brought into the immediate presence of God in the heavenly Holy of Holies, in company with their Lord Jesus. As such they would experience the promised eternal inheritance, eternal kingdom, and eternal glory, spoken of in the NT epistles.

- *The Christians living at the time of the Parousia.* The living believers in Christ would at the Parousia be changed and raised, bypassing the process of physical death, and along with their deceased brethren, they would be glorified together with Christ; they too, would put on immortal, incorruptible, glorious, spiritual, heavenly bodies; and they too, along with their deceased brethren, would receive their reward of entering the heavenly Holy of Holies to be with the Father and the Lord Jesus for ever more, enjoying to the full the same eternal inheritance, eternal kingdom and eternal glory.

I have previously examined many scriptures describing the eschatological hope of the early church, and shown that there is no distinction made by the early church between the hopes expected to be fulfilled to the deceased saints and to the living saints at the Parousia. All were expecting *the same* glorification at the Parousia, because *the same* glorification was promised to all, regardless of whether one may die before the time of the Parousia or whether one lived until the Parousia.

This teaching of the *same expectation* of the *same final blessings at the Parousia of Christ,* for deceased and living saints together, runs as a consistent theme throughout the whole NT. This being the clear teaching in the NT epistles, I have shown that there is no room at all for the idea that at the Parousia (about 70 AD) the saints alive at that time remained on earth in mortal bodies (in what is virtually still a deposit/firstfruits measure of new covenant experience), while the deceased brethren of all previous ages were raised to heavenly glory into the immediate presence of God in glorified bodies. Rather, all the Christians existing up till the coming of Jesus were taught to expect their final reward, final salvation, from the Lord at his coming. I believe that I have shown that the idea that the Parousia of Christ would bring *dissimilar fulfillments* of the *same expectations* based on the *same promises* of glory that were given to the *same people* is just not logical and does not seem to accord with the scriptural language of expectation.

The New Jerusalem.

In view of its obvious significance as an eschatological phenomenon, the meaning of the New Jerusalem, as described in the Revelation given to the apostle John, needs to be examined so as to assess its place in the scenario of the glorification of both living and deceased saints at the Parousia. In looking into this subject, I have, I believe adopted the accepted hermeneutical step of proceeding from the clear to the obscure — from the basis of the clear straightforward language and teaching of the NT epistles regarding the first Christians' expectancy of glorification with Christ in heaven, and then onto the more figurative language of the Revelation — to discover the meaning of the concept of the New Jerusalem as we find it in the Revelation. (The interpretation of a symbolic scene in an apocalyptic work must be determined by the clear teaching in the epistles, not vice versa).

The reader may wish to firstly read, as preparation, the following passages referring to the New Jerusalem and to the features contained in the New Jerusalem, to which I will refer in this chapter:

- Gal. 4:21-31;
- Heb. 11:9-10, 13-16;
- Heb. 12:18-28; Heb. 13:13-14;
- Rev. 2:7; 3:11-13, 21; 7:9-17; 14:1-5; 21:1-14; 21:22–22:5; 22:14, 19.

---

1. The General Concept of a New and Heavenly Jerusalem in New Testament Writings

The New Jerusalem is probably familiar to most people from its place in Revelation chapters 21 and 22, where it is popularly regarded as a representation of the final or consummate state for believers in the Lord Jesus Christ.

But before examining its special meaning in the Revelation, let us firstly note that the concept of a New Jerusalem exists in other epistles of the New Testament. It is known by several other expressions in the New Testament: the Jerusalem above, the city of the living God, the heavenly Jerusalem, the holy city, the great city, the holy Jerusalem. (Gal 4:26; Heb 12:22; Rev. 21:2, 9-10).

Now the concept of a New Jerusalem is presented in the New Testament under various metaphors: as a mother (and freewoman), as a bride/wife, and as the city of God. Such terminology would have been familiar to the first Jewish Christians, for in their Jewish scriptures, (what we now call the Old Testament), the earthly city Jerusalem was likewise known by these terms. The Old Testament terms however find their true or full meaning in the New Covenant, in God's plan of salvation through his Son Jesus Christ. In contrast to the earthly Jerusalem, Christians have the concept of a New Jerusalem:

- As a city, the New Jerusalem is a dwelling place for the saints, is the community of the saints; they seek it, they dwell in it.
- As a mother, the New Jerusalem (or Jerusalem above) imparts her life and spirit to her children (the saints).
- As a bride, the New Jerusalem is the people of God as a combined unity, in love and fellowship with Christ.

Let us briefly consider the New Jerusalem under these images of city, mother and bride. It will be seen that these terms all involve the concept of the New Covenant. Then we will see this City's relationship to the Kingdom of God.

(i) The New Jerusalem as the City of God

The New Jerusalem is clearly given the title "New" to differentiate it from the first and physical Jerusalem which first became of note when David defeated the Jebusites who previously possessed that area. The earthly Jerusalem was the central unifying city of the nation of Israel. It symbolized the people of the true God. Those who dwelt in it were privileged, for in this city the temple of God took pride of place. Although they knew, as Solomon had once said, that God could not be contained by the heavens let alone by a man-built temple (see 1 Kin. 8:8ff) yet they believed that God dwelt in a special way in the temple in Jerusalem. As the people prayed towards the temple, God would hear in heaven. Thus Jerusalem became known as the city of God. Jerusalem symbolized the people of God, and often God addressed his people, "O Jerusalem..."

But the earthly Jerusalem was earthly, material, temporal, and typified something higher. God has a city not made by human hands: a heavenly city, the New Jerusalem, to which all his true saints born of the Spirit belong. It is a spiritual new covenant reality, eternal in God's presence. For instance, the New Testament writer to the Hebrews said to his readers:

> [Heb 12:22-24] But *you have come to Mount Zion and to the city of the living God, the heavenly Jerusalem*, to an innumerable company of angels, 23 to a universal gathering, *to an assembly of firstborn ones who are* registered in heaven, to God the Judge of all, to the spirits of just men made perfect, *24 to Jesus the Mediator of the new covenant, and to the blood of sprinkling* that speaks better things than *that of* Abel.

Thus the heavenly city is connected with angels, with the church of firstborn ones registered in heaven, with God, with spirits of just men made perfect, with Jesus the Mediator of the New Covenant in his blood. The first Christians (pre-Parousia) had "come" to this city as a spiritual new covenant reality.

The Apostle John mentions several of the important symbolic features of this new heavenly city:

> [Rev. 21:10-14] And he carried me away in the Spirit to a great and high mountain, *and showed me the great city, the holy Jerusalem, descending out of heaven from God*, 11 having the glory of God. Her light *was* like a most precious stone, like a jasper stone, clear as crystal. 12 Also she had a great and high wall with twelve gates, and twelve angels at the gates, and names written on them, which are *the names* of the twelve tribes of the children of Israel: 13 three gates on the east, three gates on the north, three gates on the south, and three gates on the west. 14 Now the wall of the city had twelve foundations, and on them were the names of the twelve apostles of the Lamb.

This heavenly city of God is described using earthly architectural features, clearly symbolizing spiritual realities. And according to John's vision, people in the Lamb's book of life are able to enter it, and it is in this New Jerusalem that the glorified saints dwell and serve God, and God himself dwells and has his throne. (See the explicit promises for this mentioned in Revelation chapters 21 and 22). The Christians under threat of persecution and martyrdom, (particularly in Nero's days) were promised a permanent home in this city as a reward of their endurance as they waited for the Parousia of Jesus.

> [Rev. 3:12.] [The Lord Jesus said] "He who overcomes, I will make him a pillar in the temple of My God, and he shall go out no more. And I will write on him the name of My God and the name of the city of My God, the New Jerusalem, which

comes down out of heaven from My God. And [I will write on him] My new name.

This New Jerusalem is new in the sense that its revelation is new compared with the older revelation of the earthly Jerusalem, but in another sense this heavenly Jerusalem has been God's ideal since the foundation of the world. This New Jerusalem represents a heavenly realm or sphere of new covenant "architecture," in which God rules and where the light of God enlightens all, and where his people dwell and partake of its blessings of life and security and God's presence and glory. The New Jerusalem also represents the community of believers with whom God dwells and rules, and holds all in unity. The New Jerusalem then has this double sense: a spiritual sphere of new covenant realities in which God's redeemed people dwell, and also the community of believers as a unity in Christ.

As will be explained in more detail later, the association of the saints with the New and heavenly Jerusalem and their experience of its wonderful blessings has a partial measure prior to, and a consummate measure at, the Parousia of Christ.

(ii) *The Heavenly Jerusalem as a Mother and Freewoman*

The apostle Paul has a considerable amount to say about the first Christians connection with the heavenly Jerusalem:

> [Gal 4:21-31] Tell me, you who desire to be under the law, do you not hear the law? 22 For it is written that Abraham had two sons: the one by a bondwoman, the other by a freewoman. 23 But he *who was* of the bondwoman was born according to the flesh, and he of the freewoman through promise, 24 which things are symbolic. For these are the two *covenants*: the one from Mount Sinai which gives birth to bondage, which is Hagar— 25 for this Hagar is Mount Sinai in Arabia, and corresponds to Jerusalem which now is, and is in bondage with her children— 26 but *the Jerusalem above is free, which is the mother of us all.* 27 For it is written: "Rejoice, O barren, *you* who do not bear! Break forth and shout, you who are not in labor! For the desolate has many more children than she who has a husband." 28 Now we, brethren, as Isaac *was*, are *children of promise.* 29 But, as he who was born according to the flesh then persecuted him *who was born according to the Spirit*, even so *it is* now. 30 Nevertheless what does the Scripture say? "Cast out the bondwoman and her son, for the son of the bondwoman shall not be heir with the son of the free *woman*." So then, brethren, *we are not children of the bondwoman but of the free woman.*

Hagar (the slave/bondwoman, and concubine of Abraham) and Sarah (the freewoman and true wife of Abraham) represent two covenants – the old covenant, and the new covenant. These two covenants in turn find their expression or representation in two cities: the old covenant from Sinai is expressed in the earthly "Jerusalem that now exists," while the new covenant finds its embodiment in the "Jerusalem above." "The Jerusalem above" means "the heavenly Jerusalem." Jesus in Jn. 8:23 used the same Greek word *ano*, when he said that he was from "above," unlike his unbelieving opponents who were from "beneath." Paul refers to Jerusalem above as a heavenly counterpart to the earthly city. The heavenly Jerusalem represented the new covenant of liberty in the Lord Jesus, the gospel covenant involving God's grace in Christ and justification by faith in him that Paul was preaching; as compared with the existing earthly Jerusalem which was an expression of the old covenant which (because of man's fallenness) could only bring into bondage.

This heavenly Jerusalem, as embodying the life and spirit and principles of the new covenant, is called "the mother of us all" - the "all" referring to all the true believers in God and Christ - since all true believers receive their new life, salvation, and eternal happiness from the new covenant in Christ. And as individuals come, by God's grace, under the transforming influences of the new covenant and come to faith in Christ, they are nourished and have their belonging in the new covenant community of the New Jerusalem. This Jerusalem above is also referred to as "the free woman" because as the embodiment of the new covenant she holds the way and life of true liberty and reconciliation with God.

It is true to say that before the foundation of the world, God had in his mind the new covenant through the blood of his Christ who was regarded as slain before the foundation of the world for the sake of his people. He always had in his mind and heart a new covenant people, saved by his grace through Christ, a heavenly Jerusalem, whose whole manner of existence would be in the heavenly, spiritual power of the Holy Spirit. All true saints who ever existed, even prior to Jesus' incarnation, were held dear in God's ideal of a new covenant people in Christ. The first Christians, fully aware of the new covenant in Christ's blood were "children" of that new covenant, children of the "Jerusalem above."

(iii) The New Jerusalem as the Bride and Wife of the Lamb
> [Rev. 21:2, 9-11] Then I, John, saw *the holy city, New Jerusalem*, coming down out of heaven from God, *prepared as a bride adorned for her husband*.... 9 Then one of the seven angels who had the seven bowls filled with the seven last plagues came to me and talked with me, saying, "Come, I will show *you the bride, the Lamb's wife*." 10 And he carried me away in the Spirit to a great and high mountain, and showed me *the great city, the holy Jerusalem*, descending out of heaven from

God, 11 having the glory of God. Her light [was] like a most precious stone, like a jasper stone, clear as crystal.

Under the old covenant, the nation of Israel was regarded as the bride or wife or betrothed of the Lord. He had taken them into his care, to be everything to them that they could need. The terms clearly mean to express the close love and fellowship and mutual commitment which God desired to exist between Him and his people. Tragically the earthly Israel often apostatized and committed spiritual adultery by going after heathen idol-gods.

The New Testament makes it clear that the true Israel that the Lord desires to have as bride is composed of all true worshippers, those saints who have faith in him. Paul expresses his leading of the Corinthians to faith in Christ as a betrothing of them to Christ: "For I am jealous for you with godly jealousy. For I have betrothed you to one husband, that I may present [you as] a chaste virgin to Christ." (2 Cor. 11:2). Indeed the classic example of the church being likened to a bride and wife is in Paul's letter to the Ephesians:

> [Eph 5:25-27] 25 Husbands, love your wives, just as Christ also loved the church and gave Himself for her, 26 that He might sanctify and cleanse her with the washing of water by the word, 27 that He might present her to Himself a glorious church, not having spot or wrinkle or any such thing, but that she should be holy and without blemish.

Clearly then John's vision of the New Jerusalem coming as a bride for her husband represents the spiritual reality of the community of God's true people formally entering into a consummation of spiritual union and fellowship with the Lord. And the Revelation makes it clear that the time of this marital consummation (for all pre-Parousia saints) was to be at the (soon-expected) coming of Jesus. This topic will be examined in greater detail later in this article.

The concept of a New Jerusalem, then, has to do with the people of God in the New Covenant. We will further investigate features of this concept below.

2. The New Jerusalem - Firstfruits and Consummation

In Chapter 2, *New Covenant Blessings - Deposit and Fullness*, I believe that I have fairly comprehensively showed that the first Christians were experiencing what may be called the deposit and firstfruits measure of blessings of the New Covenant which had been established by the atonement and enthronement of Jesus. And for all the blessings that they were currently experiencing in a firstfruits measure, they were looking forward to a corresponding full measure of blessedness at the Parousia of Christ. At the Parousia of Christ they were expecting to enter the consummation or fullness of the New Covenant blessings which they now experienced in only a deposit/firstfruits measure.

As I pointed out in Chapter 2, under section 7. *The Peculiarity of the Deposit-Fullness Language in the New Testament*, if one happened to *only* read the Scripture verses in the NT which speak of the future fullness, one might be led to believe that none of the first Christians was yet saved or was yet a son of God, or was yet in the kingdom, etc. For example:

- 1 Thess. 5:8-9 speaks of *the hope of salvation*.
- 1 Pet. 1:5 speaks *salvation ready to be revealed* in the last time.

These verses say salvation is yet to come, and is the Christians' hope. Does that mean nobody was yet saved; that the new covenant salvation was not yet available? Certainly NOT, for other verses make it clear that the new covenant salvation was already available through faith in Christ Jesus. Believers in Christ Jesus *were already saved* and reconciled with God; e.g. Tit. 3:4-7 and Eph 2:4-6. There is but the one salvation through the completed work of Jesus Christ. However, this one salvation consists of a deposit/firstfruits measure in this life, then later a full, consummate, glorified measure. But the final phase is often spoken of as if it were a separate thing altogether.

We must be aware of this particular feature of New Covenant blessings in the NT writings — that a New Covenant blessing consists of a deposit/firstfruits measure while in this life, then a consummate, harvest measure later. The first Christians expected to experience their consummate measure at the Parousia of Christ. I believe that the *New Jerusalem of the Revelation pictures the concept of the heavenly Jerusalem in its consummate phase and manifestation.*

The Revelation's depiction of the New Jerusalem and its features may appear to be presented and promised to the first Christians in such a way as if the City and its blessings were never in existence at all before, or were never experienced before the Parousia. But the case is that the deposit/firstfruits realities of the City and its features were already present and experienced in the lives of the pre-Parousia Christians. This is an important fact to note.

In other NT letters we see that the first Christians had entered into and were experiencing the kingdom of God in a certain deposit/firstfruits measure already in pre-Parousia days, but were anticipating the time of inheriting the kingdom in its fullness at the Parousia of Christ. Similarly, they were already children of the heavenly Jerusalem and experiencing the life and Spirit of the New Jerusalem in a certain deposit/firstfruits measure, yet were looking forward to the future, promised consummate measure of heavenly Jerusalem blessedness – which latter is what is pictured in the Revelation. This will become clearer as we look as some examples of what I mean.

Here are some relevant passages concerning the concept of a new covenant heavenly Jerusalem, consistent with the firstfruits-then-harvest theme of the NT, showing that the harvest phase is what is being portrayed in the Revelation's New Jerusalem.

(i) Participation in the life and Spirit of the New Jerusalem

A. Already experiencing New Jerusalem life prior to the Parousia, i.e., in the deposit/firstfruits measure.

[Gal 4:21- 5:2] Tell me, you who desire to be under the law, do you not hear the law? 22 For it is written that Abraham had two sons: the one by a bondwoman, the other by a freewoman. 23 But he *who was* of the bondwoman was born according to the flesh, and he of the freewoman through promise, 24 which things are symbolic. For these are *the two covenants*: the one from Mount Sinai which gives birth to bondage, which is Hagar——25 for this Hagar is Mount Sinai in Arabia, and corresponds to Jerusalem which now is, and is in bondage with her children——26 but *the Jerusalem above is free, which is the mother of us all.* 27 For it is written: "Rejoice, O barren, *you* who do not bear! Break forth and shout, you who are not in labor! For the desolate has many more children than she who has a husband." *28 Now we, brethren, as Isaac was, are children of promise.* 29 But, as he who was born according to the flesh then persecuted him *who was born* according to the Spirit, even so *it is* now. 30 Nevertheless what does the Scripture say? "Cast out the bondwoman and her son, for the son of the bondwoman shall not be heir with the son of the freewoman." *31 So then, brethren, we are not children of the bondwoman but of the free.* 1 Stand fast therefore in the liberty by which Christ has made us free, and do not be entangled again with a yoke of bondage. 2 Indeed I, Paul, say to you that if you become circumcised, Christ will profit you nothing.

[Heb 12:18-24] For you have not come to the mountain that may be touched and that burned with fire, and to blackness and darkness and tempest, 19 and the sound of a trumpet and the voice of words, so that those who heard *it* begged that the word should not be spoken to them anymore. 20 (For they could not endure what was commanded: "And if so much as a beast touches the mountain, it shall be stoned or shot with an arrow." 21 And so terrifying was the sight *that* Moses said, "I am exceedingly afraid and trembling.") But *you have come to Mount Zion and to the city of the living God, the heavenly Jerusalem*, to an innumerable company of angels, 23 to the general assembly and church of the firstborn *who are* registered in heaven, to God the Judge of all, to the spirits of just men made perfect, 24 to Jesus the Mediator of the new covenant, and to the blood of sprinkling that speaks better things than *that of* Abel.

Paul makes it very clear in the above two passages: There are two covenants: a Sinai-Mosaic one of law-works and a gospel one of justification by faith in Christ.

The believers in Christ and his gospel-promise of justification by faith have not come to the fiery Mt Sinai of the old covenant – they were no longer under the law, (Rom 6:14; 7:4) – but have come to Mount Zion of the new covenant –.where they are under grace, (Rom 6:14). They are born of the Spirit and are children of the new gospel covenant, children of promise, children of the heavenly Jerusalem above, which is their "mother," in contrast to the non-believing Jews who remain under the old covenant as children of bondage. The Christians are children of the new covenant of peace with God and liberty in the Spirit, typified by the freewoman Sarah, not children of the system that brought bondage, the old covenant typified by the bondwoman Hagar. The first Christians had come to this heavenly city, this city that symbolizes the new covenant of Jesus.

B. An expected future consummate experience of entering and dwelling in and experiencing the New Jerusalem at the Parousia of Christ

[Rev. 3:12] *Him that overcometh will I make a pillar in the temple of my God*, and he shall go no more out: and I will write upon him the name of my God, and *the name of the city of my God, which is new Jerusalem, which cometh down out of heaven from my God*: and *I will write upon him* my new name.

[Rev. 2:7] "He who has an ear, let him hear what the Spirit says to the churches. *To him who overcomes I will give to eat from the tree of life, which is in the midst of the Paradise of God*.'" [The tree of life is a central feature of the New Jerusalem, ch. 22, which is here called the Paradise of God]

[Rev. 21:1-7] Now I saw a new heaven and a new earth, for the first heaven and the first earth had passed away. Also there was no more sea. 2 Then *I, John, saw the holy city, New Jerusalem, coming down out of heaven from God, prepared as a bride adorned for her husband*.... 6 And He said to me, "It is done! I am the Alpha and the Omega, the Beginning and the End. *I will give of the fountain of the water of life* freely to him who thirsts. 7 *"He who overcomes shall inherit all things*, and I will be his God and he shall be My son. [From vv. 6-7 we see the overcomers have the hope of inheriting as a near-future prospect, a share in the water of life in the New Jerusalem].

[Rev. 21:10-11] And he carried me away in the Spirit to a great and high mountain, and *showed me the great city, the holy Jerusalem, descending out of heaven from God*, 11 having the glory of God. Her light *was* like a most precious stone, like a jasper stone, clear as crystal.

There was to be a consummate coming and revelation of the concept of the New Jerusalem into which *the first Christians were expecting to enter at the Parousia*, involving an eschatological fullness of eternal life and eternal glory in God's presence. Prior to the Parousia, the New Jerusalem, signifying the new covenant kingdom, was in existence, but was experienced in a firstfruits measure.

In viewing *some of the features in the New Jerusalem of Revelation*, we discover the same theme of already experienced deposit/firstfruits becoming fullness and consummation at the Parousia. Consider the following features.

(ii) River of life in the New Jerusalem

A. Deposit/firstfruits measure of life experienced prior to Parousia

[Jn. 4:10,14] Jesus answered and said to her, "If you knew the gift of God, and whom it is who says to you, 'Give Me a drink,' you would have asked Him, and *He would have given you living water.*"... 14 "but whoever drinks of the water that I shall give him will never thirst. *But the water that I shall give him will become in him a fountain of water springing up into everlasting life.*"

[Jn. 7:37-38] On the last day, that great *day* of the feast, Jesus stood and cried out, saying, *"If anyone thirsts, let him come to Me and drink. 38 "He who believes in Me, as the Scripture has said, out of his heart will flow rivers of living water."* 39 *But this He spoke concerning the Spirit, whom those believing in Him would receive*; for the Holy Spirit was not yet *given*, because Jesus was not yet glorified.

[Rev. 22:17] And the Spirit and the bride say, "Come!" And let him who hears say, "Come!" And let him who thirsts come. *Whoever desires, let him take the water of life freely.*

Note that this last reference, in Rev. 22:17, is spoken to the churches of Asia, prior to the Parousia of Jesus; the believers could drink of water of life from the Lord Jesus already. But the visions of the new Jerusalem in chapters 21 to 22:7 concern the consummation to come, and speak of the river of life as still to come. The promise to the overcomers of living waters in Rev. 7:17 and 22:1 is in a vision of the near future and speaks of their reward of a consummate measure of life at the Parousia.

B. Consummation of life in the New Jerusalem at the Parousia of Jesus

[Rev. 7:17] "for the Lamb who is in the midst of the throne will shepherd them *and lead them to living fountains of waters*. And God will wipe away every tear from their eyes."

[Rev. 21:5-6] Then He who sat on the throne said, "Behold, I make all things new." And He said to me, "Write, for these words are true and faithful." 6 And He said to me, "It is done! I am the Alpha and the Omega, the Beginning and the End. *I will give of the fountain of the water of life freely to him who thirsts*.

[Rev. 22:1] And he showed me *a pure river of water of life, clear as crystal, proceeding from the throne of God and of the Lamb*.

(iii) The Tree of Life in the New Jerusalem

A. The tree of life, symbolic of eternal life and fellowship with God, was experienced in a deposit/firstfruits measure prior to the Parousia

Man's loss of the tree of life (Gen. 3:24) signified loss of life and fellowship with God they would have enjoyed otherwise. The term "tree of life" is not used in the following verses, but what it signifies is plainly referred to.

[Jn. 5:24] "Most assuredly, I say to you, he who hears My word and believes in Him who sent Me has *eternal life*, and shall not come into judgment, but *has passed from death into life*.

[Jn. 17:2-3] "as You have given Him authority over all flesh, that He should give *eternal life* to as many as You have given Him. 3 "And *this is eternal life, that they may know You, the only true God, and Jesus Christ* whom You have sent.

[1 Jn. 5:11-12] And this is the testimony: that *God has given us eternal life*, and this life is in His Son. 12 He who has the Son has life; he who does not have the Son of God does not have life.

[Eph. 2:17] And He came and preached peace to you who were afar off and to those who were near. 18 For *through Him we both have access by one Spirit to the Father*.

B Access to the tree of life - symbolic of access into God's fellowship and eternal life - was promised as a consummate blessing within the New Jerusalem at the Parousia of Christ.

> [Rev. 2:7] "He who has an ear, let him hear what the Spirit says to the churches. To him who overcomes *I will give to eat from the tree of life, which is in the midst of the Paradise of God.*"
>
> [Rev. 22:14] Blessed [are] those who do His commandments, *that they may have the right to the tree of life, and may enter through the gates into the city.*
>
> [Rev. 22:2] In the middle of its street, and on either side of the river, [was] *the tree of life*, which bore twelve fruits, each [tree] yielding its fruit every month.

(iv) Sonship in the New Jerusalem

A. Sonship already possessed but experienced in deposit/firstfruits measure prior to the Parousia of Jesus

We have already quoted relevant verses in Chapter 2. See for example Rom 8:15-17; Gal 3:26; 4:4-7; Eph 1:3-5. The experience of sonship was already real, but yet in deposit/firstfruits measure, for while in mortal, fallen bodies, and imperfect minds, the full glory of their status was not yet revealed.

B. Consummation of Sonship in the New Jerusalem at the Parousia

> [Rev. 21:5-7] Then He who sat on the throne said, "Behold, I make all things new." And He said to me, "Write, for these words are true and faithful." 6 And He said to me, "It is done! I am the Alpha and the Omega, the Beginning and the End. I will give of the fountain of the water of life freely to him who thirsts. 7 "He who overcomes shall inherit all things, and *I will be his God and he shall be My son.*"

The first Christians awaited the full realization of the dignity and function and happiness of sonship in relationship to and fellowship with God as Father in glory. Note again the characteristic way of expressing the future consummation in such a way that sounds as if such a relationship of sonship had not been formed yet, e.g. "he shall be my son" (Rev. 21:7), and also "eagerly waiting for the adoption as sons" (Rom 8:23); whereas in fact the first Christians rejoiced in their already being children and sons of God. Once again it is the theme of deposit/firstfruits preceding the consummation at the Parousia.

(v) God being the God of his people, and they being the people of God, in the New Jerusalem

A. Their being God's people, and His being their God, was already a reality, but experienced in a deposit/firstfruits measure prior to the Parousia of Jesus.

> [1 Pet 2:9-10] But you *are* a chosen generation, a royal priesthood, a holy nation, *His own special people*, that you may proclaim the praises of Him who called you out of darkness into His marvelous light; 10 who once *were* not a people *but are now the people of God*, who had not obtained mercy but now have obtained mercy.
>
> [2 Thess 1:1-2] Paul, Silvanus, and Timothy, to the church of the Thessalonians *in God our Father* and the Lord Jesus Christ: 2 Grace to you and peace *from God our Father* and the Lord Jesus Christ.

B. Their being God's people, and His being their God was manifested in a consummate way in the New Jerusalem at the Parousia of Jesus.

> [Rev. 3:12] "He who overcomes, I will make him a pillar in the temple of My God, and he shall go out no more. And *I will write on him the name of My God* and the name of the city of My God, the New Jerusalem, which comes down out of heaven from My God. And *I will write on him* My new name.
>
> [Rev. 21:3, 7] And I heard a loud voice from heaven saying, "Behold, the tabernacle of God [is] with men, and He will dwell with them, and *they shall be His people. God Himself* will be with them *[and will be] their God*.... 7 "He who overcomes shall inherit all things, and *I will be his God* and he shall be My son.

To have God's name written on the believer (Rev. 3:12) openly manifests the fact of his belonging to God, and God being his master, and his blessedness. "They shall be his people" means that those who already were his people prior to the Parousia, will after the Parousia be manifested in their true nature and glory as the people of the almighty and all-loving God. Similarly, "I will be their God" means that for those to whom he was already their God before the Parousia, he will after the Parousia manifest the blessings of his fellowship and the blessings of his being their God to them in heavenly, glorious ways they had never known before – in ways that, in their glorified condition, they can manage; but which before the Parousia, in their mortal condition, they could never have managed.

(vi) God's dwelling with men in the New Jerusalem

A. God's dwelling with his people in a pre-Parousia firstfruits measure of experience

> [Jn. 14:22-23] Judas (not Iscariot) said to Him, "Lord, how is it that You will manifest Yourself to us, and not to the world?" 23 Jesus answered and said to him, "If anyone loves Me, he

will keep My word; and My Father will love him, and *We will come to him and make Our home* [or dwelling place] *with him*. [This was expected after the coming of the Holy Spirit at the day of Pentecost].

[Eph 2:19-22] Now, therefore, you are no longer strangers and foreigners, but fellow citizens with the saints and members of the household of God, 20 having been built on the foundation of the apostles and prophets, Jesus Christ Himself being the chief *cornerstone*, 21 in whom the whole building, being joined together, grows into a holy temple in the Lord, 22 *in whom you also are being built together for a dwelling place of God in the Spirit.*

B. A future dwelling of God with his people in a consummate way in the New Jerusalem at the Parousia of Jesus

[Rev. 7:15] "Therefore they are before the throne of God, and serve Him day and night in His temple. And *He who sits on the throne will dwell among them.*

[Rev. 21:3] And I heard a loud voice from heaven saying, "Behold, *the tabernacle of God is with men*, and *He will dwell with them*, and they shall be His people. **God Himself will be with them** *and be* their God.

Note again the peculiarity of the firstfruits-harvest language. After Pentecost, God was dwelling with his new covenant people; yet the promise was that at the Parousia God would come to dwell with them. Is this a paradox? No, it just means that at the Parousia, the people of God would be taken into a realm of knowing the presence of God and his dwelling with them that will far surpass anything they had previously experienced of his presence and dwelling with them prior to the Parousia. Firstfruits now – later the harvest measure.

(vii) Former things passed away, all things made new, in New Jerusalem

A. In principle, this blessing was given in pre-Parousia days, and experienced in a deposit/firstfruits measure.

[2 Cor. 5:17] Therefore, if anyone [is] in Christ, *[he is] a new creation; old things have passed away; behold, all things have become new.*

[Eph. 2:10] For we are His workmanship, *created in Christ Jesus* for good works, which God prepared beforehand that we should walk in them.

[Col. 3:9] Do not lie to one another, since *you have put off the old man with his deeds,*

Prior to the Parousia, the reality of the new covenant, new creation work was but in firstfruits measure. A constant spiritual renewing was going on in the Christians, the new things of Christ were their portion. While, in the inner self, the old man had been put off, much of the old ways still had to be dealt with, and the presence of sin and the flesh and the mortality of their body showed the process was not complete in this life.

B. The consummate experiential reality of this new creation blessing – the complete eviction of every trace of the old fallenness and mortality, and full permeation with the new creation life in its glory – was expected in the New Jerusalem at the Parousia of Christ.

[Rev. 21:1-5] Now I saw a new heaven and a new earth, for the first heaven and the first earth had passed away. Also there was no more sea. 2 Then I, John, saw the holy city, New Jerusalem, coming down out of heaven from God, prepared as a bride adorned for her husband. 3 And I heard a loud voice from heaven saying, "Behold, the tabernacle of God *is* with men, and He will dwell with them, and they shall be His people. God Himself will be with them *and be* their God. 4 "And God will wipe away every tear from their eyes; there shall be no more death, nor sorrow, nor crying. There shall be no more pain, for *the former things have passed away*." 5 Then He who sat on the throne said, "*Behold, I make all things new*." And He said to me, "Write, for these words are true and faithful."

Note from all the above that the first Christians already had the blessings of the New Jerusalem in deposit/firstfruits measure; and *the promise of the special coming of the New Jerusalem in Rev. 21 and 22 represents the coming at the Parousia of the consummate manifestation of the New Jerusalem – the glory phase of the new covenant for the first Christians.*

The consummate manifestation of the concept of a New Jerusalem, described in the Revelation, pictures the great reward of new covenant fullness and glory promised to the first Christians at the Parousia — that which lay at the end of all their suffering and endurance and faithful service (even to the death) for the cause of the Lord Jesus whom they loved.

What I have discussed above is important to consider. I feel that some preterists have gone astray by interpreting the coming of New Jerusalem in the Revelation as signifying *the beginning* of the new covenant age. Instead it signifies the *consummation* of the already existing new covenant experience of the first Christians.

We must always keep uppermost in our minds the issue of audience relevance. It was for the first Christians that the Parousia was the occasion of this consummation. As I have mentioned before, we post-Parousia Christians enter this glory when we finish our earthly life. But those saints still alive at the Parousia entered it at the Parousia.

3. The New Jerusalem and the Kingdom of God

To come to a better understanding of just what the New Jerusalem signifies let us examine some scriptures that will guide us to see a clear and intimate relationship between the New Jerusalem and the new covenant kingdom of God. (Because of the large amount of space required if I were to quote fully the Scripture passages pertaining to this subject, I hope the reader won't mind too much if I just give the references for their own perusal).

(i) Parallel concepts of the heavenly Jerusalem and the new covenant kingdom of God

Consider the passage from the letter to the Hebrews contrasting life under the Mosaic or old covenant and the new covenant in Christ Jesus – Heb. 12:18-28, noting the two sections vv. 18-24 and 25-28. Note the parallelism of ideas in vv. 18-24 and vv. 25-28.

    a. In vv. 18-24 we have a comparison drawn between the Sinaitic old covenant scene and the heavenly Jerusalem/new covenant scene. This is paralleled by the comparison in vv. 25-28, between the old kingdom which is to be shaken, that consists of the things that are to be removed, (in vv. 26-27a), and the new kingdom that is unshakable and remains and which consists of things that cannot be shaken, (in vv. 27b-28). The theme of the old being replaced by the new, applies to city/covenant concept (vv. 18-24) and to kingdom concept (vv. 25-28).

    b. In vv. 18-24 we are told that the first Christians prior to the Parousia had approached/drawn near (Gr. *proserchomai*) to Mount Zion, which is the city of the living God, the heavenly Jerusalem (v.22). Their hope of actually experiencing *fully* that heavenly city had not been fulfilled yet, for they were still seeking the city to come (13:14).

This is paralleled in vv. 25-28 where we are told that they were in the process of receiving the kingdom of God, the unshakable kingdom, (v.28), which they would fully inherit at the Parousia of Christ. The theme of present, partial experience now of the new, climaxing into a near-future consummate experience of the new, applies to both the heavenly Jerusalem/new covenant scene in 12:18-24 and the unshakable kingdom scene in 12:25-28.

The parallelism here clearly implies that the heavenly Jerusalem and the unshakable kingdom are intimately connected and both concern new covenant realities in Christ.

(ii) The heavenly city and the kingdom of God both involve ultimate blessing for OT saints

Consider Heb. 11:9-10, 13-16 concerning the OT saints, such as Abraham, Isaac and Jacob; and then consider Matt. 8:11-12 and Lk. 13:28-29 in which Jesus refers to Abraham, Isaac and Jacob.

These three passages concern the hope of final blessedness of these saints. We note that the writer to the Hebrews says that this hope of final blessedness of the OT saints was to enter and experience the rest and happiness and security of the heavenly homeland with its heavenly city which God had prepared for them (instead of the pilgrim life in earthly Canaan). That heavenly city is the New Jerusalem.

Jesus' words (in the Matt and Luke passages) reveal that the hope of these ancients would find its fulfillment in their sitting down (implying rest and fellowship with God) in the consummate form of the kingdom of God which the Lord Jesus would bring at his Parousia (Matt 16:27-28).

There is therefore here a clear connection between the consummate hope of the heavenly city and the consummate hope of the kingdom of God. The kingdom of God in its consummate form at the Parousia of the Lord Jesus, and the beautiful scene in the book of Revelation of the heavenly New Jerusalem that comes at the Parousia of the Lord Jesus, both involve the consummate blessing of rest and fellowship with God. It may be said that the heavenly city, New Jerusalem of the Revelation, and the consummated kingdom of God describe the one divine eschatological reality.

(iii) The kingdom of God and the City of God are seen in the NT as something the first Christians were to seek, both to inherit and to enter

a. Seeking, inheriting and entering the kingdom of God. Believers were seeking as an ultimate goal the coming kingdom of God, in the hope of entering it and inheriting it at the Parousia of the Lord Jesus. For example:

Lk. 12:31 - seeking the kingdom of God as a priceless treasure in the heavens.
Matt 25:34 and Jas. 2:5 - inheriting the kingdom would not occur until the Lord's coming.
2 Pet 1:10-11 - entering the eternal kingdom at Christ's coming

b. Seeking, inheriting and entering the heavenly city. Believers were also seeking as an ultimate goal the heavenly city, in the hope of entering it and inheriting a place in it, all of which would occur at the Parousia of Christ. For example:

Heb. 11:14,16; 13:13-14 - seeking the heavenly city to come.
Rev. 3:11-12; 21:7 - inheriting the New Jerusalem .
Rev. 21:27; 22:12-14 - entering into the New Jerusalem.

We see in these two sets of scriptures, under sections a. and b. above, a consistent correspondence in terms of a goal to seek, an inheritance promised, and blessing to be entered. The kingdom of God and the heavenly city are *both* presented as eschatological goals or ultimate blessings which the saints are to *seek*, knowing that they are an *inheritance* promised by God, and that they must maintain a faithful ambition to *enter,* at the Parousia of Christ.

This shows that the coming consummate form of the kingdom of God and the New Jerusalem are but two different representations of the one, same divine reality. Perhaps it can better be said that the heavenly city New Jerusalem pictured in the Revelation is the expression of the consummated kingdom of God, which the people of God expected to experience at the Lord's Parousia.

(iv) The hope of the kingdom and of the heavenly city involves eternal life and resurrection

a. The kingdom and eternal life and resurrection. Believers were hoping for the consummate form of the kingdom of God in which they expected to find resurrection and inherit eternal life. For example:

Matt 19:28 - 20:1 and Matt 25:31, 34, 46 - inheriting the kingdom involves inheriting eternal life.
Acts 19:8; 23:6; 26:6-8; 28:20, 23, 30-31 - the gospel of the kingdom of God involves the hope of resurrection.

b. The New Jerusalem and eternal life and resurrection. Believers were promised the blessing of eternal life and resurrection in the New Jerusalem, at the Parousia. For example:

Rev. 2:7; 22:1-2; 22:14 - the tree of life and the river of life in the New Jerusalem.

Note: Due to sin in the original paradise of God, the Garden of Eden, man lost his life of fellowship with his Creator, pictured by his losing the right to feed on the tree of life. In the Revelation, the heavenly city, the New Jerusalem, pictures the consummated grace and victory of God, where his people are shown fully restored to a full participation of the tree of life. These verses from the Revelation thus use symbolic or figurative language to show that those residing in the heavenly city, have eternal life in its consummate form of full fellowship with God who dwells in the city.

Heb 11:9b-10, 13-19, 35, 39-40 - the hope of "the fathers" was the hope of a heavenly homeland and its heavenly city, which included the hope of a "better resurrection."

Acts 26:6-8 - Paul (guided by the Holy Spirit) in referred to the hope of the fathers as being the resurrection of the dead; it was the promise of God to them.

In Hebrews, the writer (guided by the same Holy Spirit who inspired the words in Acts), declared that the promise to the fathers, upon which they based their hope, was a heavenly city and homeland prepared by God for them, and also a "better resurrection," (i.e. better than a mere physical rising to resume an earthly life). By referring to Abraham's expectation of the resurrection of Isaac, the Hebrews writer may be hinting at the fathers' hope of a heavenly resurrection. *The point to note here from the Acts and Hebrews passages is that the Holy Spirit associates the hope held by the fathers of entering the heavenly city with the hope held by the fathers of the resurrection of the dead.*

From the parallelism above in a. and b. we see that:
- The eschatological promise/hope of the kingdom of God, included the expectation of resurrection and eternal life to be actually given to them at the Parousia of Christ.
- The eschatological promise/hope of the New Jerusalem in the Revelation also included expectation of resurrection and eternal life.

****

From the four subheadings in section 3 above, we have seen that Scripture reveals an intimate connection between the New Jerusalem and the Kingdom of God. In summary: *Both the coming kingdom of God and the coming New Jerusalem have to do with the consummation or fullness of the New Covenant founded on the atoning sacrifice and resurrection and ascension to glory of the Lord Jesus Christ.*

Everything hoped for in the coming kingdom of God is pictured in the Revelation as having its fulfillment in the New Jerusalem: resurrection, eternal life, full rest and fellowship in the presence of Almighty God. It is no wonder then that there is the call for saints to seek and to be ready to enter this consummate blessing of the New Covenant kingdom of God as pictured in the heavenly New Jerusalem.

We are confident of the following conclusion:

The New Jerusalem, also called the heavenly city, as shown in the Revelation, pictures or represents the New Covenant kingdom of God in its consummated form, which the first Christians expected to inherit at the Parousia of the Lord Jesus.

4. The Inhabitants of the New Jerusalem at the Time of the Parousia

[Rev. 21:1-3] Now I saw a new heaven and a new earth, for the first heaven and the first earth had passed away. Also there was no more sea. 2 Then I, John, saw the holy city, New Jerusalem, coming down out of heaven from God, prepared as a bride adorned for her husband. 3 And I heard a great voice out of heaven saying, Behold, the tabernacle of God *is* with men, and he will dwell with them, and they shall be his people, and God himself shall be with them, *and be* their God.

The special thing emphasized in this vision of the future given to John, is that in this coming heavenly city God began to dwell with *his people* in a blessed way which had never been possible in the history of the world before the Parousia of Jesus.

Let us look the question: Who, according to the NT writings, were expected to be the inhabitants of this heavenly city when it was revealed at the Lord's Parousia?

The number of believers living on earth at any one time is minimal compared with the far exceeding number of believers who have finished their allotted time on this earth. Consider the situation in the days just prior to the Parousia. Having experienced the benefits of the first coming of Jesus, all the deceased OT saints and all the deceased NT Christians (who had died from martyrdom and other causes), as well as all the living NT saints – all were waiting for the second coming or appearing of the Messiah to bring them all into the final/complete salvation into glory and into fellowship with God in the heavenly Holy of Holies where their forerunner, Jesus, had preceded them. They looked forward to entering into possession of the heavenly homeland and heavenly city (as described in the epistle of the Hebrews).

The apostle John in the Revelation was given insights into the new state of things that was to follow the Parousia of Christ, including the coming down of the New Jerusalem, and the tabernacle of God coming to be with men, and of their being his people and His being their God. This new state of things clearly speaks of a consummative, glorious finale in God's plan of redemption.

Now, in our preterist eschatological studies, we must not overly focus on the living saints and their blessings at the Parousia while forgetting the vast waiting multitude of previously deceased OT and NT saints who also were looking for the Parousia of the Messiah. There is a tendency in studying the coming down out of heaven of the New Jerusalem in Revelation chapters 21-22, to predominantly focus on what it means for the living saints or for us post-Parousia saints. If more consideration were given to the fact that the greater numbers of deceased believers had just as much interest in the coming of the new Jerusalem as did the living saints at that time, then it may help us to a better and more scriptural understanding of the meaning and application of the new Jerusalem to all believers.

Whatever interpretation we give to the events actioned by the Parousia of Christ, such as the coming down out of heaven of the New Jerusalem, and the dwelling of God with men, etc., it must cater responsibly for their effects on the greater number of previously deceased believers as well as for the saints who were still alive on earth at the time of the Parousia.

Consider the following people whose hopes were set on entering and inheriting the New Jerusalem at the Parousia of Jesus.

(i) The Overcomers in the seven churches of Asia and their relationship to the New Jerusalem

"Overcomers" is the term qualifying faithful Christians in The Revelation. (All faithful believers in Christ are called overcomers by the apostle John in his first epistle, 1 Jn. 5:4-5). In view of the fact that the Revelation given to the Apostle John concerned things that would shortly come to pass, then the promises made to the Christians of the seven churches (in chs 2 and 3) regarding the blessings of the new and heavenly Jerusalem, were regarded as promises soon to be fulfilled. Here are a few promises concerning their association with the coming New Jerusalem:

> [Rev. 3:12] *Him that overcometh will I make a pillar in the temple of my God*, and he shall go no more out: and I will write upon him the name of my God, and *the name of the city of my God, which is new Jerusalem, which cometh down out of heaven from my God*: and *I will write upon him* my new name.
>
> [Rev. 2:7] "He who has an ear, let him hear what the Spirit says to the churches. *To him who overcomes I will give to eat from the tree of life, which is in the midst of the Paradise of God.*'"
> [The tree of life is a central feature of the New Jerusalem]
>
> [Rev. 21:6-7] And He said to me, "It is done! I am the Alpha and the Omega, the Beginning and the End. *I will give of the fountain of the water of life freely to him who thirsts.* 7 "*He who overcomes shall inherit all things*, and I will be his God and he shall be My son. [Again the overcomers share in the New Jerusalem where the fountain of life is, 22:1].
>
> [Rev. 22:14] Blessed [are] those who do His commandments, *that they may have the right to the tree of life, and may enter through the gates into the city.*

In view of the short time frame for the fulfillment of these promises, it is reasonable to assume that many of the readers and hearers of the Revelation would still be alive when the Lord came. But the Lord also gives clear intimation in the Revelation that many Christians would be martyred before the Lord's coming. For example:

[Rev. 2:10] "Do not fear any of those things which you are about to suffer. Indeed, the devil is about to throw *some* of you into prison, that you may be tested, and you will have tribulation ten days. *Be faithful until death*, and I will give you the crown of life.

[Rev. 2:13] "I know your works, and where you dwell, where Satan's throne is. And you hold fast to My name, and did not deny My faith even in the days in which *Antipas was My faithful martyr*, who was killed among you, where Satan dwells.

[Rev. 6:9] When He opened the fifth seal, I saw under the *altar the souls of those who had been slain for the word of God and for the testimony which they held.* 10 And they cried with a loud voice, saying, "How long, O Lord, holy and true, until You judge and avenge our blood on those who dwell on the earth?" 11 Then a white robe was given to each of them; and it was said to them that they should rest a little while longer, until *both the number of their fellow servants and their brethren, who would be killed as they were*, was completed.

[Rev. 12:11] "And they overcame him [the devil] by the blood of the Lamb and by the word of their testimony, and they did not love their lives *to the death*.

[Rev. 13:7] It was granted to him [the beast] to make war with the saints and to overcome them. And authority was given him over every tribe, tongue, and nation.

Therefore the blessedness of inhabiting the coming New Jerusalem was promised by Jesus himself to all Christians, both the living and the deceased, to be fulfilled to them at his Parousia.

(ii) The saints who have come out of the great tribulation, and their relationship to the New Jerusalem.

Rev. 7:9-17 concerns a multitude of "overcomers." Their relationship to the New Jerusalem is very interesting. Remember that the Revelation was deliberately aimed at encouraging the saints who were facing extreme persecution under Nero, and who were eagerly looking for the ultimate salvation from the Lord Jesus at his Parousia. The scene presented in Rev. 7:9-17 is a preview in John's vision of the happy state of those who would come out of the coming persecutions. The saints could encourage themselves: 'I am confident in the midst of these persecutions, for after my sufferings I will experience glorious blessing at the Parousia as the Revelation given by our Lord to John shows me. It is no matter whether I am still alive at that time or if I die for my faith in the Lord before the Parousia, the revelation to John shows that I will experience wonderful blessing in the presence of the Lord at his Parousia.' Consider the blessings promised to the saints who would come out of great tribulation, as foreseen by John.

[Rev. 7:9-17] After this I beheld, and, lo, a great multitude, which no man could number, of all nations, and kindreds, and people, and tongues, stood before the throne, and before the Lamb, clothed with white robes, and palms in their hands; 10 And cried with a loud voice, saying, Salvation to our God which sitteth upon the throne, and unto the Lamb. 11 And all the angels stood round about the throne, and *about* the elders and the four beasts, and fell before the throne on their faces, and worshipped God, 12 Saying, Amen: Blessing, and glory, and wisdom, and thanksgiving, and honor, and power, and might, *be* unto our God for ever and ever. Amen. 13 And one of the elders answered, saying unto me, what are these which are arrayed in white robes? And whence came they? 14 And I said unto him, Sir, thou knowest. And he said to me, these are they which came out of great tribulation, and have washed their robes, and made them white in the blood of the Lamb. 15 Therefore are they before the throne of God, and serve him day and night in his temple: and he that sitteth on the throne shall dwell among them. 16 They shall hunger no more, neither thirst any more; neither shall the sun light on them, nor any heat. 17 For the Lamb which is in the midst of the throne shall feed them, and shall lead them unto living fountains of waters: and God shall wipe away all tears from their eyes.

This preview given to John describes the saints in a blessed heavenly situation, who had come out of the tribulation, experiencing the bliss of God's presence and the shepherding of the Lord Jesus.

Also keep in mind that this multitude includes *all* overcomers - *both those still alive on earth at the Parousia and those who became deceased/martyred prior to the Parousia.* Here we see them *all* together in the same place before the throne of God in heaven as one great multitude, having come out of the great tribulation.

Note the *consummative aspects* in this passage of scripture: this scene clearly teaches a situation and experience far higher than what these Christians could know in their normal, earthly existence, and far higher than what we post-Parousia Christians know in our earthly existence. Note their blessings:

- They are before the throne of God, serving day and night in his temple.
- God on his throne dwells in their midst.
- No more traces of the curse attached to them - no trace of hunger, thirst, harm or sorrow or tears.
- The Lamb is in their midst to shepherd and feed them.
- They have access to living fountains of water (a consummate New Jerusalem reality, Rev. 22:1).

In this scene all Christians - whether they were living or martyred by the time of the Parousia of Jesus – who suffered in, and came out of, the great tribulation are together before God in consummated bliss.

A comparison quickly shows that the blessings of these overcomers in Rev. 7:9-17 match the blessings that are revealed to John as what would exist in the new and heavenly Jerusalem in Revelation chapters 21-22 — their being before the throne of God and serving Him, 22:3; God dwelling with his people, 21:3; no curse, no tears, 21:4; 22:3; the Lamb present 22:3; 21:22; living waters, 22:1.

Therefore it seems justified to say that the vision of the overcomers in Rev. 7:9-17 (made up of all believers, whether they were alive or whether they were deceased at the time of Christ's Parousia), is a preview of those believers in the consummate blessedness of the New Jerusalem which is later pictured more fully in Rev. 21 and 22, and which came at the Parousia of Jesus.

Surely it is logical to understand that the consummated bliss that the previously deceased/martyred saints expected to experience in that paradise of God called the New Jerusalem, following the Parousia, was the same consummated bliss that the living saints expected to experience following the Parousia. Otherwise the promises of happiness in the presence of God and the Shepherd Jesus at the Parousia of Jesus following the sufferings — promises which were given to *all* the Christian readers via the apostle John in the Revelation — would have had different meanings depending on what group of Christians one belonged to at the time of the Parousia - the deceased group or the living group. Such a suggestion of double meanings is illogical and confusing.

The point to especially note is that this new Jerusalem that John sees descending from heaven is the *new home to all pre-Parousia Christians, whether they were living or deceased Christians at time of the Parousia; it is their promised reward.* It is a city in which the multitudes of deceased saints and living saints expected to find glorious life and happiness in God's presence, at the Parousia of Jesus.

(iii) The apostles and their relationship to the New Jerusalem

The apostles of the Lord Jesus would of course be amongst the "overcomers" whose hope was to enter the heavenly city of God — that consummate form of the kingdom of God. It is interesting to note that in the apostle John's vision of the New Jerusalem, he saw the names of the 12 apostles on the foundations of the city, Rev. 21:14, "Now the wall of the city had *twelve foundations*, and on them *were the names of the twelve apostles of the Lamb.*" To me, this implies, not only that the city is founded on the Word and Gospel of God as given through the apostles by inspiration of the Holy Spirit, but that the apostles themselves would be "residents" in their glorified state in this New Jerusalem at the Parousia of Christ. And we may note that it is a fact of history that many of the apostles were deceased by the time of the Parousia circa AD 70. Yet, the Parousia was the consummating time for both deceased apostles and living apostles.

(iv) The Old Testament Saints and their relationship to the New Jerusalem

Abraham and his descendants, all the believers from among the tribes of Israel, are said in the letter to the Hebrews to be looking forward to the heavenly city and heavenly homeland, Heb 11:9-10, 13-16. Note verse 16: "But now *they earnestly desire a better, that is, a heavenly country*. Therefore God is not ashamed to be called their God, *for He has prepared a city for them*."

The apostle John saw the coming New Jerusalem, having twelve gates with the names of the twelve tribes of the children of Israel written on them.

> [Rev. 21:10-12] And he carried me away in the Spirit to a great and high mountain, and showed me the great city, the holy Jerusalem, descending out of heaven from God, 11 having the glory of God. Her light *was* like a most precious stone, like a jasper stone, clear as crystal. 12 *Also she had a great and high wall with twelve gates, and twelve angels at the gates, and names written on them, which are the names of the twelve tribes of the children of Israel:*

This means that all the true saints out of Israel throughout Israel's history, would have their dwelling in this city along with their "father" Abraham, when this city was revealed at the Parousia of Christ. Not all Bible versions convey the emphasis of the definite articles in the Greek of Heb 11:10, "*he waited for the city which has the foundations, whose architect and builder is God*." Abraham looked forward to "*the* city which has *the* foundations," – the foundations of the gospel of Jesus Christ preached by the apostles, Rev. 22:14. The writer to the Hebrews is no doubt referring to the vision in the Revelation which must have been in circulation at that time. Abraham and his descendants were earnestly desiring, stretching forward to, (Gr. *orego*) their heavenly homeland, (Heb 11:16).

(v) The New Testament Saints in General and the New Jerusalem

In addition to the references in the Revelation to the Christian "overcomers," other NT epistles refer to the Christians' hope of inheriting a place in the coming heavenly city of God.

> [Heb 12:22-25] But *you have come to Mount Zion and to the city of the living God, the heavenly Jerusalem*, to an innumerable company of angels, 23 to the general assembly and church of

the firstborn *who are* registered in heaven, to God the Judge of all, to the spirits of just men made perfect, 24 to Jesus the Mediator of the new covenant, and to the blood of sprinkling that speaks better things than *that of* Abel. 25 See that you do not refuse Him who speaks. For if they did not escape who refused Him who spoke on earth, much more *shall we not escape* if we turn away from Him who *speaks* from heaven,

They had come spiritually, in a deposit/firstfruits measure, to the city, and were experiencing its life and spirit (Gal 4), but their hope was for the full consummate entrance into the city when it was revealed fully at the Lord's Parousia, as pictured in Revelation chapters 21-22. They were still seeking the city to come in its consummate reality.

[Heb 13:13-14] Therefore let us go forth to Him, outside the camp, bearing His reproach. 14 For *here we have no continuing city, but we seek the one to come.*

[Phil 3:18-21] For many walk, of whom I have told you often, and now tell you even weeping, *that they are* the enemies of the cross of Christ: 19 whose end *is* destruction, whose god *is their* belly, and *whose* glory *is* in their shame – who set their mind on earthly things. 20 *For our citizenship is in heaven, from which we also eagerly wait for the Savior, the Lord Jesus Christ,* 21 who will transform our lowly body that it may be conformed to His glorious body, according to the working by which He is able even to subdue all things to Himself.

Paul refers here in this Philippian letter to Christians having the hope of consummately partaking of their citizenship in heaven (v. 20), far higher and better than earthly things (v.19), at the Parousia of Jesus, (v. 20). He says their names are in the Book of Life (Phil 4:3). The Book of Life is a phrase used in the Revelation in connection with the New Jerusalem. Those whose names were not in the Book of Life cannot enter the heavenly city (Rev. 21:27). Anyone who took away from the words of the book of the prophecy would lose their part in the Book of Life and in the holy city, (Rev. 22:19).

Whether Paul was familiar, at this time of his writing to the Philippians, with the visions of the Revelation I do not know, but I believe the Holy Spirit, in guiding Paul to speak to the Philippians of their having a citizenship in heaven, and of their names being in the Book of Life (implying this Book recorded their right, through Jesus, to life as a citizen in the heavenly commonwealth or city), was referring to the same situation that the Holy Spirit, through John, presented in Revelation chapters 21 and 22, and the same situation as the author to the Hebrews was speaking about in Heb 11:9-10, 13-16; Heb 12:22 and Heb 13:14. Paul's "citizenship in heaven" means citizenship in "the city of the living God, the heavenly

Jerusalem," (Heb 12:22) and the "heavenly country" and "city prepared by God," (Heb 11:16).

In summary, it must be noted that the NT writings clearly convey the teaching that at the Parousia of Jesus, it was expected that all true saints that had ever lived up to that point of time — Old Testament and New Testament saints, deceased saints and living saints — would all together inherit the New Jerusalem pictured in the Revelation – the consummated kingdom of God. This is what they all were promised, and this is what all were seeking.

Note: The saints living at the time of the Parousia of Christ were expecting, according to the promises given to all, to enter into the *same* fullness and glory of the New Jerusalem as their deceased brethren would be, at the Parousia; they would be just as much glorified in the presence of God on that great occasion as the deceased brethren would be.

The study into the meaning of the New Jerusalem in the Revelation is continued in Chapter 10.

Chapter 10

The *New Jerusalem* and *Consummation for the Saints*

(Continued)

This chapter continues the study from Chapter 9 into the meaning of the New Jerusalem pictured in the Revelation of John. It is planned here to focus on some of the characteristic blessings of the New Jerusalem.

5. Facets of the New Jerusalem of the Revelation (i.e. Consummate New Covenant Blessings)

Having established that the New Jerusalem of the Revelation represents the consummate new covenant blessedness expected by the people of God, and the glory phase of the kingdom of God, let us look a bit more at the bearing of its blessings on all the pre-Parousia saints who were awaiting the Parousia of Christ, who were waiting for Christ to bring them into this heavenly city and their eternal inheritance.

Prior to the Parousia, believers could only experience a deposit/firstfruits measure of God's newness in Christ. The Revelation's New Jerusalem experience is presented as a time of total newness (21:5), where not a trace of the oldness of man's fallenness is present. Consider the following:

> [Rev. 21:1-7, 9-11a] Now I saw a new heaven and a new earth, for the first heaven and the first earth had passed away. Also there was no more sea. 2 Then I, John, saw the holy city, New Jerusalem, coming down out of heaven from God, prepared as a bride adorned for her husband. 3 And I heard a loud voice from heaven saying, "Behold, the tabernacle of God *is* with men, and He will dwell with them, and they shall be His people. God Himself will be with them *and be* their God. 4 "And God will wipe away every tear from their eyes; there shall be no more death, nor sorrow, nor crying. There shall be no more pain, for the former things have passed away." 5 Then He who sat on the throne said, "Behold, I make all things new." And He said to me, "Write, for these words are true and faithful." 6 And He said to me, "It is done! I am the Alpha and the Omega, the Beginning and the End. I will give of the fountain of the water of life freely to him who thirsts. 7 "He who overcomes shall inherit all things, and I will be his God and he shall be My son.... 9 Then one of the seven angels who had the seven bowls filled with the seven last plagues came to me and talked with me, saying, "Come, I will show you the bride, the

Lamb's wife." 10 And he carried me away in the Spirit to a great and high mountain, and showed me the great city, the holy Jerusalem, descending out of heaven from God, 11 having the glory of God.

(i) New Heaven and New Earth

John saw in his vision "a new heaven and a new earth, for the first heaven and the first earth had passed away." (21:1). John is speaking of what he saw in a vision. In a vision from God natural features or objects with which one is familiar in normal life can be seen moving or being acted upon in supernatural ways: in the Revelation we see, for example, a woman with two wings flying to escape from a serpent who spewed a flood of water from its mouth to drown her; beasts arising out of the sea; One on a white horse coming out of heaven; a city coming down out of heaven. Throughout the Revelation in all John's visions, such is the case.

The creatures and personalities and happenings that he saw in visions symbolize or represent spiritual realities and events, and by portraying them in this manner there is given a far more vivid impression of the underlying truths and natures of things than if those realities and events had just been written down as a matter-of-fact narrative. For example, rather than John just seeing an enemy empire of men, he saw a wild beast (ch 13), as did the prophet Daniel long ago, (who saw a succession of beasts, representing earthly empires). This picture emphasizes the fact that, as seen from God's true perspective, ungodly empires are beastly and devouring as to their true inner nature. The glorious woman of Rev. 12:1 in association with heaven, sun, moon and stars, is pictured so as to emphasize the heavenly status and calling of the people of God, who are not a people belonging to earth with its fallen values.

In his vision picturing the occasion of the consummation at the Parousia of Christ, John was made aware that the first heaven and first earth had passed away (21:1). "Heaven" in the Hebrew (שָׁמַיִם, *sha-ma-yim*, lit. "heavens" plural, cf. Isa. 13:13) and Greek (οὐρανὸς, *ouranos*, lit. "heaven" singular) is often used meaning "sky" and atmosphere up to the stars. In this scene that is what "heaven" means; and is to be differentiated from the spiritual heaven where God dwells, which is still in place and ever sure. So John perceived that the first world that he was familiar with – the first heaven and earth – had passed away.

In place of the first heaven and earth, John saw a new heaven/sky and a new earth. What this visionary scene looked like we cannot tell, but it was of such a vivid, beautiful nature or form that he perceived it as a new world altogether – with no sea in it. Perhaps because the sea is used in Scripture as a symbol of the restlessness that is the lot of fallen man without God, there is no place for sea in the *paradisiacal* new creation world that John saw.

In his vision, it was to a great and high mountain situated in this new heaven and new earth that John was taken by the Spirit (linking 21:1-

2 with 21:9-10), and from there John beheld the New Jerusalem descending into the beautiful scene of the new heaven and new earth – not into the old, first world. In this vision, the consummate, glorious city which he sees coming down out of heaven from God has no affinity of nature with the first world, but rather belongs to and is the central feature of this new heaven and new earth. This is all in vision, we must remember, and is not referring to any literal, physical mountain or any literal physical city coming through the sky. It is vision, symbolizing wonderful spiritual truths. So what does this new heaven and new earth symbolize, as John saw it in his vision? I believe that the new heaven and new earth represent the spiritual new covenant realm in its perfect revelation.

This will become clear as we compare the new heaven and earth with two kinds of old or first creations referred to in Scripture; viz. 1. the physical, material world of heaven and earth, whose creation is recorded in Genesis; and 2. the religious "creation" or "world" of the old covenant dispensation. I think both of these are applicable, and from examining them both we arrive at the same end as to the meaning of the new heaven and earth.

A. Comparison with material heaven and earth.

The vision given to John may picture the spiritual new covenant world, in contrast to the old or first material world – which can be called the first heaven and first earth. God created the material heaven and earth, and in that world he planted the Garden of Eden for man to dwell in and have fellowship and eternal life with God. But that creation was spoiled by sin. The vision in Revelation chapters 21 and 22 shows a spiritual recreation with many of the features of the original Eden symbolically incorporated into it. Instead of a couple of people in a garden, there is now the great city – a whole community of glorified believing people –- lacking none of the beauty of the original material garden, but containing even more that speaks of God's design and beauty such as features of gold and precious stones. And the glory of God is present in the heavenly city in a way that was not in the original earthly garden: the garden needed sun and moon, but here there is no need of these, for the glory of God illumines the city. The tree of life and the rivers of Eden are present in the spiritual New Jerusalem, symbolizing the fact that all these features in Eden find their higher and full spiritual meaning in this city.

Now this heavenly city has its place in the new heaven and new earth. Consider the principle laid down by Paul as describing God's program with man — First the natural then the spiritual (1 Cor. 15:44-46). The new heaven and new earth of John's vision refer to the consummated new covenant kingdom of God, that incorruptible, heavenly, spiritual kingdom that is not of this world, not of the old physical heaven and earth. This new heaven and new earth is of such a nature that only the saints of God can inherit, and even then they can only inherit this final, consummate heavenly form of the kingdom of God when they are in incorruptible, spiritual, heavenly bodies - as per 1 Cor. 15:50-53, 42-59, which the first Christians were expecting at the coming of Jesus.

Christians were exhorted to set their minds on "the things above" where Christ was at God's right hand, and not on "the things on the earth" (Col. 3:1-2), for the new life they had was from heaven and they were to exhibit heavenly values. They were to put to death their "members (i.e., all their past evil ways) that were on the earth," such as fornication, idolatry, anger, malice, etc. (Col. 3:4-8). The new heaven and new earth pictures that perfect realm "above" that the "born from above" Christians were connected to. The old heaven and earth represents that fallen world, this earth which gave birth, as it were, to bad ways in man. The Christians were no longer "of this world" (Jn 17:16) - the old heaven and earth - but belonged to the world above, the new heaven and earth, the spiritual new covenant realm.

So in this vision, John was shown that in respect to the New Jerusalem and the glorified saints, all things pertaining to the old, first material world had passed away. He was given insight into the full revelation and manifestation of the new heaven and earth – the consummate new covenant world above, in the spiritual sphere, which was to occur at the time of the Lord's coming (which is the time frame of this vision).

Note that John is not prophesying that the material heaven/sky and earth would physically pass away; rather this is a vision signifying spiritual realities. As far as the believers up to that point in history would be concerned, the Parousia's effect would be that the first heaven and first earth, i.e., their first world (with all the fallenness associated with that old creation), would *for them* be completely passed away, for they would no longer be inhabiting that material world; their stage of existence in "this life" (1 Cor. 15:19) in this material world, in earthly bodies, would be passed; and in its place they would be possessing their eternal inheritance in the new heaven and new earth, i.e., the consummate, spiritual, new covenant world in heaven with God and the Lord Jesus.

B. Comparison with old Israelite covenantal heaven and earth.

The vision given to John may also picture, I believe, a new heaven and earth in contrast to the old covenant "world" that incorporated the earthly Jerusalem and temple of God and its system of sacrifice and law. That the establishment of the old covenant made with Israel was known as a creation of heaven and earth is demonstrated in David Chilton's article *Looking for a New Heaven and a New Earth* in *www.preteristarchive.com*. In this article David Chilton in turn refers to the comments by the Puritan theologian, John Owen, on Isa. 51:15-16, about the creation of a religious heaven and earth using terminology borrowed from the Genesis account of the material creation:

> [Isa.. 51:15 -16] But I am the LORD thy God, that divided the sea, whose waves roared: The LORD of hosts is his name. And I

have put my words in thy mouth, and I have covered thee in the shadow of mine hand, that I may plant the heavens and lay the foundations of the earth, and say unto Zion, Thou art my people.

John Owen writes [says David Chilton]:

> The time when the work here mentioned, of planting the heavens, and laying the foundation of the earth, was performed by God, was when he "divided the sea" (Isa. 51:15), and gave the law (v. 16), and said to Zion, "Thou art my people" - that is, when he took the children of Israel out of Egypt, and formed them in the wilderness into a church and state. Then he planted the heavens, and laid the foundation of the earth - made the new world; that is, brought forth order, and government, and beauty, from the confusion wherein before they were. This is the planting of the heavens, and laying the foundation of the earth in the world. And hence it is, that when mention is made of the destruction of a state and government, it is in that language that seems to set forth the end of the world. So Isa. 34:4; which is yet but the destruction of the state of Edom. The like is also affirmed of the Roman Empire, Rev. 6:14; which the Jews constantly affirmed to be intended by Edom in the prophets. And in our Savior Christ's prediction of the destruction of Jerusalem, Matt. 24, he sets it out by expressions of the same importance. It is evident then, that, in the prophetical idiom and manner of speech, by "heavens" and "earth," the civil and religious state and combination of men in the world, and the men of them, are often understood. So were the heavens and earth that world which was then destroyed by the flood.

The fact that the old earthly Jerusalem (Babylon) has been under God's scrutiny in earlier chapters of the Revelation, as representing a corrupt old covenant Judaism and its people, and that in Chapter 21 he sees a New Jerusalem, representing a glorified new covenant people, presents a good case for regarding the first heavens and first earth that passed away (21:1) as a reference to the first covenant "world" of the nation of Israel that was formed at Sinai under Mosaic Law.

The picture of the new heaven and the new earth of Rev. 21 refers then to the new covenant kingdom – "the world to come," (Heb 2:5) – seen in its consummate form, coming into its full manifestation, in which the glorified New Jerusalem, representing the glorified people of the new covenant, has its home.

Both of these alternative meanings of the first heaven and first earth – i.e., the material creation, and the religious, covenantal creation with Israel – are superseded by the new, higher, spiritual creation called the new heaven and new earth symbolizing the spiritual new covenant kingdom of God.

Once again, though, let me mention that the first Christians were already delivered from the first covenant and already under the new covenant, prior to the Parousia. What the Revelation's symbolism is pointing to is the consummation of new covenant blessedness, at which time every trace of the old way of life was fully done away with, and everything to do with the new life in Christ was fully manifested for the first time in history.

A brief explanation of the firstfruits measure and fullness measure of the "new heaven and new earth."

Remembering the theme that we have seen in our previous studies, of a deposit/firstfruits measure of new covenant blessings, present now, preparing for the consummation measure of the new covenant blessings, to be manifested then at the Parousia, that runs through the New Testament, let me just quickly point out that I believe this theme is applicable also to the concept of the new heaven and new earth.

Just as the concept of the New heavenly Jerusalem has a deposit/firstfruits phase experienced by the imperfect first Christians prior to the Parousia of Christ and then has the consummate manifestation at the Parousia as pictured in Revelation chs 21 and 22 that the glorified first Christians were to experience, so also with the concept of the new heaven and new earth. In the case of the concept of the new heaven and new earth there is a firstfruits stage and a consummate stage of manifestation. Just as the fact of the New Jerusalem's appearance in the Revelation did not mean that none of the first Christians had experienced the reality of the concept of the New Jerusalem before, so also the fact of the appearance of the new heaven and new earth in Revelation chapter 21 does not mean that the first Christians had not partaken of the reality of the concept of the new heavens and the new earth before, in firstfruits measure and experience.

It was pointed out earlier, in Chapter 3, *The Good Things To Come*, that "the world to come" (and it constituent "good things to come") – a concept used in the epistle to the Hebrews – referred to the new covenant "world" and had a firstfruits phase experienced already through Jesus the Mediator of the new covenant, and a consummation phase expected at his second appearing. This phrase is equivalent to the concept of the new heavens and the new earth, both of them meaning the new covenant dispensation ruled over by the Messiah, the Lord Jesus. I believe that it has been incorrectly assumed that the phrase "a new heaven and a new earth" appearing in 1 Pet. 3 and Rev. 21, refers to the *beginning* of the new covenant age. Rather it is in those places referring to the expected *consummation* phase of the new covenant for the first Christians to participate in at the Parousia. It has been mentioned before that it is a peculiarity of the firstfruits-harvest language in the NT that a particular blessing can be mentioned in a verse of Scripture as a future soon-to-come blessing, which if taken at face value may suggest that the particular blessing had not been experienced at all before. But this is not the case, as we have abundantly proven, and as the language in Peter's two epistles demonstrates.

Excursion into Peter's epistles.

The apostle Peter also mentions the concept of a new heavens and a new earth: "Nevertheless we, according to His promise, look for new heavens and a new earth in which righteousness dwells," (2 Pet 3:13).

Let us consider the apostle Peter's epistles in relation to the subject of the new heaven and new earth.

Peter urges the Christians to look eagerly for the new heavens and the new earth in which righteousness dwells, at the coming of Christ, (2 Pet 3:13-14). Now note the other final blessings that are expressed in Peter's letters as the future hope of the Christians, also to be theirs at the coming of Christ:- an eternal inheritance, (1 Pet 1:3-4); a salvation ready to be revealed, (1 Pet 1:5,9); the grace being brought at the revelation of Jesus Christ, (1 Pet 1:13); the unfading crown of glory at the appearing of the Chief Shepherd (1 Pet 5:1,4); an entrance into the everlasting kingdom of the Lord Jesus, (2 Pet 1:11); the dawning of the day, (2 Pet 1:19). For all of these future blessings Peter's Christian readers were eagerly looking and waiting. All of these blessings were expected as soon-to-come consummate, final new covenant blessings at the coming of the Lord Jesus. However, although these blessings were promised by Peter as yet to come, did that mean that the believers had no experience at all of them already? Such is certainly not the case! For otherwise none of the believers would have yet been saved, or have had light or grace or righteousness, or sanctification, or any blessings in Christ. Rather, as we have seen elsewhere, it was true that the first Christians already were experiencing their inheritance in Christ, and salvation, and grace, and glory, and the kingdom of God, and the light of God in their hearts prior to the Parousia — but only in a deposit/firstfruits measure and firstfruits experience that was continually facing the guerilla warring of the flesh, sin, the world and spiritual unseen enemies. Already possessing and experiencing these blessings of the new covenant in first firstfruits measure they were longing for the glorious, consummate measure of those same blessings on the occasion of the coming of Christ.

Now since Peter includes the blessing of the new heavens and the new earth where righteousness dwells *along with these other blessings* as a hope to look forward to at the coming of Christ then it follows as a reasonable deduction that just like the others, the concept of a new heaven and new earth (i.e. a new covenant spiritual "world") has a firstfruits/deposit phase as well as a consummate phase — in keeping with the consistent theme in the whole NT of deposit/firstfruits now with the fullness coming soon at the Parousia. *Therefore, this blessing of the coming of new heavens and new earth referred to by Peter does not refer to the coming of the new covenant age per se, but to the coming of the new covenant in its consummate manifestation and eternal fullness for the first Christians at the Parousia.*

We note that Peter's Christian readers were already new creations in Christ Jesus, in the realm of the new covenant. They had been redeemed by the blood of Christ from their past futile ways (1 Pet 1:18-19), and had been sprinkled with the blood of Jesus Christ (1 Pet 1:2) – signifying their participation in the new covenant (cf. Heb 9:13-14, 16-22); they had purified their souls through faith in Christ, which faith was brought about by the sanctifying work of the Spirit, and were born anew (1 Pet 1;2, 22-23). They were already a spiritual house, a royal priesthood, God's special people of light who had received God's mercy (1 Pet 2:4-59-10), enjoying the fact that they had been returned to the Shepherd and Overseer of their souls (1 Pet 2;25); they had the Spirit of glory and of God resting upon them (1 Pet 4:13) helping them in their sufferings, as they waited for the coming of Christ; they were partakers of the divine nature, experiencing God's divine power enabling to grow in their knowing him. (2 Pet 1:2-4) These first Christians were experiencing some new covenant blessings. But they still awaited the wonderful consummation of new covenant blessedness at the Parousia, which would see them glorified in heaven in incorruptible bodies with the glorified Jesus at the right hand of God. (1 Pet 3:18, 22).

Now in regard to the matter of righteousness, which is associated by Peter with the new heaven and new earth, consider the following:

Peter's Christians readers had come to faith in the righteousness of their God and Savior Jesus Christ (2 Pet 1:1) and they were to grow (by virtue of a living knowledge of God and the Lord Jesus) in a life of righteousness, the essence of which is love (2 Pet 2:1-11). They knew "the way of righteousness" (2 Pet 2:21).

- Thus they were already experiencing Christ as their *righteousness*, (2 Pet 1:1, cf. 1 Cor. 1:30);
- They had, in Christ, died to sin and were now to live with respect to *righteousness* (1 Pet 2:24; cf. Rom 6:18-19, "bondslaves to righteousness"), aiming to be holy in their conduct as their Father is holy (1 Pet 1:15);
- They were to lay aside all unrighteousness, (e.g., 1 Pet 2:1, 11-12)
- They were to be prepared to suffer for righteousness' sake, for the name of Christ, as a Christian (1 Pet 3:14, 17; 4:14, 16)

As Paul said in his letter to the Romans, only those who are saved through faith in Christ Jesus and are in his new covenant of grace and life, can know the deliverance from being under the old covenant law and experience this inner life of righteousness by the Holy Spirit, this righteousness, peace and joy in God, which is characteristic of the new covenant kingdom of God. (See Rom 7; 8; 14:17).

Peter's Christian readers were therefore experiencing the reality of the new covenant righteousness – in its firstfruits measure of experience. Sadly while in "this life" this new life of righteousness within them was infiltrated by the remains of sin and fallenness that also dwelt within them; their condition was still far from perfect. They still had "the hope of righteousness" soon to come, like Paul said to the Galatians (5:5) – the hope of receiving the "crown of righteousness" at the Lord's coming (2 Tim 4:8); which involves the same consummate blessing as the "crown of glory" that Peter speaks of (1 Pet 5:4).

When Peter thus speaks of the hope of a new heavens and earth *in which righteousness dwells* (2 Pet 3:13), he is, (as with all the other expected consummate blessings which I mentioned above), referring to the manifestation of the consummate sphere of new covenant blessedness at the coming of Christ wherein the Christians would experience perfect righteousness – the essence of which is perfect love, seeing that God is love – with no admixture at all of anything unrighteous within them.

It may be said that in the lives of these first Christians the "old heaven and earth" had in a real sense already passed away, and for them the firstfruits of the "new heaven and new earth" of the new covenant age was already present. But these were but deposit/firstfruits blessings compared with the glory of the consummate revelation they hoped for at the Parousia of the Lord Jesus.

So when in the Revelation we read of the passing away of the old heaven and earth and the coming presence of the new heaven and earth, and similarly when we read in Peter's second epistle (ch. 3) of the saints looking for a new heaven and new earth, we are *not* to interpret this as meaning that the new covenant age had not previously been present and that it only began at the Parousia. Rather we are to understand John's vision (and Peter's) of the new heaven and new earth as the manifestation of *the glorious consummation of new covenant blessedness for the pre-Parousia saints*, that eternal heavenly new covenant realm that the first Christians would enter into at the Parousia.

The first Christians regarded themselves as strangers and pilgrims in this world.

In accordance with all our previous studies in former chapters, we can say that the consummation that Peter was looking forward to, and that John in the Revelation was referring to, was not something to be experienced on this earth, in this life, by Christians still in mortal bodies. He was speaking of the consummate form of the heavenly new covenant kingdom that flesh and blood cannot enter; where only those conformed to the image of the heavenly Man, in spiritual, heavenly, incorruptible bodies can enter (remember our studies in 1 Cor. 15, etc.).

That is why Peter refers a number of times to the first Christians as sojourners and pilgrims in this world, (1 Pet 1:1, 17; 2:11-12).

The context in which Peter uses these terms shows that the pilgrimage he is talking about is NOT a pilgrimage from the old covenant to the new covenant, as some preterists think, but a pilgrimage from this fallen world with its imperfect condition, (where ungodliness and sin are present and where they have bodies of weakness hindered by "the flesh" and where they face persecution), into the full glory of the heavenly world where the glorified Christ is, at the right hand of the Father.

The Christians felt as strangers in this world, not because they were in the old covenant age and longing for the new covenant age, as some writers suggest, but because they were born from above and were already spiritually experiencing the New Covenant age in firstfruits measure and had a heavenly citizenship; and longed to go home into the fullness of heaven. They were not at home in this world among the heathenish ways around them. They longed to put off their earthly corruption altogether and to go home into the fullness of the new covenant blessedness, into heavenly realms glorified with the Lord Jesus.

Jesus said as much in Jn. 17:16 - his followers were not of the world even as he was not of the world. Just as the Lord Jesus was glad to leave this world and go to the Father as his rightful dwelling place in glory, so also his new covenant, born-from-above followers, were to find their true home with Jesus, in God's heaven above. Consummation for the Christians can only be found where their Forerunner found it — in the sinless, perfection and glory of the Father's real presence in heaven.

Similarly, the reason Abraham and his descendants regarded themselves as pilgrims on earth was because they knew they were destined for a heavenly city and heavenly homeland that God had prepared (Heb 11).

And so in Peter's epistle he is saying, 'You Christians are born from above, and are no longer "of the world"; the divine nature is in you; you are as it were strangers and sojourners in this world; you have been called out of its ungodliness and fallenness, and are on your way to heaven, your true home; so while you are in this world, with service to do for the Lord, let your heavenly life show through, let not your conduct be like that of the world's people.'

(ii) The New Jerusalem and the great mountain

In John's vision, he was "carried away by the Spirit onto [*epi*] a great and high mountain," and there he saw the New Jerusalem descending out of heaven from God, (Rev. 21:10).

Throughout the scriptures the city of God is always associated with a mountain. The New Jerusalem is deliberately pictured as the new spiritual Eden; or Eden restored, to a higher, eternal, spiritual realm. Various features such as the tree of life, the river of water, and the mention of no more curse clearly suggest this. Now the original Garden of Eden was situated on a mountain (e.g. on a mountain plateau) from which the waters flowed to refresh the earth. (See Chapter 4 of David Chilton's *Paradise Restored* for interesting information on the fact of Eden being situated on a mountain, and the use of mountains in Scripture). In memory of Eden, throughout Scripture mountains are used as symbols of God's kingdom and place of his rule. These occasions are prophetic types or parables of the promised coming restoration of man to that holy and high fellowship with God and participation in all that is truly good, for which he was designed, and which was lost on that first physical Edenic mountain.

It is by the design of God that the earthly Jerusalem was situated in the mountains, the highest being Mt Zion. Afterwards the term Mt Zion was sometimes used as a synonym of Jerusalem and the people of Israel:

> [Psa. 48:1-3] Great *is* the LORD, and greatly to be praised in the city of our God, *In* His holy mountain. 2 Beautiful in elevation, the joy of the whole earth, *is* Mount Zion *on* the sides of the north, the city of the great King. 3 God *is* in her palaces; He is known as her refuge.
>
> [Psa. 87:1-3] Its [i.e. the city of God, Mt Zion's] foundation *is* in the holy mountains. 2 The LORD loveth the gates of Zion more than all the dwellings of Jacob. 3 Glorious things are spoken of thee, O city of God. Selah.

Mt Zion was also viewed as the dwelling place of the Lord:

> [Isa. 8:18] " Here am I and the children whom the LORD has given me! [We are] for signs and wonders in Israel from the LORD of hosts, who dwells in Mount Zion."

In Psalm 2 a more heavenly mount Zion is prophesied about, one where the Messiah would rule after his victories over his enemies:

> [Psa. 2:6-8] "Yet I have set My King on My holy mountain of Zion." "I will declare the decree: The LORD has said to Me, 'You *are* My Son, Today I have begotten You. Ask of Me, and I will give *You* the nations *for* Your inheritance, and the ends of the earth *for* Your possession.'" (see also Acts 4:23-31; 13:33)

In the book of Ezekiel, chapter 40:2, the prophet Ezekiel in a vision under the power of the Lord, was set down on a high mountain upon which he saw a temple-city, stretching southwards from where he stood; and the presence and glory of the Lord filled this temple (43:1-5); and Ezekiel was told that this was where the Lord would dwell on his throne in the midst of his people for ever (43:7); and the whole area surrounding the mountain top (on which the temple-city was situated) was to be holy; and a river with trees on either side flowed from the temple, (47:1, 7, 12). Most commentators that I have consulted state that this whole vision relates to spiritual new covenant realities under the reign of the Christ. Clearly this Ezekiel vision finds its complement/fulfillment in the New Jerusalem of the Revelation. Especially note that the city-temple is on the high mountain on which Ezekiel had been taken by the hand of the Lord.

Isaiah prophesied of the coming glory of the Lord's city established on the top of the mountains.

> [Isa. 2:2-3] And it shall come to pass in the last days, *that* the mountain of the LORD'S house shall be established in the top

of the mountains, and shall be exalted above the hills; and all nations shall flow unto it. 3 And many people shall go and say, Come ye, and let us go up to the mountain of the LORD, to the house of the God of Jacob; and he will teach us of his ways, and we will walk in his paths: for out of Zion shall go forth the law, and the word of the LORD from Jerusalem.

The New Testament also speaks of the Mount that Christians have come to. The writer of Hebrews says the first Christians had approached the spiritual antitype of the earthly Jerusalem, viz., the heavenly Mt Zion, the city of the living God, the heavenly Jerusalem, (Heb 12:22).

The faithful Christians who had been redeemed out of the earth (the symbolic 144,000) were shown in the Revelation as standing with the Lamb on Mount Zion (Rev. 14:1). Elsewhere the Lamb is shown to be in the midst of the throne of God, where a vast multitude of redeemed people is seen along with the 144,000 (Rev. 7:4, 9-10); which implies Mount Zion is where the throne of God is and where the Lamb is. Mount Zion represents the kingdom of God.

From this background, my clear impression regarding John's vision in the Revelation, of being taken by the power of the Spirit onto a great and high mountain and there seeing the New Jerusalem coming down out of heaven, is that we are to understand that the New Jerusalem comes down to rest on that great mountain. The various types throughout Scripture are thus fulfilled. The visionary scene is designed to convey the fact of the wonderful consummation of God's plan of redemption. The great and high mountain pictures the great kingdom of God, sovereign and impregnable. The Parousia, which is said in Revelation to be soon, would bring the consummation consisting of the heavenly Jerusalem coming to rest on the holy and heavenly Mount Zion. The greatest symbol of earthly Israel - the capital city of Jerusalem situated on Mount Zion - is now revealed in its infinitely higher antitype. Ezekiel's vision of the temple-city on the high and holy mount is fulfilled at the Parousia in this Revelation vision. This is a vision of the fully restored fellowship of God and man. That which was lost in the earthly Eden situated on its mount, and which was symbolically pictured in the earthly Jerusalem on its mountain, is now fully restored in the consummated, heavenly, New Jerusalem on its mountain of the new covenant kingdom of the Messiah. I am saying then that John's being taken to the high mountain means far more than that the mountain was a convenient and good vantage point for him to see the city.

Not an earthly fulfillment.
Note that the record does *not* say that John saw the New Jerusalem descending to this cursed earth on which fallen man lives and in which sin and godlessness flourish and in which even Christians still carry about the legacy of their past fallenness and sin. The fallen earth of this world has no part at this stage of the vision, for the old heaven and earth had passed away. The vision involves a mountain in the new heaven and new earth.

The vision of the New Jerusalem on the great mountain is the fulfillment of a prophetic theme running through the scriptures, and denotes a sinless, glorious condition for all the glorified saints who come to inhabit this heavenly city – this promised consummate form of the kingdom of God. The Revelation's vision describes a consummate scene in heaven, a scene of ultimate reward for the glorified, resurrected and changed saints, to be theirs on the appearance of Christ the second time with his final salvation.

Some say that the Revelation vision of the New Jerusalem signifies the New Covenant church of believers that exists now on this fallen earth, where saints are still tarnished experientially by the flesh and indwelling sin; but this interpretation is a denial of the vision's consummate meaning, a denial of its representing the condition of final, ultimate salvation. To say that it represents something existing in this fallen earth, in which imperfect Christians dwell, is to say, then, that God has not given a vision of a consummate victory in heaven anywhere in the Revelation, for everyone living on this earth still needs sanctifying, still needs a final salvation into a sinless perfect glorified state, still awaits their final reward.

Besides this, such an interpretation fails to take into account that the New Jerusalem as it is given in the Revelation is the consummated reward for all the multitude of martyred and deceased saints who were promised the inheritance of the New Jerusalem by the Lord. The New Jerusalem of the Revelation is not the symbol of the still-being-sanctified, still-being-persecuted, still-being-buffeted-by-sin New Covenant church on earth, (although this church on earth partakes of the spirit and life of the New Jerusalem in a deposit/fruits measure, as we have shown earlier), but it is the symbol of the consummated, glorified, sinless, New Covenant church of believers in heaven.

The New Jerusalem came into its official existence or manifestation *as a consummate entity* at the Parousia of Jesus. Before then, no deceased believers in all previous history had ever been glorified and perfected and fully restored to heavenly glory in conformity to God's original design for man. But at the Parousia a glorified heavenly New Jerusalem of glorified believers first came into existence.

But let it be clear that I do firmly hold that all saints living on earth in post-Parousia days are partaking of a deposit and firstfruits measure of the spirit and life of the New Jerusalem; they are "children of the freewoman," the heavenly New Jerusalem. When they die they will pass into the consummate reality and glorious fullness of the heavenly New Jerusalem as it is symbolically represented in the Revelation, into which all the pre-Parousia believers entered at Christ's Parousia.

I like James Stuart Russell's pithy comments on this scene of the New Jerusalem in the Revelation:

> "We now find ourselves surrounded by scenery so novel and so wonderful that it is not surprising that we should be in doubt where we are. Is this earth, or is it heaven? Every familiar landmark has disappeared; the old has vanished, and given place to the

new: it is a new heaven above us; it is a new earth beneath us. New conditions of life must exist, for 'there is no more sea.' Plainly we have here a representation in which symbolism is carried to its utmost limits; and he who would deal with such gorgeous imagery as with prosaic literalities is incapable of comprehending them. But the symbols, though transcendental, are not unmeaning. 'They serve unto the example and shadow of heavenly things;' and all the pomp and splendor of earth are employed to set forth the beauty of moral and spiritual excellence.

"It is impossible to regard this picture as the representation of any social condition to be realized upon earth. There are, indeed, certain phrases which at first seem to imply that earth is the scene where these glories are manifested: the holy city is said to 'come down out of heaven;' the tabernacle of God is said to be 'with men;' 'the kings of the earth' are said to 'bring their glory and honor into it; ' but, on the other hand, the whole conception and description of the vision forbid the supposition of its being a terrestrial scene. In the first place, it belongs to 'the things which must shortly come to pass;' it falls strictly within apocalyptic limits. It is, therefore, no vision of the future [i.e. modern man's future]; it belongs as much to the period called 'the end of the age' as the destruction of Jerusalem does; and we are to conceive of this renovation of all things, —this new heaven and new earth, as contemporaneous with, or in immediate succession to, the judgment of the great harlot, to which it is the counterpart or antithesis.

"Secondly, What is the chief figure in this visionary representation? It is the holy city, New Jerusalem. But the New Jerusalem is always represented in the Scriptures as situated in heaven, not on earth. St. Paul speaks of the Jerusalem which is *above,* in contrast with the Jerusalem *below.* How can the Jerusalem which is *above* belong to earth? There cannot be a reasonable doubt that the city which is here depicted in such glowing colors is identical with that which is referred to in Heb. 12:22,23: 'Ye are come unto mount Zion, and unto the city of the living God, the heavenly Jerusalem, and to an innumerable company of angels; to the general assembly and church of the firstborn, which are written in heaven, and to God the Judge of all, and to the spirits of just men made perfect.' Clearly, therefore, the holy city is the abode of the glorified; the inheritance of the saints in light; the mansions of the Father's house, prepared for the home of the blessed.

"Once more, this conclusion is certified by the representation of its being the dwelling-place of the Most High Himself: 'The Lord God Almighty and the Lamb are the temple of it;' 'the throne of God and of the Lamb shall be in it;' 'his servants shall serve him, and they shall see his face.' In fact, this vision of the holy city is anticipated in the catastrophe of the vision of the seals, where the hundred and forty and four thousand out of all the tribes of the children of Israel, and the great multitude that no man could number, are represented as enjoying the very same glory and felicity, in the very same place and circumstances, as in the vision before us. The two scenes are identical; or different aspects of one and the same great consummation.

"We therefore conclude that the vision sets forth the blessedness and glory of the heavenly state, into which the way was fully opened at the 'end of the age,' (Heb. 9:26, Gr. συντελείᾳ τῶν αἰώνων), according to the showing of the Epistle to the Hebrews." (from *The Parousia* on the *Online Bible* CD)

(iii) *The New Marriage Union*

[Rev. 21:2, 9-11] Then I, John, saw the holy city, New Jerusalem, coming down out of heaven from God, *prepared as a bride adorned for her husband....* 9 Then one of the seven angels who had the seven bowls filled with the seven last plagues came to me and talked with me, saying, "Come, I will show *you the bride, the Lamb's wife*." 10 And he carried me away in the Spirit to a great and high mountain, and showed me the great city, the holy Jerusalem, descending out of heaven from God, 11 *having the glory of God.*

The fact of the New Jerusalem appearing as a bride has been referred to briefly in Chapter 9, but here I wish to give further emphasis on this as a consummative event. Clearly, John's vision of the New Jerusalem coming down out of heaven from God as a bride for her husband represents the spiritual reality of the community of God's true people formally entering into a consummation of spiritual union and fellowship with the Lord. All believers who had existed up to this time in history (deceased and living) were to enter this marital consummation at the (soon expected) coming of Jesus.

Believers prior to the Parousia of Christ were already "married" or "joined" to the Lord in a life-giving union, and they were "one spirit with him," (e.g. Rom 7:4; 1 Cor. 6:17). But we may say that the believers' experience of this marriage bond or union was only in a firstfruits/deposit measure. Their overall imperfect condition limited their experience of this wonderful reality. The vision in the Rev. 21 speaks of a time of consummation when the company of believers were to meet the Lord in a glorious newness and fullness and consummation.

In Rev. 19:1-9, John was shown the lead up to this coming of the Bride. He heard the "Alleluias" given to the Lord by a great multitude in heaven proclaiming the Lord as the author of salvation and worthy of being ascribed with all glory and power; "for the Lord God Omnipotent reigns!"

Their praise arises on the occasion of the completed judgment of the "great harlot," (apostate Jerusalem), for God "has avenged on her the blood of his servants shed by her" (Rev. 19:2). (Amongst this multitude would be the martyred saints of Rev. 6:9-11, who cried out for God to avenge them). The twenty-four elders and the four living creatures who were before the throne of God in Rev. 4 and 5, here add their praise along with the great multitude (Rev. 19:3-4). Then a voice calls on all the Lord's servants to praise him. (v.4). At this call, a great multitude proclaim God's praise and proclaim that now – since the Lord's Parousia has brought to an end the false harlot – the time of the marriage supper has come and the true wife (betrothed) "has made herself ready," (v.7). This bride is composed of the saints, (v. 8). After the brief excursion of Rev. 19:11-20:15 detailing further matters of judgment, the theme of the New Jerusalem as a bride resumes in Rev. 21:2, where she is viewed as "prepared as a bride adorned for her husband." ("Prepared" in 21:2 [NKJV] is from the same Greek verb (Gr. ἑτοιμάζω, hetoimazo) as "made ready" in 19:7 [NKJV]).

The New Jerusalem is seen *adorned with the glory of God* (21:2, 10-11). Note this emphasis on the bride's being adorned with glory; she is a glorious bride. Following the Parousia of Christ, the New Jerusalem, comprising all the saints who had existed up to that point in history, is presented before God and the Lord Jesus. This is that climactic occasion looked for by all the first Christians: viz. that at the Parousia of Jesus they would be presented "faultless, before the presence of His glory with exceeding joy," (Jude 24). Note that the climax of Christ's sanctifying the bride, the church, is to present her to himself as a perfect bride:

> [Eph 5:25-27] Christ also loved the church and gave Himself for her, 26 that He might sanctify and cleanse her with the washing of water by the word, 27 *that He might present her to Himself a glorious church, not having spot or wrinkle or any such thing, but that she should be holy and without blemish.*

The scene in Rev. 21 and 22 pictures the time when the glorified Jesus presents the church to Himself "*a glorious church,*" (Eph 5:27). The believers prior to the Parousia had been called with the hope of being "glorified together with Christ," called "to his own kingdom and glory," to "appear with Jesus in glory" when he was manifested; and this vision in the Revelation pictures this fulfillment. The New Jerusalem Bride, representing the people of God, comes adorned with glory to be with her husband. The previous earthly afflictions are now replaced by "the incomparable weight of glory."

Part of the adornment of glory that the "glorious church" of God would have is their glorified, heavenly bodies, for only by their being in a glorified, spiritual and heavenly condition, in the image of their husband, could the marital union be consummated and they enjoy unfettered fellowship in heavenly realms. At the Parousia the awaited resurrection/transformation of deceased and living saints into heavenly, glorified bodies occurred which fitted them for living in the realm of the consummate and heavenly form of the kingdom of God:

[Phil 3:20-21] For *our citizenship is in heaven, from which we also eagerly wait for the Savior, the Lord Jesus Christ*, 21 *who will transform our lowly body that it may be conformed to His glorious body*, according to the working by which He is able even to subdue all things to Himself.

[1 Cor. 15:42-44, 47-50] So also *is* the resurrection of the dead. *The body* is sown in corruption, it is *raised in incorruption*. 43 It is sown in dishonor, it is *raised in glory*. It is sown in weakness, it is *raised in power*. 44 It is sown a natural body, it is *raised a spiritual body*. 47 The first man *was* of the earth, *made* of dust; the second Man *is* the Lord from heaven. 48 As *was* the *man* of dust, [i.e. subject to dishonor, weakness, naturalness and earthliness - IH] so also *are* those *who are made* of dust; and as *is* the heavenly *Man*, [i.e. incorruptible, glorious, powerful, spiritual, heavenly - IH] so also [*will be* (no verb here in the Greek)] those *who are* heavenly. 49 And as we have borne the image of the *man* of dust, *we shall also bear the image of the heavenly Man*. 50 Now this I say, brethren, that flesh and blood cannot inherit the kingdom of God; nor does corruption inherit incorruption.

In such a manner as described by Paul in the two passages above, the New Jerusalem is "made ready as a bride adorned for her Husband" (Rev. 21:2), bearing the image of her Beloved, and "having the glory of God," (Rev. 21:11), .

But there is another fascinating aspect of fulfillment here. Already I have alluded to the fact that many of the features in the heavenly city remind one of similar features in the original Garden of Eden. Indeed, the New Jerusalem vision is designed to teach that what was begun and lost in the garden is now restored and brought to consummation in the heavenly city. There is in the New Jerusalem vision of the Revelation a fulfillment of what the bringing of Eve to Adam in the original Eden typified. The apostle Paul in Eph 5:31-32, using a quote from Gen. 2:24 describing the case of the union of Adam and Eve, refers to marriage between husband and wife (firstly demonstrated in the case of Adam and Eve) as picturing the mystery of the union of Christ and his church. The marriage in the Garden of Eden situated in its mountain, now finds a wonderfully higher antitype in the assembly of God's people, in the form of the New Jerusalem, being brought as a fully adorned bride to Christ her husband on the mountain of the consummate kingdom of God. Such is the scene of consummation expected at the Parousia of Christ.

The New Jerusalem Coming Down out of Heaven from God

Consider the description of the New Jerusalem as "coming down out of heaven from God." Is there significance in this expression? I can suggest a couple of ideas.

Firstly, the fact that the New Jerusalem is "out of heaven from

God" signifies that it has come from his presence, that God is its origin, its caretaker, and its preparer. The company of the saints composing the New Jerusalem Bride are "not of the world," but are "born from above" and "born of God."

Secondly, the picture of the city "coming down" out of heaven from God, signifies that special ideal of God – of a glorified people for his name, conformed to the image of his Son – previously hidden (as far as its full revelation goes) in God, is now being manifested for all his angels and all his saints to see it. For never in all of history has God revealed fully his glorious ideal lying behind his creation of man.

Thirdly, the fact that in John's vision the bride came down out of heaven from God to the great mountain prepared to meet her husband, would seem to imply that the bride was with God in heaven being prepared prior to the coming down, i.e. being revealed, as "a bride prepared for her husband." This makes me think that just prior to the episode in Rev. 21:2, all the saints, living and deceased, had been taken from the earthly realm into heaven and there prepared for their manifestation in glory with Christ.

Possibly it was just before the event of the bride's coming in Rev. 21:2 that the deceased and living believers were "caught up together," as Paul talks about in 1 Thess 4:17, and prepared for their meeting the Lord Jesus and being with him forever. Possibly the occasion in Rev. 14:14-16 of the Son of Man reaping the harvest refers to his taking up his living saints from the earth, to prepare them, along with raised deceased saints, as members of his bride, whose preparedness is then announced in Rev. 19:7 following the destruction of earthly Jerusalem (Babylon).

I would not be dogmatic about this. But whatever our interpretation may be on this, what is clear is that the NT scriptures declare that both deceased and living believers together were expecting to be presented before the Lord as his bride, as those composing the New Jerusalem, as those prepared by an adornment of glory. (For more on language, "coming down out of heaven from God," see at the end of section (5) below.

(iv) The Tabernacle of God with Men

Ever since the fall of man and his first sense of shame before God and ever since the first couple was driven out of the garden of Eden on its pristine mountain, with the subsequent loss of the Edenic presence of God with them and the loss of fellowship between the Creator and his created people, (and the cherubim and sword-like flame were put at the gate to guard the way back to the tree of life), there has been the understanding by spiritual men that the greatest privilege man could have was for God to pardon his sins and restore man to a position where God and man would dwell together again in reconciliation and unhindered fellowship. To have God dwell in the midst of his people and to be their God was the greatest blessing. Sadly the appreciation of this privilege and blessing was short-lived in all the Old Testament history. It is amazing to see the condescending grace of God in his repeatedly making specific promises of dwelling with and among his people.

In Moses' days, it was the introduction of the three main features of Jewish worship – tabernacle, priesthood and sacrifice – (all designed and made and operated according to the pattern given to Moses by God), that enabled the Lord to dwell among his people, and to be their God. Clearly these features are symbolic of the person and atoning work of the promised Messiah.

> [Ex 25:8-9] "And *let them make Me a sanctuary, that I may dwell among them.* 9 "According to all that I show you, *that is*, the pattern of the tabernacle and the pattern of all its furnishings, just so you shall make *it*.
>
> [Ex 29:42-46] "*This shall be* a continual burnt offering throughout your generations *at* the door of the *tabernacle of meeting* before the LORD, where I will meet you to speak with you. 43 "And *there I will meet with the children of Israel*, and *the tabernacle* shall be sanctified by My glory. 44 "So I will consecrate the tabernacle of meeting and the altar. *I will also consecrate both Aaron and his sons to minister to Me as priests.* 45 "*I will dwell among the children of Israel and will be their God.* 46 "*And they shall know that I am the LORD their God*, who brought them up out of the land of Egypt, that I may dwell among them. I *am* the LORD their God.

In David's days, with the tabernacle resident in Jerusalem, the city of Jerusalem became known as the city of God, and the place where God dwelt among his people.

> [Psa. 46:4] *There is* a river whose streams shall make glad *the city of God, The holy place of the tabernacle of the Most High.* 5 *God is in the midst of her*, she shall not be moved; God shall help her, just at the break of dawn.
>
> [Psa. 132:13] For *the LORD hath chosen Zion; he hath desired [it] for his habitation.*

Prophets warned the people of Israel and Judah that God's judgment would come upon them for their spiritual idolatry. Their prophecies of judgment were tempered with prophecies of restoration where the dwelling of the Lord in Zion, in the midst of his people, was the central blessing. These were speaking of a higher reality that the physical temple in physical Jerusalem.

> [Joel 3:16-18] The LORD also will roar from Zion, And utter His voice from Jerusalem; The heavens and earth will shake; But the LORD will be a shelter for His people, And the strength of the children of Israel. 17 "*So you shall know that I am the*

LORD your God, dwelling in Zion My holy mountain. Then Jerusalem shall be holy, and no aliens shall ever pass through her again." 18 And it will come to pass in that day *That* the mountains shall drip with new wine, The hills shall flow with milk, And all the brooks of Judah shall be flooded with water; A fountain shall flow from the house of the LORD And water the Valley of Acacias.

[Zech. 2:10] Sing and rejoice, O daughter of Zion: for, lo, I come, and *I will dwell in the midst of thee*, saith the LORD.

[Zech. 8:3] Thus saith the LORD; *I am returned unto Zion, and will dwell in the midst of Jerusalem: and Jerusalem shall be called a city of truth; and the mountain of the LORD of hosts the holy mountain.*

These Old Testament prophecies are fulfilled through the Messiah, Jesus, as God came to dwell with his new creation people, the true "Israel of God" who are a "new creation" of God, (Gal 6:15-16). Consider in particular the prophecy of Ezekiel, focusing on the Messiah, the true Seed of David (Rom 1:3), and the covenant of peace (new covenant), and the dwelling of God in their midst:

[Ezek 34:22-25; 37:24-28] "therefore I will save My flock, and they shall no longer be a prey; and I will judge between sheep and sheep. 23 "I will establish one shepherd over them, and he shall feed them—*My servant David. He shall feed them and be their shepherd.* 24 "And I, the LORD, will be their God, *and My servant David a prince among them*; I, the LORD, have spoken. 25 "*I will make a covenant of peace with them*...37:24 "*David My servant shall be king over them,...* 25 ...and *My servant David shall be their prince forever.* 26 "Moreover I will make *a covenant of peace* with them, and it shall be *an everlasting covenant* with them; I will establish them and multiply them, *and I will set My sanctuary in their midst forevermore.* 27 "*My tabernacle also shall be with them; indeed I will be their God, and they shall be My people.* 28 "The nations also will know that I, the LORD, sanctify Israel, when *My sanctuary is in their midst forevermore.*""

Clearly, it was a central feature of God's purpose from the beginning of creation to have his dwelling place among his people. In the New Testament, following the incarnation and atoning work of Jesus as the promised Messiah – the Greater David – and his ascension to heaven to his Father, these Old Testament prophecies began to be fulfilled. The Lord Jesus reigned as Lord over his people. The physical Jerusalem, physical tabernacle/temple and old covenant are superseded by the church, and the new covenant – the everlasting covenant, also called the covenant of peace, And God took up his dwelling place in the midst of his people, in their hearts and lives. The worship of God, said Jesus, was no longer to be attached to a place, but was to be in spirit and truth.

> [Jn. 14:22-23] Judas (not Iscariot) said to Him, "Lord, how is it that You will manifest Yourself to us, and not to the world?" 23 Jesus answered and said to him, "If anyone loves Me, he will keep My word; and My Father will love him, and *We will come to him and make Our home* [or dwelling place] *with him.*
> [Eph 2:19-22] Now, therefore, you are no longer strangers and foreigners, but fellow citizens with the saints and members of the household of God, ...built on the foundation of the apostles and prophets, *Jesus Christ Himself being the chief cornerstone, 21 in whom the whole building, being joined together, grows into a holy temple in the Lord, 22 in whom you also are being built together for a dwelling place of God in the Spirit.*

But because of his people's still bearing the legacy of the fall in their bodies and minds, fellowship with God could never be perfected while they dwelt on this earth in mortality and corruption. Apostle Paul, perhaps the greatest Christian missionary who ever lived, nevertheless felt his imperfection and groaned in his present body with a longing to experience full redemption of the body, and to share in the glory with Christ, where he could enter into his full sonship before his heavenly Father. (Rom 8:23).

The vision in Rev. 21-22 of the New Jerusalem pictures the full consummate restoration of man into the fellowship with God as fully functional sons of God, (Rev. 21:7). The blessings of God's tabernacle being with men, that is, of God's dwelling in the midst of his people and being their God and their being his people, were known in a limited and deposit/firstfruits measure prior to the Parousia of Christ; however the fullness of these blessings was eagerly expected to be revealed and experienced in their ultimate liberating power and glory when Christ came with his final salvation, when he brought them into his eternal kingdom and eternal glory.

The promise in Rev. 3:11-12 to the overcomers was a permanent home in the heavenly New Jerusalem; they would be in the temple where the presence of God is and would enjoy fellowship and association with God always. This was not to do with deposit/firstfruits measures of blessings, but with the consummate fulfillment of the prophecies/promises of dwelling with God, and God dwelling with his people.

> [Rev. 3:11-12] "Behold, I am coming quickly! Hold fast what you have, that no one may take your crown. 12 "He who overcomes, *I will make him a pillar in the temple of My God*, and he shall go out no more. *And I will write on him the name of My God and the name of the city of My God, the New Jerusalem*, which comes down out of heaven from My God. And *I will write on him* My new name.

In the vision of what was to occur in the near future regarding the saints who had come out of the great tribulation, it is said:

> [Rev. 7:15] "Therefore they are before the throne of God, and *serve Him day and night in His temple*. And *He who sits on the throne will dwell among them.*

And later John saw a vision of the fulfillment of the ages-long promise of perfect restoration of fellowship with God.

> [Rev. 21:3] And I heard a loud voice from heaven saying, "Behold, *the tabernacle of God is with men*, and *He will dwell with them, and they shall be His people. God Himself will be with them and be their God.*
> [Rev. 21:22] But I saw no temple in it [i.e. New Jerusalem], for the Lord God Almighty and the Lamb are its temple.
> [Rev. 22:3-4] And there shall be no more curse, but *the throne of God and of the Lamb shall be in it*, and His servants shall serve Him. 4 They shall see His face, and His name [shall be] on their foreheads.

Again the mention in Rev. 21 and 22 of the materials such as gold and precious stones in the city, and the tree of life and the river, all are symbolically declaring that this vision of what would occur for all saints at the Parousia of Jesus, this dwelling of God with his people in a consummate way, is a full recovery, on a far higher plane, of that dwelling together of God and man at the original creation in the garden of Eden. The Edenic situation was a physical type of the far greater spiritual and heavenly reality in Christ represented by the New Jerusalem.

The scene of the New Jerusalem in the Revelation thus represents the blessedness of the consummate phase (in contrast to the deposit/ firstfruits phase) of his people dwelling with God and God dwelling with his people; a consummation that was/is not possible for those on earth still in their mortal, earthly bodies.

(v) The Throne of God

> [Rev. 21:5; 22:1, 3] Then *He who sat on the throne* said, "Behold, I make all things new." And He said to me, "Write, for these words are true and faithful." 22:1 And he showed me a pure river of water of life, clear as crystal, proceeding *from the throne of God and of the Lamb*.... 3 And there shall be no more curse, but *the throne of God and of the Lamb shall be in it*, and His servants shall serve Him.

Throughout the whole Bible the throne of God is always pictured as in heaven. From his throne in heaven Almighty God rules the universe and especially his kingdom in the lives of his people. The New Jerusalem vision in the Revelation represents the glorified people of God in heaven in the presence of God. They had the awesome privilege of being in the presence of the throne of God.

Following his atoning work on earth, the Lord Jesus ascended to heaven to the throne of his Father:

> [Heb. 10:12] But *this Man*, after He had offered one sacrifice for sins forever, *sat down at the right hand of God*,
> [1 Pet. 3:22] *[Jesus] has gone into heaven and is at the right hand of God*, angels and authorities and powers having been made subject to Him.
> [Rev. 3:21] Jesus said, "...*I overcame and sat down with My Father on His throne.*"

Throughout the Revelation, the throne of God and the Lamb in heaven is the sphere of sovereign rule; the sphere in which the angelic beings live and serve and worship.

> [Rev. 4:1-5, 9-11] After these things I looked, and behold, a door *standing* open in heaven. And the first voice which I heard *was* like a trumpet speaking with me, saying, "Come up here, and I will show you things which must take place after this." 2 Immediately I was in the Spirit; and behold, *a throne set in heaven, and One sat on the throne.* 3 And He who sat there was like a jasper and a sardius stone in appearance; and *there was* a rainbow around the throne, in appearance like an emerald. 4 Around the throne *were* twenty-four thrones, and on the thrones I saw twenty-four elders sitting, clothed in white robes; and they had crowns of gold on their heads. 5 And from the throne proceeded lightnings, thunderings, and voices. Seven lamps of fire *were* burning before the throne, which are the seven Spirits of God.... 9 Whenever the living creatures give glory and honor and thanks to *Him who sits on the throne, who lives forever and ever*, 10 the twenty-four elders fall down before Him who sits on the throne and worship Him who lives forever and ever, and *cast their crowns before the throne*, saying: 11 "You are worthy, O Lord, To receive glory and honor and power; For You created all things, And by Your will they exist and were created."
> [Rev. 5:6, 13] And I looked, and behold, *in the midst of the throne* and of the four living creatures, and in the midst of the elders, *stood a Lamb* as though it had been slain, having seven horns and seven eyes, which are the seven Spirits of God sent out into all the earth.... 13 And every creature which is in heaven and on the earth and under the earth and such as are in the sea, and all that are in them, I heard saying: "Blessing and honor and glory and power [Be] *to Him who sits on the throne, And to the Lamb*, forever and ever!"

[Rev. 7:9-12, 15, 17] After these things I looked, and behold, a great multitude which no one could number, of all nations, tribes, peoples, and tongues, *standing before the throne and before the Lamb,* clothed with white robes, with palm branches in their hands, 10 and crying out with a loud voice, saying, "*Salvation belongs to our God who sits on the throne, and to the Lamb!*" 11 *All the angels stood around the throne* and the elders and the four living creatures, and fell on their faces before the throne and worshiped God, 12 saying: "Amen! Blessing and glory and wisdom, Thanksgiving and honor and power and might, *Be* to our God forever and ever. Amen."... 15 "*Therefore they are before the throne of God, and serve Him day and night in His temple.* And *He who sits on the throne will dwell among them....* 17 "for *the Lamb who is in the midst of the throne will shepherd them* and lead them to living fountains of waters. And God will wipe away every tear from their eyes."

[Rev. 14:1, 3, 5] Then I looked, and behold, a Lamb standing on Mount Zion, and with Him one hundred [and] forty-four thousand, having His Father's name written on their foreheads.... *3 They sang as it were a new song before the throne, before the four living creatures, and the elders*; and no one could learn that song except the hundred [and] forty-four thousand who were redeemed from the earth.... 5 And in their mouth was found no deceit, for *they are without fault before the throne of God.*

[Rev. 16:17] Then the seventh angel poured out his bowl into the air, *and a loud voice came out of the temple of heaven, from the throne, saying, "It is done!"*

In a scene set around the throne in heaven there was, as well as praise for God's destroying the enemy Babylon, the great announcement of the marriage of the Lamb and his bride.

[Rev. 19:4-9] And the twenty-four elders and the four living creatures fell down and *worshiped God who sat on the throne,* saying, "Amen! Alleluia!" 5 Then *a voice came from the throne, saying,* "Praise our God, all you His servants... 6 And I heard, as it were, the voice of a great multitude, as the sound of many waters and as the sound of mighty thunderings, saying, "Alleluia! For the Lord God Omnipotent reigns! 7 *"Let us be glad and rejoice and give Him glory, for the marriage of the Lamb has come, and His wife has made herself ready."* 8 And to her it was granted to be arrayed in fine linen, clean and bright, for the fine linen is the righteous acts of the saints. 9 Then he said to me, "Write: 'Blessed *are* those who are called to the marriage supper of the Lamb!'" And he said to me, "These are the true sayings of God."

Then following the announcement in 19:4-9 there comes the vision of the fulfillment:

> [Rev. 21:2, 5; 22:1, 3] Then I, John, saw the holy city, New Jerusalem, coming down out of heaven from God, prepared as a bride adorned for her husband.... 5 Then *He who sat on the throne* said, "Behold, I make all things new." And He said to me, "Write, for these words are true and faithful." 22:1 And he showed me a pure river of water of life, clear as crystal, proceeding *from the throne of God and of the Lamb*.... 3 And there shall be no more curse, but *the throne of God and of the Lamb shall be in it*, and His servants shall serve Him.

The New Jerusalem has as its centre the throne of God and of the Lamb. There is only one throne of God previously mentioned many times in the Revelation – the throne of God in the temple of God in heaven.

Jesus ascended to heaven, to the heavenly throne of the Father, and throughout the Revelation, as shown in the selection of verses above, the throne of God and the Lamb are always set in heaven, in the heavenly temple of God, where God's angelic servants wait on him. And there is no reason to suppose that the throne of God and of the Lamb spoken of in Rev. 21 and 22 has any different meaning.

The New Jerusalem has its situation in heaven before the throne of God where the Lord Jesus is - at the right hand of the Father. To the Father's presence was where Jesus said he was going when he left earth, (e.g. Jn. 14:28 as one example of many. See Chapter 5, *Going to the Father and into His Glory*), and that was where he was going to prepare a place for his disciples. The whole context of Jn. 14:1-6 is that Jesus would return to take his disciples to be with him in the presence of the Father; his whole atoning work was to enable men to come to the Father (Jn 14:6; 1 Pet 3:18), not just in spirit while they lived on earth, but to come to the Father in heaven just as really and fully as Jesus did when he finished his allotted time on earth.

Jesus' promise to the overcomers, regardless of whether they would die as martyrs before the Parousia, or whether they remained alive until the Parousia, was that at the Parousia they would be granted to sit with Jesus on his throne just as he overcame and sat down with his Father on His throne.

> [Rev. 3:21] "To him who overcomes I will grant to sit with Me on My throne, as I also overcame and sat down with My Father on His throne."

Where did Jesus sit down? On the right hand of the Father in heaven, on that throne which is in the heavenly temple of God which is seen often in the Revelation. The overcomers - whether living or deceased by the time of the Parousia, it made no difference in the end - did not expect to be remaining on earth in their mortality after the Parousia; rather they expected to be with Jesus, the Lamb who dwells at the throne of God. Did the dead overcomers go to heavenly glory at the Parousia? Yes. Then so did the living overcomers at the Parousia; for all overcomers were promised the same glorious inheritance.

The saints of Rev. 7:9-17, seen as having come out of the great tribulation, were seen before the throne of God in His temple, serving Him there. We have noted before that this scene in Rev. 7 is the same scene expanded on in Rev. 21 and 22.

The remnant of Rev. 14:1-5 were seen with the Lamb before the throne of God. In the Revelation the Lamb and the throne of God in heaven are inseparable. This remnant of Rev. 14, who had the Father's name written on their foreheads, are certainly among the saints of the New Jerusalem, where the servants of God are with the Lamb before the throne of God, and who have the name of God on their foreheads, Rev. 22:3-4. This whole consummation scene of glorified saints is certainly not describing believers still on earth in mortal bodies, but glorified believers in heaven with the Lord Jesus.

Someone may again raise the question: Why does it say John saw the New Jerusalem *descending out of heaven from God*, if it was to have its situation in heaven with God? Does it mean that the New Jerusalem is not in heaven? I have given some suggestions at the end of section (4) above. But here are, what I feel, are some other guiding points.

Firstly, this wording cannot contradict the clear teaching elsewhere that the throne of God and the Lamb are situated in heaven and are never promised anywhere in the New Testament to leave heaven. And so, seeing that the New Jerusalem is situated with the throne of God and the Lamb in its midst, it must mean that the New Jerusalem must be a heavenly reality.

Secondly, in the letter to the Hebrews, the hope of the first Hebrew Christians was to enter the heavenly Holy of Holies where their forerunner Jesus had gone ahead of them to prepare the way for them all to follow after him, at his Parousia. This was the glory that the many sons were to be brought into - the same glory that Jesus had in heaven in the Father's presence. And as previous studies have shown, the expectation of the saints at the Parousia was to enter the fullness of heaven and in a glorified state to be with Jesus and the Father. So the interpretation of the vision cannot contradict that.

Thirdly, keep in mind that this is a vision. Movement in a vision may not refer to actual equivalent physical movement in real life, but is symbolic of spiritual realities. To illustrate the fact that one must not press the physical details or movements of a vision too much, consider the following. In Rev. 21:2 the New Jerusalem was seen "descending out of (Gr. *ek*) heaven from (Gr. *apo*) God." In Rev. 19:1-9, the praise service and the announcement of the marriage of the Lamb occurred in heaven before him who sits on the throne. That is, the throne of God is in heaven and the bride is in heaven. Now the city which is at one moment with God in heaven where God's throne is, and there announced as ready for the marriage, in the next moment descends out of heaven from God (21:2), and yet is said a bit later to have God dwelling in the city and his throne situated in the city (21:3, 5, 22; 22:1,3). To press the physical aspects here, gets one involved in a paradox. For, to say that the city descended out of heaven from God and out of that heaven where the throne of God was, and then a moment later to say that God was dwelling in the city and had his throne in the city, leads to the questions: Did the city not actually physically depart from God after all, if it was with him before and now is with him again? Or if it did descend from heaven from God, did God and his throne suddenly descend out of heaven too, (without John being shown it), such that God and his throne now actually dwell in the city which is not in heaven anymore? The latter cannot be true! Because for evermore, God reigns supreme from his throne in heaven.

Remember: This is a vision and one cannot press the physical details. The descending of the city from God portrays certain spiritual realities, such as its new manifestation originating from God; while the next scene of the city being in heaven with God and his throne portrays other realities, especially that the New Jerusalem is a heavenly reality in God's immediate presence. This may seem a paradox if this was to do with physical entities in this world, but it is not dealing with physical movements visible to this physical world. This is all dealing with spiritual realities in the consummate kingdom of God, and in such a sphere the vision presents no paradox at all.

In one sense the city comes from God out of heaven, denoting that it is a heavenly entity designed and made by God alone and dependent on him alone for its being and light and life. The vision of its coming signified to John the coming of its full manifestation, not suggesting any real physical movement. In another sense, the city never leaves God in heaven, for he and his throne dwell in it; or rather, the city is built around him and his throne in his temple in heaven. The heavenly throne of God and the Lamb with its angelic attendants is ever firm in the same situation over the universe, as is portrayed throughout Scripture.

(vi) The Hope of Entering the Heavenly Holy of Holies Fulfilled

This scene in Rev. 21 and 22 also describes the fulfillment of the Christians' hopes of entering the true Holy of Holies in the heavenly temple, into the Fathers' presence where the Lord Jesus dwells and also the angels. This particular aspect is part of the eternal inheritance described in the letter to the Hebrews. It is the references to the temple in the New Jerusalem that highlights this fulfilled promise.

While the pre-Parousia Christians had an intimate fellowship with the Father through Christ and by the Spirit's enabling, (e.g. Eph 2:18), it was but a foretaste, a firstfruits measure, of what they hoped for — the going into the Holy of Holies where the Father dwelt in heaven, in just as real a manner as their forerunner and pioneer, Jesus, had entered that holiest place in the heavenly tabernacle before them.

Consider the following verses in Hebrews expressing the hope of entering the Holy of Holies in the heavenly temple:

Christ entered the heavenly tabernacle and Holy of Holies (into God's presence) upon which the Mosaic tabernacle was patterned, and later Solomon's temple.

> [Heb 8:1-5] Now *this is* the main point of the things we are saying*: We have such a High Priest, who is seated at the right hand of the throne of the Majesty in the heavens, 2 a Minister of the sanctuary and of the true tabernacle which the Lord erected, and not man....* 4 For if He were on earth, He would not be a priest, since there are priests who offer the gifts according to the law; *5 who serve the copy and shadow of the heavenly things*, as Moses was divinely instructed *when he was about to make the tabernacle.* For He said, "See *that* you make all things *according to the pattern* shown you on the mountain."
>
> [Heb 9:11-12] But Christ came *as* High Priest of the good things to come, *with the greater and more perfect tabernacle not made with hands, that is, not of this creation.* 12 Not with the blood of goats and calves, but with His own blood *He entered the Most Holy Place* once for all, having obtained eternal redemption.
>
> [Heb 9:24] For *Christ* has not entered the holy places made with hands, which are copies of the true, but *into heaven itself, now to appear in the presence of God for us*;

The hope of the Hebrew Christians was to enter that same heavenly tabernacle and Holy of Holies, just as really as Jesus their forerunner did.

> [Heb 6:19-20] *This hope we have* as an anchor of the soul, both sure and steadfast, and *which enters the Presence behind the veil,* 20 *where the forerunner has entered for us, even Jesus*, having become High Priest forever according to the order of Melchizedek.
>
> [Heb 10:19-25] Therefore, brethren, *having boldness to enter the Holiest by the blood of Jesus*, 20 by a new and living way which He consecrated for us, through the veil, that is, His flesh, 21 and having a High Priest over the house of God, 22 let us draw near with a true heart in full assurance of faith, having our hearts sprinkled from an evil conscience and our bodies washed with pure water. 23 Let us *hold fast the confession of our hope* without wavering, for He who promised is faithful.

Now the use of the word "tabernacle" is used in the above passages rather than the word "temple," in describing God's dwelling place in heaven, because the writer to the Hebrews was specifically contrasting the Mosaic covenant with the new covenant inaugurated by Jesus; and in Moses' days the special emblematic dwelling place of God on earth was called the tabernacle. Later under Solomon the larger structure that he built was called the temple. As we come to the relevant passages (mentioned below) in the Revelation we will find that the word "temple" is primarily used of God's dwelling place in heaven, as the antitype and the reality of the Old Testament type. The tabernacle in heaven in the letter to the Hebrews is the same as the temple in heaven in the book of the Revelation.

Consider the promise to the overcomers in the Revelation of a place in the temple of God in heaven.

> [Rev. 3:11] "Behold, I am coming quickly! Hold fast what you have, that no one may take your crown. 12 *"He who overcomes, I will make him a pillar in the temple of My God, and he shall go out no more.* And *I will write on him the name of My God and the name of the city of My God, the New Jerusalem*, which comes down out of heaven from My God. And *I will write on him* My new name."

This promise is that Christian overcomers, (both living and deceased saints at the Parousia), would be granted at the Parousia a permanent dwelling in the heavenly temple of God which is in the New Jerusalem.

Consider the vision in which John saw a the future scene of the saints who had come out of the great tribulation:

> [Rev. 7:14-15] "These are the ones who come out of the great tribulation, and washed their robes and made them white in the blood of the Lamb. 15 "Therefore *they are before the throne of God, and serve Him day and night in His temple. And He who sits on the throne will dwell among them.*

Many times throughout the Revelation the temple of God in heaven is referred to as the place of God's immediate presence and the place of his throne from which He rules the universe, and from which the angels are sent out on their missions, (see Rev. 4:5, 6, 10; 7:11; 11:19; 14:15, 17; 15:5, 6, 8; 16:1, 17).

It was into this heavenly temple and to the throne of God in the heavenly Holy of Holies that the Lord Jesus entered following his work of atonement on earth. And it was into this same heavenly temple, the True Holy of Holies, that the first Christians were hoping to enter at the Parousia of Christ. Then the promise of their coming to the Father (Jn. 14:6) would be totally fulfilled.

At the sounding of the seventh trumpet, signaling the time of God's victory over his enemies (after the judgments on apostate Jerusalem and Israel), and signaling the time of the saints to receive their reward, we have the interesting statement:

> [Rev. 11:19] Then the temple of God was opened in heaven, *and the ark of His covenant was seen in His temple.* And there were lightnings, noises, thunderings, an earthquake, and great hail.

James Stuart Russell in *The Parousia* comments on this verse:

> The symbolical representation in the last verse [Rev. 11:19] seems susceptible of a satisfactory explanation. At the very moment of the doom of Jerusalem, when city and temple perish together, — when all the ceremonial and ritual of the earthly and transitory are swept away, the temple of God in heaven is opened, and the ark of His covenant is seen in the temple. That is as much as to say, the local and temporary passes, but is succeeded by the heavenly and eternal; the earthly and figurative is superseded by the spiritual and the true. We have in this representation a fine comment on the words of the Epistle to the Hebrews, 'the way into the holiest of all was not yet made manifest, while as the first tabernacle was yet standing.' But no sooner is the 'first tabernacle' swept away than the temple in heaven is opened, and even the sacred Ark of the Covenant, the shrine of the divine Presence and Glory, is revealed to the eyes of men. Access into the holiest of all is no longer forbidden, and 'we have boldness to enter into the holiest by the blood of Jesus.'

Now the events in the vision of Rev. 11:19 occur at the Parousia of Christ – the same time in history that the events that are pictured in the vision of the New Jerusalem in Rev. 21 and 22 are to occur. In the New Jerusalem there is access to the Holy of Holies presence of God.

The temple in the New Jerusalem

At a first reading of Rev. 21:22 there seems to be a contradiction here, for while the promises to the Christians had to do with their entering the temple of God in the New Jerusalem, the word in Rev. 21:22 says that there was no temple in the New Jerusalem:

> [Rev. 21:22] But I saw no temple in it, for the Lord God Almighty and the Lamb are its temple.

But this seeming contradiction is solved if we consider that the whole New Jerusalem was pictured as a giant cube resembling the cubic shape of the earthly Holy of Holies in the tabernacle of Moses and the temple of Solomon.

[Rev. 21:16] The city is laid out as a square; its length is as great as its breadth. And he measured the city with the reed: twelve thousand furlongs. Its length, breadth, and height are equal.

This implies that the whole city was the holy sanctuary of God. There was no separate temple or Holy of Holies structure in the vision of the New Jerusalem because a separate structure would imply that the presence of God within that structure is not freely accessible to all, which was the case in the earthly structures – where only the special priests had access to the holy place, and only the high priest had access to the Holy of Holies and then only once per year. In the New Jerusalem God's presence is everywhere and all its inhabitants are in immediate fellowship with Him. *All is temple, all is Holy of Holies, for God fills all.* Indeed it may be said that the Lord God Almighty and the Lamb are its temple; for all his saints are in his presence and his presence fills all the city.

In the New Jerusalem there is no temple in the sense of a particular structure, for God is the temple; the saints who were promised permanent access into the temple of God find themselves brought at Jesus' Parousia into the immediate presence of God in the New Jerusalem; there is no separating veil, and no privileged elite priesthood; all his people in the New Jerusalem see his face, and dwell in his light and glory, all of which speaks of the highest privilege of access to the Father where Jesus lives as the saints' high priest and forerunner and savior.

(vii) All Things New

[Rev. 21:3-5] And I heard a loud voice from heaven saying, "Behold, the tabernacle of God *is* with men, and He will dwell with them, and they shall be His people. God Himself will be with them *and be* their God. 4 And God will wipe away every tear from their eyes; there shall be no more death, nor sorrow, nor crying. There shall be no more pain, for *the former things have passed away*." 5 Then He who sat on the throne said, "*Behold, I make all things new*." And He said to me, "Write, for these words are true and faithful."

Regarding the wonderful condition and circumstances of the inhabitants in the New Jerusalem, John hears a loud voice from heaven saying that all the former things associated with their earthly condition have passed away; and God on his throne confirms that voice by himself saying, "Behold, I make all things new."

The former things have passed away

Prior to the Parousia the apostle Paul could speak of the present believers as new creations in Christ Jesus, in whom the old things had passed away, and all things had become new, (2 Cor. 5:17). The old Godless life has finished, and a new life in Christ Jesus has begun. Yet it is clear he is not meaning that they were experientially perfect, for elsewhere he has to exhort believers to put away the old ways and adopt the new ways of love and peace, etc. And Paul himself confesses the real groaning within himself to be rid of his old corruption and instead to experience full redemption and full sonship, (Rom 8:23). In other words, the fact that in Christ the old things had passed away, was only being experienced in a firstfruits measure while in this life. He was expecting the full demonstration of his total freedom from all the old state of things at the Parousia. And that final time is what is expressed in Rev. 21:4. At the Parousia, the full manifestation, the full experiential reality, was given of the fact that in Christ the old, former state of things had passed away.

"The former things have passed away" for the saints in the New Jerusalem at the Parousia of Christ. There will be nothing that will cause them sadness or pain in their consummated, glorified condition. "God will wipe away every tear from their eyes; there shall be no more death, nor sorrow, nor crying. There shall be no more pain, (21:4). "And there shall be no more curse," (22:3). "They shall neither hunger anymore nor thirst anymore; the sun shall not strike them, nor any heat; for the Lamb who is in the midst of the throne will shepherd them and lead them to living fountains of waters. And God will wipe away every tear from their eyes," (7:16-17).

Suffering from outside causes has passed away.

In Rom 8:17-18, 35-39 and 2 Cor. 4:7-18, Paul expressed his expectation that at the coming of Christ, he and fellow Christians would be taken out from under the weight of suffering, affliction, and persecution they were under and brought under the "far more exceeding and eternal weight of glory." This hope is fulfilled in the New Jerusalem.

Suffering from inside causes has passed away.

In the New Jerusalem there is no more groaning and sorrow arising from inner conflict in a believer due to indwelling sin in the flesh, something which Paul hoped to be rid of at the Parousia. Freedom from his imperfect condition was part of the glory he was looking forward to, (Romans chapters 7–8, esp. 8:19-23). The first Christians were expecting that their humiliated bodies, "the body [which] is dead because of sin" would no longer bother them but would be changed/transformed into glorious bodies, by the power of Christ and the Holy Spirit (Phil 3:20-21; Rom 8:10-11).

This consummate New Jerusalem leaves no room for any aspect of the "old, former things" which were attached to the believers as leftovers, or as a legacy, from their unconverted, unregenerated days. All things related to man's fallenness, such as weakness in body, mind, and spirit, indwelling sinfulness, mortality, worldliness or earthliness of any kind, would be passed away. As Paul says, "flesh and blood cannot inherit the kingdom of God [in its consummate, spiritual nature]; nor does incorruption [i.e. men or believers in corruptible bodies] inherit incorruption [i.e. the incorruption and holy spirituality of the consummated heavenly kingdom], (1 Cor. 15:50). And the New Jerusalem represents the consummate form of the kingdom of God. No unhappy aspect associated with flesh and blood life on earth is present in the New Jerusalem. The mention of no more death being the portion of those in the New Jerusalem at the Parousia, reminds one of the note of victory that would sound at the Parousia of Christ:

> So when this corruptible has put on incorruption, and this mortal has put on immortality, then shall be brought to pass the saying that is written: "Death is swallowed up in victory." (1 Cor. 15:54)

It is to be noted that in the context of 1 Cor. 15, corruption, dishonor, weakness and naturalness (materiality) characterize man and his body as the image of fallen, earthy Adam; while incorruption, glory, power and spirituality characterize redeemed men and his new body when raised/transformed fully into the image of the heavenly Man, the Lord Jesus.

"No more death" in the New Jerusalem means its inhabitants reign in life, in resurrection, glorified, spiritual bodies, together with the Lord Jesus in his glorious body. This actual victory over death was the portion of the pre-Parousia saints of all past ages, at the Parousia of Christ. This verse of victory in 1 Cor. 15:54, while potentially true in Christ for all *post-Parousia* Christians, cannot be proclaimed as experientially accomplished while they are still on earth in a mortal, sin-affected condition, but will be proclaimed over them as each in their order finishes their allotted time on this earth, and physically dies, at which time they are then raised incorruptible and glorious to join their previously deceased but now raised brethren in heaven with the glorified Christ.

Behold, ...all things new

As mentioned above, Paul said those in Christ were new creations, and the old had passed away and all things had become new. The first Christians prior to the Parousia had the firstfruits of the newness that was in Christ Jesus. They were undergoing a constant renewing (e.g., Col. 3:10; Rom 12:2). Christians had already commenced a new creation life in peace and fellowship with God, who was dwelling with and in them, and they were partaking of the refreshing rivers of living water by the Holy Spirit. But that was the deposit/firstfruits measure, while they were still in earthy corruptible bodies and partially renewed minds and while sin and imperfection was still a legacy in them from Adam. Their hopes were focused on the glorification with Christ at his Parousia, when they would be presented to Christ totally conformed to his image. The New Jerusalem represents the glorious consummation of the restoration of his people back to himself. It is the time of the consummation of their newness in Christ proclaimed in Rev. 21:5, as God says, "Behold, I make all things new."

On the authority of God himself, those believers composing the New Jerusalem – all believers of Old and New Testament days who had ever existed up until the time of the Parousia – were to experience "all things new" at the Parousia of their Lord. When God on his throne says, "Behold, I make all things new," He means just that! — a completed newness of body, soul and spirit, that perfectly suits the Christians for fullness of life in the consummate kingdom of God before the throne of God. All believers in the New Jerusalem are before the Lord in a perfect, blameless, glorified condition, as represented by the beautiful and precious stones and gold and pearls that are in the city.

The "all things new" in the New Jerusalem includes the consummate blessing of eternal life and fellowship with God, pictured by God's dwelling place being with men and God dwelling with men, (Rev. 21:3), and by the tree of life and the river of the water of life (Rev. 22:1-2). These features symbolize the fact that in the New Jerusalem, all that was lost by man in the garden of Eden, where man had unhindered fellowship with God and where there was the tree of life and the rivers irrigating the land, is now recovered, plus much more! After Adam and Eve's fall in the Garden of Eden they were barred from the garden; the close fellowship with the Lord was lost; and the cherubim and a swordlike flame guarded the entry so that no one could re-enter. In the vision of the New Jerusalem all believers are back in a greater paradise, in the closest fellowship with their God and enjoy sinless service and worship, partaking of an eternal life pictured by the tree of life, and the river of the water of life.

The "all things new" includes the fulfillment of that hope of glory held by the first Christians (e.g. Rom 5:2. See my Chapter 4, *The God of Glory and the Hope of Glory*). When the New Jerusalem would come at the Parousia, as foreseen by John in the Revelation, glory is a key characteristic. The glory of God adorns the people of God. The glory of God illumines the city. This is the occasion when the first Christians have their glorified bodies like the Lord Jesus and experience to the full consummate measure, their citizenship in heaven. The saints would have their hope of glory fulfilled in the New Jerusalem at the Lord's return. It is in this consummate form of the kingdom of God, that the saints will be crowned with the unfading crown of glory (1 Pet 5:4). And all of God's sons will be fulfilled as they are brought to final glory (Heb 2:10) where their glorified Lord Jesus is. The scene is beautiful and complete: "The city had no need of the sun or of the moon to shine in it, for *the glory of God illuminated it. The Lamb is its light*. (Rev. 21:23).

The "all things new" includes the sixteen aspects of consummate blessedness listed in Chapter 2, expected by the first Christians at the Parousia; namely:

1. *Full Salvation* - fully into God's will and purpose, where all presence of sin and fallenness and imperfection is gone.
2. *The Crown of Righteousness* - fully conformed to the image of Jesus Christ the righteous.
3. *The Crown of Eternal Life* - where all is life in union with

God, experiencing the divine nature with no trace of death and fallenness.
4. *Full Sonship* - full experience of living as God's glorified sons, no un-son-like aspects present at all.
5. *Redemption* - total reclamation from every part of the legacy of death, fallenness and corruption and sin derived from the fall of Adam.
6. *The Kingdom of God* - complete experience of the reign of God within, where all is of Christ, where all of his characteristics have full sway within, with no "flesh" warring against the Spirit.
7. *Fullness of Light with Christ* - fullness of divine light within, no trace of darkness of mind or heart.
8. *Participation in the New Jerusalem* - partaking of heavenly blessedness with all God's people in God's majestic presence.
9. *Reigning with Christ* - the raised saints are completely taken up with Christ's interests in complete Christ-likeness, ruling in his name over all he gives them to rule over.
10. *Rest and Comfort with God* - perfect joy and peace within the heaven of God's presence, with all evil influence no longer present.
11. *God's Dwelling with His People* - enjoying His wonderful presence in ultimate reality.
12. *Access and Fellowship with God* - full, clear fellowship, totally uncluttered by sin, the flesh, and mortality.
13. *Knowing and Seeing God and his eternal realities* - undimmed knowing and appreciating Him.
14. *Marriage-Union with Christ* - Christ completely the real life and happiness of believers.
15. *Resurrection/Transformation and Glorification with Christ* - complete capacity to inhabit and experience the wonders of heaven with God in glorified-resurrection bodies.
16. *The Crown of Glory* - full glorification together with the glorified Jesus where He dwells.

The Revelation was given particularly to prepare and encourage the first Christians to endure the great tribulation of the Neronic persecutions. Who can imagine the sufferings of being burnt alive, or of being fed to wild beasts, of being treated as outcasts of society? But they were willing to bear it for the sake of the Lord and his gospel. They had the visions of the Revelation to encourage them that whether they lived or died they would all soon, when their Savior came for them, be ushered into the heavenly city, the New Jerusalem. The terrible evil of earthly suffering would be finished and would suddenly seem of comparatively small weight as it was exchanged for the far exceeding weight of glory and of life in that glorious city of the living God.

6. A Brief Summary of the Meaning of the New Jerusalem Vision

From the above discussion in Chapters 9 and 10 about the New Jerusalem, let me now summarize the main points.

i. I believe that the New Testament clearly presents the New Jerusalem vision in the Revelation as a representation of *the consummate glorious form of the new covenant kingdom of God and the glorified people of God*, which was expected at the soon coming Parousia of Christ. Prior to the Parousia of Christ, the saints had only a deposit/earnest/firstfruits measure of New Jerusalem–New Covenant blessings; they were expecting the consummate, harvest measure of blessings, pictured in the Revelation's New Jerusalem, at the coming of Christ.

ii. Old Testament and New Testament saints were *expecting to enter together* this eternal inheritance represented by the New Jerusalem in the Revelation. The OT saints were looking forward eagerly to their inheritance in the New Jerusalem, the heavenly city: in it they were to experience their homeland that they could not find on earth. The first Christians in the NT were likewise promised their inheritance in the New Jerusalem, the city to come. In the Revelation numerous promises and encouragements were given to build up their hope and confidence in such a glorious inheritance. The Parousia of Christ was to bring about a glorious and heavenly change to ALL saints who had existed up to that point in history. It is clear that the expectation was that the coming Parousia of Christ would occasion a consummative new experience and condition of those Christians still alive at the time of the Parousia which would be no different at all, but just the same as, the new experience and condition of the saints who were deceased before the time of the Parousia. At the Parousia of Christ, all believers who had lived up to that point in history would share alike in the glory of the New Jerusalem in the heavenly realms before the throne of God.

iii. It is important to see the significance of the Parousia of Christ introducing the New Jerusalem as *the heavenly city and the bride of Christ*. Until the Parousia of Christ, no saint in all of history had received their final salvation and eternal reward, no one had been glorified, no one had been resurrected into their heavenly state, no one had entered the heavenly Holy of Holies into the immediate presence of God. The saints at best had a deposit, earnest, firstfruits, and foretaste of a consummation about to come at the Parousia. The NT epistles make it clear that the Parousia of Christ was to bring in the long awaited consummation. The coming of New Jerusalem signifies the coming of the revelation and manifestation of the consummate glory state in heaven that was not in place previous to the Parousia of Christ.

"We are thus led to the conclusion, alike from the teaching of the Apocalypse and the rest of the New Testament scriptures, that in the days of St. John the Parousia was universally believed by the whole Christian church to be close at hand. It was the promise of Christ, the preaching of the apostles, the faith of the church. We are also taught the significance of that great event. It marked a new epoch in the divine administration. Until that event took place the full blessedness of the heavenly state was not open to the souls of believers. The Epistle to the Hebrews teaches that until the arrival of the great consummation something was wanting to the full perfection of them who had 'died in faith.' The same thing is taught in the Apocalypse. Until the 'harlot city' was judged and condemned, the 'holy city' was not prepared as the habitation of the saints." [James Stuart Russell in *The Parousia*, Part 3 The Parousia in the Apocalypse, Epilogue]

At the Parousia of Christ, which was expected before that messianic generation passed away, there was to be an entrance *en masse*, as one great assembly, of all OT saints and all NT saints, (deceased and living) – all saints who had ever existed up till that point in history would pass into the glory of God, into His heavenly kingdom to appear before him and live before him forever in consummate blessedness. Herein is the significance of the Revelation's vision of the New Jerusalem.

This examination of the meaning of the New Jerusalem and its inhabitants, fully harmonizes with the themes running through the other New Testament epistles that I have sought to highlight in previous chapters, viz., that all living and deceased believers who ever existed prior to the Parousia were expecting the Parousia of Christ to give them the same final salvation and the same glorification together with Christ. There is no reason to suggest that the believers living at the time of the Parousia of Christ expected anything less at the Parousia than the same glorification in heavenly bodies in the presence of the Lord that the deceased brethren expected. ALL had the same promises made to them regarding the consummate blessings coming at the Parousia of Christ.

7. The Relationship of Post-Parousia Believers to the New Jerusalem of the Revelation

Having examined the expectancy of the first (pre-Parousia) Christians at the Parousia, an important question now is: What of the post-Parousia Christians, that is, all the people who have come to faith in Christ since the Parousia of Christ circa AD 70 (including us modern Christians alive today) – what is our relationship to the New Jerusalem of the Revelation?

(i) The New Jerusalem of the Revelation is NOT fulfilled in Christians in this life, while they are living on earth.

The first Christians' hope was always to leave "this life" with its imperfection, sin, and other limitations, and be raised into heaven. The NT makes it clear that the first Christians knew they could never experience the consummation of the kingdom of God, the Revelation's New Jerusalem, while in this fallen world in their fallen bodies. To think otherwise defies all meaning of consummation and glorification and final salvation.[1] The best one can experience in this life is the deposit/firstfruits measure of the new covenant blessedness. The New Jerusalem expresses the consummate manifestation of the kingdom of God that "flesh and blood" (i.e. man in his mortal body) cannot inherit.

We post-Parousia Christians while in this life in our mortal bodies are yet only in the deposit/firstfruits phase of New Covenant experience and blessing. For we have not been glorified, nor can we be, while we are in these mortal bodies, the way the first Christians were glorified at the Parousia.

So if, according to the expectation presented in the New Testament epistles, all pre-Parousia believers were taken to heaven into the glory of the New Jerusalem at the Parousia, and if the consummation New Jerusalem is not fulfilled in us post-Parousia believers while we are on earth, then what is the relationship of all post-Parousia believers to the New Jerusalem?

(ii) The New Jerusalem of the Revelation is a delightful hope for post-Parousia Christians

In regard to this matter, the following comments on Rev. 14:13 give significant light:

[Rev. 14:13] *'And I heard a voice from heaven saying unto me, Write, Blessed are the dead which die in the Lord from henceforth: Yea, saith the Spirit, that they may rest from their labors; and their works do follow them.'*

All this is clearly indicative of the near approach of the final catastrophe. There is one expression, however, in the last quotation which calls for explanation, viz. the announcement respecting the blessedness of the dead who die in the Lord *from henceforth*. This 'henceforth' [Gr. *ap arti*] is the emphatic word in the sentence, and must have an important significance. It is not simply that the dead in Christ are safe or happy, but that, from and after a certain specified period, a peculiar blessedness belongs to all those who thenceforth die in the Lord.

It is not unreasonable in itself, and it appears, moreover, to be the distinct teaching of Holy Scripture, that the great consummation which closed the Jewish age had an important bearing upon the condition of all who subsequently to that period, 'die in the Lord.' We have seen (see Russell's remarks on Heb. 11:39-40 in *The Parousia*, Part 2) that previously to the redemptive work of

Christ the state of the pious dead was not perfect. They had to await the accomplishment of that great event which constituted the foundation of their everlasting felicity. The saints of the old dispensation 'obtained not the promise.' They died in *faith*, but did not possess the inheritance. 'God provided something better for *us*, that they without us should not be made perfect.' So wrote the author of the Epistle to the Hebrews on the verge of the great consummation. The plain meaning of this is that the *Parousia* marked the introduction of a new epoch in the condition of the departed saints and the prospects of all who after that epoch commenced should die in the Lord. 'Blessed are such' *from henceforth*. That is to say, they should not have to wait, as their predecessors had, the arrival of the period when the promise should be fulfilled. They should enter *at once* into 'the rest which remaineth for the people of God.' The way into the holy place has now been made manifest; there is immediate rest and reward for the faithful departed; 'they rest from their labors; for their works do follow them.'

This important passage would be totally inexplicable but for the light thrown upon it by Heb. 4:1-11 11:9,10,13,39,40.

(Comments by James Stuart Russell in *The Parousia*, in *Part 3 The Parousia in the Apocalypse* (from *Online Bible* CD and website).

Following Russell's explanation in the quote above, we note that the Parousia introduced a new epoch. This consummate glory represented by the New Jerusalem of the Revelation, this access into the heavenly Holy of Holies, was first set in place at the Parousia of Christ. On the occasion of the Parousia of Christ, in one sudden blessed moment all prior saints from all ages since the creation of the world, who had been waiting for this glory to be set in place for them, entered into and possessed their promised inheritance.

In the time following the Parousia, the blessedness that the pre-Parousia Christians entered at the Parousia would be fulfilled to the post-Parousia Christians *when they died. "Blessed are the dead which die in the Lord from henceforth."* When we post-Parousia Christians die, we won't need to wait for some future crisis, like the deceased pre-Parousia Christians did, who had to wait for the Parousia before they would be glorified and resurrected. Upon our death we are immediately resurrected into the consummate glory of the New Jerusalem to join the rest of the glorified believers in heaven. Note that the blessedness of the consummate glory-state is NOT stated to be for post-Parousia believers while they are alive on earth. *Blessed are the dead...* They experience the *blessedness* when they die. We have the happy knowledge that the realm of glory set up by the Lord at his Parousia, is fully ready for us to enter when our allotted time on earth is completed.

I would imagine this truth must be music in the ears of those preterists who have been taught that they had their final salvation already, but have been disillusioned by seeing so much of fallenness still in their lives. Be encouraged brethren, your final salvation, your real entrance into the consummate New Jerusalem will come, and be assured it will not be an objective, covenantal thing, but a radical, real resurrection, real experientially glorious thing, really seeing the glory of God in the company of millions of other glorified believers in heaven. Remember this: the apostle Paul was a better Christian than any modern preterist; his hope was to enter an inestimable glory-state, free from all trace of sin, experiencing the fullness of his adoption as a son, in a glorious, incorruptible, spiritual body. There is no way in this wide world, that Paul's hope can be reduced in meaning to mean that Paul would have been fulfilled at the Parousia by having no more than what the modern preterists have who say that they have the consummation now on earth. Dear preterist friend, our hope of glory is not fulfilled yet; don't pretend it is or you'll be gravely disillusioned; the glory that is our portion, which Paul and his brethren received at the Parousia and which they are enjoying in heaven, is still to come for us. Blessed are we when we die, when our time on earth in concluded, because then we'll join Paul and all the others in real glory and consummation.

(iii) We post-Parousia Christians experience the firstfruits measure of the New Jerusalem in this life

For all of us post-Parousia Christians, while we are on earth in these bodies we are in a deposit/firstfruits measure of New Covenant blessing, just like the first Christians were prior to the Parousia of Christ. We like the Galatian Christians are "children of the Jerusalem above," born of the Spirit, having the firstfruits of the New Jerusalem in us, awaiting our possession of the eternal inheritance in the heavenly New Jerusalem in its consummate form.

Meanwhile we, as Christians who have a deposit/firstfruits measure of new covenant blessings, find our food in the scriptures that were written by apostles, who were men of deposit/firstfruits blessedness; who wrote to their Christian brethren who were also people of deposit/firstfruits blessedness.

Let us be encouraged as we remember that our experiences of God, even while in this deposit/firstfruits stage of blessedness, can be wonderfully real, more than our mortal frames can handle at times, as is evidenced in the many spiritual Christian revivals that have occurred down through the centuries. The Holy Spirit desires to fill our lives as He filled the lives of the early apostles and the first Christians, and to work great things in this sad world. Let us be encouraged as we remember that the same Holy Spirit by whom the first Christians were sealed for glory, abides in us as our Comforter. We must not underestimate the power of the deposit and firstfruits measure that God has for us to experience during this life.

It is an exciting thing to me that in that first century, the Lord really did come just as he said; and that all pre-Parousia believers (deceased and living) were taken to glory to be forever with their Lord, just as he said. And I know that when my allotted time on earth is spent, the Lord will grant me the blessedness of sharing in the consummate form of the New Jerusalem just like all of those pre-Parousia believers did at the Parousia of Christ, and just like all post-Parousia believers have who have lived and died since the time of the Parousia.

(iv) We post-Parousia Christians walk in the light of the consummate New Jerusalem

Consider the words about the nations of the saved in the vision of the New Jerusalem in the Revelation:

> [Rev. 21:24-27] And the nations of those who are saved shall walk in its light, and the kings of the earth bring their glory and honor into it. 25 Its gates shall not be shut at all by day (there shall be no night there). 26 And they shall bring the glory and the honor of the nations into it. 27 But there shall by no means enter it anything that defiles, or causes an abomination or a lie, but only those who are written in the Lamb's Book of Life.

In the wonderful vision of the New Jerusalem in Revelation chapters 21 and 22, in addition to the inhabitants who are in the city serving the Lord in his temple, there are "the nations of those who are saved" who walk in its light and bring their honor and glory into it. These nations remind me of the post-Parousia believers who are alive on earth at any given time, while the saints in the city are the glorified believers who have finished their allotted time on earth. The post-Parousia saints alive on earth are like that nations of the vision; they walk in the light of the consummate glory, but are not yet glorified inhabitants who can live in it as such. The post-Parousia Christians alive on earth - the nations of those who are saved - bring their prayers and praises into God's temple, they spiritually come to His throne of grace to find grace and mercy to help them in their need. As believers on earth die they themselves become part of the glorious gifts that are brought into the city of God. The gates of the heavenly city are ever open for us believers on earth to have spiritual access to God while we live on earth, and are open for us to fully and completely enter when we die. Sooner or later all of us believers on earth, (the nations that are saved), whose names are in the Lamb's book of life, shall permanently and fully enter the heavenly city in a glorified form. Until then we walk in its light, i.e. walk in the sense of its absolute reality as our hoped-for heavenly homeland; walk now as its children, partaking of its life and spirit in a deposit/firstfruits measure while we are on earth; walk in the light of its divine realities and truth. In reality, to walk in the light of the heavenly Jerusalem is the same as walking in the light of the Lord himself because the Lord is the light of that city and the Lord is our light. However the glorified believers in the heavenly Jerusalem know his light in a fullness, while we on earth have the capacity for a firstfruits measure of light.

What can I say to end this, but to praise our wonderful God and Father of our Lord Jesus Christ who has "blessed us in Christ with every spiritual blessing in the heavenly places." For "from Him, and through Him and to Him are all things." To him be the glory forever. Amen.

Footnotes

For those interested, here are some further remarks enlarging on my assertion that the consummate manifestation of the New Jerusalem of the Revelation is *not* fulfilled in us post-Parousia Christians in this life, while living on earth. In saying this I realize that I am opposing a popular preterist "remained-on-earth" view (as I have coined it), that teaches a consummation now in this life on earth.

Audience Relevance

Consider the hermeneutic of audience relevance in looking at the final salvation and consummation promised at the Parousia of Christ. To receive final salvation *at the time of the Parousia* of Christ was the promise made to, and the expectation of, *the pre-Parousia saints*, (OT and NT saints, living and deceased) – that is, all the saints whose history was brought to a crisis at the Parousia.

Now to say, as some preterists popularly teach – that everything that was fulfilled to *pre-Parousia* Christians *on the occasion of the Parousia* is fulfilled now to *post-Parousia* Christians *while living in this life on the occasion of their coming to faith* in Christ Jesus – simply has no validity. It is absolutely at odds with what I said in point 7.(i) above, that mortal men in this life cannot know God's consummation and glorification. 1 Cor. 15:50 flatly states that "flesh and blood" cannot inherit the Kingdom of God, nor can corruption inherit incorruption. They are two separate realms of flesh and spirit. One on earth in the fleshly realm cannot have everything that pertains to the afterlife in the spiritual realm. There is a much fuller inheritance that waits until our passing from this realm of "flesh and blood" and corruption to that other realm of incorruption and the Kingdom of God in the spiritual realm.

The *deceased pre-Parousia saints* received *their real resurrection and glorification in heaven in the real immediate presence of the Father and Christ Jesus on the occasion of the Parousia (as did the living Christians, except they were "changed," bypassing death, rather than resurrected from the dead).* There *is no scriptural authority* (that I can see) that allows anyone to say that *on the occasion of faith* in Christ, *post-Parousia believers on earth* immediately receive their final salvation and resurrection and glorification *while still living on earth in their mortal bodies.*

For how can living-on-earth post-Parousia Christians claim to have in this life, a so-called final salvation, resurrection, etc., when *their* version of a final salvation, and glorification, etc., is a *different type* from what the NT speaks of and from what the deceased pre-Parousia saints received on the occasion of the Parousia? The deceased (along with the living) pre-Parousia saints got the real, experiential thing, of sinless glory in heaven; but the so-called final salvation, and glorification, etc. claimed by some preterists to be in the possession of living-on-earth post-Parousia Christians is a different type altogether – called "covenantal," and which is non-experiential, and which can coexist with sin, weakness, corruption and mortality within the modern believer. This sure doesn't sound at all like the real final salvation, resurrection and glorification expected by the pre-Parousia saints.

Now, opposite to my view, some preterists popularly teach that the Revelation's New Jerusalem consummation is currently possessed by post-Parousia Christians living on earth in their earthly bodies *prior to their death*. But I believe that all the studies in this book show that no post-Parousia Christian can experience the promised glory while on earth in this life prior to their physical death.

Note: The only saints who have ever been given the promise and privilege of entering and experiencing the consummate manifestation and glory of the New Jerusalem in heaven prior to their death were the pre-Parousia saints who were living at the time of Christ's coming, and even then they could not, did not, enter that promised glory while living in their mortal bodies; they were "changed," bypassing the normal process of death, and were given incorruptible, glorious, spiritual, heavenly bodies, (the same as for the deceased brethren), in order for them to inhabit the New Jerusalem of the Revelation.

There is the glaring fact that *post-Parousia believers living on earth* now *do not* experientially have what the *pre-Parousia deceased saints* got at the Parousia, nor what the pre-Parousia living Christians expected to get at the Parousia.

A mistaken view of the significance of the New Jerusalem in the Revelation

There appears to me to be a popular misinterpreting of Revelation's portrayal of the coming of the New Jerusalem and the new heavens and the new earth, to mean *the beginning* of the New Covenant age, instead of the [correct] meaning, viz., the *consummation* in heaven of the already existing New Covenant age, and consummation of New Covenant blessings which had already been present in a firstfruits measure in the first Christians' lives.

With this (mis)interpretation of supposing that the New Covenant age *began* at the Parousia one necessarily has to somehow manipulate or accommodate the language of consummation regarding the New Jerusalem in the Revelation in order to apply it to imperfect believers still on earth, in order to make it fit the truth that all post-Parousia believers on earth are under the New Covenant. The logic of this (mis)interpretation is:

"Since we post-Parousia believers are Christians, then we are under the New Covenant; and since the descending of the New Jerusalem of the Revelation represents the *coming* and *beginning* of the New Covenant age and the New Covenant church, then the significance of the Revelation's New Jerusalem *must* be already fulfilled in the church now on earth, and in Christians on earth, or else we would have to deny that we are under the New Covenant."

Upon this reasoning, the consummation theme and consummation language and features of the New Jerusalem which occur in the Revelation (discussed in Chapters 9 and 10) have to be accommodated and applied in some "spiritual way" or "covenantal way" to us on earth who are really and experientially not in a perfect condition, nor showing the consummate features described in the New Jerusalem, but who are still only in a deposit/firstfruits measure of New Covenant blessings like the pre-Parousia Christians were prior to the Parousia.

Such a mistaken interpretation has no grounds when one sees that the pre-Parousia Christians already were in the New Covenant age, inaugurated by the atonement and enthronement of the Lord Jesus; and were no longer under the law; but were experiencing a deposit/firstfruits/earnest measure of New Covenant blessings ever since Jesus' ascension to heaven and the Holy Spirit descended to the saints, (see Chapters 1 and 2). And the coming of the new heaven and earth and the coming of the New Jerusalem and the promised final salvation all have to do with the coming of the consummate manifestation, the fullness, the harvest, of the New Covenant blessedness — a consummation that involved all pre-Parousia believers being taken to a heavenly realm that flesh and blood cannot inherit.

Chapter 11

Firstfruits and Harvest —
Pre-Parousia and Post-Parousia Christians

In this final chapter I wish to briefly look, firstly, at the theme of "firstfruits" in the New Testament, particularly from the perspective of the pre-Parousia church being a firstfruits saved people anticipating a great harvest of post-Parousia saved people; and then, secondly, at how this theme illuminates the reputation of the Lord Jesus Christ as heir of the nations.

1. The firstfruits theme in the New Testament
The theme of the firstfruits may be considered from *two aspects*: One descriptive of blessings; the other descriptive of a people.

A. The firstfruits - descriptive of the measure of new covenant blessings experienced by Christians while living on earth:

[Rom. 8:23] Not only [that], but we also who have the *firstfruits* of the Spirit, even we ourselves groan within ourselves, eagerly waiting for the *adoption*, the *redemption of our body*.

This subject has been thoroughly examined in the previous chapters. The pre-Parousia Christians were experiencing the new covenant in a firstfruits measure; they had the firstfruits of the Spirit. They were experiencing the new creation life in Christ; righteousness, peace and joy in the Holy Spirit; an at-peace conscience before God due to sins forgiven; the joy of being children and sons of God; fellowship with the Father and the Son; communion of the Holy Spirit; the experience to some degree of victory over indwelling sin and the rising within them of the fruit of the Spirit. They were getting a taste of all of these new covenant blessings that would be fully theirs after entering heaven. While they were in their mortal bodies on earth, they could only know such blessings in a limited way – in a deposit-guarantee measure, and a firstfruits measure.

They groaned because of the legacy of fallenness still remaining in them; they longed for total deliverance from every trace of sin and fallenness, for the full, consummate experience of their redemption in Christ, for the full experience and revelation of their sonship, for obtaining glorious, heavenly, spiritual bodies capable of inhabiting heaven in the presence of God. They expected this hoped-for total deliverance and fulfillment in glory to come to them on the occasion of the Parousia of Christ, which we preterists believe took place circa AD 70.

And as I have shown from the scriptures, while we *post*-Parousia Christians are living on earth in our mortal bodies, we too have limited capacity, and also only experience the new covenant blessings in a deposit and firstfruits measure. We too groan because of our imperfection and sinfulness, although thankful that we are experiencing the Lord's sanctification. We post-Parousia Christians look forward, upon our physical death, to experiencing the same total deliverance from all trace of sin and evil and mortality and entrance into the same glory in heaven, that the pre-Parousia Christians were blessed with at the Parousia.

B. The firstfruits – a saved new covenant pre-Parousia people:

It is particularly regarding the theme of the firstfruits, not as a measure of the new covenant blessings they were experiencing, but as it applies to the pre-Parousia church as a people, that I wish to focus attention on in the rest of this chapter.

In the first days of the gospel, of those people who were the first in a particular province or country to become born-again believers in Christ Jesus, the term "firstfruits" was applied. In accordance with the full idea behind the Greek word (ἀπαρχή, *aparchee*) translated "firstfruits," this means that those people were *not only the first results of the gospel of Christ in that province, but were also an indication and guarantee of many further people of that province also coming to faith in Christ Jesus through that gospel.* For example,

> [1 Cor. 16:15] I urge you, brethren——you know the household of Stephanas, that it is *the firstfruits of Achaia*, and [that] they have devoted themselves to the ministry of the saints.

In his epistle, James refers to a larger group than just that of a particular province or country. He said:

> [Jas. 1:18] Of His own will He brought us forth by the word of truth, that we might be a kind of *firstfruits of His creatures*.

The "we" who are the firstfruits in James' mind may either mean the Jews who were believing into Christ Jesus, or that generation of believers generally (Jew and gentile) who were believing into Christ Jesus through that first great wave of apostolic gospel ministry throughout the Roman world. Regarding the term "firstfruits" used by James in this place, commentator Albert Barnes suggests the meaning in his commentary on the New Testament:

> "...under the gospel, those who were addressed by the apostles had the honor of being first called into his kingdom as a part of that glorious harvest which it was designed to gather in this world, and that the goodness of God was manifested in thus furnishing the firstfruits of a most glorious harvest..." (Albert Barnes, *Commentary on the New Testament*, from the *Online Bible* CD available from www.OnlineBible.net).

With the above ideas in mind, regarding the use of the term "firstfruits" as descriptive of an advance-group of people preparatory to the coming of many more, I believe that it is helpful to think of the whole short-lived pre-Parousia church as a firstfruits group. What was accomplished in them under the gospel of the new covenant, made them not only the first people in history in whom such blessings were accomplished, but they were also a token, a guarantee, of the far larger harvest of *post*-Parousia people who, after the Parousia circa AD 70, would be saved – people from all the nations of the world "for all generations of the age of the ages" to come (Eph. 3:21).

Consider the picture of victory in Rev. 14:1-5, which I believe was given primarily for the benefit of the persecuted pre-Parousia church as a preview of the soon to come victory for the pre-Parousia saints at the Parousia of Christ – which is, as many preterist commentary writers have repeatedly shown, the theme of the whole book of Revelation, and indeed the theme of all the other New Testament end-time predictions as well.

> [Rev. 14:1-5] Then I looked, and behold, a Lamb standing on Mount Zion, and with Him one hundred and forty-four thousand, having His Father's name written on their foreheads. 2 And I heard a voice from heaven, like the voice of many waters, and like the voice of loud thunder. And I heard the sound of harpists playing their harps. *3 They sang as it were a new song before the throne*, before the four living creatures, and the elders; and no one could learn that song except the hundred and forty-four thousand *who were redeemed from the earth*. 4 These are the ones who were not defiled with women, for they are virgins. These are the ones who follow the Lamb wherever He goes. *These were redeemed from among men, being firstfruits to God and to the Lamb.* 5 And in their mouth was found no deceit, *for they are without fault before the throne of God.*

This group of 144,000 redeemed saints with Christ the Lamb on Mt Zion in Rev. 14:1-5, was mentioned earlier in the Revelation from an earthly point of view (in Rev. 7:1-8). I agree with David Chilton's analysis in his commentary on the Revelation, *Days of Vengeance*, that this remnant group of Israel, of whom the apostle John "heard" that they were sealed for God, (Rev. 7:1-8), is in actual fact representing the church of the true Israel, and is inclusive of the great multitude from all nations of the world that he then "saw" in a state of glory before the Lamb at the throne of God (Rev. 7:9-17) – a preview of the glorified saints at Christ's Parousia. Commenting on the 144,000 in Rev. 7:1-8, Chilton says,

> Seen from one perspective, the Church is the new, the *true,* Israel of God: the sons of Jacob gathered into all their tribes, full and

complete. From another, equally true perspective, the Church is the whole world: a great multitude redeemed from every nation and all tribes and peoples and tongues. In other words, the 144,000 are the Remnant of Israel; yet the fulfillment of the promises to Israel takes place through the salvation of the world, by bringing the Gentiles in to share the blessings of Abraham (Gal. 3:8). The number of the Remnant is filled by the multitudes of the saved from all nations. [David Chilton, *Days of Vengeance*, p. 214] (Emphasis in the original)

Chilton later comments on this saved group or 144,000 in Rev. 14:1-5 (quoted above) –

That the 144,000 are regarded as members of the Church, and not ultimately as a separate category of ethnic Israelites, is underscored by John's combination of previous imagery. We were told before that the 144,000 are sealed on their foreheads (7:3), while it is all Christ's overcomers who have His name and the name of His Father written on their foreheads (3:12) [*see also 22:4 - IH*]. The 144,000, therefore, belong to the Church, the army of overcomers. Yet they are also a special group: the Remnant-Church of the first generation. (p. 355) ...A precise statement of those who comprise this group, however, is given in the next phrase: These have been purchased from among men as first fruits to God and to the Lamb. The expression first fruits refers essentially to a sacrifice, the offering up of the first harvest of the land to the Lord, claimed by Him as His exclusive property (Ex. 22:29; 23:16, 19; Lev. 23:9-21; Deut. 18:4-5; Neh. 10:35-37; Prov. 3:9-10); these Christians have offered themselves up to God's service for Christ's sake. More than this, though, the New Testament uses firstfruits to describe the Church of the Last Days, the "first-generation" Church (Rom. 16:5; 1 Cor. 16:15), especially the faithful Remnant from the twelve tribes of Israel (Jas. 1:1, 18): "The confessors and martyrs of the apostolic Church, who overcame by reason of their testimony and the blood of the Lamb, are thus declared to be *a first fruits,* a choice selection out of the innumerable company of saints. The purpose of this Apocalypse was to give special encouragement to these virgin spirits." [David Chilton, *Days of Vengeance*, p. 357] (Emphasis in the original)

So, from a preterist point of view, I believe it fair to say that the holy group of 144,000 in Rev. 14:1-5 represents "the Israel of God" (Gal 6:16) composed of pre-Parousia Christians (Jews and gentiles), foreseen by the apostle in a place of victory with Christ in heaven. *They were viewed as firstfruits.* The Lord's design in the Revelation is to encourage the first, pre-Parousia church that, in spite of the threat of awful persecution, their

Lord was in control and would bring them full salvation and victory at his Parousia.

Notice in John's preview of the soon-to-come victory of redeemed pre-Parousia saints in glory in Rev. 14:1-5, that the saints are "redeemed from the earth" and "redeemed from among men." This is consistent with the preterist taken-to-heaven view of pre-Parousia saints at the Parousia. At the Parousia they received the completeness of their redemption, as they were literally taken from the fallenness of earth, and from men still living in imperfection in the world, to be with Christ in glory. In view of their experiencing the completeness of their redemption, they are seen by John as singing a new song, which only the fully and consummative redeemed can sing.

The pre-Parousia church, made up of 40 years worth of saved people mainly from within the then Roman world, was taken to heaven at the Parousia c. AD 70 and there glorified together with Christ to reign with him over the earth. They were the privileged ones of the Messianic generation, who as a group of living and deceased saints, were all at once raised to heavenly glory at the Parousia, being given new heavenly, spiritual bodies that could inhabit God's presence in heaven.

The pre-Parousia people were the firstfruits; and the post-Parousia people were the harvest

While commentator Albert Barnes, as a futurist, has a different view of the timing and the actual people viewed by John in Rev. 14:1-5, yet his understanding of the meaning of their being called a *firstfruits* group is helpful to my preterist taken-to-heaven interpretation:

> *Being the firstfruits unto God....* The meaning here would seem to be, that the hundred and forty-four thousand were not to be regarded as the whole of the number that was saved, but that they were representatives of the redeemed. They had the same characteristics which all the redeemed must have; they were a pledge that all the redeemed would be there. (Barnes, *ibid.*, comments on Rev. 14:1-5)

As the first ones to be fully, experientially redeemed (as e.g. Rom 8:23) at the Parousia of Christ, the pre-Parousia believers were the privileged firstfruits of the great crop of believers to come after the Parousia. *As the firstfruits in glory, the pre-Parousia church (from 40 years worth of gospel preaching) pointed to and guaranteed the future, extended, post-Parousia harvest of thousands of years' worth of people from all over the earth* who would be saved and, after their individual lifetimes on earth, would be individually taken to the same glory in heaven as what the pre-Parousia firstfruit people entered at the Parousia. In that realm of glory, called in Jesus' parable the Lord's "barn" and "the kingdom of their Father" (see Matt 13:30, 43), both the pre-Parousia "firstfruits" of the crop of the saved, and the post-Parousia rest of the crop of the saved, would share together with the glorified Christ in the presence of the Father.

Christ Jesus, as the first to be resurrected and glorified in heaven, was/is the firstfruits of all the redeemed of all history (pre-Parousia and post-Parousia saints) (1 Cor. 15:23). The pre-Parousia church, as the first group in Christ to be resurrected and glorified at Christ's Parousia, was the firstfruits of the coming harvest of post-Parousia Christians who also would be resurrected and glorified in their time.

The principle or pattern of spiritual life that was demonstrated in the firstfruits pre-Parousia church - namely, that of having a firstfruits measure of new covenant blessings while in this life on earth in mortal bodies, followed by the harvest measure of blessings when taken to heaven - is the same principle or pattern that operates in the harvest-field of post-Parousia Christians down through the centuries.

This fact of the firstfruits people having been taken to the Lord in glory at the Parousia about AD 70, is of great encouragement to us post-Parousia Christians. For we have the assurance that the promised consummate measure of grace and power of the Lord that we are expecting in our lives when we die, has already been demonstrated and proven to be completely reliable and efficacious in the case of the firstfruits pre-Parousia saints. He gathered that firstfruits group, consisting of the apostles and all the pre-Parousia church, to himself in glory at the Parousia; and we need have no doubt that he is willing and completely able to gather all of us post-Parousia believers to himself in glory at our set times, and give us new immortal bodies in which to dwell in heaven.

This idea of the Lord's proven ability in the case of the firstfruits, leads into my next related topic of the Lord's reputation.

2. The Lord's reputation as heir of the nations – honored by the pre-Parousia firstfruits theme

A. The nations are destined as the Lord's inheritance.

The Lord's desire is to have the nations of this world as his inheritance, conformed to his image, glorified together with him.

In Psalm 2 we have the wonderful promise of God to the Messiah of his inheriting the nations:

> [Psa. 2:7-9] 7 "I will declare the decree: The LORD has said to Me, 'You are My Son, Today I have begotten You. 8 Ask of Me, and I will give You the nations for Your inheritance, And the ends of the earth for Your possession. 9 You shall break them with a rod of iron; You shall dash them to pieces like a potter's vessel.'"

And a point to note here in v. 9: from what I can find, everywhere that the idea of a nation or nations being called an inheritance of the Lord, it is in a good and positive connotation. So although, verse 9 of Psa 2 speaks about breaking the stubborn nations, it is a breaking with the purpose of subduing them into humility and faith so that they will really be his people, his inheritance that he will rejoice over, and be glorified in throughout all ages.

And in Psalm 22, which amazingly pictures our Lord Jesus' death on the cross for sinners, the wonderful outcome of the Lord's rule is presented: the nations will become his people.

> [Psa. 22:27-28] 27 All the ends of the world shall remember and turn to the LORD, and all the families of the nations shall worship before You. 28 For the kingdom is the LORD'S, And He rules over the nations.

This is similar to the picture seen in Ezekiel 47 where the little trickle of water becomes a mighty river baptizing all the nations.

And in Isaiah chapter 49, we have the Messiah, the Servant of the LORD, speaking of God's choice to give him, not only Israel, but also the nations as his reward and inheritance:

> [Isa. 49:5-6] 5 "And now the LORD says, Who formed Me from the womb to be His Servant, To bring Jacob back to Him, So that Israel is gathered to Him (For I shall be glorious in the eyes of the LORD, And My God shall be My strength), 6 Indeed He says, 'It is too small a thing that You should be My Servant To raise up the tribes of Jacob, And to restore the preserved ones of Israel; I will also give You as a light to the Gentiles, That You should be My salvation to the ends of the earth.'"

And in view of the mission of the Messiah's uniting sinners to God, the voice of God speaks in Isaiah 45 with a prophetic command that will be fulfilled:

> [Isa. 45:22] "Look to Me, and be saved, All you ends of the earth! For I [am] God, and [there is] no other.

It is against this background of God's giving the nations to the Messiah as his inheritance, that we are to understand the significance of the Lord Jesus' declaration:

> [Matt. 28:18] And Jesus came and spoke to them, saying, "All authority has been given to Me in heaven and on earth.

And we have the great words speaking of Christ's rule as prophesied in Psalm 110 and repeatedly shown in the New Testament as being fulfilled in Christ Jesus after his ascension to heaven to the Father:

> [Psa 110:1-2] The LORD said to my Lord, "Sit at My right hand, till I make Your enemies Your footstool." 2 The LORD shall send the rod of Your strength out of Zion. Rule in the midst of Your enemies!

B. Calling out a people for his name from the nations commences

In the book of the Acts, Luke commences by saying that in his former account, i.e. in his gospel account, he had recorded all that Jesus *"began* both to be doing and teaching" (Acts 1:1). The clear implication is that in the Acts, Luke recorded what Jesus *continued* to be doing/accomplishing and teaching, by the agency of the Holy Spirit sent to his followers in his name. As *Robertson's Word Pictures* (incl. on the *Online Bible* CD) explains:

> Jesus "began" "both to do and to teach" (Gr. ποιεῖν τε καὶ διδάσκειν). Note present infinitives, linear action, still going on, and the use of "te kai" binds together the life and teachings of Jesus, as if to say that Jesus is still carrying on from heaven the work and teaching of the disciples which he started while on earth before his ascension. The record which Luke now records is really the Acts of Jesus as much as the Acts of the Apostles. Dr. A. T. Pierson called it "The Acts of the Holy Spirit, " and that is true also. The Acts, according to Luke, is a continuation of the doings and teachings of Jesus.

In the account of the Acts, we see the Lord Jesus ruling in his authority as Mediator of the new covenant and gradually gaining a people for himself, as an inheritance, from different countries of the world.

The rule of Jesus Christ was felt among the Israelite nation after Pentecost, as thousands of Israelites believed into Jesus as the Christ and as Lord. Later, Jesus showed he had remembered the Samaritans from his time on earth; and he directed Philip to preach the gospel in Samaria, and Jesus turned many to believe in him as the Christ, and they were saved through faith in him. Later, Jesus' rule was manifested in the case of the God-fearing gentiles (Cornelius and his household) who were sympathetic to the Jewish religion. The Lord showed Peter that he was out to save gentiles as well as Jews. The Jewish-Christian leaders in the church in Jerusalem were amazed that God should be granting gentiles the grace of repentance. The Lord Jesus, surprisingly to all, brought the evil Pharisee Saul to faith in him; and he directed Saul, now called Paul, to take his gospel to various other nations of the Roman world. We see the Lord Jesus claiming his inheritance out of many nations, as many came to faith in Christ through Paul's preaching. As James said, (Acts 15:14), the Lord was calling out "a people for his name." Just as in the Old Testament, the nation of Israel was called the Lord's inheritance, now in that first messianic generation we see the Lord calling out a people, an inheritance, for himself, from many nations.

C. The full revelation of the glory of his people (his inheritance) is not during this life on earth

The decades passed from the time of Pentecost when the new covenant commenced its operation, and the Lord had been saving people from many nations. His saved people from many nations were recognized as the Lord's people and his inheritance by the graces of repentance and faith, regeneration and sanctification that were manifested in their lives (e.g. 1 Thess 1:2-5).

However, so far, his people had only tasted the firstfruits of the Lord's new covenant blessings, and they were still experientially very imperfect in holiness and knowledge of God. Although in a true sense, as just mentioned, these saved people were manifested as belonging to the Lord Jesus as his inheritance during their lives on this earth, it could be rightly said that the *full* proof had not yet been given that they were his. The contents of the privilege of being his inheritance had not yet been *fully* revealed and demonstrated (the theme in Rom. 8:17ff). That full proof would require actual experiential entrance into those promised blessings. *Not until he had brought them completely home into the glory of heaven and full conformation to his image, would the truth that they were his inheritance be fully and indisputably demonstrated.* Paul's groanings in Romans 8 are to the effect "Lord, we are your inheritance, but your possession of us, your restoring us, has not yet been fully revealed while we remain as we are - with the legacy of the fall still so evident in us, limiting and hindering our holiness and experiential union with You; we feel it acutely that *we are not yet conformed to God's appointed destiny for us as your people*."

It may sound like a play on words, but the following axiom needs to be noted: *It is only when the saints receive in consummate measure their inheritance from God, that they can be fully manifested as the inheritance of God.* And this cannot occur while remaining in an imperfect condition on this earth.

Similarly, the fact that Jesus was appointed as the heir of the nations, as their Lord and Savior in every way, with total power to save and provide for them, could not be *fully* revealed and demonstrated until he proved it by bringing them home to be with him in glory.

So there awaited a great dual interdependent revelation:

- *the full revelation of the believers of many nations as the Lord's inheritance, and*
- *the full revelation of Jesus' power to consummately save, as the heir and Lord and Possessor of his people.*

But while all his saved people (deceased and living) from out of the nations continued in a not-yet-glorified condition, not yet in resurrection, glorified bodies, then this dual revelation was still awaited.

D. The method and time-factor involved in the dual consummate revelation of the Lord's inheritance from among the nations, and the Lord's power to fully save

The promises were that he would inherit the nations, but until he brought them home into perfect glory, totally delivered from every trace of sin, his inheritance was not ready to dwell with him in heaven, and his victory on their behalf was not yet fully manifested. How long was his inheritance going to have to wait?

The way in which the Lord chose to display his power to completely save his inheritance – his redeemed from all the nations of the world – was *NOT* the way of waiting until the literal end of time and literal end of the world and then to manifest his full salvation all at once upon all saints who have ever lived from creation to the end of the world. This is the futurist view of eschatology and the Parousia. Under the modern futurist scheme, even now nearly 2000 years since Pentecost, it has to be acknowledged that not yet has there appeared even one glorified saint who has received fully his/her eternal inheritance and who subsequently has become fully manifested as the Lord's inheritance; nor has the Lord been *fully* revealed as actual heir and Lord, for he has brought no one to glory yet.

Rather, according to the preterist interpretation of the time-expectancy statements in the NT, the Lord's way of bringing his inheritance to full salvation and glorification, was to firstly completely save a firstfruits portion of his inheritance in an operation involving the saints from creation to the time of the Lord's Parousia about AD 70, all at once in one great multitude. Then, after the Parousia, the Lord would individually take each believer home to glory when they physically died, and the Lord would continue this saving work among the nations over all post-Parousia future years, drawing more and more people to himself as new members of his inheritance With this interpretation, there has been already a proven demonstration about AD 70 of the Lord's consummating power upon a firstfruits "sample" of redeemed people. And all of us post-Parousia people can know that we do not have long to wait until we enter the same guaranteed glory. We only have to wait the term of our natural life on earth, and then we'll be fully revealed as his inheritance in glory in heaven, just like the pre-Parousia saints were on the occasion of the Parousia!.

E. A promised first century Parousia — the Lord's reputation at stake

It is not hard to imagine that many Christians needed much encouragement during those early days of Christianity, surrounded as it was by apostate Judaism and pagan culture throughout the Roman Empire. Faith in this Savior Jesus Christ did not necessarily save one from trials of life, nor from persecution and suffering from pagans, nor from illness and death, nor from poverty (– for indeed, Christians who truly followed Jesus and refused to partake in the idolatry of emperor worship faced rejection and refusal of employment). And then in the midst of this was the consciousness of an inner warfare of the flesh and the Spirit within them; dying to self didn't come easily; victory over sin, didn't occur over night; bad habits sometimes died slowly.

The early Christians were exhorted to persevere in their faith and hope; for the Parousia of Christ was not far away, they were told. The coming of the Lord, would occur before that messianic generation passed away, so Jesus promised. The readers of the New Testament epistles were told that some of their number would still be alive when Christ came. They were promised complete deliverance and glory on the occasion of the soon-expected Parousia of Christ.

Until the Parousia, the Lord had not perfected in glory any of his people that he had saved out of the nations; he had not brought any of his people completely home so as to fully reverse the tragedy of the fall of man in Adam. But he did promise his first disciples that he would do so before that present generation passed away. *The Lord Jesus' reputation was at stake. Would he complete his promise to fully save his people to the uttermost?*

One is reminded of the exodus of the Israelites out of Egypt. The Lord told Moses that His desire and plan was to bring his people out of bondage in Egypt, in order to bring them into the promised land of milk and honey in Canaan, (e.g. Ex 3:8, 17). However, after the successful exodus out of Egypt, all did not go smoothly. When at times it looked as if the plan to bring the redeemed Israelites into the Promised Land might fail (due to the Israelites' sins), Moses was greatly concerned about the Lord's name or reputation. He prayed that the Lord, for the Lord's name's sake, would continue with his people and bring them into the promised land; otherwise all would see a God who could only half-finish his plan; a God who could bring his people out of bondage in Egypt, but lacked the power to bring them into their promised home in Canaan. (see e.g. Ex 32:11-14; Num 14:11-16). Even so, the Lord Jesus had brought his people out of bondage to sin and estrangement from their loving Father, and they were now experiencing new life in a firstfruits measure in fellowship with him; and the question now was, could he bring them completely into the promised land of heavenly glory, and totally put behind them all traces of Egypt (so to speak) from their lives?

The Lord Jesus, the Mediator of the new covenant, was to demonstrate on the occasion of his Parousia, that his name was greater than every name that could be named, and that his new covenant with his people would never fail:

- *He would vindicate his name, he would vindicate his new covenant, and he would vindicate his people's faith in him.*

> • *He would show his great saving power by saving, firstly, the pre-Parousia saints as a firstfruits people from many nations. This event is proof and guarantee of his power to save many thousands more from all over the world in the future post-Parousia days, years, centuries and millennia.*

At the Parousia, a magnificent spectacle occurred - much to the amazement of the great host of observing angels. Eph 3:10-11 says that angelic authorities were beholding God's manifold wisdom being demonstrated as he worked out his eternal purpose in the church. Angels rejoiced in heavenly praise (Lk. 2:8-14) as they witnessed God's plan commencing in the incarnation of their Lord, the Son of God, in Bethlehem. And now, at Christ's Parousia, this heavenly host would observe God's plan in Christ being demonstrated in its consummate phase upon his pre-Parousia people – revealing a fully restored and glorified people of God, for the first time in all of earth's history.

At the Parousia, the Lord Jesus gathered together all his redeemed pre-Parousia children (deceased and living) from amongst the Jews, the Samaritans, the gentiles from throughout the Roman world and anywhere else, and brought them all home to heavenly glory all at the one time as one great multitude. As their Perfecter (Heb 12:2), he now perfected them. He promised that he would and now he proved that he could complete their salvation.

He proved at the Parousia, by his work in fully saving his pre-Parousia people into heaven itself, that the new covenant in his blood is victorious, is fully reliable, and is the one and only fully efficacious covenant that truly and completely restores fallen man to God's designed destiny.

The world didn't have to wait until some future end of time or end of the world, before the full saving power of Christ to save his inheritance could be proved. He proved his ability at the Parousia, by displaying it in the case of a firstfruits of his inheritance. *What he displayed there in them, was the example and pledge that he could and would do it for everyone else to come in the future; and that the power of his new covenant would completely avail for everyone else who believed in him.*

Until the Parousia, the completive or consummative power of Christ had never been demonstrated. Believers had lived in the promise of it. At the Parousia the Christ, Jesus, was truly vindicated as the complete Savior and Lord of his people, through his bringing his pre-Parousia people completely to glory.

Jesus' reputation was also at stake in regard to his prophecies of judgment to come upon the apostate Jewish people, (e.g. Matt 23:32-36; Lk. 11:50-51; 19:41-44; 21:20-24; 1 Thess 2:14-16). Up until the Parousia that promised judgment had not arrived. The anti-Jesus Jewish hierarchy could no doubt feel they had grounds to mock the warnings of Jesus, as they saw for decades no results from Jesus' promises of judgment upon them. But his enemies' evil was punished and Jesus' righteousness was vindicated at the Parousia, when at his coming, the Roman armies was used by the Lord as his rod to punish them. The judgment that fell on an apostate Jerusalem, at the Parousia of Christ, c. AD 70, was "the sign [that appeared] of the Son of man [reigning] in heaven" Matt 25:30.

But it was not outward human enemies that were dealt with by Christ's victory in the case of the pre-Parousia saints. Every evil demonstrated in Christ's outward enemies, actually had lodging in "the flesh" of every Christian. To get rid of an outward enemy Pharisee was one thing, but a more profound victory was for Christ to get rid of every trace of Pharisee spirit in his people's souls. The greatest enemies lie within every man's own heart. And in the case of the pre-Parousia saints, Christ Jesus delivered them at his Parousia from all inward as well as all outward enemies. He "brought many sons into glory" where they were made completely "holy and blameless before him in love" (Eph 1:4).

F. The significance of the Parousia and the victory displayed in his firstfruits pre-Parousia people

The significance of the overthrow of Jerusalem and the temple at the Parousia of Christ is momentous. It signaled and broadcast to the world, that the Mosaic old covenant economy, (and indeed, any method of so-called salvation based on human works and merit) had no legitimate with the Lord as a means of salvation. Up till this time, although the new covenant was prevailing throughout the Roman empire, no official action by God upon the relics of the Mosaic economy had taken place – the temple stood as always, the priesthood still functioned, the animal sacrifices still were being offered; the average Jew assumed that the God of their fathers was still their God, and they looked with disdain upon the heretical sect of Jesus the Nazarene. To all outward appearance it could be thought that the LORD, known as the God of Israel, was still confined to exclusive dealings with Israel, and that for a gentile to worship Israel's God, he would have to join the Jewish/Judaic system.

But the new covenant economy that had commenced like a small piece of leaven in Jerusalem, had been spreading its effects gradually throughout the world, despite being much opposed by the Jews (who failed to see that Jesus had fulfilled the old covenant requirements), and opposed later by the Romans. At the Parousia the new covenant in Christ Jesus was exalted for all to perceive that it was fully in force as God's appointed and only way of salvation for men on earth of every nation, and that no holy mountain nor Jerusalem of the Jews was at all necessary for the true worship that the Father desired.

Although Jesus had been reigning as Mediator of the new covenant ever since his ascension, it was at his Parousia that the worldwide implications of his reign were placarded to the world. At the Parousia it was clearly demonstrated that His salvation was not confined within the limits of a shadowy, typical, Mosaic or Judaic economy, but extended in new covenant power to all the nations of the earth. I believe this is the significance lying within the songs of praise in the Revelation that anticipate the occasion of the Parousia: for example,

> [Rev. 10:7; 11:15-18] but in the days of the voice of the seventh angel, whenever he is about to sound *his* trumpet, the mystery of God would be finished, as He declared to His servants the prophets.... 15 Then the seventh angel sounded *his* trumpet, and there were great voices in heaven, saying, "The kingdom of this world have become *the kingdom* of our Lord and of His Christ, and He shall reign forever and ever!" 16 And the twenty-four elders, those before the throne of God who sit on their thrones, fell on their faces and worshipped God, 17 saying: "We give You thanks, O Lord God Almighty, The One who is and who was, because You have taken Your great power and have begun to reign. 18 The nations were angry, and Your wrath has come, and the time of the dead, that they should be judged, and that You should reward Your servants the prophets and the saints, and to those that fear Your name, to the small and to the great, and to destroy those who destroy the earth." (English *Majority Text* Version)

The Lord is here designated in v. 17 as "The One who is and who was," (according to the *Majority Greek* text and the *Nestle Greek Text*). The extra epithet, "and who is to come," that is normally used (Rev. 1:4,8; 4:8; 16:5) is not used here because in this vision the Coming One was viewed as having come.

The "mystery of God" (10:7), i.e. the mystery of the gospel, that had been made known in the world, especially by the apostle Paul – viz., the fact that Jews and gentiles were united as one man in Christ, as one inheritance belonging to Christ, under the one salvation by the Lord Jesus and together destined for glory – was finished/completed/fulfilled (Gr. τελέω, *teleo*, Rev. 10:7) at the Parousia of Christ — in the case of the first Christians, that firstfruits group, to whom the Revelation was specifically written. At the Parousia a marvelous completion occurred as all pre-Parousia believers composed of Jew and gentile were brought together into their glorious destiny in the consummate manifestation of the kingdom of God. Here it was ultimately shown that there is no difference between Jew and gentile as far as salvation in Christ is concerned.

Although the Lord had been reigning as Lord of the new covenant since Pentecost, it was at the Parousia that his reign was gloriously magnified. In this anticipatory vision of the time of Jesus' defeat of his enemies, and of his fully delivering his pre-Parousia people and bringing them to heavenly glory, the heavenly elders in the passage above praise him as if he had *begun* to reign (v.17). This is not meaning that they felt he had not been reigning at all before his Parousia, but it is a relative term, implying that, in his bringing things to a consummative phase and fully revealing his power at his Parousia against all his enemies and upon his firstfruits pre-Parousia people, the FULL, *victorious nature* of his redemptive, new covenant reign was being revealed for the first time in history.

It was indisputably demonstrated at the Lord's Parousia – though virtually declared by his death and resurrection and ascension (e.g. Col. 2:15; Eph 1:20-21) – that the kingdom of this world, which the devil had boasted to be in charge of (Matt 4:8-10), since he (the devil) had held blind and spiritually dead sinners in his grasp, was in fact under the Lord Jesus' control. The nations were destined to be Jesus' inheritance, as the Father had gifted them to him, and no devil could stop him!

At the Parousia thousands of saved people from many nations were perfected, consummately saved into the promised heavenly glory, as a firstfruits, as a pledge, of the many more millions to be similarly brought to glory afterwards. The mediator of the new covenant was truly reigning over the nations, which are his inheritance! So at the Parousia of Christ we have these magnificent aspects:

- Jesus was vindicated against his enemies among the Jews (within the province of seventh trumpet lies the seven bowls that signal the end of Babylon [apostate Jerusalem]),
- it was confirmed that the limited Jewish, Mosaic economy had no more place in God's economy.
- the new covenant was honored and confirmed as God's chosen way to save believers out of every nation in the world, and that the Lord Jesus was to inherit all nations of the world.
- all pre-Parousia believers (Jew and gentile, living and deceased) were brought into their glorious destiny in the consummate manifestation of the kingdom of God in God's presence.
- the Lord Jesus was proved to be the Perfecter of his people; was vindicated as truly reigning with the saving power and love to bring his saved people home to consummate glory in heaven
- the consummate phase of the kingdom of God was established in heaven – firstly, for the *pre*-Parousia church as the Lord gathered them to himself at the Parousia; and secondly, in preparation for all *post*-Parousia Christians of all future centuries to enter into (at the end of their lives on earth), and there join the glorified family of God.

Conclusion

In view of the above, we post-Parousia Christians are to have the utmost confidence in our Lord Jesus Christ. He is ruling in us as his people; he is ruling over the nations today, calling out a people for his name – using us as his people to preach, speak, and live out his gospel in the world, to pray and intercede for his lost ones to be gathered in. And when the term of our natural lives, and the term of our service in this life, is completed, we each one individually will be raised into our glorious consummate inheritance with Christ in heaven. Every day and every night there are many Christians who are graduating out of their earthly phase, the deposit-firstfruits phase, of Christian life into the glory phase of the New Jerusalem depicted in Rev. 21 and 22 where they join the already glorified, perfectly happy, family of saints in heaven in the light and glory of the Lord's immediate presence. There, all our dreams will be more than fulfilled. What grace is ours in Christ Jesus! But until then, "Lord, fill us by your Holy Spirit and your divine nature, so that we may be the best servants, the best channels of blessing, that we can be to a needy world."

Appendix

"The Perfect" in 1 Cor. 13:10 and its (non-) relation to the Canon

"And when that which is perfect may come, then that which is in part shall become useless." [1 Cor. 13:10, Young's Literal Translation]

I wish to examine the clause contained in 1 Corinthians 13:10 - "when that which is perfect is come" (KJV). I believe that an accurate exegesis of 1 Cor. 13 confirms the taken-to-heaven view already detailed in the previous chapters of this book: that is to say, "that which is perfect" describes a state and condition which can only be had in heaven, out of this earthly sphere of mortality and imperfection, and this was what the first Christians were expecting to enter at the Parousia of Christ. I hope to show that "the perfect" came for the pre-Parousia Christians, collectively, en masse, at the Parousia, while for post-Parousia Christians "the perfect" comes individually upon their physical death.

In Chapter 13 of 1 Corinthians, Paul shows the great significance of true Godlike, God-inspired love. Consider the three divisions in 1 Corinthians 13.

- In verses 1-3 he shows that only with love as the driving force can any gift or service have value. Gifts and services are to be employed as the servants or implements of love. Such gifts, knowledge and services that men may be tempted to boast of, are not ends in themselves; they bring no real good without the power of love being in them. Love, seeking the highest well-being of the ones loved, is the central issue.
- In verses 4-7, Paul describes some of the beautiful qualities of true love, many of which the Corinthian believers were failing in.
- In verses 8-13, Paul focuses on the issue of love's operation with respect to the partial and the perfect states of the Christians' existence. Love is to be valued above all other elements in the Christian life, as it alone is everlasting, while all other elements are partial and therefore temporary.

Focus on 1 Cor. 13:8-13

It is this third division (1 Cor. 13:8-13) that I wish to focus on, wherein verse 10 contains the term "the perfect." Here it is (and I have included 14:1 as well):

[1 Cor. 13:8 - 14:1] (Young's Literal Translation) –
13:8 The love doth never fail; and whether there be prophecies,

they shall become useless; whether tongues, they shall cease; whether knowledge, it shall become useless;
13:9 for in part we know, and in part we prophecy;
13:10 and when that which is perfect may come, then that which is in part shall become useless.
13:11 When I was a babe, as a babe I was speaking, as a babe I was thinking, as a babe I was reasoning, and when I have become a man, I have made useless the things of the babe;
13:12 for we see now through a mirror obscurely, and then face to face; now I know in part, and then I shall fully know, as also I was known;
13:13 and now there doth remain faith, hope, love-these three; and the greatest of these is love.
14:1 Pursue the love, and seek earnestly the spiritual things, and rather that ye may prophecy

In this passage Paul makes a number of statements to emphasize the preeminence of love. Remember that chapter 13 has the purpose of emphasizing the preeminence of God's kind of love over all other seemingly important elements that men may be tempted to boast about and to have a sense of achievement about.

Having shown in verses 1-3 the preeminence of love over all other elements - in that all other elements only have their relevance as existing for the service of love - Paul then shows in verses 8-13 the preeminence of love by declaring the fact that all gifts and knowledge and ministries are of temporary relevance compared to the everlasting relevance of love. Elements such as the knowledge, miracles, etc., that were being experienced by the Christians only belong to and are only suited to "the partial" phase of a Christian's life, while, contrastingly, love is of supreme significance operating through the partial and on into the perfect phase.

The meaning of partial and perfect will become clearer as we study this passage. It must be kept in mind that Paul has not set out here to discourse on the nature of the partial and the perfect as such, but has introduced these topics in the context of his aim to highlight the significance and prime importance of love over all other things that Christians may boast about. To get them to focus on true love, God's kind of love, was the apostle Paul's aim in addressing these new Christians in Corinth.

Exposition of 1 Cor. 13:8-13 regarding "the partial" and "the perfect"

1. The enduring nature of love versus the temporary nature of other elements

"Love never fails, never falls powerless; never is without effect" (1 Cor. 13:8a).

All these meanings are accurate renderings of the Greek verb "ekpiptei" [ἐκπίπτει, in *Greek Received Text*] which qualifies love. I believe that Paul is using a figure of speech here, (called "Tapeinosis" in Greek, or "Demeaning" in English) ,where a negative or diminished sense is applied to a thing in order to actually emphasize the positive or greatness of that same thing. In saying, "Love never fails," Paul is actually emphasizing the fact that love will always continue, will always have its central place, will always be of prime importance in any work, will for ever be effective and fruitful.

As we progress through this passage, we see that Paul's message is that love always will continue as the factor of crucial importance, both through the partial phase of Christian life that Paul and his fellow Christians were experiencing in his days when he wrote, and into the perfect phase which those Christians were looking forward to.

"...whether there be prophecies, they shall become useless; whether tongues, they shall cease; whether knowledge, it shall become useless," (1 Cor. 13:8b, *YLT*).

In contrast to love which never fails and which will always endure and be operative, other elements in the Christian life are not so enduring. The time will come, says Paul (1 Cor. 13:8), when:

- "prophecies...shall become useless, be rendered inoperative, be brought to an end," [Gr. καταργέω, katargeo]; - unlike love.
- "tongues...shall cease" [Gr. παύω, pauo]; - unlike love.
- "knowledge...shall become useless, be rendered inoperative, be brought to an end" [Gr. καταργέω, katargeo]; - unlike love.

So, implies Paul in verse 8, don't go boasting about things that are mere temporary things, but rather focus on partaking of God's unfailing, everlasting love.

2. The Perfect compared with the Partial

Why will these other elements such as prophecy, tongues and knowledge (to mention just a few of the more problematical areas in this Corinthian church) be brought to an end, and be rendered inoperative and useless, as compared with love which will always last and be relevant? Why will they not last as long as love lasts? The reason Paul gives is:

"For *in part* we know, and *in part* we prophesy; 10 and *when that which is perfect may come*, then that which is *in part* shall become useless/be brought to an end [Gr. καταργέω, katargeo]," (1 Cor. 13:9-10, *YLT*).

"For our knowledge is imperfect, and so is our prophesying; 10 but when the perfect state of things is come, all that is imperfect will be brought to an end." (1 Cor. 13:9-10, *Weymouth*)

To understand Paul's explanation in vv. 9-10, let us firstly examine some of his terms.

The Greek behind the words "in part" in verse 9 is *"ek merous"* (ἐκ μέρους). The noun *"merous"* has the basic idea of a part, portion, or division of a whole (*Analytical Greek Lexicon*, Bagster, 1977). The Greek phrase *"ek merous"* is used adverbially to mean: in part, partially, imperfectly – as opposed to that which is whole and complete. "We know and prophesy in part, partially, imperfectly, in a limited way."

In verse 10, we again have *"ek merous,"* but this time in an adjectival sense, with the definite article "the" in front of it, but with no qualifying noun following it; the noun is understood or implied (a common occurrence in the Greek). To make sense in English a noun or noun phrase must be added. The phrase in Greek, *to ek merous* (τὸ ἐκ μέρους), can be translated as "the partial state of things," or "that which is in part."

The Greek translated as "that which is perfect" (v.10) is *"to telion,"* where *"to"* means "the," and *"telion"* is an adjective with the general meaning of "brought to completion, fully accomplished, fully developed, fully realized," (Bagster's *Analytical Greek Lexicon*), as opposed to what is partial and limited. There is no qualifying noun in the Greek, following the adjective *telion*, - the noun is understood or implied. We may input a noun to make better sense in English, such as "the perfect state."

Paul's implied exhortation in verse 8 is: Don't boast in the various gifts, etc, you may have, for they are all temporary and will pass away; rather value more that permanent quality of the undying, unfailing love. "But Paul," an inquirer is bound to ask, "Why do you say that such things that we pride ourselves on and which are so important to us will finish and pass away?" An expanded version of Paul's answer is (1 Cor. 13:9-10):

> "9 For we know in part, partially, imperfectly, in a limited way, and we prophesy partially, imperfectly and in a limited way. And partial, imperfect and limited things cannot have undying, everlasting relevance; they serve, by their very nature, a temporary purpose. 10 Indeed, when the consummate, fully realized, perfect state of things may come, then the partial, imperfect and limited state of things will have served its purpose and will become irrelevant, useless, and so will cease and be done away with."

In verses 9-10, a partial and limited state of things, (comprising partial and limited elements such as the knowledge, prophecies, and tongues which the Corinthians boasted of), is contrasted with the expected complete, consummate, fully realized, perfect state of things soon expected. There is a unity between the partial and the perfect in that they both concern the kingdom of God and the new covenant, however there is also a real difference in that the partial is only a small portion and imperfect representation as compared with the great, perfect, full reality in Christ.

There are elements in the Christian life in this world that are suited to the partial, imperfect state of things, that are not suited to the coming perfect state of things - for example, the knowledge and prophecy and tongues valued by the Corinthians. Love, however, is relevant and suited to and vital and necessary for both the partial state of things that now is and the state of the perfect state of things that is to come.

3. The Meaning of "the Perfect (State of Things)"

By the term "the perfect" (Gr. *to telion*) in 1 Cor. 13:10 I believe Paul is referring to the consummate, glory phase of new covenant blessings, which the pre-Parousia Christians held as their hope, which they expected to be fulfilled in their lives at the Parousia of the Lord Jesus. I have written fairly extensively about this hope of glory in previous chapters.

Consider Jesus and "the perfect" in the Epistle to the Hebrews
The Lord Jesus is the Perfecter [Gr. *teleiotees*] (Heb 12:2) of the Christians' faith and life. The first Christians were expecting the Lord to come soon in their day, to apply to them his final, consummate phase of salvation: to perfect them, to bring into being the perfect state of things for them. Consider Heb. 11:39 - 12:2:

> And all these [OT saints], having obtained a good testimony through faith, did not receive the promise, 40 God having provided something better for us, *that they should not be made perfect* [Gr. *teleioo*] *apart from us.* 12:1 Therefore we also, since we are surrounded by so great a cloud of witnesses, let us lay aside every weight, and the sin which so easily ensnares us, and let us run with endurance the race that is set before us, 2 looking unto Jesus, the author and *finisher* (or *perfecter*; teleiotees) of our faith, who for the joy that was set before Him endured the cross, despising the shame, and has sat down at the right hand of the throne of God. [Heb. 11:39 - 12:2]

The context of Heb 11:39-40 gives the understanding that being made perfect (spoken of in v.40) is equivalent to receiving [the fulfillment of] the promise mentioned in 11:39. What promise was that? Answer: The promise whose fulfillment the fathers were longing for but didn't receive in their lifetimes - viz., the promise of the heavenly country and city prepared by God, and the better resurrection (11:9-10, 13, 16, 35). The context of Hebrews shows that this heavenly country is the sphere in which the promised "rest of God" (ch. 4) would be had - that "rest" that the Hebrew Christian readers were being exhorted to hope in and stay loyal for.

This passage in the Hebrews epistle then points out (in 12:1-2) that Jesus is the Perfecter/the Completer of the waiting Old Testament saints and the Perfecter of the waiting first Christians. The writer says that it was God's plan to not make perfect the OT saints apart from those first NT Christians. They were to be perfected together. They - the OT saints and the pre-Parousia NT saints - were expecting to be made perfect at the Parousia of Jesus, when he would appear with salvation. At the time of this epistle, both groups were awaiting this perfection of being raised into the consummate blessing of the heavenly city and country, into the rest of God, into the heavenly holy of holies where Jesus their forerunner had entered previously for them.

Jesus is the Perfecter (Heb 12:2) of his saints, and the perfection that he would provide his OT and first NT saints was the perfection that he himself, as their forerunner, entered into after his time of trial on earth - glory with the Father in the heavenly holy of holies. Jesus is the one who is able to save to the uttermost (Heb 7:25). (The Greek underlying "to the uttermost" implies "to completion/perfection in all respects."). The Christians of those pre-Parousia days were expecting to experience this salvation into perfection in all respects, at the Parousia of Jesus.

Under the Holy Spirit's inspiration, "the perfect" spoken of as the Christians' hope in 1 Cor. 13:10 is the same hope of perfection by Jesus the Perfecter in the epistle to the Hebrews.

From 1 Corinthians itself we can gather what "the perfect" or consummate state was to be and when it was expected.

The timing of the coming of "the perfect."

In 1:7-8 Paul thanks God "that you [i.e. the Corinthian Christians - IH] come short in no gift, eagerly waiting for the revelation of our Lord Jesus Christ, 8 who will also confirm you to the end, that you may be blameless in the day of our Lord Jesus Christ." The grace-gifts of God are a help to the first Christians' edification as they wait for the coming of the Lord Jesus. Comparing this with 13:8-13, which mentions that the gifts belong to the partial state of things that will end for the pre-Parousia Christians when the perfect comes, confirms that, for the pre-Parousia saints, the coming of the Lord Jesus is the occasion when the perfect comes.

The nature of "the perfect."

Man was designed in the beginning to manifest and know the glory of God: "he (man) is the image and glory of God" (11:7). But sadly, man fell away from God and failed to realize the dignity of his high calling, (indeed in Adam "all sinned and come short of the glory of God," Rom 3:23), but the salvation in Christ has been granted by God's amazing grace to rectify this terrible problem of man's imperfection.

Paul could say of these Corinthian believers in Christ, who formerly were pagans: "But you were washed, but you were sanctified, but you were justified in the name of the Lord Jesus and by the Spirit of our God, (6:11). And Paul thanked God that the Christians had been "called by God into fellowship with His Son," the Lord Jesus (1:9).

This fellowship with the Lord Jesus was a spiritual reality: Paul states that it involved being "joined to the Lord...one spirit with Him" (6:17). Now it is important to see that the Lord Jesus is "the Lord of Glory" (2:8). So the believers were in a union of spirit and fellowship with the Lord Jesus, the Lord of Glory. This is Good News for fallen man, because God had planned this gospel union with Christ (the Lord of Glory) in order that the believers in union with him might be brought to glory - "But we speak the wisdom of God in a mystery, the hidden wisdom which God ordained before the ages for our glory" (2:7).

For man to be brought to perfection and completion, he must be brought back to the glory that God designed him for; he needs to share in the glory of the Lord Jesus Christ. Salvation is for this purpose.

A believer in the Lord Jesus is in His kingdom, i.e. in the kingdom of God. Paul preached this gospel of the kingdom. In this earthly life believers partake of the firstfruits of the kingdom of God, but the first Christians were looking forward to the Parousia of Jesus bringing them into the consummate phase of the kingdom. (Refer to chapter 2, "New Covenant Blessings - Deposit and Fullness"). It is of this consummate phase of the kingdom that Paul says, "Now this I say, brethren, that flesh and blood cannot inherit the kingdom of God; nor does corruption inherit incorruption," (1 Cor. 15:50). Paul explains that to enter this consummate, glory phase of the kingdom, the Christians need glorified bodies. While there is anything in them that has the stain of sin, of "the flesh," of death, of anything to do with the fall of man, then a Christian has not yet reached experiential completeness or perfection, he is not yet fully "home" where he belongs. Paul explains in 1 Cor. 15 that at the Parousia all (pre-Parousia) saints - both living and deceased - would be transformed in such a manner that would equip them spirit, soul and body for fellowship in glory with the glorified Lord Jesus. The perfection or completion that would occur at the Parousia, would involve, in the case of living saints, a great change: (see 1 Cor. 15:42-53)

- their bodies of *corruption* would be changed into incorruptible bodies,
- their bodies of *dishonor* would be changed into glorious bodies,
- their bodies of weakness would be changed into bodies of power,
- their bodies of natural makeup would be changed into spiritual bodies,
- their bodies of earthiness would be changed into heavenly bodies, such that,
- as they had borne the image of the man of dust, they would now bear the image of the heavenly Man
- they would put on immortality and incorruption

This was "the perfect" that Paul expected and referred to in 1 Cor. 13:10. The perfect state is also that state of things where God is all in all (1 Cor. 15:28). The God-all-in-all state is that which prevails where the saints have had every enemy within and without totally, experientially subjected to the Lord Jesus Christ and the saints have been glorified together with Christ in heaven in the Father's presence. The perfect or God-all-in-all state that the pre-Parousia saints expected to enter at the Parousia was a state where there was nothing in them that was not of God, but where everything in them was holy, filled with God's life and power. Such a state cannot exist while Christians are on earth where they are still subject to numerous enemies within and without, and while so much that is not of God still affects their inner life and outward behavior.

At the Parousia, this perfect/complete/consummate state of things would come for the pre-Parousia saints: they would then be complete in that "kingdom and glory" to which God had called them through the Lord Jesus (1 Thess 2:12); they would then have fulfilled their hope of "obtaining the glory of our Lord Jesus Christ," to which God had called them, (2 Thess 2:14).

The Partial/Firstfruits and the Perfect/Consummation

"The perfect" of 1 Corinthians 13:10 is therefore another name for the consummate, glory phase of the new covenant that those pre-Parousia Christians were expecting at the Parousia of Christ. Already I have demonstrated in previous articles that the pre-Parousia Christians were partaking of the new covenant in a deposit and firstfruits degree of blessedness. At the Parousia they were expecting the full payment and the full harvest of new covenant blessings, which would consist of full glorification together with Christ in heaven in their glorified, incorruptible, spiritual bodies, being conformed to the image of Christ, living with Christ in the heavenly holy of holies, fully revealed as sons of God, free from all death and fears.

"The partial state of things" (or "that which is in part") and "the perfect state of things" spoken of in 1 Cor. 13, are the counterparts of the deposit/firstfruits phase and the full consummation phase of new covenant blessedness spoken of elsewhere in the NT, and which has been the subject of previous chapters of this book.

Also, "the perfect" refers to the perfect state of love in heaven

Having said the above about the perfect state of consummate glory, I feel that there is also an added dimension to the meaning of "the perfect" as it appears in the context of 1 Corinthians — an added dimension which relates to the community aspect in the church. "The perfect" in 1 Cor. 13:8 refers to more than just the glorified state of believers as individuals, but to the glorified state of believers in their unity and love together.

Consider the large amount of effort Paul has expended in this letter endeavoring to get the Corinthian Christians to see the folly of their disagreements and careless manner towards fellow brethren. Even at the communion meal, there was failure of brotherly love. In the function of spiritual gifts there was lack of loving harmony. (The old worldly pollution of self-importance so often pervades our modern churches too). Paul reminds them in chapter 12 of their baptism in ONE Spirit into ONE body to try to get them to feel their oneness and that all use of gifts and ministries should be done in love for mutual edifying as fellow members. Paul wants them to love one another.

In the present time of the partial, the time of the firstfruits, while love should be preeminent, the fact is that in the nature of things it can't perfectly be so, because of the remaining presence in believers of "the flesh." But in the perfect state of things, when the perfect has come, "the flesh" will be gone, sin will be gone, and ignorance will be gone — all that hinders the true and full and perfect lordship of love will be gone. Love will be preeminent and all the brethren will perfectly love each other in their glorified state in heaven. As I mentioned earlier, the theme in Paul's chapter 13 is that love is the crucial issue, both now in the partial phase and in the perfect phase. Because love will be fully manifested as the very atmosphere of heaven in the perfect state of things, we had better get acquainted with love now in this preliminary stage.

This perfect state of things, of glory in heaven together in perfect love is also the subject of Ephesians 4:13, "till we all come to the unity of the faith and of the knowledge of the Son of God, to a perfect man, to the measure of the stature of the fullness of Christ," which I believe describes a heavenly state, not something that will be manifested on earth. When there is complete absence of immaturity, and of the presence of sin and the flesh, only then would full experiential conformity to Christ be manifested. (Note: In the passage Eph 4:11-16, verses 11-12 and 14-16 is a continuing sentence referring to the edifying that occurs while on earth in the partial phase, or the firstfruits stage of things, where imperfect saints still require sanctifying and renewing in knowledge: the "in order that" of verse 14 qualifies the verbs "equipping" and "edifying" of verse 12. Verse 13 is virtually a parenthesis, and refers to "the perfect" state of things that was to come, as the end of their earthly trial and labors).

4. The Meaning of "The Partial (State of Things)"

"For in part we know" (1 Cor. 13:9), or "we know partially, imperfectly."

The knowledge of God and of his ways and of his Word that is presently possessed, while good and helpful when held and used in love, is nevertheless of a form that is adapted to human minds which, although undergoing a renewing, are still very ignorant and lacking the capacity of perceiving the full reality of things. "Flesh and blood" is not able to inherit the kingdom of God, (1 Cor. 15:50); that is, man in his earthy condition, although alive in his spirit through the righteousness of Christ and the work of the Holy Spirit, is yet bodily (which includes his material brain) unable to enter or appreciate the fullness of the kingdom of God in its heavenly, spiritual, glorious reality. Man needs raising to a heavenly condition in order to enter such an elevated sphere.

The Corinthians' Problem regarding Knowledge.

Knowledge and wisdom were something of an issue in the church. The wrong and worldly emphasis on knowledge by some had the tendency to detract from the purity and simplicity of the gospel. We gather from some of Paul's statements, that there were those in the Corinthian church who were tempted to adapt the Christian gospel to fit it with their ideas of Greek philosophy and rhetoric, and were tempted to imagine that accumulating knowledge made them superior to others of lesser knowledge.

Chapter 8 of Paul's letter concerns those who flaunted their 'superior' knowledge with disregard and to the hurt of the conscience of less knowledgeable brethren. There was a problem due to those members who were claiming superiority of knowledge in things to do with idols and foods, but lacking the love to handle that knowledge. The knowledge they possessed, was actually being selfishly prided upon, their knowledge was just puffing themselves up, instead of wisely being used in love to build others up. Paul exhorts in 1 Cor. 8:1, "...We know that we all have knowledge. Knowledge puffs up, but love edifies. 2 And if anyone thinks that he knows anything, he knows nothing yet as he ought to know."

In the section 1:10 to 4:21 there runs a theme of there being disagreements among the church members regarding what teacher had the best teaching. The Paul-ites and the Apollos-ites and the Cephas-ites and the Christ-ites all argued that they had the better knowledge of doctrine, etc. You are still carnal, says Paul, while you brag about your knowledge like you are doing (3:1-4). For what can mere knowledge accomplish? Nothing; for all depends on God's exerting his power to give life and growth (3:6). Paul warns: "Let no one deceive himself. If anyone among you seems to be wise in this age, let him become a fool that he may become wise" (3:18), and explains, "Now these things, brethren, I have figuratively transferred to myself and Apollos for your sakes, that you may learn in us not to think beyond what is written, that none of you may be puffed up on behalf of one against the other. 7 For who makes you differ from another? And what do you have that you did not receive? Now if you did indeed receive it, why do you boast as if you had not received it?" (4:6-7).

And to those who felt they were superior to Paul and didn't need Paul's visits and teaching anymore, he gave the challenge: "Now some are puffed up, as though I were not coming to you. 19 But I will come to you shortly, if the Lord wills, and I will know, not the word of those who are puffed up, but the power. 20 For the kingdom of God is not in word but in power" (4:18-20).

Christian knowledge is very partial in this life. That is why Paul frowns upon any Christians boasting about their level of knowledge. Because while on earth Christians are in a partial state of things, their knowledge can only be imperfect and partial. It is a fact of life that even though the inner, spiritual work of God produces truth in the inward parts resulting in real life, worship and service, Christians are still below God's standard while in this world in these fallen bodies. Our ability to perceive and hold the truth is partial and often faulty. Often without meaning to, we Christians can easily say what the truth is, but our lives betray the fact that we don't fully behave the truth. Our love for God and people is partial in this life. Our knowledge (intellectual and spiritual) is indeed very partial. And our ability to possess and use our knowledge in the way of love as described in 1 Cor. 13 is also very partial.

That is why Paul advises his readers not to boast about their present knowledge as if it is an end in itself, as if it is a means to promote one's superiority over others. This is to forget: 1. That the present knowledge one has is a temporary, partial element compared with everlasting love, and 2. That knowledge is to be employed in and by love for it to have real value. Love continues to rule when the perfect comes, but the present partial knowledge will be rendered inoperative, brought to an end, eclipsed by a heavenly, spiritual knowledge that cannot be imagined here on earth.

"In part we prophesy" (v. 9), or "we prophesy imperfectly, in a limited way."

Prophecy as used in 1 Cor. 12-14, I tend to understand as a Holy Spirit anointed application, teaching and opening up the meaning of the scriptures already possessed, (perhaps like Peter did on the day of Pentecost), rather than of foretelling the future or of revealing or composing new scripture. Paul encouraged prophesying, motivated by love, among the congregation as a great way of edifying the saints. Clearly the prophesying that Paul was advocating was not to do with the inspiration or writing of the scriptures themselves. There were many prophets, or rather those used in prophesying, in the churches of those days (e.g. Acts 11:27-28; 13:1-3; 15:32; 1:8-9; and 1 Cor. 12; 14) who were used by God to encourage, strengthen and guide the brethren, but who were not in any way pretending to put forth their teachings as if they had the authority of new scriptures, and certainly the Holy Spirit did not see fit to record these prophecies as part of the canon.

We see also in 1 Corinthians 12 and 14 that the gift of tongues with interpretation when rightly used could also encourage the congregation in the things of God, but once again, not in the way of introducing new scripture truth.

The Corinthians' Problem regarding Prophecy and Tongues.

From Paul's discussion in 1 Corinthians chapters 12 to 14, one gathers that some of the Christians were not using the gifts of prophecy and tongues under a motivation of love for edifying their brethren, but were operating in a rather selfish way to boost their own egos, to proclaim their superiority over less-gifted members. Paul counters this by showing in chapter 12 that every member of a body has its place and is important to the whole, that self-vaunting is not of love, and is not considering the body. He urges them to operate their gifts and ministries in love as contributive members of the same body, for building up the whole.

Paul says here in 1 Cor. 13 that the education, exhortation and comfort (1 Cor. 14:3) from the scriptures as applied and explained by anointed prophesying, while good and beneficial in its place, was still *only a partial means of communication adapted to or suitable to men in a partial, imperfect state of things. Prophecy (anointed exposition, etc.) is limited and can still only put across spiritual realities in the form of human words and concepts*, whereas the perfect revelation that was to come - a revelation that would be adapted to glorified, incorruptible, spiritual saints in heaven - would no longer require partial, imperfect methods such as prophecy to convey knowledge.

Similarly, the gift of tongues, like prophecy, would no longer be a relevant nor suitable means of communication in the sphere of the perfect where a divine illumination and heavenly communication would be operative, far above what is possible in this earthly experience.

"The partial shall be done away" v. 10.

When the consummate state of things has come, then that which is in part and imperfect (such as our partial knowledge, and our partial, imperfect perception of God and his ways, and the partial, imperfect manifestation of truth and love in lives, and the imperfect gifts and other means of conveying knowledge), shall be done away, brought to an end, rendered useless. Something unimaginably greater will take its place of all we know on earth.

Paul singles out in particular the three elements - knowledge, prophecies and tongues - because it was in the area of these three elements in particular that there was some conflict in the Corinthian church. All conflict was the outcome of the failure to love (in the way of 1 Cor. 13:4-7) and failure to use said gifts and knowledge in a loving way. So Paul takes up these three elements of prophesy, tongues and knowledge which were troublesome areas and in 1 Corinthians 13 brings at least *two main important truths* to help get things in true perspective. These truths are relevant in principle to any other elements of life that man may boast in as something that makes him feel self-important:

1. Gifts and knowledge, etc. are of *temporary significance*, compared with love which is of *unending significance*. There is coming a time when the perfect state will have come. And in that perfect state, love will still be the operative life-force (for love is as eternal as God is, for God is love), but love will no longer need the services of elements that were only adapted to and suitable for the time of the partial and firstfruits phase of new covenant life — that less-than-perfect phase that continues for as long as men are still in earthy bodies, with minds still largely in an ignorant condition and in constant need of renewal to know and follow God and to oppose the incipient corruption still in their "flesh." When the perfect state has come, love will operate using new heavenly means yet to be revealed, means far higher in nature than those on earth, heavenly means adapted for a heavenly, spiritual, incorruptible, glorious, consummate sphere of existence.

2. All gifts and knowledge, etc., are not only of temporary significance, but during the temporary time in which they are operative they are of *implemental significance*, in the service of love, for love is of *ultimate significance*. So all gifts and knowledge, etc., are not ends in themselves, for of themselves they can accomplish nothing. They are to be regarded as implements or servants of love. Love is the only ultimate, abiding power, and the only acceptable underlying motive, in any service. All other elements, such as prophecy, tongues and knowledge, are not ends in themselves; they are for the service of love; they are implements of love, by which love can accomplish its design of working for the well-being of all concerned. To boast about possessing the implement is totally unprofitable and unreasonable if there is not a power to use it and a right reason for having it and using it. The implement can accomplish nothing of itself. But where God is, with his power, and where His love is, as the guiding principle and reason for the implement's existence, those implements can achieve good, and can edify the saints. Paul is not advocating the use of love instead of gifts of the Spirit and gaining of knowledge; but is advocating the use of love-empowered gifts and knowledge rather than gifts and knowledge without love.

It was only because there were problem areas in the church regarding the use of knowledge, prophecies and tongues outside the motive of love that Paul has cause to mention them in 1 Cor. 13. The principle behind Paul's argument in 1 Cor. 13 could just as well be employed in getting into perspective any other elements in church life that could be misused by some as a means of self-aggrandizement or creating a party spirit. There may be differing views on theological subjects and on the timing of the Lord's coming; on the use of creeds, catechisms, preferred types of church governments and of church singing, hymns and/or choruses; views on the duties of the deaconate, eldership and minister, etc. All of these elements (over which there may be arguments in churches), Paul would say, may have a partial contribution to one's Christian life if they are recognized and used in love and wisdom, for the blessing of others; but realize that all such knowledge is partial and temporary compared to a perfection of glory and love in heaven that we hope to experience, and that such things exist during this life for the service of love, as love deems it best to employ them; they are not ends in themselves. (I am not denying the need to uphold the true faith in the Lord Jesus Christ against heresy; but even there the principle of "love your enemies" abides. We are not out to win our cause as such, to prove our point or our superiority - religious "flesh" enjoys a good cause - but we aim to guard the church, to help others to a better understanding of God and his truth for their well-being; we aim to "speak the truth in love.")

5. The Illustration of Childhood to Adulthood

Continuing with our study in 1 Corinthians 13:8-13, Paul illustrates his teaching of the partial phase passing into the perfect, such that the partial is rendered inoperative and unnecessary when the perfect comes, by two illustrations. The first concerns childhood to adulthood; the second (regarding partial knowledge versus complete or full knowledge) will be presented in point 7 below:

> [1 Cor. 13:11] "When I was a child, I talked like a child, felt like a child, reasoned like a child: when I became a man, I put from me childish ways." (*Weymouth's* Translation)

Speaking in the first person, Paul said that as a child he spoke, felt/understood and reasoned like a child. The fact is that such a type of speaking, thinking and reasoning, while imperfect and limited in comparison to adult ways, was nevertheless suitable, proper, and necessary as a part of growing up as a child. But when he became a man, an adult, he "put away, brought to an end, rendered inoperative (Gr. καταργέω, *katargeo*, see vv. 8 and 10 above) childish ways." A child has a limited capacity to comprehend many things and to know how to behave in many ways. An adult has a greater capacity to comprehend things in the world and to behave in appropriate ways in this world.

We have in this illustration the subject of a social human being - but presented in two phases of his existence. There is a partial, not-mature phase of social development and a mature phase of social development, in the context of functioning in this world.

From the context the application is clear: The human child phase, with its limited capacity for human knowledge and behavior, is parallel to the Christian in the partial phase of new covenant blessings, for such a Christian has in this life only a limited capacity for knowing and appreciating God and walking in holiness. The human adult phase with its more mature capacity for human knowledge and working in this world, is parallel to the Christian who enters the consummate phase of the new covenant blessings, in which he is relieved of all mortality, corruption, sin, the flesh, spiritual dullness, that previously limited his spiritual capacity to know and appreciate God. In the consummate phase of blessedness, the Christian's capacity to know and walk with God is beyond our present limited imagination.

Paul is likening his graduation from childhood into adulthood in the social setting of this world to his expected spiritual graduation from his partial Christian experience into a consummate, perfect state of things in heaven on the occasion of the Lord's Parousia. Paul is giving an implicit exhortation here, in the context of the childish boasting of some of the Corinthians: "Don't go pridefully boasting about what you have and know, for remember we are at present in the partial, firstfruit stage of Christian blessing; and what we have and know now is mere child's play (reverently speaking) compared with what lies ahead for us when the consummate state of things comes on the occasion of the Lord's Parousia. To pridefully boast and act superior before fellow believers is just as silly as a little child boasting of how wise and knowledgeable he is, when all along any adult is far superior to him."

Note that Paul is likening his and his Corinthian brethren's present Christian experience to a child-level compared to what he and they could expect to enter when the perfect state came at the Parousia. (If that is how Paul felt about his walk with God, how then should we (who are far less experienced) view our level of knowing God? We haven't risen to the level of experience with God that Paul had in his pre-Parousia days, and which he calls his childhood level.)

6. The Illustration of Obscurity to Clarity of Vision

"For we see now through a mirror obscurely, and then face to face." [1 Cor. 13:12a *Young's Literal Translation*]

"For the present we see things as if in a mirror, and are puzzled; but then we shall see them face to face." [1 Cor. 13:12a *Weymouth's Translation*]

In those days, they didn't have glass mirrors with good reflections like today; they were made of polished steel, which gave an imperfect, blurred reflection. One would have to carefully puzzle out the image. The image was a poor representation of the real subject.

Paul is meaning by this illustration that to compare what we perceive of God and his glory now while in the firstfruits, partial phase of new covenant experience with what we will perceive when the perfect state of things comes on the occasion of the Parousia, is like comparing one's vision of a blurred image in a metal mirror with seeing the real object in full clarity.

There is in the present, the perception and acknowledgment of true and good things - the things of God, and the person of Christ, etc., but the perception is unclear, obscure, puzzling, (the Greek literally is *en enigmati* = in an enigma). Mind you, what we do see of the glory of Christ is wonderful enough to draw our souls from unbelief to faith in Christ; but our perception of God and his things is nevertheless imperfect, compared to the heavenly clarity and glory in which we will perceive them with a glorified mind in the perfect state of things.

While they are living on this earth in mortal, earthy bodies, still infected with the dregs of the flesh and sin, the Christian's spiritual vision and capacity to receive the things of God is very imperfect. When the perfect comes, the things of God would be seen in a complete, clear manner, in accordance with the fact that then the saints would have glorified, incorruptible, spiritual bodies like the Lord Jesus' glorious body, and their spiritual vision would be perfect: their vision would then be like the Lord Jesus' vision.

While there is no object to the verb "see" in the Greek, I believe that it can be understood as things of God and also of Christ. "Now we see [Christ and the things of God] dimly...but then [we shall see Him and the things of God] face to face." The phrase "face to face," signifies "every thing being seen in itself, and not by means of a representative or similitude," (*Adam Clarke's Commentary on the Bible*). There will be nothing [-no flesh, no sin, no weak earthy brain, no lack of spiritual power, etc.] between us and the face of things, nor between us and the face of Christ; we shall then be acquainted with ultimate reality, of which in the present we have only vague spiritual and mental conceptions.

7. To Partly Know and To Fully Know

"now I know in part, and then I shall fully know, as also I was known" [1 Cor. 13:12b *Young's Literal Translation*]

For the present the knowledge I gain is imperfect; but then I shall know fully, even as I am fully known. [1 Cor. 13:12b *Weymouth's Translation*]

In verse 12b Paul summarizes succinctly his theme of the previous verses, and of the two illustrations of childhood to adulthood and obscurity to clarity of vision. The partial and imperfect phase of new covenant blessing that is now present will come to an end and be superseded by the consummate state of new covenant blessedness.

The verb "to know" is used three times in this sentence (v. 12b), translating two related Greek verbs which, as used in this context, must be given their distinction. The first occasion - "now I know in part" means to know in a general sense (intellectually and experientially, Gr. *ginosko*), the second and third occasions - "then I shall fully know" and "as also I am fully known" means to know and to recognize in a full and thorough sense (Gr. *epiginosko*). (Refer to the *Online Bible* Greek Lexicon; and *Robertson's NT Word Pictures*).

Paul is talking of his whole acquaintance with the things of God and his fellowship with God himself. Now, he says, I know imperfectly, partially, in a limited way, in an unclear and - compared to what is to come - in what may be called a spiritual child-level degree, the things of God and God himself; but then, when the consummate state of things comes at the Parousia of Jesus, I shall fully know and recognize, in a complete and unlimited way, the things of God and God himself: I shall know with a heavenly clarity of vision, in what may comparatively be called a spiritual adult-degree. I shall fully know God and his things in a manner that will resemble the way in which God has fully known me - that is, with a heavenly clarity, with a heavenly, spiritual understanding and appreciation that far exceeds what is possible to mortal man in this earthly life.

8. Love continues always

"And now abide faith, hope, love, these three; but the greatest of these is love," (1 Cor. 13:13).

Love never fails, and will always will have its effect (v.8) and ever remains and continues (v.13). When "the perfect" has come and the saints begin their heavenly, glorified life with Christ, all the earthly and (therefore) temporary gifts and helps and means of gaining and imparting knowledge that love employed for the saints' growth in the pre-perfect period on earth will be no longer needed nor applicable, but the love that ruled on earth and which used these earthly elements, will continue to rule in the heavenly realms, but in a far more manifest and glorious way than it did on earth in the partial phase or the firstfruits phase of the new covenant.

Love is the power sustaining faith and hope. Some commentators say that these other two qualities, faith and hope, will also continue (v. 13) even when the perfect is come, (but in a far higher nature) because there will ever be occasion for confidence and expectation in God in heaven among the angels and His children as He everlastingly opens up new vistas of His infinite perfection and glory for all his creatures to enjoy.

9. Who was perfected when the perfect came?

Keeping in mind the description and meaning of "the perfect" discussed above, this question has two separate answers depending on which side of the Parousia a saint exists.

Pre-Parousia believers. In my previous articles examining the hope of the first Christians, the answer to this question is clarified: the perfect came for all pre-Parousia saints - deceased and living - at occasion of the Parousia (c. AD 70). This is the primary reference in regard to the original readers to whom the NT epistles were written. As they expected, their hope of glory was fulfilled at Christ's appearing. Until that occasion, the first Christians lived as partakers of the new covenant in its partial, deposit/firstfruits stage. At the Parousia all pre-Parousia saints, all together, entered the perfect, consummate phase of the new covenant in heaven, to experience the Lord in his glory; and there the partial elements of this life were no longer needed or relevant.

Post-Parousia Christians. Since the Parousia in AD 70, the perfect state of things comes for all post-Parousia saints when they physically die. At their death they individually enter the same perfect, consummated state and condition in heaven that the pre-Parousia saints entered en masse at the Parousia. Until their death, all post-Parousia Christians partake of the new covenant in a deposit/firstfruits measure, and their lives involve the partial and imperfect elements, just as in the case of the pre-Parousia Christians prior to their change at the Parousia. (The church today is still fighting over doctrines, gifts, knowledge, etc., just like the pre-Parousia Corinthians).

Post-Parousia believers are still in the state described in Rom. 8:10, "And if Christ [be] in you, the body [is] dead because of sin; but the Spirit [is] life because of righteousness." And as long as we remain in this earthly physical realm, we still await our spiritual, glorified, heavenly bodies.

The Lord Jesus, at his Parousia, formally set up for his people the state of glory, his consummated kingdom: and firstly, all believers who had ever lived prior to the Parousia (millions since creation) entered that heavenly glory at the Parousia Secondly all believers who would ever live consequent to the Parousia enter their perfect blessedness individually upon their death (that is, when their allotted time on earth is finished). "Blessed are the dead who die in the Lord from hence forth" (i.e. from the time of the Parousia), (Rev. 14:13): this blessing qualifies all post-Parousia Christians, because since the time of the Parousia the heavenly glory is a prepared reality awaiting their entrance when they die.

10. Perfection not possible while saints remain on earth

I realize that here I enter a controversy with the "remained-on-earth" brethren, for they say that the whole church on earth (i.e. including the post-Parousia church) entered perfection at the Parousia; that since the Parousia all people, as soon as they receive Jesus as Lord and Savior, enter the perfect and glorified state, and see the Lord face to face, etc. I believe that I have shown in the comments above regarding 1 Cor. 13, as also in the rest of this book, that such a position in just not true to fact, and makes confusion of the scriptures, and takes away the true hope of true glory in the heavenly realm after death that is expressed throughout the scriptures.

How do we compare with Paul?

But let me see how this "remained-on-earth" view of the perfect fares if we do a comparison of our modern day preterists' lives with the life and views of the apostle Paul. In doing this comparison I do not mean to be mocking toward brethren of the opposing view, but I just wish to apply some simple logic to critically analyze the position, so that others reading this article may understand the differences and implications.

Old *Matthew Henry* says in his comments on 1 Cor. 13:9 –

> Our best knowledge and our greatest abilities are at present like our condition, narrow and temporary. Even the knowledge they [i.e. the first Christians - IH] had by inspiration was but in part. *How little a portion of God, and the unseen world, was heard even by apostles and inspired men! How much short do others come of them!* [emphasis mine - IH]

Even the great apostle admitted that until the Parousia came, and until the perfect came, he was partaking of the partial, imperfect phase of knowing, seeing and appreciating God and the things of God. He implies that his graduation from a child's ways (i.e. its level and ability of speaking, knowing, thinking and reasoning) into his present adult's ways, provides a similitude of how he anticipates he will feel about things when the perfect will have come. From the perspective of his then perfect state, what he now possesses will seem, relatively speaking, like a mere child's imperfect and partial level of knowledge, appreciation, and grasp of God, having no more use to him because he will have outgrown such a partial view of things, and will be experiencing a far higher form of experience, knowledge and fellowship with God than he ever imagined.

Note that when Paul was speaking of when the perfect will have come, he is talking about *the perfect as a reality that would be known, felt, seen, experienced - a wonderful experiential reality where all past ways of knowing God that he had enjoyed as an apostle would be put away, would be finished with, because he would have graduated to living in a new and perfect realm of love and heavenly knowledge far exceeding anything he had known on earth.* Nowhere does Paul suggest that the perfect he was anticipating was just a covenant change, or just an objective change more or less in God's sight, but which would leave him and his readers still in an earthly realm knowing and serving God much the same in experience as he/they did before the perfect came.

11. Some questions to ponder:
Comparison of our prayer life with Paul's.

Who of us post-Parousia believers (including both futurist and preterist believers), would honestly say that we match Paul in his prayer-life: do we not all study his prayers as recorded in the NT, in order to understand how and for what we are to pray? Yet these are prayers of a man only in the firstfruits level of new covenant life, of a man who admits that he only had a dim view of God, and was imperfect in knowledge and understanding, of a man who was looking for something far higher - the perfect. Let us not pretend that the perfect has come to us, and that we are perfected with the perfection that Paul longed for at the Parousia, when our prayer life does not match that of Paul in his pre-Parousia, partial-phase of life.

Comparison of our knowledge with Paul's.

Who of us would honestly say that we match Paul in his spiritual knowledge of God and God's ways: do we not spend countless hours during our Christian life in study of Paul's epistles with the help of many commentaries, and listen to hundreds of sermons expounding Paul's letters, all in order to try to appreciate his teaching? Yet Paul said his knowledge of God and God's ways was but imperfect, partial, dim, on a child's level, compared with what he anticipated to experience when the perfect came. What preterist minister has no need to employ the use of study, commentaries, lexicons, in his attempts to grasp the firstfruits-level knowledge of Paul? Does the preterist minister feel his congregation so "fully knows" that he feels no need to explain Paul's epistles to them? Let us not pretend that the perfect has come to us, or that we are perfected with the perfection that Paul expected at the Parousia, when our knowledge is far short of the apostle's pre-Parousia, partial, imperfect knowledge.

Comparison of our holiness with Paul's.
Who of us would dare say that we, individually, and our churches, collectively, fully function according to the standard set down in the NT: of selfless love and holiness, doing all for the glory of Christ in humility and joy, with longsuffering and endurance, with no bitterness, coveting, pride or gossip - as Paul exhorts and expects his pre-Parousia readers to function in? Don't we all still need to be reminded and taught about loving one another? Don't we all fall short of manifesting the qualities of love described in 1 Cor. 13:4-7? Don't differences in interpretation over scripture still arise even in preterist churches and between preterist ministers? Let us not then pretend that the perfect has come, or that we are perfected with the perfection that the pre-Parousia church expected at the Parousia, while our lives and spirituality are no better than that in the pre-Parousia churches, and while we still need the daily teaching of pre-Parousia scriptures (part of "the partial") to guide us in right living.

Post-Parousia Christians are in the realm of the partial and firstfruits.
The truth is: While we are still in the realm of opinions and taught knowledge, while we are so much needing to be taught and to learn the teachings in the pre-Parousia scriptures - about God, Jesus, salvation, about how to live a good Christian life, etc - while we still need all these helps, while we still carry around the legacy of mankind's fallenness and sin in death-bound bodies, we remain in the sphere of what Paul called the imperfect, the partial; and we are still awaiting the perfect to come. In no way can it be said while we are in this life on earth that we post-Parousia Christians, (whether preterists or futurists), "fully know even as also we have been fully known," or that we now "see face to face" with God and heavenly realities with undimmed vision. By these terms Paul is talking about a level of knowing God and the reality of his fellowship and his divine nature, in a perfection of love, in a perfection of body and mind, beyond anything possible to mortal, imperfect man.

If he were alive today, and visited us, would the apostle Paul recognize that, in our present-day preterist churches on earth, the perfect for which he so ardently longed had come and was present in our lives?? Or would he recognize churches who were but still infants in the knowledge of God - churches who, just like the churches in his days, needed his teaching and counseling, who needed further sanctification, who had not yet even come up to the standard of his partial-phase holy life, let alone the standard of the perfect he was looking forward to?

12. The condition of post-Parousia saints
There are a couple of very important questions that we post-Parousia saints need to ask ourselves at this point. "What is the condition of those people on earth who have become Christians *following* the time of the Parousia c. AD 70? Do they have a deposit/firstfruits measure, or the consummate measure, of new covenant blessedness?"

How do our lives as modern-day Christians measure up to the list of expected consummate blessings that I have mentioned in this book?

Apostles Paul, John and Peter and the other first Christians whom we admire in the NT writings were only in the deposit/firstfruits stage of their Christian experience, and were longing for the ultimate fullness of the eternal inheritance which the Parousia of Christ would bring them into. If *they* were only in the pre-Parousia deposit/firstfruits stage, and if it is true that all post-AD 70 Christians (including us of the twenty-first century) who have arisen on earth since the Parousia, have not surpassed them in spiritual maturity, then can we post-Parousia Christians claim to be beyond a deposit/firstfruits experience of the new covenant?

Consider the spiritual greatness of the apostle Paul, and his love, prayer-life, service and vision of Christ in whom he gloried. Paul's level of spiritual maturity was something that none of us could honestly claim to have reached. Yet, in the midst of what we think of as his high level of spiritual experience with Christ, Paul himself felt that it was just the firstfruits/deposit stage of Christian experience. Paul said he only saw spiritual realities dimly, he only had a partial knowledge; he implies that spiritually speaking he was as a child, and that just as in human, natural affairs a child comes to a stage when he puts away childish things and enters adulthood, even so at the Parousia of Christ he would put away the child-stage of seeing dimly and knowing partially and enter a fullness and completion in spiritual matters, (1 Cor. 13:10-12). Paul groaned within himself for release from his fallenness and desired a graduation from a deposit measure of his salvation-experience; he longed for his full manifestation as God's son, when the corruption would be gone and the exceeding glory of God was revealed to him and in him, (e.g., Rom. 8). Yet who of us can claim to be higher in spirituality than the pre-Parousia Paul?

Since we post-Parousia Christians readily identify with the weaknesses and dullness and imperfection of Paul and the Christian readers of his epistles — like them, living still in earthy bodies carrying all the signs and symptoms of fallenness — then we have no authority to claim anything more than that we are in a similar condition with the pre-Parousia Christians; that is, that we are yet, while on earth, in a deposit/firstfruits level of spiritual experience with Christ. (Although, to the praise of God's grace, new creation life is at work in us, sanctifying us).

Consider this also: Since the AD 70 Parousia of Christ, there have been produced countless sermons, Bible commentaries, Christian books, Bible study guides and booklets (including by preterist preachers and writers) all endeavoring to impart to post-Parousia believers an understanding of, and to exhort post-Parousia believers to rise to, the spiritual maturity prescribed in *the writings of the NT deposit/firstfruit writers - writings that were originally directed to deposit/firstfruit Christians.* Yet even with all this wealth of instruction and example available to us post-Parousia Christians, what pastor or minister (including preterist ones) can say that either he himself or his people (including preterist people) have fully comprehended intellectually and spiritually and experientially and behaviorally the deposit/firstfruit doctrines and directions of the NT, initially intended for deposit/firstfruit believers?

In all honesty, who then can legitimately claim that any Christian living on this earth in their fallen, earthy bodies since AD 70, has passed beyond the deposit/firstfruits stage of Christian, spiritual experience with God as exemplified in the NT pre-Parousia apostles and other Christians?

If a Christian has any connection with - the presence of sin and a groaning within himself due to the internal war between the flesh and the Spirit; any connection with - corruption, death, darkness, sorrow, tears, fears, spiritual insensitivity and ignorance, lack of love and lack of the other fruit of the Spirit, impatience or unkindness or selfishness, falling short of the glory of God in spirit, soul and body, falling short of loving God with all one's heart, soul, mind and strength, imperfect fellowship with God (Father, Son and Holy Spirit), etc., etc., — if a Christian has any connection with these unhappy aspects, — no matter how mature a Christian he is, — then by the authority of the inspired writings of apostle Paul, who with his fellow Christians felt all these same unhappy aspects in themselves, it is logical to say that such a Christian still has the signs and symptoms of, and has not yet progressed further than, the deposit/firstfruits stage of Christian, spiritual development that the first Christians were in prior to the Parousia, and has certainly not yet entered into the all-glorious, consummate phase of new covenant blessedness that the first Christians were expecting to receive and experience at the Parousia.

The pre-AD 70 saints alone had the unique privilege of all of them at once entering the glory of the eternal inheritance on the occasion of the Parousia. For all saints who have arisen on earth since the Parousia of Christ in AD 70, individually, at their physical death, each post-Parousia Christian enters the glory of their eternal inheritance, leaving the deposit/firstfruits stage behind forever.

13. "The Perfect" and the New Testament Canon

[1 Cor. 13:10] "and when that which is perfect may come, then that which is in part shall become useless."

Canon is the technical word used to describe the full list of books comprising our Bible, (Old Testament and New Testament) regarded as inspired by God, and accepted as the providing the complete authoritative message of God concerning doctrine and practice for the Church of God.

A Traditional Interpretation regarding the Canon and "the Perfect"
Many futurists (Calvinistic and Arminian) in past history - who did/do not believe that the Parousia occurred back then in the first century AD – understood "the perfect" to refer to the completed canon of the New Testament. And then they reason thus: Since the perfect thing – the NT

canon – has come, then it must be that the partial things – spiritual gifts, etc. – have passed away and no longer have relevance since the apostolic era. But I note this: as far as I am aware, although these futurist commentators and theologians may have felt that the charismatic gifts had served out their purpose in the apostolic age because now the completed canon had come, none of them have felt the further need to say that the Paraclete-ministry of the Holy Spirit expired after the apostolic age, (excepting his inspiring the scriptures to be written), as do some modern-day preterists.

As former *futurists* adopted the *preterist* view, it seems that some of them (especially the "remained-on-earth" preterists) have brought along with them their old traditional understanding regarding the canon as "the perfect" that Paul mentions in 1 Cor. 13:10, and have merely adapted it (with little or no change) to fit in with their new preterist view. Those who were formerly Amillennialists tend to take this approach. Some now add to their former idea about the cessation of the gifts (because of the presence of a completed canon) the further idea of the cessation of the indwelling of the Holy Spirit in believers as their Paraclete because of the completed canon and their perfection-on-earth assumption. Under this "remained-on-earth" view, the completed canon concept forms part of the perfect state of things that came to the church on earth at the Parousia. This remained-on-earth view argues that we post-Parousia believers no longer need the partial elements of Christian life that the pre-Parousia believers required because we now, since the Parousia, have "the perfect," and are perfected.

Reminder of the correct meaning of "the partial."

But, on the basis of the exegesis of 1 Cor. 13 above (and in accordance with my exegesis of the many expectancy statements in the NT in previous articles), it has to be said that *"the partial," as used by Paul, is not about gifts as such; "the partial" is about our whole life experience of knowing, loving and serving God while in this mortal frame on this earth.* The mention of spiritual gifts in 1 Cor. 13 was in a sense, incidental, alluded to only because there were particular problems in that area in the church and so were convenient examples to the point of demonstrating the importance of love. In the overall sense of Paul's words, "the partial" in this whole view of our Christian life and knowledge, has *not* passed for us post-Parousia Christians, *nor* has the perfect come for us post-Parousia Christians still living on earth as it came for the pre-Parousia Christians at the Parousia who entered heaven and glory.

A More Scriptural and Logical Look at the Canon as it relates to "the Perfect" of 1 Cor. 13:10

From what I consider to be the scriptural, preterist, taken-to-heaven view of things, I don't believe that this canon-closed at AD 70 argument (nor, of course, the perfect-on-earth argument) can be used in the aforementioned manner at all.

Note: In what I will say below about the canon of Holy Scripture, I do not wish to be misunderstood! I have no intention to diminish the sacredness and importance of the Bible. I affirm my belief in it being fully inspired by God (in its original languages), as the Holy Spirit moved men to write; and that by means of the Word of God the Holy Spirit convicts and saves and sanctifies his people and enables them to know God.

Based on the "taken-to-heaven" view of the Parousia event, here are *some reasons for my belief that the completed canon is NOT a part of "the perfect" of 1 Cor. 13:10, that came at the Parousia of Christ:*

1. It Was Being "Taken To Heaven" Which Perfected Them

According to the (scriptural) "taken-to-heaven" view, it was the occasion of the Parousia of Christ – by taking the pre-Parousia Christians to glory out of the earthly realm – that rendered the partial phase of Christian life no longer needed and no longer operative; *not* the completed canon on earth, nor any thing else appearing on earth.

It was by their being taken into glory in heaven to be with the glorified Christ, at the Parousia, that the pre-Parousia Christians would enter the realm of fully knowing as also they had been fully known, and that they would see with full clarity face to face instead of dimly and obscurely, as per 1 Cor. 13:10-12. The perfect state, (that Paul said would render previous knowledge, gifts, means of edification, etc., no longer necessary), was not expected to be a perfection on earth but a perfection accomplished in the saints in heaven. It wasn't the canon on earth, or anything else on earth, that rendered pre-Parousia saints perfect in knowledge and vision; rather it was the coming and power of the Lord.

2. Saints Were Not Told To Wait/Watch For a Completed Canon

In addition to #1, there is no mention at all that I can see in all the NT letters that the pre-Parousia Christians were taught to look for, or wait for, a completed canon at all, let alone a completed canon to come before or at the Parousia to bring them to maturity or perfection.

It would seem that Paul's reference to the scripture in 2 Tim 3:15-17 was what we now call the Old Testament; nevertheless my point is that Paul viewed the scriptures that the church already possessed as profitable to make a man of God fully fitted out, and thoroughly equipped for every good work. The Bereans searched these scriptures daily as Paul preached to them the word, (Acts 17:11). In the early church there also was a recognition of Paul's letters being classed as part of scripture (2 Pet 3:15-16), and to be read as authoritative (Col. 4:16). Paul urged the saints to let the word of God dwell in them richly (Col 3:16). To the Ephesian elders, (c. AD 58, not long before his imprisonment in Rome), Paul gave exhortation to remain loyal to Christ, reminding them of his ministry among them:

> I kept back nothing that was helpful, but proclaimed it to you, and taught you publicly and from house to house, 21 testifying to Jews,

and also to Greeks, repentance toward God and faith toward our Lord Jesus Christ. 27 For I have not shunned to declare to you the whole counsel of God. (Acts 20:20-21, 27).

He had shared "the whole counsel of God" with them, as far as it had been revealed to him by the Spirit.

In all of the apostles' concern to preach Christ, there is nowhere that the saints are taught that they were to earnestly wait for further scriptures to be written, in the hope that the full complement would soon become available to them. Paul nowhere hints that "the whole counsel of God" that he had taught in the churches was insufficient, and that they needed to wait until God caused further inspired scriptures to be written, before they could be perfected and glorified together with Christ. At any given time no man had any idea of how many new covenant scripture writings God the Holy Spirit was yet to inspire, so no one could know whether to expect more to be written, or when they had a completed canon.

I see no scripture verse that gives a reason for the idea that Paul's use of "the perfect" in 1 Cor. 13:10, includes the idea of the completed canon. As mentioned in #1, the pre-Parousia Christians' hope of glory depended solely on the coming of Christ for them, who would take them into their inheritance of incorruptible, spiritual, glorious bodies, and bring them to the Father, to be with him forever in the heavenly holy of holies. Such a hope of glory is nowhere implied as being dependent for its fulfillment on the presence of a completed canon on earth. The hope of glory was in existence before the notion of a completed NT canon ever existed.

3. Apostles Do Not Connect Parousia with Completed Canon

I understand that (according to preterist studies, at least) all the gospels and epistles that we now have in the completed canon of the New Testament were written and were in circulation as individual entities *prior to the Parousia of Jesus* - including the Revelation by John. We have hints that Peter and the writer to the Hebrews already had knowledge of the Revelation of John when they wrote their epistles.

Even though all the individual writings of the New Testament were written and available *before* the Parousia, there is no record of the believers thinking that because of this the perfect had already come, or that they had thereby already been perfected. The completed canon was therefore not part of the perfect state they were waiting for while enduring Nero's evil persecutions; they were waiting for glorification with Christ at his coming. There is no mention at all that they were expecting the Parousia to be the occasion of making up a completed canon. It is true though, that no more scripture was written after the Parousia.

4. Church Did Not Have a Clear Concept of a Completed Canon

But even more than this is *against* the notion that a completed canon was regarded by the first church as part of the expected perfect that was to come at the Parousia. The fact is that the very concept of selecting and grouping a complete and unique collection of inspired writings, distinct from all other religious but uninspired documents floating around, does not seem to have been recognized prior to the second century AD.

It was not until "towards the close of the second century that awareness of the concept of a canon and scriptural status begins to reveal itself in the thought and activity of Christians." (D. F. Payne, "Canon of the New Testament," in *The New Bible Dictionary*, Ed. J. D. Douglas, Intervarsity Press, 1962, p. 196). That is, the awareness of the need to clarify a canon did not arise until 100 years after the Parousia of Christ. The Christians worked on this task of clarifying a canon, and by the third century AD, the Christians had gathered a list of books and epistles that were acknowledged as authoritative, but not yet a completed list. In regard to the fourth century, E. F. Harrison says,

During this period the church came more and more to a position of unanimity regarding the canon. Eusebius (260-340) lists only James, Jude, 2 Peter, 2 and 3 John as disputed books (antilegomena). Cyril, Bishop of Jerusalem (315-386), accepts all but the Revelation. Athanasius, Bishop of Alexandria, in his 39th Festal Epistle (367), is the first to cite all 27 books. (E. F. Harrison, "The Canon of the New Testament," a Supplement in *Analytical Concordance to the Bible* by Robert Young, LL.D. William B. Eerdmans Publishing Company, Michigan, 1979).

In the fourth century AD, (viz. 367 AD) the canon as we know it today was defined. So it needs to be taken into account that the Parousia did not bring in the completed canon, as part of "the perfect" that the pre-Parousia Christians were waiting for to perfect them; and that the church at that time, while recognizing epistles, etc., that they regarded as scripture, did not then have a concept of a canon, so couldn't have been expecting the Parousia to bring such a canon into being, or that the canon would bring perfection.

5. A Completed Canon Has Not "Perfected" Anyone

Besides the above, there is the fact that the mere existence or presence of a completed canon in itself has never perfected anybody. Even if a completed canon did come at the Parousia, that would still not account for the fact that the pre-Parousia Christians expected to be raised to heaven into a perfection of knowing and seeing and loving far surpassing anything they had known before on earth - as Paul said would happen at the coming of "the perfect." The mere fact of a complete canon, even though it contains the full written revelation of God to us, does not at all mean a mature or perfect church on earth. (I discuss the subject of the objective, written truth and its relation to truth living and powerful in the inward parts of man in another article available from the author entitled, "The Paraclete and the Truth.")

Thousands of homes down through the centuries, I am probably right to say, have had a completed canon of the Holy Bible in them, which in no way guaranteed that its owners were even converted, let alone perfected. Millions of Christians possess the completed canon of the Holy Bible, having the complete revelation by God regarding Jesus, and yet no one can claim to be perfected by the mere possession of it. This was where the Jews in Jesus' day and Paul's day got themselves into trouble. For they thought that their custodianship and possession and study of the Bible (the Old Testament) marked them out as unique among the nations of the earth. Yet for all their exacting study and memorizing of it, such mere knowledge of the Bible never matured them enough even to recognize Jesus as their Messiah. The knowledge of the full canon, doesn't guarantee maturity. For example, a simple believer with a deep heart knowledge of the essentials of who Jesus is and what he has done for them, may have a more sincere, and real love and dependence upon the Lord, than a theology professor at a university who knows Biblical Hebrew and Greek and has a grasp of all the latest doctrinal arguments and knows the teaching of the canon from front to back. In the very nature of things the presence of the canon, in itself, could never be "the perfect thing" that the pre-Parousia saints were waiting for.

And let's be honest — post-Parousia Christians who have a completed canon, including us preterists today, can not thereby claim our need for knowledge and teaching is past, for it clearly is not past. But Paul said when the perfect came a Christian would fully know, and wouldn't need the kind of teaching we are still needing today. We are absolutely *not* able to say, "The perfect has come; I have been perfected; because I have the completed NT canon I now know fully even as I have been fully known." The fact is that we do not yet know as we are known; we, with all our scholarship, are still struggling to get a better knowledge of the New Testament scriptures that the pre-Parousia Christians possessed (who had none of our commentaries and books!!). Knowledge has not yet been rendered useless or inoperative to us post-Parousia Christians alive on earth, for we greatly feel our need for teaching and knowledge and sermons and commentaries to help us grow in our faith.

Consider this also: While the existence of the canon is of immeasurable value, the fact is that its completion and formation in AD 367, no more perfected the church who possessed it at that time, than did the available scriptures in Peter's and John's days perfect those first Christians. The existence and possession of the written scripture portion of the epistle to the Ephesians, did not guarantee the maturity of the church in Ephesus in the knowledge and practical outworking of the doctrines and exhortations contained in that epistle. (We read of the Ephesians' lack of love in Rev. 2:1-7). Similarly, the existence and possession of Paul's epistles (portions of scripture) by churches in Asia (including the Ephesian, Laodicean [note Col 4:16], Colossian), did not ensure the maturity of the churches in Asia in the doctrine of those scripture letters by Paul; for consider Paul's lament toward the end of his life, 2 Tim 1:15, "all those in Asia have turned away from me," and the sad condition of the Laodicean church in Rev. 3.

Now if the presence of one or more epistles of scripture then, did not mature the recipients in the doctrines of those epistles, when they had the Paraclete to call upon for help, there is no reason to think that suddenly having 27 NT writings together as a canon can bring to maturity those who possess them or that they will be able to abide in the doctrines contained in the whole 27 of them - especially when (as some suppose) they don't even have the Paraclete to call upon for help! The coming of the completed canon, even if it had been formed and recognized by the time of the Parousia, cannot be that for which Paul longed and expected at the Parousia of Jesus as that which would bring a perfection that would produce in the waiting pre-Parousia Christians a knowing and a seeing surpassing all types of knowing and seeing that they had previously experienced.

It is a fact, too, as I am sure many Christians have realized, that the more deeply one comes to know the teachings of Holy Scripture, the more one is made to feel how little real knowledge one actually has. No sooner than one feels established in some teaching, the Lord by his illumination sooner or later will show one that one's depth of understanding is very minimal. Also, far from the canon making one feel he has reached perfection, the more its message is felt in the heart and conscience, the more one becomes aware of one's imperfection. A surface and intellectual knowledge of scripture can puff up and maybe make one feel mature and knowledgeable; but a true Spirit-guided knowledge of scripture humbles one to the dust. When one reads the biographies of the most saintliest men in the Christian church down through the centuries, one will see that the more they knew the whole canon of scriptures (under the illumination of the Holy Spirit), and knew the God of those scriptures, the more they became aware of how much they did not know; and the more they despaired of the corruption and imperfection they found within themselves.

Far from the completed canon being something to do with perfection, history proves the sad case that in the hands of mortal, imperfect man, (including mortal, imperfect Christians – which all Christians are while on this earth), the canon often becomes the object of evil religious wars and bitter argument. Men can think themselves most orthodox, fighting for the meaning of words and doctrines which they think they see in the canon of scripture, and yet all the while be failing in the most basic fundamental realities of true Christianity that are taught in that same canon – denial of self, taking up one's cross, and love to Christ, and love to others, even to one's enemies. The lesson of 1 Corinthians 13 is so often forgotten. So numerous are the occasions in history of canon-believing Protestants happily, and so very orthodoxly and righteously, rising up to condemn, physically abuse, and even murder those for whom Christ died – simply because of different interpretations of the same canon. The flesh can be so religious with a complete canon. It scares me, and challenges me: what are my motives for writing. I would rather not have written any of these articles at all if I thought they would just be for a show of intellectual juggling, competing with another man's act. My sincere hope in writing is to help others to a better trust and hope in, and loving-fellowship with, the Lord Jesus and the Father, as the Holy Spirit sees fit to bless.

Conclusion

Perfection for believers, as mentioned in 1 Cor. 13:10, can only be had by being totally raised out of this life's mortal frame, into the glorification that consists of having immortal, spiritual heavenly bodies in heaven in consummate union there with Christ Jesus and the Father.

While we post-Parousia Christians are on earth in our mortal bodies, we are subject to the same partial and deposit/firstfruits phase of new covenant experience as were the pre-Parousia believers. But we must never despise this partial, deposit/firstfruit stage of knowing our God, for it is a necessary part of God's overall plan for his people; and we must remember that there are scriptures enough to show that we are to have a wonderful fellowship with our great loving God in this life in the power of the Holy Spirit.

Post-Parousia Christians are to find encouragement in the fact that the NT hope of glory together with Christ, is our portion just as it was for the pre-Parousia brethren. The difference of course lies in the timing and circumstances of the fulfillment of this hope:

- For the pre-Parousia saints, their hope of glory was fulfilled en masse at the Parousia of Christ; that was the occasion when the perfect came for them.
- For us post-Parousia Christians, our hope of glory will be fulfilled individually on the occasion of our physical death, upon the end of our allotted time on earth; then we enter that same perfection and glory in heaven that the pre-Parousia saints entered into at the Parousia.

The End

This book and over 100 other fine
Preterist resources are available from:

International Preterist Association

Ask For A Free Information Packet

The FREE information packet includes:
- "What Is the Preterist View?" article
- Book List and Order Form (over 100 books and other resources available)
- Media List (audio, video and CD/DVD)
- Information about other new or featured resources and upcoming events of interest

How to Contact IPA:
- Browse Our Web Site: www.preterist.ORG
  - Read, copy and print articles stored there
  - Buy Books & Media (VISA, M/C, Discover accepted)
  - Ask Questions
  - Contact Other Preterists Online
- Email: preterist1@aol.com
- Toll-Free (orders only) **1-888-257-7023** (USA only)
- Traditional Mail (see IPA postal address below)

International Preterist Association, Inc.

122 Seaward Avenue • Bradford, PA 16701-1515 USA
(814) 368-6578 (for all other calls)